Bridging Health, Environment, and Legalities:

A Holistic Approach

Siddharth Kanojia
O.P. Jindal Global University, India

A volume in the Advances in
Medical Education, Research, and
Ethics (AMERE) Book Series

Published in the United States of America by
IGI Global
Medical Information Science Reference (an imprint of IGI Global)
701 E. Chocolate Avenue
Hershey PA, USA 17033
Tel: 717-533-8845
Fax: 717-533-8661
E-mail: cust@igi-global.com
Web site: http://www.igi-global.com

Library of Congress Cataloging-in-Publication Data

Names: Kanojia, Siddharth, 1989- editor.
Title: Bridging health, environment, and legalities : a holistic approach / edited by Siddharth Kanojia.
Description: Hershey, PA : Engineering Science Reference, [2024] | Includes bibliographical references and index. | Summary: "This book aims to shed light on the intricate relationship between human health, the environment, and the legal frameworks that govern our societies. It intends to delves deep into the multifaceted interactions and consequences that arise from the interplay of these three crucial domains"-- Provided by publisher.
Identifiers: LCCN 2023049174 (print) | LCCN 2023049175 (ebook) | ISBN 9798369311783 (hardcover) | ISBN 9798369311790 (ebook)
Subjects: LCSH: Environmental health. | Public health--Social aspects. | Social policy. | Economic policy.
Classification: LCC RA565 .B755 2024 (print) | LCC RA565 (ebook) | DDC 362.1--dc23/eng/20231201
LC record available at https://lccn.loc.gov/2023049174
LC ebook record available at https://lccn.loc.gov/2023049175

This book is published in the IGI Global book series Advances in Medical Education, Research, and Ethics (AMERE) (ISSN: 2475-6601; eISSN: 2475-661X)

British Cataloguing in Publication Data
A Cataloguing in Publication record for this book is available from the British Library.

All work contributed to this book is new, previously-unpublished material.
The views expressed in this book are those of the authors, but not necessarily of the publisher.

For electronic access to this publication, please contact: eresources@igi-global.com.

Advances in Medical Education, Research, and Ethics (AMERE) Book Series

ISSN:2475-6601
EISSN:2475-661X

MISSION

Humans are living longer now than ever as a result of advances in the medical field. Having the tools available to train knowledgeable and ethical future generations of doctors and medical researchers is essential to continuing to advance our understanding of the human body and develop new ways of treating and curing sickness and disease.

The **Advances in Medical Education, Research, and Ethics (AMERE)** book series highlights publications pertaining to advancements in pedagogical practice for developing future healthcare professionals, research methods, and advancements in the medical field, as well as moral behavior and practice of healthcare professionals, students, and researchers. Featuring research-based book publications that are highly relevant to the healthcare community, this series is ideally designed for library inclusion at medical universities and research institutions as well as personal use by medical professionals, researchers, and upper-level students entering the field.

COVERAGE

- Clinical Research
- Conflicts of Interest
- Ethics in Medicine
- Healthcare Pedagogy
- Medical Curricula
- Medical Simulation
- Patient Data
- Professional Development
- Research Methods
- Scientific Misconduct

IGI Global is currently accepting manuscripts for publication within this series. To submit a proposal for a volume in this series, please contact our Acquisition Editors at Acquisitions@igi-global.com or visit: http://www.igi-global.com/publish/.

The Advances in Medical Education, Research, and Ethics (AMERE) Book Series (ISSN 2475-6601) is published by IGI Global, 701 E. Chocolate Avenue, Hershey, PA 17033-1240, USA, www.igi-global.com. This series is composed of titles available for purchase individually; each title is edited to be contextually exclusive from any other title within the series. For pricing and ordering information please visit http://www.igi-global.com/book-series/advances-medical-education-research-ethics/132365. Postmaster: Send all address changes to above address. Copyright © 2024 IGI Global. All rights, including translation in other languages reserved by the publisher. No part of this series may be reproduced or used in any form or by any means – graphics, electronic, or mechanical, including photocopying, recording, taping, or information and retrieval systems – without written permission from the publisher, except for non commercial, educational use, including classroom teaching purposes. The views expressed in this series are those of the authors, but not necessarily of IGI Global.

Titles in this Series

For a list of additional titles in this series, please visit:
www.igi-global.com/book-series/advances-medical-education-research-ethics/132365

Advances, Challenges, and Trends in Veterinary Science Teaching
Kutty Kumar (Sri Venkateswara Veterinary University, India) and Ramesh Babu Potu (Sri Venkateswara Veterinary University, India)
Medical Information Science Reference • copyright 2024 • 300pp • H/C (ISBN: 9781668472514) • US $325.00 (our price)

Bioethics of Displacement and Its Implications
Manuel Lozano Rodríguez (American University of Sovereign Nations, Spain)
Medical Information Science Reference • copyright 2023 • 386pp • H/C (ISBN: 9781668448083) • US $270.00 (our price)

Cases on Teaching Pharmacology to Complementary and Alternative Medicine Students
Muhammad Shahzad Aslam (School of Traditional Chinese Medicine, Xiamen University Malaysia, Malaysia)
Medical Information Science Reference • copyright 2023 • 209pp • H/C (ISBN: 9781668478288) • US $295.00 (our price)

Handbook of Research on Instructional Technologies in Health Education and Allied Disciplines
Manuel B. Garcia (FEU Institute of Technology, Philippines) Mildred Vanessa Lopez Cabrera (Tecnológico de Monterrey, Mexico) and Rui Pedro Pereira de Almeida (University of Algarve, Portugal)
Medical Information Science Reference • copyright 2023 • 439pp • H/C (ISBN: 9781668471647) • US $425.00 (our price)

For an entire list of titles in this series, please visit:
www.igi-global.com/book-series/advances-medical-education-research-ethics/132365

701 East Chocolate Avenue, Hershey, PA 17033, USA
Tel: 717-533-8845 x100 • Fax: 717-533-8661
E-Mail: cust@igi-global.com • www.igi-global.com

Table of Contents

Detailed Table of Contents

Chapter 1

    Tatjana Kochetkova, O.P. Jindal Global University, India
    Gianluigi Segalerba, Universidade de Coimbra, Portugal

The emergent trend of granting legal personhood to natural entities – environmental personhood – is a promising approach to nature's conservation. This inquiry explores its philosophical foundations and prerequisites for successful implementation. It argues that, along with a strong legal framework, its efficacy largely depends on the transition from anthropocentric to ecocentric values and on the appearance of a new ecological identity or eco-self. Critical for implementing the rights of nature are the ecocentric shift in culture and the consequent abandoning the "skin-encapsulated ego" in favor of the ecological self. This shift is what environmentalists strive for but couldn't achieve until now. To fill this gap, attention is given to one among the several traditions which can practically guide the identity transformation, namely Tantra yoga with its embeddedness in the natural world. It explains Tantra yoga's psycho-somatic methodology as a promising eco-spiritual practice to deal with current ecological challenges and to restore our planet's health by evoking biophilia.

Chapter 2

    V. S. Gigimon, Maharashtra National Law University, Mumbai, India
    R. S. Darsana, Maharashtra National Law University, Mumbai, India

Environmental impact assessments (EIA) evolved in ignorance of health concerns. Health impact assessments (HIA) have evolved to cater to health impacts of projects. Due to the intricate relationship between environment and health, integrating Health impact assessment and environmental impact assessment would be more cost-effective and practical. In the implementation of major projects, health impact assessment gains importance as there is large displacement of people, environmental changes, and related health hazards. This would enable a sustainable approach to properly handle the environment, health, and human well-being. This chapter analyses the meaning and scope of health impact assessment, its advantages, and challenges. It describes why India needs an integrated approach considering the socio-economic and demographic situations.

Chapter 3

Anny Gabriela Molina Ochoa, O.P. Jindal Global University, India
Maria Camila Duque Gomez, O.P. Jindal Global University, India
Santiago Weil Silva, O.P. Jindal Global University, India

This chapter explores the climate migration phenomenon and its legal framework in Latin America, studying some of its possible drivers and how these have a notable incidence in the global south. The chapter is centered on the Latin American region, providing a panorama of the geographical characteristics that make it particularly vulnerable to natural disasters and climate-related events, being these drivers of climate migration. The chapter also gives a view of the social, economic, and political conditions that make Latin America more susceptible to suffering human rights violations, which has an impact on the capacity of the countries to protect climate migrants and adds to the vulnerability of the region. The chapter also links this phenomenon to the existing legal framework, starting from the international instruments to later approach the domestic legislation and developments of the Latin American countries, revealing the lack of a harmonized regional instrument to protect climate migrants.

Chapter 4

Parimal Kumar Roy, Bangladesh Public Administration Training Centre, Bangladesh

This study reflected the author's one-decade professional journey in Bangladesh when he worked on the urban local body. Nevertheless, the author's sensuality with high empathy is that alleviating the urban primary health issues requires a governing department—Urban Health Unit. The urban local body is always under capacity to provide health services in terms of sustainability. In this sense, development agencies like ADB, DFID, and UNFPA anticipated the projects and accelerated the primary health care services under urban local bodies' capacities to downsize health pressure in secondary and tertiary health levels. As a result, assertive public participation and time-befitting policy implications were shaky to do so. For this drive, this study dives into ethnographic methods—participant observation and in-depth interviews with project personnel and public representatives in five urban local bodies of Bangladesh to write this chapter for policy recommendations, ab initio, on urban health issues to establish an Urban Health Unit to achieve SDG 3.

Chapter 5
Pranjal Khare, O.P. Jindal Global University, India
Hemendra Singh, O.P. Jindal Global University, India
Paridhi Sharma, O.P. Jindal Global University, India
Shalinee Vishwakarma, O.P. Jindal Global University, India

This chapter deals with the concept of Environmental Impact Assessment (EIA) in India and Canada. It scrutinizes the effectiveness of EIA regulatory frameworks in both the countries on the touchstone of extent of public participation, engagement with indigenous communities, and the integration of healthcare aspects. The analysis reveals a nuanced landscape wherein Canada serves as a model for comprehensive and well-structured EIA practices, whereas India grapples with challenges in implementation and enforcement. Canada excels in inclusivity by actively involving the public and indigenous communities in decision-making processes. In contrast, India faces hurdles in achieving meaningful public participation particularly in marginalized communities. The study emphasizes the need for contextualization in EIA frameworks and raises questions about improving public engagement and healthcare integration globally.

Chapter 6
Nishika Bhatia, O.P. Jindal Global University, India
Siddharth Tandon, State Bank of India, India

The world is witnessing rapid advancement in healthcare. As a consequence, the amount of biomedical waste generated globally is growing at an exponential rate. However, management of the biomedical waste (BMW) still remains a difficult challenge. Mismanagement of BMW has alarming and life-threatening ramifications to human health and the environment. Key steps of BMW management are waste segregation, collection, treatment, and safe disposal. Leading international health organisations emphasise segregation at source as an important focus point to improve BMW management. In this chapter, the authors will study a BMW management network in an Indian healthcare facility. The different steps of BMW management will be analytically modelled and simulated. The importance of segregation at source will be investigated and a post-segregation policy with a penalty framework will also be suggested. The authors also conduct numerical experiments to test their model and suggestions. This computational study establishes the importance of accuracy in segregation to improve efficiency of BMW management.

Chapter 7

Himanshi Bhatia, Symbiosis Law School, Symbiosis International University (Deemed), Nagpur, India & Maharashtra National Law University, Nagpur, India

The impact of the environmental deterioration is known to the world with the series of catastrophic damages and events. The discourse on the criminal intent behind man-made disasters is often regarded as a quixotic quest by various scholars and states. This study aims to examine this conundrum concerning the unsuitability of the ecocide as an international crime. It will analyze the profuse hesitation of the states and the international community on preventing environmental destruction. It argues that the presence of inter-linkages of criminal intent and elements while committing the acts deteriorates the environment. The concluding section briefly explores the questions on the urgency of criminalization, the level of regulation, the national and international administrative fallacies on environmental crimes, and above all, the feasibility of "ecocide as an international crime."

Chapter 8

Akash Bag, Adamas University, India
Pranjal Khare, O.P. Jindal Global University, India
Paridhi Sharma, O.P. Jindal Global University, India
Souvik Roy, Adamas University, India

In India, the idea of the polluter pays principle (PPP) is frequently used in environmental court cases. Though it is widely used, little scholarly research has been done on its conceptual limits and the difficulties it faces when applied to the Indian judicial system. This chapter examines decisions made by the National Green Tribunal (NGT) to close this information gap. This research examines three important aspects of PPP that can be identified from NGT examples. First, it explores how the definitions of "pollution" and "polluter" have changed over time, as demonstrated by several examples. Second, the chapter examines the techniques used by the NGT to determine compensation. Finally, it analyzes the justification for PPP implementation, as explained by the NGT in various instances.

Chapter 9

Piyush Pranjal, O.P. Jindal Global University, India
Vani Singhal, O.P. Jindal Global University, India
Soumya Sarkar, Indian Institute of Management, Ranchi, India
Tanvi Aggarwal, O.P. Jindal Global University, India

Mental health illnesses have assumed pandemic proportions, especially post-COVID, adversely impacting society and the global economy. The effect is more pronounced in India, ailing with inadequate mental healthcare infrastructure and management. The mental health illness burden is a drag on the achievement of SDGs as well. Spiritual care, religious-healing, and faith-healing have recently received greater emphasis in research and practice. Several practices within each are either proven support systems or cures. There is, however, a globally recognized downside that it is unregulated, which provides room for misuse and abuse, which are rampant. The current chapter demystifies the nexus between mental health, SDGs, and spiritual care, and necessitates a call for sagacious legal advocacy.

Chapter 10

Kalpana Sharma, Chaudhary Bansi Lal University, Bhiwani, India

Sustainable behaviour entails considering the need to protect the environment for current and future generations while also considering economic, environmental, and social development. Also, this is one of the goals of positive psychology to investigate the psychological consequences of such behaviour. As per previous studies, practising pro-environmental and altruistic activities can lead to higher levels of happiness, and thrifty consumption can result in a feeling of fulfilment and intrinsic motivation. For this research, a total number of 200 university students completed general ecological behavioural scale and happiness scale. Statistical analysis includes t, Pearson r, and regression analysis. Results showed that sustainable behaviour had a considerable impact on the "happiness" element. Males are more involved in sustainable behaviours as compared to females, and also had a higher mean score on the happiness scale. Furthermore, the participants' satisfaction was significantly predicted by all elements of sustainable behaviour.

Chapter 11

Richa Kapoor Mehra, O.P. Jindal Global University, India

Historically, evidence is available to make us understand the fact that nature has also played a therapeutic role in our lives by benefiting our mental health as well as physical health. The present study will address a concern: How can nature healing occur if a person suffers from chronic disease or is disabled? Through this chapter, an attempt has been made to provide a solution via digital or virtual reality tools, equip disabled patients, and give them a reel feeling of nature. Those who cannot go out and get the real feel of nature can make use of virtual reality tools to heal themselves with technology. Also, the present chapter will address the question, can virtual exposure to nature be equivalent to real exposure? Further, an attempt is made to discover how technological advancement is benefiting our lives, equipping us in the best possible ways. The prime concern here is to unfold how technological advancement and digital revolution have influenced the way we relate to the environment.

Chapter 12

The chapter explores the transformative implications of the tech-driven unification of health, environment, and legal domains, emphasizing the profound impact on societal well-being. It delves into the ethical considerations that arise, balancing the collective good with individual privacy rights, addressing biases in artificial intelligence, and ensuring transparent and inclusive technological practices. Global collaboration, exemplified by India's contributions, becomes pivotal in addressing challenges that transcend borders. Looking ahead, the chapter envisions a future of innovation with advancements in predictive technologies, interoperability, and immersive experiences. It underscores the necessity of a human-centric approach, drawing insights from India's diverse landscape. The conclusion is not a static endpoint but a juncture where collaborative efforts paint a vision of a harmonious, resilient, and sustainable future, with India playing a crucial role in this ongoing narrative of global collaboration and responsible technological integration.

Chapter 13

There has been an increase in the hazardous waste trade amongst countries of the world; consequently, two approaches have emerged over time. India follows the principles laid down by the Basel convention and incorporates the safeguard of PIC. The hazardous waste (management and transboundary movement) rules, 2016 incorporates the safeguard and regulates the movement of hazardous waste to and from India. Despite the stringent procedural requirement there have been cases wherein hazardous waste has been dumped in India. Research Foundation for Science

Technology and Natural Resources Policy v. Union of India (1995) is one such case wherein waste oil was imported in India while being labelled as lubricating oil. The waste oil had to be destroyed in India by way of incineration because other measures were not deemed feasible by the Apex court. A similar thing happened in 2018 in the case of P.P. Electronics v New Delhi (Import & General). The chapter analyses the law, highlights the gaps and challenges and provides remedy for preserving public health in India.

The Maldives, an island nation with a low elevation, is especially susceptible to the consequences of climate change, including rising sea levels, stronger storms, and coral reef degradation. Thereby, it has been committed to reducing greenhouse gas emissions and adapting to climate change under the terms of the Paris Agreement and has actively participated in the international climate negotiations. In reference to this, this chapter aims to assess the implementation and impact of the Paris Agreement on climate action in small island developing states including the Maldives. The primary objectives of this chapter are to analyze the specific commitments and contributions of the Maldives under the Paris Agreement, to assess the effectiveness of the Maldives' adaptation efforts in response to climate change, and to evaluate the progress made by the Maldives in meeting its mitigation targets.

Preface

In an era defined by the inextricable interlinking of our actions and their consequences, we are confronted with unprecedented challenges to our planet's health, environment, and legal frameworks. The culmination of climate change, biodiversity loss, acute pollution, and diverse health crises, both acute and chronic, underscores the urgency for collective action.

Bridging Health, Environment, and Legalities: A Holistic Approach delves into this complex web of relationships, recognizing the imperative need for a holistic perspective. Authored by Siddharth Kanojia, this comprehensive reference book traverses the multifaceted interactions between human health, the environment, and the legal structures governing our societies.

This book isn't confined to academic circles alone; it is a vital resource for researchers, public health practitioners, policy makers, environmental and conservation organizations, legal practitioners and advocates, and general readers alike. It addresses critical topics including the intricate relationship between health, environment, and legal frameworks, legal mechanisms for environmental protection, the impact of environmental pollution on human health, environmental justice and health disparities, sustainable development and health, and much more.

The aim is to offer insight into the interconnectedness of these domains and provide actionable solutions that benefit our interconnected world. As we navigate the complexities of our time, understanding these interconnections becomes paramount. This book is an invitation to explore, analyze, and ultimately contribute to the collective endeavor of nurturing a healthier, more sustainable future for all.

ORGANIZATION OF THE BOOK

Chapter 1: Environmental Personhood: Philosophical Foundations in Tantric Ecology

This chapter dives into the emergent concept of environmental personhood, exploring its philosophical roots and the necessary cultural shift from anthropocentrism to ecocentrism. It highlights the importance of an ecological identity and how traditions like Tantra yoga offer practical guidance in this transformative process, crucial for addressing ecological challenges.

Chapter 2: Integrating Health Impact Assessment and Environmental Impact Assessment: A Catalyst for Sustainable Development and Public Health in India

Focusing on India, this chapter examines the need for integrating Health Impact Assessments and Environmental Impact Assessments. It emphasizes how this integration can lead to a more sustainable approach, particularly in major projects, acknowledging the intricate link between environment, health, and societal well-being.

Chapter 3: Exploring the legal framework of climate migration in Latin America

Centered on Latin America, this chapter delves into climate migration and its legal aspects, highlighting the region's vulnerability to natural disasters. It discusses the socio-economic and political conditions impacting the region's capacity to protect climate migrants, revealing gaps in existing legal frameworks.

Chapter 4: Role of Urban Local Body to Ensuring Primary Health Care: A Case of Bangladesh

Drawing on real-life experiences, this chapter discusses the challenges faced by urban local bodies in providing primary health care. It emphasizes the need for an Urban Health Unit, exploring the implications of development projects and public participation in addressing urban health issues.

Chapter 5: A Comparative Study of Environmental Impact Assessment (EIA) Practices in India and Canada

Comparing EIA practices in India and Canada, this chapter scrutinizes public participation, engagement with indigenous communities, and healthcare integration. It sheds light on the nuanced differences between the two countries' approaches, stressing the necessity for contextualization and improved engagement globally.

Chapter 6: An Analytical Study of Biomedical Waste Management in Indian Healthcare

Addressing the challenges of biomedical waste management in India, this chapter presents an analytical model and simulation of waste management steps. It emphasizes the significance of waste segregation at the source, proposing policies and penalties to enhance efficiency.

Chapter 7: 'Buried into Oblivion': Ecocide as a Crime Against Humanity

This chapter explores the concept of ecocide as an international crime, dissecting the reluctance to recognize environmental destruction as criminal. It touches upon the link between criminal intent, environmental deterioration, and the feasibility of ecocide as an international crime.

Chapter 8: Examining the Application and Challenges of the Polluter Pays Principle: A Focus on India's Environmental Adjudication

Focusing on India, this chapter examines the Polluter Pays Principle in environmental court cases. It delves into the evolution of definitions, compensation techniques, and justifications for its implementation by analyzing decisions made by the National Green Tribunal.

Chapter 9: Mental Health, SDGs, and Spiritual Care - A Call for Legal Advocacy

Highlighting mental health challenges and their impact on SDGs, this chapter explores spiritual care's role while emphasizing the need for regulation. It discusses proven support systems within spiritual care and calls for prudent legal advocacy to address misuse and abuse.

Chapter 10: Sustainable Behavior: Endorsing Happiness

Examining the link between sustainable behavior and happiness, this chapter showcases how pro-environmental actions positively impact satisfaction levels. It discusses gender differences in sustainable behavior participation and their implications on happiness.

Chapter 11: Technology as a Means to Bridge the Gap Between Humans and Nature

This chapter explores technology's role in providing nature therapy to those unable to access it physically. It examines virtual reality's potential in healing, comparing its effectiveness to real exposure and addressing technological advancements' impact on human-nature relations.

Chapter 12: Synergizing Horizons - The Tech-Driven Unification of Health, Environment, and Legal

Envisioning a technologically-driven unification of health, environment, and legal domains, this chapter discusses ethical considerations, global collaboration, and India's role in technological integration. It foresees a harmonious future through responsible technological advancements.

Chapter 13: Preserving Public Health: Strengthening Hazardous Waste Rules for a Safer Future

Focusing on hazardous waste management, this chapter analyzes India's regulations, highlighting gaps and challenges. It examines key cases, emphasizing the importance of robust rules for public health preservation.

Chapter 14: Guardians of Atolls: Examining the Paris Agreement's Role in Climate Change Mitigation and Resilience in the Maldives

Centered on the Maldives, this chapter evaluates the country's commitment and progress under the Paris Agreement. It assesses mitigation efforts, adaptation strategies, and the effectiveness of climate action in small island nations like the Maldives.

Each chapter offers a unique perspective, examining critical intersections between health, environment, and legal frameworks, contributing to the broader conversation on holistic approaches to global challenges.

IN SUMMARY

As we draw the curtains on this comprehensive exploration into the intricate relationships between health, environment, and legal frameworks, the depth and diversity of insights presented across these chapters affirm a singular truth: our world's challenges are deeply interwoven.

From philosophical foundations in environmental personhood to the application of technological innovations bridging human-nature gaps, each chapter illuminates a facet of the complex tapestry that binds our well-being to the environment and legal structures.

The urgent need for a shift in perspectives, from anthropocentrism to ecocentrism, echoes through discussions on climate migration, hazardous waste management, and the implementation of impactful agreements like the Paris Agreement.

Moreover, the call for integrated assessments—combining health and environmental impacts—resonates as a practical step towards sustainable development, particularly in regions vulnerable to environmental upheavals.

We've ventured into the realms of law, examining the application of principles like the Polluter Pays Principle, while also probing the frontiers of potential legal frameworks to protect our planet and its inhabitants, be it through criminalizing ecocide or strengthening hazardous waste regulations.

The journey through these chapters has been a testament to the diversity of challenges faced globally and the necessity of collaborative, inclusive, and innovative approaches in tackling them.

As editors, our aim has been to present a compendium that not only informs but also inspires action and collaboration among diverse stakeholders—academicians, policymakers, practitioners, and concerned citizens. The multifaceted nature of these challenges demands a collective effort, transcending borders and disciplines.

In this ongoing narrative of global collaboration, innovation, and responsible stewardship, each contribution serves as a clarion call to heed the interconnectedness of health, environment, and legalities—a call to embrace holistic approaches in safeguarding our collective future.

May this compendium serve as a catalyst for ongoing dialogues, policy reforms, and transformative actions, fostering a world where the health of our planet and its inhabitants is nurtured through thoughtful, inclusive, and sustainable practices.

Chapter 1
Environmental Personhood:
Philosophical Foundations in Tantric Ecology

Tatjana Kochetkova
O.P. Jindal Global University, India

Gianluigi Segalerba
iD https://orcid.org/0009-0004-6127-4248
Universidade de Coimbra, Portugal

ABSTRACT

The emergent trend of granting legal personhood to natural entities – environmental personhood – is a promising approach to nature's conservation. This inquiry explores its philosophical foundations and prerequisites for successful implementation. It argues that, along with a strong legal framework, its efficacy largely depends on the transition from anthropocentric to ecocentric values and on the appearance of a new ecological identity or eco-self. Critical for implementing the rights of nature are the ecocentric shift in culture and the consequent abandoning the "skin-encapsulated ego" in favor of the ecological self. This shift is what environmentalists strive for but couldn't achieve until now. To fill this gap, attention is given to one among the several traditions which can practically guide the identity transformation, namely Tantra yoga with its embeddedness in the natural world. It explains Tantra yoga's psycho-somatic methodology as a promising eco-spiritual practice to deal with current ecological challenges and to restore our planet's health by evoking biophilia.

DOI: 10.4018/979-8-3693-1178-3.ch001

ENVIRONMENTAL PERSONHOOD: PHILOSOPHICAL FOUNDATIONS IN TANTRIC ECOLOGY

The environmental crisis is one of the greatest problems of our times. Many solutions have been undertaken, both on national and global levels, including global environmental legislation, such as the Paris Agreement on Climate change, the conventions on biodiversity conservation, and the national environmental policies, ranging from anti-pollution measures, to curbing carbon emissions to species and habitat conservation. However, they all seem to reach limited results in their application. The environmental crisis continues.

This chapter looks at a new turn among the various solutions to humanity's self-destructive behavior – i.e., the idea of Environmental Personhood, reflecting on its philosophical assumptions. Furthermore, here we discuss a possible way to give it sufficient cause and effect by extending cultural support and relying on biophilia as an inborn psychological affiliation with other living forms and ecosystems. For this, we turn to the Indian school of Tantra yoga, which can promote the attitude and identity leading to the desired cultural shift from Ego to Eco, and thus, as we will argue below, can help us solve the environmental crisis and can make environmental personhood work.

ENVIRONMENTAL PERSONHOOD IN LEGAL TERMS

The essence of Environmental Personhood is the attribution of legal rights to natural entities, an idea first proposed by Christopher Stone in his 1972 article, "Should Trees Have Standing—Toward Legal Rights for Natural Objects." Stone argued that it is necessary to grant legal personhood to natural entities, in a way which is similar to the way in which legal rights

have been extended, in the course of history, to women, children, minorities, or corporate entities.

There is a growing trend of granting legal personhood to natural entities, i.e., environmental personhood. Over the decades, Stone's idea has brought about a revolution in legal thinking, thus foregrounding the legal rights of nature. It was implemented for the first time in 2008 by Ecuador when the fundamental rights of the natural ecosystem were introduced into the constitution. Thus, Article 10, Section 2 of the Constitution states: "Nature shall possess the rights recognized for it by the Constitution." Furthermore, within Chapter 7 (Articles 71–74) of the Constitution of Ecuador, the rights encompass the entitlement to comprehensive reverence for its existence, as well as for the preservation and rejuvenation of its life cycles, structure, functions, and evolutionary mechanisms.

Two years later, in 2010, a similar recognition of nature's rights was established in Bolivia through the "Law of the Rights of Mother Earth". This legislation establishes a "Defensoría de la Madre Tierra," (i.e. "Protection of Mother Earth") analogous to the institution of a human rights ombudsman, "Defensoría del Pueblo" (Łaszewska-Hellriegel, 2022).

The vision behind these constitutional changes – which environmentalists passionately embrace – is that natural entities and ecosystems should not be seen as mere property but as entities with their own rights, e.g., the right to exist and flourish. However, critics have raised concerns about its practical implementation, which is common for new legal developments.

The main point of contention and perhaps the weakest aspect of the concept of environmental personhood lies in the need to appoint a representative—a person or an organization—to act on behalf of the environmental person. The quality of this representation is crucial to ensure the efficacy of environmental personhood. For instance, how can one ensure that the Bolivian nature's rights ombudsman, "Defensoría de la Madre Tierra," will function properly? In other words, what will guarantee that the new legal rights will receive sufficient force and effect? According to O'Donnell and Talbot-Jones study of the legal rights of rivers (2018), the crucial factor for the success of environmental personhood is giving it sufficient force and effect.

Achieving sufficient force and effect for nature's legal rights requires a broader change in the mindset towards natural entities, envisioning them not as property but as subjects of legal rights. For this change, the crucial factor is the social context, including transparency in implementation and governance, freedom from corruption, a strong legal framework, and an ecological shift in public mindset.

Already Christopher Stone, (1972) in his seminal paper on the rights of nature, argued about the need to change the foundations of our worldview – i.e., to give up the view that Nature is "a collection of useful senseless objects" and to give up our sense of separateness from the universe, restoring the ancient ability to love nature. Stone argues about the need to change the underlying vision of nature. Moreover, it is the experience of humans in relation to nature that needs to change. In order to change the philosophical foundations of our worldview, we need first to examine it, which is the subject of the next section.

ENVIRONMENTAL PERSONHOOD, RIGHTS OF NATURE, AND PHILOSOPHICAL ORIGINS

The concept of Environmental personhood is not only a point of heated legal discussion, but also the watershed line between two major philosophical and ethical views. It is where Anglo-American philosophy, sceptical about extending legal rights beyond the rational agency, clashes with a holistic philosophy, which strongly supports environmental agency.

Thus, Anglo-American philosophy of the 20th to 21st century generally avoids working on the Rights of Nature and the existing discourse tends to criticize it, as Jeremy Gilbert pointed out in his multi-disciplinary overview of the origins of the rights of nature (Gilbert et al., 2023). Nevertheless, many Anglo-American philosophers remain skeptical toward the idea of granting rights to nature, arguably because of the absence of attributes they consider essential for legal agency, such as autonomy, rationality, or free will.

The dismissive reaction of mainstream Anglo-American philosophy to the idea of the rights of nature appears to be a specific case of anthropocentrism, i.e. the view that only humans are intrinsically valuable while the rest of living beings are instrumental to their needs. It is anthropocentrism, as Lynn White argued, which is largely responsible for the environmental crisis (White, 1967). In opposition to that, the concept of environmental personhood is ecocentric and sees intrinsic value not only in humans but also in natural entities. Anthropocentric envisioning the universe as purely instrumental, contributes, in the words of one of their opponents, Max Weber, to the "disenchantment of the world (2004, p. 30)" Disenchantment denotes the lost meaning of reality because of the elimination of depth in our mainstream epistemological paradigm. Max Weber explained "the disenchantment of the world" as the eclipse of magical beliefs about nature as part of the more general process of "rationalization" which he saw as the defining feature of modernity in the West." [1]Another opponent of disenchantment, Nobel prize winner for literature Herman Hesse ironically portrayed the loss of meaning as a consequence of denigrating compromise (1968):

"The men of principled simplicity

Will have no traffic with our subtle doubt.

The world is flat, they tell us, and they shout:

The myth of depth is an absurdity!

.....in order to peacefully coexist

Let us strike one dimension off our list

...The third dimension is dispensable."

However, as psychologists Bettelheim and Zelan argue, "the dimension of depth cannot be dispensed" (Bettelheim & Zelan, 1981). Only those experiences "endowed with some visionary qualities and magic meaning" are likely to become an enjoyable and important part of one's life (Bettelheim & Zelan, 1981). This observation, based on children's reading experiences, is equally extendable to adult activities, because within each adult there is 'an inner child,' who continues to live in the unconscious mind. Just like reading, any human activity, if it lacks depth, is unlikely to be enjoyed and sustained. Similarly, the protection of the rights of nature, to be vital, must also maintain depth and meaning. Indeed, if nature is perceived without depth, i.e., as an external material object, one gets emotionally disconnected and hence is unlikely to protect nature for its own sake. But the aim of "environmental personhood" is to protect nature *for its own sake*, envisioning it as an intrinsic value, irrespective of its pragmatic uses. Hence, environmental personhood is a move to overcome anthropocentric bias in legal thinking as well as to re-enchant the world.

The opponents of the "the disenchantment of our worldview," – like Carl Gustav Jung, Roberto Assagioli, Abraham Maslow, Ken Wilber, Mishael Washburn, Starhawk, Vandana Shiva, search for meaning and wonder, as well as for the sacred reality within the natural one. They embrace spirituality as an essential part of this process, viewing it as an interconnected force that can heal Mother Earth and re-enchant the world (Khanduja, G. 2017).

The supporters of the Rights of Nature embrace the traditions, which challenge the reductionist worldview and associate it with the origins of the current environmental crisis.[2] Reductionism and anthropocentrism go hand in hand in neglecting the intrinsic value of nature and denying its rights. Indeed, reductionism investigates nature exclusively from a third-person perspective, which is incomplete. It can be claimed that a truly comprehensive approach must embrace all dimensions of reality, which implies having also first-person and second-person perspectives, as they are directly experienced as present and indispensable dimensions of reality.

The origins of the justification of the rights of nature can be traced back to such comprehensive views – Romanticism, Transcendentalism, Daoism, Indian classical philosophical systems, and Buddhism. These traditions consider that agency needed for entities to be subjects of legal rights goes beyond rationality, and claim that entities like rivers or mountains, while not possessing rationality in the ordinary sense, have enough spiritual value and inner depth to be legal persons.

This also goes in agreement with the ancient experience of rivers and mountains as sacred. Moreover, it aligns with the opinion of ecophilosophers, starting with Aldo Leopold's call to think like a mountain,[3] or Arne Naess' positions, supported by contemporary environmentalists such as Vandana Shiva. A prominent critic of Western reductionism, Vandana Shiva provides extensive justification for the rights of nature, arguing that nature is an agent in a philosophical sense.

DENIAL OF THE BIOSPHERE

Let us consider why Anglo-American mainstream approach neglects nature's rights. Neglect of nature's rights not only derives from anthropocentrism and associated reductionism but also underlies the global environmental crisis.

The current ecological crisis is frequently equated with the destruction of the biosphere – humanity's life support system. However, this is not entirely accurate. Indeed, the biosphere as the total sum of all ecosystems on this planet can hardly be destroyed by human activity, because it will survive, even if in viral or bacterial form, no matter which human-made disaster may occur (Wilber, 2001). For instance, neither nuclear war nor climate change, whatever harm to civilization it may bring, will eliminate bacteria from the Earth's surface. However, the current ecological crisis *"can alter the biosphere in such a way that it may not support human civilization anymore"* (Wilber, 2001, p.311).

Therefore, it makes sense to define the current ecological crisis as a neurotic *denial* of the biosphere, rather than its destruction (Wilber, 2001, ibid). Similar to how a neurotic denies – or represses – one's interconnectedness with one's own body, in the same way the collective mentality of the contemporary mainstream denies human embeddedness in the biosphere[4]. This denial is not a matter of words (verbal behavior), but rather of an actual decision to externalize the environmental costs of economic activities and of the unwillingness to pay for environmental restoration.

While mainstream media and politicians keep paying lip service to sustainability, in reality, the environmental costs of carbon emissions continue to be externalized, which is tantamount to an actual denial of the biosphere, comparable to a neurotic denial of bodily needs and sensations. Arguably, its root cause is an identity characterized by a sense of absolute separateness from everything else, called "skin encapsulated ego" (Watts, 1969, p. 24). This identity type represses its interconnectedness with the surrounding web of life.

This repression is a product of alienated lifestyles, typical of industrialized civilization. Such lifestyles force people to close themselves up from industrialized surroundings and leave them longing for natural areas, which may be out of reach. The situation of being constantly sensorily and informationally overloaded by noise, crowds, chaotic traffic, air pollution, stream of online messages, ads, news, and phone calls – all this makes one switch off one's senses, wear anti-pollution masks, put on ear plugs, or isolate themselves in homes and offices, attempting to block the stressful artificial environment, just to remain sane, as was pinpointed already by Georg Simmel. [5]

An example of the practical denial of the biosphere is when General Motors 'killed' of its electric vehicles (EVs) in the early 2000s. It was described in the American documentary film "Who killed the Electric Car?" directed by Chris Paine (2006). [6] Even though its EV's were clearly better for the climate than petroleum cars, and clients liked them, GM partners, mostly petrol producers, found them threatening to their revenues and decided to stop them.

In spite of these EVs clearly being better for the climate than petroleum cars, GM partners, mostly petrol producers, saw them as a threat to their revenues and decided to stop them.

Furthermore, General Motors' destruction of its electric vehicles (EVs) in 2003 is also a case of "skin encapsulated ego" (Watts, 1969, p. 24) repressing embeddedness in the biosphere. When GM slopped all its functioning EVs, their clients protested, wanting to keep using them and even offering GM to buy all their EV from the lease. The general motive behind the destruction by GM of its own EVs was profit: as EVs need less maintenance and do not require petroleum, they undermine the interests of the gas and oil industry, currently accused of hiding from the public information about climate change which they knew as early as in 1979. In the same year 1979 an Exxon study claimed that fossil fuels "will cause dramatic environmental effects" in the near future (Supran, 2022). When in the 2020s these data became public a stream of lawsuits against US oil and gas companies started, and now they may be held responsible before the law. [7] Another similar case is when a few investors made a fortune by taking full advantage of the impending subprime mortgage crisis in the US in 2007-2008. When they early in advance found out about the impending mortgage crisis, they never attempted to avert it.

Thus, the US oil industry was hiding the climate change data for decades because it prioritized its own short-term profit above everything else, be it the long-term survival of humankind or the global ecosystem. This is an exemplary case of the aforementioned "skin-encapsulated ego".

The "skin-encapsulated ego" stands behind the US oil industry's attempts to hide facts about carbon emissions' impact on climate change: it supports dumping toxic waste whenever possible, biopiracy, and other abuses of ecosystems, prioritizing own short-term profit above global survival. A satirical portrait of such identity is Adam McKay's comedy movie "Don't Look Up!" from 2021 about a US president failing to deflect a comet which was going to destroy planet Earth because the comet in question contained precious minerals they wanted to exploit. As one can see, such a structure of individual identity is socially destructive. It has been widely criticized by environmentalists, who brought persuasive ethical and practical arguments about the need to change, to phase out the fossil fuels industry and to find ecological stability.

However, the backlash against the environmental movement is still persistent. The denialists of climate change are not convinced by the rationality of curbing climate change. As one can see from debates with climate denialists, they are hardly persuaded by rational arguments (Bretter and Schulz, 2023). Indeed, there are limits to persuasion and understanding via concepts and words, and words frequently do not change what we are: they do not modify our identities. This is perhaps the ground why environmentalists failed to achieve ecocentric shifts until now.

Philosophers claim that "for the betterment of our society, we have to look not through an anthropocentric lens, but through the ecological lens" (Barman, 2022, 8736).[8] However, all these claims have little impact on the actual corporate behavior, and economic and business actions. Environmental destruction continues, and even in the most obvious cases, such as ambient air pollution, which comes from traffic and industry that most people can smell directly, and has obvious bad health effects, the rational arguments are powerless (Singh et al., 2010). This is because actual human behavior is a complex outcome of cognitive, emotional, conscious, and subconscious factors, and identity plays a role as well. So, explaining why egocentric behavior is irrational or ecocentric behavior rational will not guarantee a behavioral change.

In fact, rational arguments have not accomplished a cultural difference until now. Egocentric identity cannot be renounced via rational arguments because emotions and experience play a big role in each type of identity, but it can be outgrown. Indeed, real personal growth is required, with experiences that deepen our perception and bring us back to our nature. A different approach is needed that can change identity through practices and experiences more than arguments.

A possible effective approach to ecological shift is to tap on biophilia – an inherent human affinity for nature (Wilson, 1986). This innate connection serves as a powerful motivator for environmental action. According to this theory, the human inclination to connect with nature and other living beings is intrinsic (Wilson, 1986). Early evidence supporting this idea came from Ulrich's (1984) study, which revealed that patients recovering from gall-bladder surgery in a suburban Pennsylvania hospital experienced faster recovery and required fewer painkillers when their rooms had "windows offering views of natural landscapes" compared to those facing a plain brick wall. Remarkably, it was later discovered that even images of green landscapes had a positive impact on patients' well-being. The point of this observation is to prove that the need for nature is a vital human instinct.

Biophilia stands as a fundamental driving force behind environmental activism and the public's call for conservation efforts, deeply ingrained in the values of various cultures. Strengthening this innate connection with nature could potentially be achieved by honing our sensory perception.

Biophilia seems to play a crucial role in daily green actions, like tree planting, caring for birds or maintaining hobby gardens, and caring for pets or street animals. Biophilia appears to motivate all green activities, from climate change resistance to biodiversity conservation.

While the potential for biophilia is inborn, it is not equally distributed among people. Clearly, environmentalists are strongly motivated by biophilia and by the consequent hope to restore the flourishing of ecosystems. Under democratic regimes, having political leaders with biophilia lead to more efficient green policies. A good example was US President Teddy Roosevelt, a passionate hiker and nature lover, who, for the first time in history, implemented environmental legislation, expressing the concerns of the environmentalists.

The growth of biophilia would exemplify the currently sought shift from an Egocentric identity to an Ecocentric one. The prevalent egocentric identity is transient and seems to be already in the process of being replaced. As David Ulansey has demonstrated, we are living in times of far-reaching cultural transition and spiritual transformation: the very structure of individual identity is shifting profoundly (2000). Showing parallels between Hellenistic times and our ongoing globalization and individualization, Ulansey concludes that today again, like two thousand years ago, a new personal identity is emerging, one defined in relation to global cyberspace and breaking away from all local ties, changing its relation to body and materiality.

In other words, the ongoing transformations make us feel the growing need to plug into archaic dimensions, denied to us, as said James Morley (2008), "by the alienated lifestyles of industrialized civilization." This may be explained, as Russian philosopher Berdyaev mentioned, by the fact that during transitional times, social conditioning becomes looser and allows the expression of the archaic dimension. More specifically it is found in Yoga, understood as "a system of contemplative practices that emphasizes *the somatic incarnate domain of human experience neglected by the religious mainstream* (italics ours) (Morley, 2008). To further explore how this system helps us along this ongoing transformation, let us examine, in the next section, one aspect of Yoga: Tantra. [9]

WHY TANTRA?

Can Yoga in its Tantric form become the missing link in environmentalists' efforts to accomplish the shift from Ego to Eco? Even though Tantra appeared in times when nobody thought of ecological devastation, and is ultimate goal is not environmental protection, but spiritual liberation, Tantric practices can promote biophilia and thus help strengthen environmental personhood.

Tantra is one among several psycho-somatic reflective practices which can be supportive of environmental personhood. The related practices include, among others, Shinto and Taoist meditative training. For instance, one of them, Neidan meditation, was described in the ancient Taoist text rediscovered by R. Wilhelm, who recognized it as essentially a practical guide to the integration of personality (Lü, et al., 2014). Moreover, Francis of Assisi, who saw the Divine incarnation manifested in the entire natural world, also seems to follow a path of sacred immanence (Rohr, 2014). Such writings have as their final goal the crossing of the anthropological border – i.e., the maximization of human potential – by renouncing the limitations of the human condition to achieve spiritual liberation. This final goal, which we could term "Enlightenment," is of essential importance, as ecocentrism and green values both manifest aspects of the self-realizing or enlightened consciousness.

Since, however, it is impossible to embrace all available approaches at once, one of them – Tantra yoga – is here singled out for special consideration. As a practice, Tantra is an ancient Indian tradition whose exact age is not established, though we know that it precedes Rigveda. An umbrella term for several Indian philosophies, rituals, and yogic practices, Tantra is present in several schools of Hinduism, Jainism and in Vajrayana Buddhism. Its earliest written appearance is in Hymn 10.71 of the Rigveda (Padoux, 2017). As a written tradition, it encompasses a vast and diverse body of texts from around the 8th century AD onwards.

It is still discussed how Tantra is different from non-Tantric approaches in Hinduism and Buddhism. A Tantra scholar, Andre Padoux, wrote that Tantra entails a divergence from the Vedic tradition via the application of *Kundalini* yoga, different from classical Patanjali's yoga (Padoux, 2017). Various experts agree that Tantra is a genuine and unconventional path to spiritual liberation, which stands in contrast to Vedic tradition (Dupuche, 2003).

There are two traits of Tantra which make it worth considering for the justification of the rights of nature and for making ecological shifts in culture and individual identity.

- The first is Tantric *ontology*, which is liberating, implementing the path of sacred immanence and psychological integration into nature, hence promoting/grounding biophilia.
- The second one, and even more important, is the Tantric method, Yoga, as the path of *psycho-somatic practice*. In the face of Tantra, we turn to a tradition that not only chases depth, but it has a specific "know-how": it teaches its adepts to perceive the depth in nature and in one's own body. The phenomenological slogan "to the things themselves" is more applicable to

Tantra yoga than to phenomenology in the opinion of James Moorley (2008). Tantric yoga entails an experiential phenomenology of the body, and in the process of such phenomenological study of own body, a yogin creates a new entity, a "subtle or yogic body". Therefore, Tantric practice intends, among other things, to overcome the body-mind split, and hence enhances biophilia and integration into nature. This is because, as we will argue further, the psychological integration with nature occurs via one's integration between body and mind.

TANTRA AS ONTOLOGY

While various holistic philosophies provide a justification for the rights of nature, we suggest here that the possible contribution of Tantric philosophy is worth considering independently. An example is the two-way exchange between Tantra and eco-philosophy, as presented in the works of Vandana Shiva, Rita Dasgupta Sherma, Jeffrey Lidke, Kunt Jacobsen, Ian Whicher, and Christopher Key Chapple.

There are several essential affinities between Tantra and ecophilosophy, including the celebration of all aspects of life, the elevation of the feminine principle linked to materiality and the liberation of the female gender from the constraints of 'fertility and nurturance alone,' the affirmation of natural phenomena as a manifestation of the Goddess, the articulation of a discourse of empowerment for the marginalized, the veneration of the body and its sensations, and the rejection of a spirit/matter dichotomy (Sherma, 1998; Lidke, 2009; Kochetkova, 2022a). Tantra's practical dimensions embrace egalitarianism, feminism, ecology, and the immanent divinity of the natural world.

Contemporary readings of Tantra by ecofeminists such as Rita DasGupta Sherma, Jeffrey Lidke, Starhawk, and Vandana Shiva bring out its potential to foster ecosystem flourishing and contribute to a more harmonious society.[10]

Vandana Shiva applies the idea of *śakti* as primordial and all-persuasive energy while exploring ecological issues—water management, agriculture, women's rights, indigenous rights, and seed patenting. She views *śakti* as manifested in a dialectical interplay of two partners: Prakriti, or Nature, and Purusha, or Spirit. Nature as Prakriti is inherently active, a powerful, productive force in the creation, renewal, and sustenance of all life. From the perspective of Prakriti, Shiva redefines productivity as "the creation and not destruction of life," applying Prakriti as an epistemological criterion to assess real knowledge (Shiva, 2016). She uses the concept of Prakriti to explore the roots of major ecological and social issues. The vision of Prakriti as the agent who creates all life leads to an argument justifying the rights of nature and granting legal personhood to natural entities.

The tantric practice remains relevant in today's environmental and cultural contexts, for instance, because belief in *śakti* forms the basis of sacred groves, which are protective of biodiversity and can contribute to the spiritual and psychological well-being of their visitors. This tradition of treating certain areas as sacred has helped protect biodiversity throughout Indian history and stays relevant today.

Crucially, not all schools of Indian philosophy choose the "path of sacred immanence" (integration into the natural world). Out of the two basic Indian philosophical perspectives on liberation (moksha), to wit: escaping and transcending the world vs. integrating into it, Tantra predominantly validates integration. This gives Tantra (more specifically, Shakta Tantra) an affinity with emancipatory eco-philosophy.[11] In fact, though some Indian philosophical systems identify Nature as a source of bondage (and thus favor the "transcending path"), Tantra offers an alternative hermeneutics which "affirms the embodied world as the field of liberation" (Lidke, 2008).

TANTRA AS SOMATIC CONTEMPLATIVE PRACTICE: BODY AND ECOLOGY

Can Tantric practice enable a shift from egocentric to ecocentric self? This possibility exists because Tantra "emphasizes the somatic incarnate domain of human experience neglected by the religious mainstream" (Morley, 2008).

What really makes Tantra stand out among holistic traditions is its being primarily a somatic contemplative practice. Indeed, Tantric meditative and yogic practice is directed at achieving personal transformation, associated with yogic self-realization or liberation while alive. In Tantra, this happens while fostering embeddedness in the natural world.

Indeed, Tantra's practice is directed, first of all, at arriving at "the things themselves" (Husserl, 2001, p. 168) – backing the things the way they are experienced, and favoring an unbiased, non-dualistic consciousness, and a somatic experience deeply embedded in the surrounding world.

It is somatic yoga practice or living body experience in Tantra, that offers a way out of the "skin encapsulated ego" (Watts, 1968) and reconnects us to the web of life, by means of practical work on the development of consciousness and yogic integral body-mind.

Hence, the overcoming of transcendental idealism distinguishes both yoga from its mainstream tradition and acknowledges that this is the basis for a radically *embodied* approach to spirituality (Moorley, 2006).

The path of sacred immanence can be illustrated by the works of Abhinavagupta, an outstanding representative of Kashmir Shaivism, who lived between 960 and 1020

C.E. In his encyclopedic work, Tanrtāloka, 'The Light on and off the Tantras', he makes an overview of the existing Tantras of his time. What may appear surprising, is the attitude of the famous Abhinavagupta to the Kula ritual. The most extreme among Tantric rituals of his time, the Kula ritual involves the transgression of many religious taboos, proposing the use of wine, meat, and intercourse with women of the lowest castes as a path to ultimate liberation.

Despite being an intellectual authority of his time, Abhinavagupta esteemed the alternative Kula ritual highly, placing it almost at the top of divine revelation (Dupuche, 2006). Kula's subversion of castes and conventions appears as an efficient means to undermine dualism. It is resemblant of Renaissance carnival, it is subversively an impulse to remove artificial boundaries, overcoming the distinction between purity and impurity.[12] For the liberated consciousness, all reality is pure: this is the implication of the Kula ritual. As Dupuche observes (2006, p. i.):

"The Kula ritual leads the practitioner to ever more exalted stages of the mantra finally to reach the highest level of consciousness, the experience of mantravyiipti, the 'pervasion of the mantra'. The person who knows this pervasion knows that he is Bhairava. The supreme mantra of consciousness is none other than the mantra SAUH, the supreme goddess Para, which expresses both the supreme reality.

In this way Abhinavagupta breaks down the dualism between sacred and profane, ritual and ordinary life so that the Kula practitioner is liberated while alive, his every act is worship, and his every word is mantra."[13]

The point of the Kula ritual in the initiate empowering oneself to "experience *sudden enlightenment (alamgrāsah)."*

"His anxiety to conform to the orthodox religion (śaṅkā) will abruptly dissolve, taking with it all trace of the lower, dualistic experience of reality. Throwing off the unenlightened inhibition (pāśavayantranā) which has contaminated his awareness he will penetrate to the nondual consciousness which is absolute reality and the state of liberation."[14]

In Sanderson's analysis of the Kula rituals, the transgression of prohibitions, including the use of 'impure' substances and sexual intercourse with exactly the type of partners which official religion would condemn – including blood relatives – is a powerful way to overcome socially constructed distinctions of pure/impure, high/low, and hence to arrive at non-dual awareness, discovering deities within own body (Sanderson, 2022).

As a result of overcoming dualism, one becomes aware of one's deeper self as divine, who encompasses the entire universe and affirms the universe as all sacred. This integrated consciousness may present a link to an ecocentric shift in the culture, and to the ecological self as individual identity. In the words of 8th-century Tantric, Saraha:

"Here [in my body] are the Ganga and the Yamuna... here are Prayaga and Varanasi, here the Sun and the Moon. Here are the sacred places, the pithas... Never have I seen a place of pilgrimage and an abode of bliss like my body" (Padoux, 2017).

Here, Saraha envisions the body as a microcosmos, a homology of the universe, containing the entire reality within itself, including the biosphere. Therefore, the specific type of liberation sought in Tantra is not an escape from the world but a deeper integration within and inside the natural world. Thus, Tantra seems likely to foster the ecological self, because Tantric somatic contemplative practice is intensely aware of its interconnectedness with nature and more capable of creating a strong commitment to environmental protection. Hence, the shift to both ecocentric public ethics and ecological self can occur via somatic awareness and overcoming alienation from the body.

TANTRIC PERSPECTIVE ON BODY

Tantric perspective on the human body is an object of the growing interest of neuroscientists, who look for ways to link the first and third-person perspectives on the body (Venkatraman, et al, 2001). Neuroscience itself studies the body from an objective or third-person perspective. But it misses the other perspectives, i. e. the first person, and the second person, which also have to be included for a comprehensive view. Hence, neuroscience turns to Tantra, which examines the body through immediate experience or the "I-perspective," – the first-person perspective. It contrasts with neurology's third-person perspective that treats the body as an object ("it").

Tantra advocates for a more comprehensive approach that integrates three distinct perspectives: the first-person perspective (experiential), the second-person perspective (hermeneutic and communicative), and the third-person perspective (physiological and material). This holistic approach seeks to bridge the gap between our subjective experience of the body and its objective, scientific understanding (Kochetkova, 2022a).

One central concept in Tantra is the idea of the "subtle body," which is set apart from the "gross body" (Venkatraman et al., 2019). The subtle body is believed to reflect an "interoceptive map of the nervous system" (Venkatraman et al., 2019). This concept aligns with the contemporary understanding of interoception, which encompasses a wide range of internal sensations, including those related to the heart, lungs, taste, and vision.

In Tantric philosophy, the subtle body is conceptualized as a flow of primaeval divine energy known as Kundalini. It consists of a network of "centers", or "nodal points" called chakras, interconnected by channels known as "Nadi." Interestingly, recent scientific studies suggest that the Tantric concept of "chakras" can have some parallels with experiential aspects of neurological functioning. Essentially, the chakras cannot be reduced to physical objects but rather represent intricate aspects of our subjective experience. For instance, there is a connection between the nervous control of the heart and social behaviour; likewise, there is a link between irritable bowel syndrome and a patient's emotional reactivity to words. This body-mind connection corresponds to the chakra approach (Venkatraman, et al., 2021.)

Furthermore, Tantric practices prove to induce relevant changes in the structure and function of the nervous system of the practitioners. Advanced yogis and Tantric adepts can exert conscious control over typically autonomous bodily functions, including pulse and heart rate variability, body temperature, and blood pressure (Venkatraman et al., 2019).

Tantra offers a unique perspective on the human body, emphasizing the integration of subjective, objective, and relational viewpoints. It posits the existence of a subtle body, linked to the nervous system, and explores how its practice can bring about remarkable changes in the body-mind connection, challenging conventional notions of bodily autonomy and control (Venkatraman et al., 2021, p. 1190.).

TANTRA AND BIOPHILIA

One of the outcomes of awakening the Kundalini energy is an enhanced awareness of one's connection with the natural world, which is perceived as intricately linked to one's own body. This perspective envisions the entire universe as paradoxically contained within the individual's physical form, akin to David Bohm's concept of a "holographic universe," (1980) where each part contains the whole, often referred to as Indra's net. Current research suggests that human well-being is significantly influenced by the environment (Jimenez et al, 2021). However, conventional natural science often expresses this connection in abstract terms that may not directly impact our personal experiences.

In contrast, Tantric yoga provides a means to directly sense the environment, transforming the "subtle body" into a tangible and lived experience and fostering a deep connection with the natural world. Practitioners begin to perceive natural elements filled with vibrant colors, sounds, shapes, and scents, a crucial aspect of discovering meaning and forming attachments. Through this process, the boundary between self-care and care for the environment dissolves, giving rise to biophilia.

The tantric practice of Kundalini can foster biophilia by reestablishing a profound bond between individual consciousness and the natural world, as recognized by contemporary eco-psychologists. This connection is made possible because, within the Tantric perspective, the universe is conceived as a unified energy field known as Šākti or divine power. The human body is an integral component of this universal energy field since it mirrors the very structure of the cosmos. Consequently, the "subtle body" is not an object but rather a flowing stream of energy within the all-encompassing "Šākti" field, and Tantric embodiment becomes an integral part of the Earth's biosphere and the broader cosmic reality.

The ecological crisis of our era presents both an environmental and a psychological challenge, necessitating a shift in mainstream individual consciousness from self-identification with the narrow confines of the "ego" (Watts, 1994, p. 76) to a more expansive ecological self. Tantric practice aligns seamlessly with the principles of eco-psychology, facilitating the reconnection and transformation of personal consciousness "from ego to Eco" through the journey of personal growth (Danon, 2019, p. 8).

The ecological self, represented as "Eco," is attained through three crucial dimensions: (1) a downward reconnection with all living beings, (2) an inward reconnection involving a profound understanding of one's true essence, and (3) an upward reconnection with the ultimate, transhuman reality (Danon, 2019, p. 10). Tantric practice fully embraces all three these elements, guiding adept individuals to reconnect with fellow living beings, with their intrinsic nature, and with the transcendent ultimate reality.

Of course, there is a gap between a psycho-somatic meditative practice, like Tantra yoga, on the one hand, and social reality, including economy, politics, and technology, on the other. This gap will most likely remain, at the same time, Tantric practice can inspire ecological shifts in society, embracing cleaner technologies, internalization of environmental costs, and giving sufficient force and effect to environmental personhood.

Furthermore, the shift to the ecological self would require reshaping the modern lifestyle. Apart from the standard program of maintaining a high quality of objective environment – the anti-pollution measures to keep clean air, water, and soil, it also necessitates dedicated attention to two things: to one's body and to natural ecosystems as an experiential, subjective, aesthetic, and spiritual reality.

Attention to one's body, or body-mind integration can be implemented by practicing movement, yoga, and overall healthy living. The second element is giving equal warm care to the natural entities in one's proximity. Hence, a lifestyle comes about which involves living within reach from natural areas – forests, lakes, rivers, or waterfalls – and includes frequent walks in natural areas, while being intensely aware of them, being actively involved in nature protection such as civil action and also mindful activities with gardening, and caring for natural ecosystems, like protecting wild birds in one's immediate surroundings.

A possible approximation of the ecological lifestyle can be found in the Himalayan Iyengar Yoga Center (HIYC) in Himachal Pradesh, which is directed by Yoga Master Sarat Aurora. One of the authors followed courses in this center recently: they teach to reflect on inward sensations while performing asanas. So, the aim does not consist in performing asana as physical exercise, but in directing awareness and reflection to the inward sensations while doing asana: therefore, the role of the mind is crucial. Consequently, it feels like authentic yoga in contrast to merely physical asana practice. This is akin to qigong, another practice in which the object of meditation is the inward sensations during practice.

The HIYC is located in one of the ecologically cleanest areas of the Himalaya and is surrounded by a large and beautiful garden. Along with yoga, the center offers courses in organic gardening from a meditative perspective. The ecological concern is inherent there, as part of the lifestyle of participants of the center, a lifestyle which is simple, deep, and enjoyable, prioritizing quality over quantity. The mindset of the center is ecological by virtue of being meditative.

PSYCHOLOGICAL AND MENTAL HEALTH IMPLICATIONS OF *ECO-TANTRA*

The motivation to implement the rights of nature is associated with the psychological embeddedness in natural surroundings, equally supportive of mental health and well-being. As research has demonstrated, immersing oneself in pristine natural environments, like mountains or waterfalls, can significantly relieve stress and enhance subjective well-being, facilitating personal growth and self-realization (Wang, 2023). The exact mechanisms behind this positive influence remain obscure. Fortunately, Tantric philosophy can shed some light on this issue by offering valuable insights into understanding the workings of this profound connection. As a type of eco-spiritual practice, Tantra can also address mental health issues such as depression and burnout, frequent in hectic urban lifestyles characterized by disconnection from nature.

The Tantric way to alleviate human suffering involves deeper integration and embodiment in the entire universe, including the cultivation of gratitude for being in the world, a mandala-based vision of interconnectedness, and the practice of cultivating the sense of connection to local landscapes (Lidke, 2009).

CONCLUSION

The concept of environmental personhood originated as a more evolved response to the need for our species to control their self-destructiveness. Its philosophical foundation implies ecocentric values and outlook. However, an obstacle to implementing ecocentrism is that many people are still motivated by their egocentric identity ("skin-encapsulated ego"). To change this personal identity to its counterpart, the "ecological self," is, in our opinion, an important way to broaden the social support of environmental protection, and to green the popular culture.

Why is the formation of an "ecological self" so crucial for implementing environmental personhood and its final target – i.e., controlling environmental destruction and securing our planetary future? Because of all possible styles of personal identity, the ecological self is probably the most appropriate for promoting environmental protection. Such ethical and personal identity change involves a deep ecocentric transformation of our culture, prioritizing planetary and human health in their interconnectedness.

Ecocentrism, which provides a philosophical foundation for environmental personhood, is grounded in several holistic philosophical traditions that envision nature as a manifestation of an all-permeating substance. Tantra is one such school, promoting spiritual liberation through deeper integration with the natural world – the path of sacred immanence. It influences eco-feminist and sustainability thinking within contemporary responses to ecological crises. Tantric yogic practice enhances bodily awareness, thus restoring psychological connection to nature. Biophilia is one of the strongest motivations for protecting the rights of nature, and it can be evoked by Tantric psycho-somatic meditative practice. Embracing Tantric eco-spirituality is a promising approach to address current ecological challenges and restore our planet's health.

STUDY/ REVISION QUESTIONS

1. What is environmental personhood? Explain the concept and its history.
2. What is Tantra? How human-nature connection is presented in Tantra as a micro-macro-cosmic correspondence?
3. What is Sacred Immanence and how is it present in Tantra?
4. What is biophilia? How is it relevant for environmental protection?
5. How Tantric practice can be relevant for inspiring environmental protection?

REFLECTION/ DISCUSSION QUESTIONS:

1. What do you think are philosophical assumptions and implications of the legal concept of environmental personhood?
2. How do you envision a connection between the ecological self, mental health, and environmental protection?
3. How Tantric yogic practice relates to psychophysical health and personal development, in your view?
4. Why do you think Tantric yogic perspective on body is an object of the growing interest of neuroscientists?
5. Do you think that Tantric practice may promote the re-enchantment of human relation to nature? Why?
6. Is Biophilia able to provide sufficient support for the enactment of environmental personhood? On what grounds?

REFERENCES

Barman, M. (2022). Arne Naess Reflection of Eco-Centrism and Deep Ecology with Utilitarian and Deontological Defense against Anthropocentric Theory. *Journal of Positive School Psychology*, 6(3), 8736–8739.

Bettelheim, B., & Zelan, K. (1981). *On Learning to Read: The Child's Fascination with Meaning*. Alfred A. Knopf.

Bretter, C., & Schulz, F. (2023). Why focusing on "climate change denial" is counterproductive. *PNAS Nexus*, *120*(10), e2217716120. doi:10.1073/pnas.2217716120 PMID:36853937

DanonM. (2019). "From Ego to Eco": The contribution of Ecopsychology to the current environmental crisis management. *Visions for Sustainability*, 12, 8-17. https://doi.org/ doi:10.13135/2384-8677/3261

Dupuche, J. R. (2003). Abhinavagupta: The Kula Ritual, as Elaborated in Chapter 29 of the Tantrāloka, Motilal Banarsidass Publishers, ISBN 81-208-1979-9.

Gilbert, J., Soliev, I., Robertson, A., Vermeylen, S., Williams, N. W., & Grabowski, R. C. (2023). Understanding the Rights of Nature: Working Together Across and Beyond Disciplines in Human Ecology. *Human Ecology: an Interdisciplinary Journal*, *51*(3), 363–377. doi:10.1007/s10745-023-00420-1

Giménez, T. V. (2023). The rights of Nature: The legal revolution of the 21st century. *MOJ Ecology & Environmental Sciences, 8*(3), 97–115. doi:10.15406/mojes.2023.08.00280

Hesse, H. (1968). Magister Ludi, Glass beads game, Engl. Transl. by Holt, Rinehart & Winston.

Husserl, E. 2001, [1900/1901]. Logical Investigations. Ed. Dermot Moran. 2nd ed. 2 vols. London: Routledge.p. 168

Jimenez, M. P., DeVille, N. V., Elliott, E. G., Schiff, J. E., Wilt, G. E., Hart, J. E., & James, P. (2021). Associations between Nature Exposure and Health: A Review of the Evidence. *International Journal of Environmental Research and Public Health, 18*(9), 4790. doi:10.3390/ijerph18094790 PMID:33946197

Khanduja, G. (2017). Prakriti and Shakti: An Ecofeminist Perspective. *Jindal Journal of Public Policy, 3*(1), 105-14. ISSN 2277-8743

Kochetkova, T. (2022a). Environmental management in transition: Lessons from tantra. In: (Eds.) P. Gupta, S. P. Sahni & T. Bhatnagar, Spirituality and Management: From Models to Applications. Springer Singapore.

Kochetkova, T. (2022b). The impact of ideas on bodily processes. Lessons from mantra techniques. In (Eds). G. Enthoven, S. Rudnicki & R. Sneller, Towards a Science of Ideas, An inquiry into the emergence, evolution and expansion of ideas and their translation into action. Vernon Press.

Łaszewska-Hellriegel, M. (2023). Environmental Personhood as a Tool to Protect Nature. *Philosophia, 51*(3), 1369–1384. doi:10.1007/s11406-022-00583-z

Leopold, A. (1949). *A Sand County almanac. And sketches here and there.* Oxford University Press.

Lidke, J. (2017). *The Goddess Within and Beyond the Three Cities: Śākta Tantra and the Paradox of Power in Nepāla-Maṇḍala.* Printworld.

Lidke, J. S. (2009). Towards a Theory of Tantra-Ecology. In C. K. Chapple (Ed.), DANAM Conference. *Yoga and Ecology: Dharma for the Earth: Proceedings of Two of the Sessions at the Fourth DANAM Conference, held on site at the American Academy of Religion.* Deepak Heritage Books, Deepak Heritage Books.

Lü, D., Richard, W., & Jung, C. G. (2014). The secret of the golden flower: a Chinese book of life. Mansfield Centre., OCLC 105755408.

Morley, J. (2008). Embodied Consciousness in Tantric Yoga and the Phenomenology of Merleau-Ponty. *Religion and the Arts*, *12*(1-3), 144–163. doi:10.1163/156852908X270980

O'Donnell, E. L., & Talbot-Jones, J. (2018). Creating Legal Rights for Rivers: Lessons from Australia, New Zealand, and India. *Ecology and Society*, *23*(1), 7. doi:10.5751/ES-09854-230107

Padoux, A. (2017) *The Hindu Tantric World: An Overview*, Chicago University Press, https://doi.org/ doi:10.7208/chicago/9780226424125.001.0001

Rohr. Fr. R. (2014). *Eager to Love: The Alternative Way of Francis of Assisi*. Hodder & Stoughton.

Sanderson, A. (2017). Ritual Transgression in Kaula Trika, https://amritananda-natha-saraswati.blogspot.com/p/ritual-in-kaula-trika.html

Sherma, R. D. (1998). Sacred Immanence: Reflections of Ecofeminism in Hindu Tantra. In L. E. Nelson (Ed.), *Purifying the Earthly Body of God. Religion and Ecology in Hindu India* (pp. 89–132). SUNY Press.

Shiva, V. (1993). *Ecofeminism*. Zed Books Ltd.

Shiva, V. (2016). *Staying Alive: Women, Ecology and Development*. North Atlantic Books.

Simmel, G. (1950). The Metropolis and Mental Life. In K. H. Wolff (Ed.), *The Sociology of Georg Simmel* (pp. 409–424). The Free Press.

Singh, S., Kaur, A., & Kaur, N. (2010). Environmental Degradation — A Case Study of Ambient Air Quality in Some Industrial Pockets of Punjab, *National Seminar on Management of Natural Resources and Environment in India,* Organized by GAD Institute of Development Studies, Amritsar, (pp. 564-75).

Starhawk (1999). *The Spiral Dance*. 20th edition, Harper.

Starhawk (2013) *The Earth Path: Grounding Your Spirit in the Rhythms of Nature,* HarperOne.

Stone, C. D. (1972). Should Trees Have Standing—Toward Legal Rights for Natural Objects. *Southern California Law Review*, *45*, 450.

Supran, G. (2023). Assessing ExxonMobil's Climate Change Communication, https://www.europarl.europa.eu/cmsdata/162144/Presentation%20Geoffrey%20Supran.pdf

Tabuchi, H. (2023). Maui Sued Big Oil in 2020, Citing Fire Risks and More, The New York Times.

Ulansey, D. (2000). Cultural Transition and Spiritual Transformation: from Alexander the Great to Cyberspace. In T. Singer (Ed.), *The Vision Thing: Myth* (pp. 213–231). Politics, and Psyche in the World.

Ulrich, R. S. (1984). View Through a Window May Influence Recovery from Surgery. *Science, 224*(4647), 420–421. doi:10.1126/science.6143402 PMID:6143402

Venkatraman, A., Nandy, R., Rao, S. S., Mehta, D. H., Viswanathan, A., & Jayasundar, R. (2019). Tantra and Modern Neurosciences: Is there any Correlation? *Neurology India, 67*(5), 1188–1193. doi:10.4103/0028-3886.271263 PMID:31744942

Wang, S., Blasco, D., Hamzah, A., & Verschuuren, B. (2023). Tourists and 'philosophers': Nature as a medium for consciousness and transcendence in spiritual tourism. *Annals of Tourism Research, 99*, 103543. doi:10.1016/j.annals.2023.103543

Watts, A. (1969). *Psychotherapy East and West*. Ballantine Books.

Weber, M. (2004). *The vocation lectures* (D. S. Owen & T. B. Strong, Eds., LivingstoneR., Trans.). Hackett Pub.

White, L. Jr. (1967). The historical roots of our ecological crisis. *Science, 155*(3767), 1203–1207. doi:10.1126/science.155.3767.1203 PMID:17847526

Wilber, K. (2001). *Sex, Ecology, Spirituality*. Shambhala.

Wilson, E. O. (1986). *Biophilia. The human bond with other species*. Harvard University Press.

ENDNOTES

[1] See more on disenchantment at https://www.cambridge.org/core/books/abs/subject-of-modernity/disenchantment-of-the-world/D4917EDEFA7216B908FD65749FE7826E).

[2] Reductionism is a worldview which considers that all complex entities or wholes can be reduced to a minimum of elementary particles. Also, in the reductionist view, the higher level of meaning (consciousness, mind), can be reduced to the lower level, consisting of elemental parts.

[3] Aldo Leopold, an early pioneer of the rights of nature, recognized the energy flow in the living world when he wrote: "Land is not merely soil; it is a fountain of energy flowing through a circuit of soils, plants, and animals" (Leopold,

1949, p. 216). His understanding of the Land as a self-organizing fountain of energy, dependent on physical energy while surpassing it, laid the foundation for recognizing the rights of nature in contemporary society, strikingly akin to Shiva's vision.

4   One may wonder whether this neglect of the environment is a denial or just a wrong order of priorities. Denial does look on suffice as a wrong order of priorities. For instance, an ill smoker who finds that stopping smoking is not a priority is close to denying the problem.

5   Already Georg Simmel described the modern sensory overload in his work *The Metropolis and Mental Life* (1903). He envisioned "an urban landscape of constant sensory stimuli against which the city-dweller must create a barrier in order to remain sane" (Simmel, 1903). On the contrary, staying in wild and beautiful natural environments opens our senses to the scale of sounds, colors, smells which are enjoyable and welcome. Of course, not every city forces us to encapsulate in our inner world to avoid being overloaded. There are green suburbs, city parks, and the growing trend to build eco-cities, which are clean, green, and home to a variety of living species.

6   "Who Killed the Electric Car? (2006)". Box Office Mojo. Retrieved October 19, 2023.

7   Thus, in 2020 Maui County filed a lawsuit "seeking damages from Exxon, Chevron and other giant oil and gas companies, accusing them of a "coordinated, multifront effort to conceal and deny their own knowledge" that the burning of fossil fuels would heat the planet to dangerous extremes." Hiroko Tabuchi, (2023).

8   For instance, a philosophically oriented environmental movement, Deep Ecology, presented convincing rational arguments against anthropocentrism. One of such arguments was derived from the scientific relational model of ecology, and it demonstrated "the interconnection and interdependence of everything that is alive" (Barman, 2022, p. 8737). As a result, it is not logical to set humans as ends and the rest of living beings as instruments or means.

9   "So, while being the most ancient of all psychological systems, yoga is simultaneously the holistic health paradigm of the future, a practical yet contemplative health practice." (Morley, 2008).

10 Some core works of these thinkers include Vandana Shiva's books Ecofeminism (1993) and Staying Alive: Women, Ecology, and Development (1988), Jeffrey Lidke's The Goddess Within and Beyond the three Cities: Sakta Tantra and the Paradox of Power in Nepala Mandala (2017), Rita DasGupta Sherma's Hermeneutics and Hindu Thought: Toward A Fusion of Horizon (2008), Starhawk's The Earth Path: Grounding Your Spirit in the Rhythms of Nature

(2004) and article Feminist, Earth-based Spirituality and Ecofeminism, in book ed Plant. Healing the Wounds: The Promise of Ecofeminism, pp.174-185.

[11] Shakta Tantra is a tradition in Shakti worship, a trend in Tantrism which identifies the supreme reality with Shakti, a female consort of Shiva. There are number of overviews of Shakta Tantra, one of which is by Jeffrey Lidke (2017) The Goddess Within and Beyond the Three Cities: Śākta Tantra and the Paradox of Power in Nepāla-Maṇḍala. The origins of Shate Tantrism are ancient and still discussed, while the mentions of Shakta Tantra appear at least in the 6th century CE and flourished during the late Middle Ages.

[12] Tantric practice of contact with impurity as a means to enlightenment is resemblant to the writings of Mikhail Bakhtin on Renaissance carnival as a spectacular feast of inversion and parody of high culture, which inspires ecstatic transgression of boundaries in altered states of consciousness. The carnival consciousness is also aspiring for non-duality, akin to the sudden enlightenment sought in Tantric rituals.

[13] In Tantric rituals mantra appears as a tool for the control of the manifested word, "mantra is envisioned to awaken the unconscious power of the human mind" (Kochetkova, 2022b, p. 63).

[14] A. Sanderson, *Ritual Transgression in Kaula Trika*, at https://amritananda-natha-saraswati.blogspot.com/p/ritual-in-kaula-trika.html

Chapter 2
Integrating Health Impact Assessment and Environmental Impact Assessment:
A Catalyst for Sustainable Development and Public Health in India

V. S. Gigimon
Maharashtra National Law University, Mumbai, India

R. S. Darsana
Maharashtra National Law University, Mumbai, India

ABSTRACT

Environmental impact assessments (EIA) evolved in ignorance of health concerns. Health impact assessments (HIA) have evolved to cater to health impacts of projects. Due to the intricate relationship between environment and health, integrating Health impact assessment and environmental impact assessment would be more cost-effective and practical. In the implementation of major projects, health impact assessment gains importance as there is large displacement of people, environmental changes, and related health hazards. This would enable a sustainable approach to properly handle the environment, health, and human well-being. This chapter analyses the meaning and scope of health impact assessment, its advantages, and challenges. It describes why India needs an integrated approach considering the socio-economic and demographic situations.

DOI: 10.4018/979-8-3693-1178-3.ch002

INTRODUCTION

Health is an indispensable component of human well-being. It encompasses physical, mental, and social dimensions. Healthy populations are the foundations of prosperous and thriving societies. A proper healthcare system ensures increased productivity, economic growth, and social cohesion. In its ambit, health includes not only disease treatment and prevention; but also aspects such as access to healthcare services, adequate living conditions, sanitation, nutrition, pollution-free environment, housing, etc. Health is also interconnected with other domains such as education, poverty alleviation environmental stability etc. Therefore, health plays a pivotal role in moulding quality of life and contributes to the overall development of societies.

Right to health is an internationally recognized Human right, finding its base in the Universal Declaration of Human Rights, the International Covenant for Economic, Social and Cultural Rights, and Constitution of the World Health Organisation. These instruments envisage the highest attainable standard of health for every human being. Thus, health has to be given utmost priority by states in policy formation. However, this importance of health is largely overlooked by policymakers. While extensive policies are framed on various issues such as national security, economic stability, and infrastructural development, health considerations are often neglected. Thus, leading to weak disease prevention strategies, increased health disparity, increased healthcare costs and decreased productivity. A healthy population would mean a skilled and knowledgeable workforce. They would be better resilient to infectious diseases and epidemics. Health is an important determinant of a nation's prosperity and well-being and therefore it is imperative that policymakers incorporate health considerations into the decision-making process. In this fast-growing world health is affected by non-health sectors and this impact have to be given due regard by stakeholders. (Fehr et al., 2014; Kemm et al., 2004)

Globalization has contributed to accelerated colonisation and developmental progress. New inventions and innovations have revolutionized all areas of life. With the rise in urbanization and industrialisation we now have well-built roads, different transportation mechanisms, dams, mines, buildings etc. which has eased lifestyle and helped mankind progress. However, this comfort has its own consequences such as pollution, climate change, soil erosion, etc. These impacts therefore revealed the necessity to give due regard to sustainability.

Governments therefore started monitoring the environmental impacts of human activities and brought effective remedial measures. Environmental Impact Assessments (EIA) were thus introduced to analyse the impact of any project, plan, or policy on the environment. EIAs are mandated by most of the countries before implementation of any mega project. EIAs would evaluate the potential harms of a project on the environment. This would provide decision-makers a holistic view of the potential effects of a project through which they may form informed decisions on whether to accept, reject, or modify the proposed project. EIAs therefore helps to bring balance between development and protection of biodiversity and ecosystems.

Environment is an important factor concerning human health. Natural environments have a direct influence on human health and well-being. Air, water, biodiversity, food security, etc are important determinants of health. Therefore, any interference with the environment would also have necessary repercussions on human health.

But EIAs fall short of adequately addressing the impacts of large projects on human health.(Bhatia & Wernham, 2008; Harris-Roxas et al., 2012) Despite the close relation, health considerations are not given due relevance in EIAs. In case of any project, a large population would be displaced. Not only are they moving out of their natural environment, but their settling in a different area may also lead to crowding and increased use of natural resources, putting them at a risk of vector borne and infectious diseases. Their access to good quality food, air, and water is also a challenge. Any developmental project would include construction activities. which would affect the air quality, soil fertility, flora, and fauna. It would also affect transportation and vehicle traffic. Thus, the threat to the health of nearby populations is apparent. Hence it becomes necessary to assess the health impacts of projects as well so that projects may be implemented giving top priority to citizen health. This is where Health Impact Assessment (HIA) becomes relevant.

According to WHO, "Health Impact Assessment is a practical approach used to judge the potential health effects of a policy, programme or project on a population, particularly on vulnerable or disadvantaged groups." (*Health Impact Assessment.*)

It is a systematic process conducted by health professionals, scientists, health care practitioners, social scientists and other stakeholders to assess the health impacts of projects on the health of populations so as to give a holistic understanding of how various factors can affect public health. This ensures that the decision makers give due regard to health-related considerations also while policy making.

HIAs take into account the impact of programmes, projects or policies on the health of the population. It is a structured process analysing large scale data and bringing together various stakeholders and expertise aim to analyse the potential consequences of a proposed project and suggest changes so as to mitigate those hazards.(Wernham, 2011) Thus, there would a balance between human health and development.

HIAs incorporate the broad definition of health as defined by WHO and therefore covers a wide ambit of areas including transportation, housing, land use, mining and construction activities and many more. In the absence of HIAs, projects and policy making would continue to be carried out without paying attention to the health of the citizens. This would result in problems such as spread of diseases, inability to access healthcare services, pollution, malnutrition and also other adverse health conditions such as respiratory issues or diabetes.

HIA has a wide ambit covering various sections of the society. It therefore would consider the impact of projects on the vulnerable and marginalised communities and ensure their needs and aspirations are also acknowledged. By integrating health considerations of various sectors, such as transportation, energy etc., it promotes a healthy environment supporting physical activity, access to health care and overall, wellbeing. It also facilitates collaboration between stakeholders and experts from various backgrounds, thus ensuring transparency and inclusiveness. HIA is also a precautionary step towards health hazards reduces health care costs.

It also takes a holistic approach by taking into account various exposures and health effects. Integrating HIA into EIA can assess health impact, sustainability and viability of various projects and diminish health disparities. It encourages inter sectoral responsibility for health by facilitating collaboration between various agencies. This would address the public concerns relating to both environment as well as health in an efficient and cost-effective manner.

In the global scenario, many countries do carry out HIAs, but it is largely as a voluntary process. It is also interesting to note that promotion of health and wellbeing is one of the criteria for EIAs, but it is overlooked and ignored. Legal or regulatory mandates for HIA are only found in few countries such as Canada, Australia, France, Lithuania, Thailand etc.

Developing countries, like India, are the worst hit by the adverse health impacts due to urbanisation and climate change. Considering the rate of infrastructural activity being carried out, it becomes necessary that health impacts also be given due weight along with environment so that population would be able to properly enjoy the benefits of the developmental activities.

An important consideration here is that very few HIAs have been conducted in India. There is no legal requirement for HIA in India. On the other hand, EIAs are mandatory; any developmental projects need environmental clearance. Where Sustainable development is being sought for, it becomes imperative that there be an initial evaluation on the potential health impacts be done to come up with adequate solution. Considering the transboundary threats to health such as climate change, it is high time that HIAs be part of the policymaking. Thus, HIA is an absolute necessity in India.

Public health is the most important area requiring governmental intervention. But unfortunately, it is the one that is not appropriately dealt with in policymaking. This chapter studies the necessity to interrelate HIA and EIA in India owing to the large number of developmental activities being carried out. In a country like India where the public health sector is lagging behind, integrating HIA and EIA would be more beneficial. Considering the state of affairs of the public health domain, a policy in this respect can ensure sustainability and well-being.

Integrating HIA and EIA gives a holistic assessment on the impact of projects. Consideration of both health and environmental makes policy decision more comprehensive and people friendly. Owing to the close connection between health and environment, there would be common factors of assessment as well as similarities in processes. The integrated approach would therefore cater to healthier communities by mitigating the risks before they become prominent. Moreover, a cumulative assessment would be beneficial for long-term planning and sustainable development. It would simplify decision making and bring down health disparities. The combined approach consolidates both environmental sustainability and public health.

ANALYSING ENVIRONMENTAL IMPACT ASSESSMENT AND HEALTH

Environmental Impact Assessments were a response to the growing global concerns over environment conservation. The National Environment Policy Act (NEPA) 1969 of the United States was the first legislation mandating EIAs.(Wernham, 2011) Many nations including both developed and developing countries mandate EIA before implementation of any plan.

Simply put, EIA is a systematic process that analyses the potential environmental impact of a proposed project before its implementation.(Glasson et al., 2012; Morgan, 2012; Wathern, 2004). This process assesses the possible consequences on the environment by considering factors such as air and water quality, biodiversity as well as social aspects. This would therefore help in evaluating the significance of the project by giving due consideration to its benefits and detriments. It also aims to provide measures to reduce the negative impacts thereby promoting sustainable practices. EIA also involves bringing together multiple stakeholders in the decision-making process. It caters to the concerns of the local community and all interested parties. Ultimately, the decision-makers are forced to consider alternatives which are less environmentally damaging alternatives. Thus, balancing demands of development and environmental protection in an equal manner.

EIA is a multi-stage process.(Glasson et al., 2012; Morgan, 2012; Wathern, 2004). The first step, called scoping, is where the boundaries of assessment are determined. The key environmental issues are identified by involving the various stakeholders. Scoping helps in prioritizing the most important issues through consultations with local residents, community leaders, interest groups and other organizations. Once the focus of the assessment is determined, the next step is the collection of baseline data. This involves gathering of background information on environmental and socio-economic conditions. Baseline studies would lay down the foundations on which the impacts of the project may be later measured. They would establish the descriptions of various environmental parameters to which subsequent prediction would be attempted as to the change in values. In the next step of impact prediction, experts evaluate the potential impacts by analysing various scenarios and parameters. Experts identify the direct, indirect, short term and long-term consequences and cumulative impacts. Based on the findings the project would be assessed and mitigation measures would be suggested so that there is minimum environmental damage. The findings are documented (in the form of an Environmental Impact Statement (EIS)) and made available for public consultation. Based on the reports or findings, a decision would be made as to whether or not to proceed with the project or bring in appropriate modifications. The project would then be monitored to ensure compliance with environmental policy. This is also essential to keep track of any impacts that may not have been initially predicted but is endangering the environment. Hence prompt decisions may be made to reduce these harms since a study on the conditions have already been made.

However, the impacts on health have rarely been assessed. Health risks due to socio economic changes are inadequately covered by EIAs.(Thondoo & Gupta, 2021) Public health and environmental factors such as transportation, land use, housing, energy production, etc. are closely connected since they are causes for a wide variety of health conditions. However, in decision-making & policy formulation, this influence on health are not given enough importance, and plans are made without involving health experts. Health aspects are rarely incorporated while conducting EIAs.(Bhatia & Wernham, 2008; Wernham, 2011) The Stockholm Declaration, recognized this relation between human well-being and environmental issues laying down the stepping stone for global environmental protection measures which also addresses health concerns. (Thondoo & Gupta, 2021)

Considering the close connection between health and the environment, there would be common determinants involved in assessment. Carrying out environmental assessments by including health factors would therefore save time and costs. It first becomes essential to analyse the scope and advantages of health impact assessments before examining the need for integrating Health Impact Assessment and Environmental Impact Assessment.

A STUDY ON HEALTH IMPACT ASSESSMENT

Health Impact Assessment is a structured process that identifies the potential health effects of a policy, program or project.(Thondoo & Gupta, 2021; Wernham, 2011) Like EIA, HIA also involves multiple stages beginning with the screening. It is assessed as to whether HIA is needed by considering the availability of data and health information to be used. In the scoping stage, the plan for HIA is developed by identifying the potential risks & benefits. This is done based on stakeholder inputs, literature review, and expert opinion. Assessment of the health impact is made in the next stage by bringing all baseline studies of affected populations. It lays down the existing conditions that affect health and analyses the potential harms the proposed project decision would have. Once the health effects are identified, appropriate recommendations are made for effective management and mitigation of these harms. The findings are thereafter reported to decision-makers and affected communities. The decision-makers would then have evidence-based information on which the project may be carried on through a plan where health risks to the community are reduced to the minimum. The next step is monitoring and evaluation where the effectiveness of recommendations are evaluated and the predictions are compared with the actual impacts. (Dua & Acharya, 2014; Kemm, 2013; Thondoo & Gupta, 2021; Wernham, 2011)

Conducting HIA will give evidence-based information on the potential health impact of any project. This would help to refine policy decisions at the planning stage itself so that negative health impacts could be minimised. It would therefore prevent health hazards before they occur. Thus, public health and wellbeing would become the top priority of the decision makers. By recommending changes in policies, it also optimizes positive health outcomes. This would foster public trust in governance. Moreover, it aligns with the principles of sustainable development and avoids hasty short-sighted decisions which would adversely affect health of the population.

HIA offers a mechanism to minimise the health risks of a proposed project. (Thondoo & Gupta, 2021) With enough empirical evidence, the viability of the plan can be determined by prioritizing health of the people. Moreover, the authorities and public health officials could be well-equipped to manage and handle any crisis based on the predictions made in the assessment and environmental disasters may also be properly tackled. In the absence of HIA large projects would be carried out without any heed to health concerns thereby threatening the overall survival of the community. Thus, HIA can be an efficient tool in achieving this Global Sustainable Development Goals which provide for promotion of healthy life and well being of all ages.(Thondoo & Gupta, 2021) Health is viewed in the most widest sense by considering social, economic and cultural influences.(Bhatia & Wernham, 2008)

HIA is done by considering multiple determinants of health such as pollution, waste management, nutrition, construction, transportation, housing, disease prevention and protection and also social factors such social cohesion and economic opportunities. (Thondoo & Gupta, 2021) It also integrates various stakeholders which includes affected communities, vulnerable populations, public health experts as well as experts in other fields.(Wernham, 2011) Therefore, a holistic study would be conducted that fosters informed decision-making. It also helps in understanding and promoting health among different age groups by using the various indicators and determinants.

HIA also presents a lot of challenges which can be defeated in the presence of a legislative framework and technical expertise. Identifying the relevant health determinants to carry out the assessment is very crucial, considering the available resources and the time frame within which the assessment has to be completed. The numerous factors involved has to be properly prioritised. Capturing and comprehensively analysing these determinants can be combined, requiring interdisciplinary collaboration and based on technical expertise. The boundary of the assessment ought to be identified depending on the type of project that is to be carried out.

HIA relies heavily on accurate and up-to-date information to assess baseline health conditions, identify vulnerable populations, and predict potential impacts. In some cases, there may be gaps in data accessibility or reliability, hindering the precision of the assessment. A question which needs attention is 'who' will carry out the assessment, thus necessitating the training of individuals and also the establishment of organizations. Planning agencies and public health organisations along with the health ministry has a major role to be played to establish a robust mechanism. The connected problem to this issue is funding wherein the health departments should be actively involved. The private sector, especially national and multinational corporations would have much to do in this respect.(Wernham, 2011)

Further, engaging diverse stakeholders, including communities, policymakers, and experts, requires effective communication, cultural sensitisation, and a commitment to transparency. Disparities in power dynamics and the inclusion of marginalized voices can pose additional challenges, potentially leading to incomplete assessments, that do not fully capture the range of perspectives. Time and resource constraints represent another significant challenge in the implementation of HIA since it involves data collection, analysis and engagement of stakeholders. In practice, tight project schedules or limited financial resources can compromise the depth and breadth of evaluation. This challenge is particularly important in rapid development projects where decisions are often made under tight deadlines. Challenges also may arise in translating HIA findings into actionable recommendations and ensuring their integration into policy and project development. Decision-makers may lack awareness of the importance of HIA or face competing priorities, potentially relegating health considerations to secondary status. Further, the inclusion of HIA into the decision-making process would also have to counter bureaucratic hurdles.

TRACING THE DEVELOPMENT OF HIA
IN THE GLOBAL SCENARIO

The international recognition of HIA can be traced to the Ottawa Charter of Health Promotion, 1986. However, the Gothenburg Consensus Paper, 1999 gave HIAs more precision and clarity.(Bhatia & Wernham, 2008; Thondoo & Gupta, 2021) The Amsterdam treaty led to the crystallization of HIAs in the European Union. The Jakarta Declaration on Health Promotion, 1995 also stressed on HIA as a means to promote social responsibility for health.(Ahuja, 2007) WHO also played an important role in the growth of HIA with the Bangkok Charter on Health Promotion, 2005 and other guidelines issued from time to time.(Kemm et al., 2004; Thondoo & Gupta, 2021) The United Nations Environmental Programme is actively engaged in capacity building and HIA Policy development. The International Association for Impact Assessment integrates researchers and practitioners worldwide and aims to develop integrated impact assessment policies.(Ahuja, 2007) In addition to these various private bodies and organizations also work for implementation of HIA and have contributed much to its evolution and growth. (Ahuja, 2007; Thondoo & Gupta, 2021)

In the European Union, the Gothenburg Consensus Paper is responsible for streamlining HIA process. It gives an extensive definition by framing it to be a combination of procedures which are used to judge the potential effects of a policy, program or project on the health of the population and the distribution of effects within the population; and identifies 4 values based on which HIA ethics revolve namely democracy, equity, sustainability and ethical use of evidence.(Kemm, 2013) Democracy means the right of participation wherein those who would be affected by a decision have the right to be involved in the decision-making process. Equity focuses on analysis of the impact of decisions not just in aggregate, but as to how various sections of the population are affected. These sections may be characterized based on multiple factors such as gender, age, socio-economic status, ethnic background, etc. HIA should focus on clearly defining the positive and negative impacts of a project on the different groups of the population. This ensures that the voices of every section especially vulnerable and marginalised sections are not ignored. As per the principle of sustainable development, a complete and holistic assessment is to be conducted by taking into account short-term, long-term, direct as well as indirect impacts. Any decision ought to be taken considering the needs and aspirations of future generations as well. Ethical use of evidence means honest use of qualitative and quantitative data based on scientific disciplines and methodologies. The assessor has to rely on literature as well as expert opinions. Any conflict of evidence should be reported and evidence should not be suppressed. (Kemm, 2013)

HIAs are still not a mainstream part of the public health sector. Even though they are carried out in many countries, only a very few nations offer a legislative mandate;

in others, it is largely voluntary. The way HIA is perceived and implemented also varies across countries.(Kemm, 2013) For example, the European notion of HIA is based on the Gothenburg Consensus Paper definition and principles, whereas Australian view of HIA focuses on the "impact of chemical, biological, physical, or social agent on a specified human population under a specified set of conditions and for a certain time frame."(Kemm, 2013)

Countries such as France, Germany, Thailand etc. have standalone legislations and nations such as Cambodia, the United States, Canada, New Zealand etc. have integrated HIAs into the procedures of EIA.(Thondoo & Gupta, 2021) However, there are no uniform standards on which HIAs are carried out based on any best practices. Hence, HIA processes vary in methodology and type.(Kemm et al., 2004; Thondoo & Gupta, 2021) Though HIA is gaining global recognition, it is not implemented in many countries due to absence of a uniform regulation or practise that can be adopted like that for EIA. Therefore, even those countries which have adopted HIA polices are unable to enjoy the benefits of HIA since there is no international standard. Hence there is a need for an international recognition for HIA through a convention or protocol.

INTEGRATING HIA INTO EIA

Integration of HIA into EIA recognises the interconnection between environment and health. It would provide a holistic understanding of how variations in environment affects health of communities. The process of data collection, analysis and reporting would be refined by avoiding duplication of efforts. It basically would refines the existing statutory mechanism to strengthen impact assessments. Since EIAs already involve collaboration of multiple institutions, integration with HIA would mean scrutiny by multidisciplinary experts which would provide a broad and improved analysis. Integrated approach also would provide better understanding of the various social determinants of health which may help in reducing health disparities and promote health equity. This can lead to formulation of new policies and regulatory measures that focus on the promotion of health.(Bhatia & Wernham, 2008)

In the United States, the first reported case of integrating HIA into EIA can be seen in North Slope Borough, Alaska during the late 2000. The North Slope Oil and Gas Development project raised concerns among the indigenous communities about the health impacts experienced by them which included nutritional impacts, contaminant-based issues etc. The Alaska Inter-Tribal Council along with the Bureau of Land Management and Minerals Management Service worked together in successfully incorporating health concerns into EIA. HIA was conducted by utilising the public health data; by conducting public meetings as well as through literature review. The public health experts were therefore able to outline the extend of impact and come out with appropriate recommendations. The health impacts found include dietary changes (due to displacement of subsistence animals); diabetes; cardiovascular diseases; transmission of infectious diseases and also social strain and cultural changes which may lead to increased access to drugs and alcohol. As a result, new measures of mitigation and monitoring of health indicators, contaminants, environment and foods. Recommendations also included monitoring and mitigation strategies of health impacts in case of oil spills. (Bhatia & Wernham, 2008)

HIA would therefore be a cost-effective and resource-saving mechanism. Since the number of projects taken up is at a rise every day, especially those that affect large populations, integration of HIA and EIA would ease the burden on the state. It also would lead to recommendations and mitigation plans which cater to public health demands as well as environmental concerns.

It would strengthen public participation in decision making by addressing the needs of the affected communities. It would also enhance stakeholder collaboration with active involvement of communities, interest groups, and experts in the various fields. Thus, promoting transparency and accountability. Another advantage of integration is that it provides better risk assessment and helps in formulation of risk management strategies which considers both health and environmental aspects.

Moreover, the combination of HIA and EIA would ensure that the decision-making process is in tune with the goals of sustainable development as well as climate change. It is high time that health and the environment are considered together and not in isolation. This would also enable long-term sustainability wherein only those projects which aim in the well-being of current and future generations are promoted.

THE INDIAN SCENARIO

In India, EIAs are governed by the Environmental Impact Assessment Notification (first issued in 1994) under the Environment Protection Act, 1986.(Ahuja, 2007; Pradyumna, 2015) The Notification has undergone various amendments catering to changing environmental concerns. Environmental clearance is mandatory for various categories of developmental activities which include mining, thermal power plants, airports, transport, tourism, etc. Though EIA and HIA are much similar HIA is only at a nascent stage. EIAs do seek health-related information relating to the impact of hazardous materials; changes in disease prevalence; changes due to land use, solid waste, etc. However, a comprehensive assessment of the adverse effects and suitable recommendations for tackling these impacts is absent. Further public health experts and healthcare organisations have no role in EIA. Therefore, health remains out of the primary focus of EIA in India.(Ahuja, 2007)

In terms of health and health policy, India still has a long way to go. Though the Health Ministry has been implementing various policies and programs, to improve healthcare, a substantial population of the country is yet to receive basic health needs due to poverty. The intensity of poverty as per the Multidimensional Poverty Index in India is 44.39%. (*India-National-Multidimentional-Poverty-Index-2023.Pdf*, 2023) Policies and schemes of the governments have led to a lot of improvements such as reduced mortality rate, eradication of disease, etc. However, a huge population of the country has not received the benefits of these schemes. Many remain malnourished and do not have access to even primary healthcare facilities. Many live in unhygienic living conditions which is detrimental to their immune system making them vulnerable to diseases and epidemics.(Ahuja, 2007)

India has yet to completely absorb the fact that health is influenced by decisions beyond the health sector. HIA is yet to be part of the policy-making process in India. While nations worldwide have adopted and are in practice of HIA, only very few HIAs have been conducted in India in which the state has a very minimal role. (Dua & Acharya, 2014)

Being a developing country, India is accustomed to large projects being implemented, which are increasing every day. These span across various industries such as transportation, natural resource development, housing, manufacturing, etc. Large projects would involve the displacement of a large population. This would substantially change their way of life, the resources they would use and consume as well as their livelihood. Such a transition not only affects their socioeconomic status but would also have health consequences. Similarly, people living near factories or mines would continuously be exposed to toxic chemicals and polluted atmosphere, which in the long run is detrimental to not only the present but also future generations.

Disasters such as Bhopal Gas Tragedy, Kodaikanal Mercury Poisoning, Kolkata Flyover Collapsing etc. shows the need to incorporate health concerns in the planning process. HIA would provide a complete picture as to the consequences in case the plan fails. Thereby, adequate prevention and mitigation plans could be made which makes all stakeholders prepared in case of a health crisis. Another important point is that the health impacts of many projects may not be as apparent as in the cases above. Many would be subtle and would develop only over a period of time. Environmental changes due to construction can result in vector-borne diseases. Any developmental activity such as mining, laying of electricity lines, oil pipelines, construction of roads, railways, highways, etc. would have a significant impact on the population living nearby. Furthermore, health impacts would continue even after the implementation of projects which therefore requires close and thorough monitoring. Hence, experts play a crucial role in providing a sophisticated analysis. Considering India's population, health situation, and the growing number of projects that neglect their health impacts, introducing HIA as a legislative measure is very important.

To properly understand the need for HIA policy in India, two case studies are done. In the first, HIA was conducted and it was able to prevent a larger harm. The second case study shows the extent of damage caused due to lack of proper planning.

Konkan Railway Project

There are not many HIAs conducted in India.(Dua & Acharya, 2014) One example where HIA proved to be beneficial in mitigating harm is the Konkan Railway Project. (Dua & Acharya, 2014; Kumar & Shetty, 2017) This was one of the biggest railway projects in India which aimed at improving rail connectivity along the Konkan coast in the Western Ghats which stretches through the states of Maharashtra, Goa, and Karnataka. The railway line covers a distance of 760 kilometers, running from Roha near Mumbai to Thokur near Mangalore. The project has significantly reduced travel time and has facilitated economic development and tourism.

This was also one of the most challenging railway projects in India since the construction had to be carried out in difficult terrain and climatic conditions. The project required the construction of numerous bridges, tunnels, and railway stations. Although the project's initial plan was laid down in the 19th century, due to the challenges and costs, the project officially began during the 1990s. It became operational in phases and the first passenger train started running in 1998. (Kumar & Shetty, 2017)

The climatic conditions in the region is characterised by heavy rainfall and high humidity which favour mosquito breading and in the spread of malaria in the nearby areas. The area being prone to malaria outbreak which was another challenge that had to be addressed.

Environment Impact Assessment was conducted but it did not provide any reference to the impacts of the project on the disease prevalence and spread. Hence there arose a need for conducting HIA separately for a better understanding of the health risks. The HIA teams focused on assessing the causes of increased malarial infection due to the migrant workforce and also investigated water stagnant points in the construction sites which enabled mosquito breeding. Based on the findings appropriate modifications were suggested to prevent water stagnation and mosquito breeding. Appropriate advice in engineering were given such as efficient drainage systems; anti-mosquito septic tanks at stations and staff quarters; proper demolition of water tanks used for once construction of bridges are over; use of reusable fiber glass in trains etc. (Kumar & Shetty, 2017)

The HIA helped in understanding the root causes of the spread of vector-borne disease and its spread. It took a complete view by analysing the effect of the migration of workforce into the area. Thus, HIA helped in preventing an outbreak due to the timely intervention.

The Konkan HIA example reveals the importance of HIA in policymaking and planning. It shows the need for conducting HIA before the implementation of the project so that necessary impacts may be anticipated and countered. In the absence of such a plan, the project would have continued without considering health factors. The resulting health crisis would have been cumbersome not only to the public but also to the State.

Sterlite Copper Smelt Plant

The Sterlite Copper Smelter Plant, located in Thoothukudi, Tamil Nadu, India, was a copper smelting facility owned and operated by Vedanta Limited, a subsidiary of the Vedanta Resources conglomerate. The plant was established in the late 1990s and became one of the largest copper smelting facilities in India. It played a crucial role in meeting the country's demand for copper. The plant employed a copper smelting process to extract copper from copper concentrates. The process involved the use of high-temperature furnaces to melt and refine copper ore, releasing by-products such as sulfur dioxide and other pollutants. (Govindarajan, 2018; Pandi-Perumal, 2022)

Since its inception, it has been a subject of public opposition. Local communities raised environmental and health concerns. The emissions from the smelting process caused respiratory issues, skin diseases, and other health problems among the local people. Villagers reported water contamination. Many people suffer from cancer and other deadly problems. A health study conducted by the Tirunelveli Medical College revealed that a huge amount of population living in a 5km radius from the planet suffer from respiratory diseases; Menstrual disorders were reported in women and ground water contamination was also reported. However, these studies were not able to specifically attribute the cause of the diseases to Sterlite Copper. The plant was permanently closed down in 2018 by the State Government citing public health concerns. Even the Environmental Clearance Report showed minimal damage to the environment and nearby population. Despite closing of the plant, health problems and disease prevalence still continue in the area. (Pandi-Perumal, 2022)

These case studies therefore reveal the potentials of HIA wherein a proper study was able to prevent a health crisis and the lack of one, led to halt of crucial economic resource. Conduct of HIA would have given proper insights as to the root cause of the health concerns. The construction of such plants would significantly affect the nearby population. Once it becomes operational, the adverse impact that it would have on the environment as well as the health of populations also needs to be considered. Large-scale projects would therefore need large scale impact assessments to have a complete understanding of the nature and core of the problem. HIA would tally all the health determinants and would have provided for a balanced approach which promoted health on one hand and contributes to economic prosperity on the other.

HIA would have properly predicted the impacts and the areas where caution needs to be taken.

Analysing the methodologies and techniques in other countries was a difficult task. The number of reliable and official sources with accessible materials are very less. HIA reports (other than a few) were either not available in the public domain or were not accessible. However, Good Practice guidelines which are industry specific have been published by various organisations. (Bank, 2018; *Health Impact Assessment. A Guide for the Oil and Gas Industry.*, 2016; *HIA_in_Planning_Exec_Summary.Pdf*, 2020)Therefore, accessing recent HIAs and a facilitated analysis was not possible.

WAY FORWARD

India is therefore in need of a regulatory framework for Health Impact Assessments in the form of legislation or guidelines. Majority of the people in India belong to poor and underprivileged sections whose basic health demands such as access to healthcare; adequate food, water and amenities; access to fresh air and water, etc. remain unsatisfied. These populations suffer the most due to major projects. Displacement and lifestyle changes directly impact health. These may have long-term effects and could lead to disabilities. In the Indian scenario where the health disparity is very high, integrating HIA and EIA would be a more pragmatic approach. The legislative framework should define a specialized agency that would govern the impact assessment process. Thus, a robust mechanism could be placed the focus of which is promoting health and wellbeing of all sections of the society.

Due to the influence of other sectors on health. which are largely overlooked, it is necessary to promote collaboration between various Government Agencies as well as other stakeholders. This can contribute to reduced costs and processing time. A paradigm shift in the way development is conceived and carried out is required for the integration of HIA and EIA; it is not only a technical process. The practical examples served as a reminder that good coordination, community involvement, and recognition of the social determinants of health are just as important to success as analytical expertise.

An integrated approach in the hands of a specialized agency would provide a holistic assessment of health and environmental factors. This will not only facilitate informed decision nations but also will give due importance to social impacts. The Decision of such an agency would provide a model to upcoming developmental projects to give enough significance to health & environmental points. In the long run, the country would benefit from projects that promote sustainability, health, and well-being of people. The specialized agency can facilitate data collection, and monitoring in one go without any duplication making the whole process efficient. (Ahuja, 2007)

Such an agency would also be able to involve multiple stakeholders such as members of local bodies, members of NGOs, interest groups, and other organizations. The needs of the affected communities would also be better acknowledged. This would ensure reduced costs and better utilization of resources. In such an approach, the matter is not just the responsibility of a single ministry, and therefore resource constraints may be overcome.(Ahuja, 2007) Moreover, funds may also be pooled from various sources. Such an agency would also promote public-private partnerships.

Along with this, it is also essential that there be guidelines on the conduct of HIA. Due to the varied projects undertaken spanning different industries whose scope and impacts are dependent on multiple factors; it is imperative that good practises be adopted so that the scope of HIA can be properly streamlined. Therefore, health indicators may be prioritise giving due importance to the project and the available time and resources. It would also help in delineating the geographical limits of the assessment.

This can be illustrated by taking the case of the HIA in the Boone Boulevard Green Street Project, Atlanta Georgia.(US EPA, 2015) The city of Atlanta had a combined sewage system where stormwater and sanitary discharge flow together to enter a treatment facility and then is discharged to a nearby waterbody. This has been detrimental to many rivers and streams. As a part of implementing green infrastructure of the US Environmental Protection Agency (EPA) a project called as the Boone Boulevard Green Infrastructure Conceptual Design was developed for converting underutilised roadways and to redirect stormwater from roadway to raingardens before flowing into the combined sewer system. The HIA relied on publicly available data, empirical and science based literature and followed rigorous analysis methods by including health professionals and stakeholders. Stakeholder participation was facilitated through email, phones, public flyers etc. There were also public meetings and community members involving members of the community as well as other organisations. Training programmes were organised. The core team consisted of EPA Staff, researchers from the Centre of Disease Control and Prevention as well as students who were residents of the community. By comparing with other HIAs, the team identified the geographical scope to be half a mile radius around the project site since this would give optimal results in regards to impact. By analyses of the available data (at the national level) 12 determinants were identifies which included water quality, flood management, climate, air quality, traffic safety etc. The team therefore framed appropriate recommendations catering to the demands of all stakeholders. Hence, the benefit of the project was received by the community with strategies to combat potential health risks.(US EPA, 2015)

CONCLUSION

After the Industrial Revolution, the world witnessed rapid urbanization leading to various developmental activities. New inventions paved the way for human progress. Slowly the negative impacts of developmental and infrastructural activities were realised and measures were taken to curb these negative impacts. The environmental impact due to depletion of natural resources, deforestation, and pollution revealed the need for a balance between development and sustainability. Therefore, environmental protection measures were envisaged on national and international forums. Hence strategies were developed to reduce environmental degradation. Environmental Impact Assessments arose as a preventive mechanism. They fostered a mechanism whereby adverse environmental impacts may be prevented. Decision-makers can therefore analyse if the benefits outweigh the risks through a bigger picture. EIAs have been carried out in most of the countries globally, and have proved to be an efficient tool in achieving the goal of sustainability.

Health cannot be considered independent of other influences. Any new project or plan for development always have health outcomes. However, these outcomes are never taken up in mainstream decision-making. At its core, Health Impact Assessment acknowledges the influence of non-health sectors on health. It recognizes the fact that any lifestyle change, which may be induced or voluntary, would have a necessary impact on health and stresses on the need to prevent or mitigate any adverse impacts. The environment is the core of human survival. Any change in the chain of survival and environmental conditions would therefore affect human health. Increased cases of asthma due to air pollution is just a simple example. Despite this connection, health remained an outsider to Environmental Impact Assessments. Though the promotion of health is one of the objectives of EIAs, the extent of the impact of any project on health was never thoroughly analysed. HIAs are however concerned with the health impact of policies.

Developing countries undergo large-scale infrastructural activities and it is high time that health considerations be given due importance while conducting impact assessments. This is where integrated assessments play a role. Integrating HIA and EIA would kill two demons in one go. Due to the presence of common determinants, integrated assessments would avoid duplication of efforts. Moreover, a holistic view of the public concerns may be obtained and appropriate decisions made. Public consultation is an important element in both EIA and HIA and therefore integration would prove to be more practical and useful. EIA itself is a process that brings together various stakeholders and technical expertise. Integrating HIA would promote larger stakeholder collaboration and would increase the involvement of experts from various fields. Moreover, this would uplift collaboration of various ministries and departments.

While this would be the best solution, there are numerous challenges which could be resolved with proper planning and monitoring. Groundwork has to start from academic settings and then move upwards. This will promote efficient decision-making and bring up long-term and quality mitigation strategies. It is essential to provide thorough rules and instruments specifically designed for the Indian setting. These materials ought to provide useful approaches, handle contextual difficulties, and guarantee a uniform methodology for integrated evaluations. Integration would not be successful in a setting where there is no collaboration among ministries and other stakeholders. Decisions ought to be taken by considering the demands of the affected communities. Decision-makers ought to be far-sighted and should think beyond the immediate health impacts. Hence, health would also be an important consideration while developing projects and policies and thereby there would be a promotion of sustainable projects which holistically cover environmental and health impacts. Since environmental and health issues are dynamic, research must be done continuously. It is crucial to fund multidisciplinary research projects that investigate new problems, evaluate the efficacy of integrated techniques, and provide insights for adaptable tactics.

Standardized methodology development, awareness campaigns, and capacity building are all necessary for effective implementation. Stakeholder engagement needs to go from being a ceremonial activity to becoming a vital component of decision-making, especially with local communities. In the context of sustainable development, trust is a vital resource that policymakers may cultivate by promoting a culture of transparency, responsibility, and inclusivity.

Growing technologies such as artificial intelligence, remote sensing, etc. can refine methodologies of assessment and can would enhance the predictions of assessment. These technologies contribute to more robust, efficient, and data-driven assessment processes, enabling better-informed decision-making and fostering sustainable development. They can enhance accuracy and efficiency of the assessment process.

By intertwining considerations of human health and environmental well-being, the integrated approach provides a more sophisticated understanding of the intricate relationship between development initiatives and the health of communities and ecosystems wherein India would scale up in the index of better healthcare and development. In the current global scenario where there are border threats to health raised by climate change, impact assessment has a huge role in preventing health crises.

An important point to be addressed is the lack of international consensus in the case of HIA, like that of EIA. Uniform standards can only be established, in the presence of an international framework. Until then, incorporation of national guidelines would enhance the country's path to sustainability.

REFERENCES

Ahuja, A. (2007). Health Impact Assessment in Project and Policy Formulation. [JSTOR.]. *Economic and Political Weekly, 42*(35), 3581–3587.

Bank, A. D. (2018). *Health Impact Assessment: A Good Practice Sourcebook.* Asian Development Bank. https://www.adb.org/documents/health-impact-assessment-sourcebook

Bhatia, R., & Wernham, A. (2008). Integrating Human Health into Environmental Impact Assessment: An Unrealized Opportunity for Environmental Health and Justice. *Environmental Health Perspectives, 116*(8), 991–1000. doi:10.1289/ehp.11132 PMID:18709140

Dua, B., & Acharya, A. S. (2014). Health impact assessment: Need and future scope in India. *Indian Journal of Community Medicine, 39*(2), 76–81. doi:10.4103/0970-0218.132719 PMID:24963222

Fehr, R., Viliani, F., Nowacki, J., & Martuzzi, M. (2014). *Health in impact assessments: Opportunities not to be missed.* World Health Organization. Regional Office for Europe; WHO IRIS. https://iris.who.int/handle/10665/137369

Glasson, J., Therivel, R., Chadwick, A. J., & Chadwick, A. (2012). *Introduction to environmental impact assessment* (4th ed.). Routledge.

Govindarajan, V. (2018, April 6). *'Every house has a sick person': Why people in Tuticorin are opposing Vedanta's copper smelter.* Scroll.In. https://scroll.in/article/874441/every-house-has-a-sick-person-why-people-in-tuticorin-are-opposing-vedantas-copper-smelter

Harris-Roxas, B., Viliani, F., Bond, A., Cave, B., Divall, M., Furu, P., Harris, P., Soeberg, M., Wernham, A., & Winkler, M. (2012). Health impact assessment: The state of the art. *Impact Assessment and Project Appraisal, 30*(1), 43–52. doi:10.1080/14615517.2012.666035

Health impact assessment. A guide for the oil and gas industry. (n.d.). Ipieca. https://www.ipieca.org/resources/health-impact-assessment-a-guide-for-the-oil-and-gas-industry

Health impact assessment. (n.d.). WHO. https://www.who.int/health-topics/health-impact-assessment

HIA_in_Planning_Exec_Summary.pdf. (n.d.). UK Government. https://assets.publishing.service.gov.uk/media/5f85b628e90e07329a8dbf81/HIA_in_Planning_Exec_Summary.pdf

India-National-Multidimentional-Poverty-Index-2023.pdf. (n.d.). NITI. https://niti.gov.in/sites/default/files/2023-08/India-National-Multidimentional-Poverty-Index-2023.pdf

Kemm, J. (Ed.). (2013). *Health impact assessment: Past achievement, current understanding, and future progress* (1st ed.). Oxford University Press.

Kemm, J., Parry, J., & Palmer, S. (2004). *Health Impact Assessment.* Oxford University Press. doi:10.1093/acprof:oso/9780198526292.001.0001

Kumar, K., & Shetty, D. R. (2017). Health Impact Assessment: Recent Developments and Challenges. *International Journal of Health Sciences and Research, 7*(11), 296–306.

Morgan, R. K. (2012). Environmental impact assessment: The state of the art. *Impact Assessment and Project Appraisal, 30*(1), 5–14. doi:10.1080/14615517.2012.661557

Pandi-Perumal, S. R. (2022). Sterlite Copper: Much Ado About Nothing, all the while Ignoring the Elephant in the Room? SSRN *Electronic Journal.* doi:10.2139/ssrn.4106810

Pradyumna, A. (2015). Health Aspects of Environmental Impact Assessment Process in India. *Economic and Political Weekly, 50*(8), 57–64.

Thondoo, M., & Gupta, J. (2021). Health impact assessment legislation in developing countries: A path to sustainable development? *Review of European, Comparative & International Environmental Law, 30*(1), 107–117. doi:10.1111/reel.12347

US EPA. O. (2015, July 15). *Proctor Creek Boone Boulevard Health Impact Assessment (HIA) Final Report* [Reports and Assessments]. EPA. https://www.epa.gov/healthresearch/proctor-creek-boone-boulevard-health-impact-assessment-hia-final-report

Wathern, P. (Ed.). (2004). *Environmental impact assessment theory and practice.* Routledge.

Wernham, A. (2011). Health Impact Assessments Are Needed In Decision Making About Environmental And Land-Use Policy. *Health Affairs, 30*(5), 947–956. doi:10.1377/hlthaff.2011.0050 PMID:21555479

Chapter 3
Exploring the Legal Framework of Climate Migration in Latin America

Anny Gabriela Molina Ochoa
O.P. Jindal Global University, India

Maria Camila Duque Gomez
O.P. Jindal Global University, India

Santiago Weil Silva
O.P. Jindal Global University, India

ABSTRACT

This chapter explores the climate migration phenomenon and its legal framework in Latin America, studying some of its possible drivers and how these have a notable incidence in the global south. The chapter is centered on the Latin American region, providing a panorama of the geographical characteristics that make it particularly vulnerable to natural disasters and climate-related events, being these drivers of climate migration. The chapter also gives a view of the social, economic, and political conditions that make Latin America more susceptible to suffering human rights violations, which has an impact on the capacity of the countries to protect climate migrants and adds to the vulnerability of the region. The chapter also links this phenomenon to the existing legal framework, starting from the international instruments to later approach the domestic legislation and developments of the Latin American countries, revealing the lack of a harmonized regional instrument to protect climate migrants.

DOI: 10.4018/979-8-3693-1178-3.ch003

INTRODUCTION

During recent years, climate variability has increased in occurrence and magnitude. There is a link between climate events such as flooding, hurricanes, and landslides with climate change and the increase in global temperature (WMO, 2021). As well, human interaction accelerates natural warming and cooling cycles. According to the World Meteorological Organization, in 2022, "the global annual mean near-surface temperature exceeded the pre-industrial average by approximately 1.15 °C, increasing from 1.02 °C to 1.28 °C" (WMO, 2022). Scholarly approaches have studied it as anthropogenic climate change, which has consequences for the living and organization of human communities. One of the responses of human societies to changes in living conditions is to move, making climate change a driver for migration (Pan, 2020).

Environmental issues can affect living conditions and motivate human response by relocation. For the purposes of this chapter, these issues will be named as drivers. There are multiple drivers that have been identified by literature, but this chapter will approach two of them: natural disasters and resource scarcity (Wyman, 2013). The first one encompasses a series of events, such as hurricanes, floods, earthquakes, and wildfires, with devastating consequences that can forcefully displace entire communities (Pan, 2020). The second one also directly impacts living conditions, and the barriers or lack of access to natural resources can gradually force the relocalization of individuals and communities (Reuveny, 2007).

Migration is defined as the movement of communities and individuals to settle in another location (European Parliament, 2023). The causes for this displacement can be multiple, but they can be divided into voluntary and involuntary reasons. The first one refers to those relocations due to the individual's willingness, for example, to work or study abroad. The second refers to forced movements due to social issues like economic distress, political unrest, and violence (UNESCO, 2021). These two categories sometimes overlap because of the multiple circumstances and contexts leading individuals and communities to migrate, making it a multidimensional phenomenon that calls for a holistic approach.

Migration has been recognized as a global issue by the United Nations Department of Economic and Social Affairs (UNDESA), which in 2021 reported that globally, there are around 281 million international migrants, which means individuals that are not living in their country of origin (UNDESA, 2021). Migration as a process impacts various aspects of human life, and the vulnerability of the displaced individuals makes them prone to multiple forms of human rights violations. Migrants are considered a vulnerable group due to several factors that can trigger or arise out of the migration process, like poverty, discrimination, xenophobia, violence, and gender inequality. Other situations arising from the displacement are connected to social consequences, including family rupture or separation (IOM, 2020). These situations occur when migrating individuals or families face significant challenges maintaining their social connections and support networks. This disruption affects the stability and continuity of family and social life and often leads to emotional distress, as Kirmayer portrays in her 2011 study, where the mental health of a group of migrants was studied through the process of obtaining refugee status, the results of this study show differences in family structure, acculturation, and intergenerational problems, among other situations (Kirmayer et al., 2011).

Regarding the international recognition of displaced individuals and the legal protection they require, there is a narrow scope of who must be protected by the receiving State and the status they obtain as refugees. According to the definition drawn in the 1951 Convention relating to the Status of Refugees and its Protocol from 1967, a refugee is an individual fearing persecution based on race, religion, nationality, social group, or political opinion. The individual is outside their home country and unwilling or unable to seek protection in the countries of transit and the destination country (UNHCR, 2011). Considering this, only a specific group among all migrants fits within the category of refugee; the rest of the migrants that are not included in the special status do not receive the same protection that refugees have under specific international treaties and conventions.

Considering the emerging events related to climate variability driven by climate change and the effects that it can have on displacing people, like the ones reported by the Internal Displacement Monitoring Centre (IDMC, 2021), which reported that globally, 23.7 million people experienced displacements in 2021 as a result of cyclones and floods, it is essential to acknowledge climate change, and the events induced by it, as relevant drivers and factors of global migration. Given this panorama, this chapter will explore climate migration, defined as the movement, voluntary or involuntary, of individuals or communities from their place of residence within the same country or internationally, originating from the change in living conditions due to acute or chronic events caused by climate change (IOM, 2019).[1]

Forced-displaced people suffer from a situation of vulnerability, which creates a necessity for a robust legal framework that allows states to respond appropriately and address the possible vulnerabilities and risks that migrants suffer, especially those involving the fundamental human right to life and other linked human rights like the right to health, as has been indicated by the World Health Organization, who recognized the importance of guaranteeing migrants rights and granting them universal health coverage (WHO, 2022).

As this chapter will show, climate migration is still to be acknowledged as an independent issue that requires specific and direct action, especially in the global south, which faces the challenges of developing countries, like poverty, lack of essential services, and inequality. Additionally, Latin America, which is part of the global south, is vulnerable to the effects of climate change (OCHA, 2023). The region suffers from social vulnerability while being susceptible to the impacts of climate change; these impacts will be explained in *Section I: Exploring the Latin American region context* of this chapter.

Finally, the objective of this chapter is to explore the current legal framework surrounding climate migration in Latin America from the international instruments that have been ratified by the countries of the region and that are currently applied to the national legislation of those countries, following the chapter sequence, this will be done in *Section II: Exploring the Legal Framework,* and the findings will be explored in *Section III: Conclusions.*

Section One: Exploring the Latin American Region Context

The Latin American region is generally vulnerable to various social, environmental, and economic factors, including social problems that impact various aspects of people's lives. Regarding these social issues, the region faces high levels of inequality and informal employment, leading to a lack of formal job opportunities, insufficient social protection, and unequal distribution of resources, exacerbating the problem of inequality (Pizarro, 2001). Due to poverty, among other factors, Latin America faces enduring economic challenges. The Social Panorama of Latin America and the Caribbean in 2022 reveals that approximately 201 million individuals live in poverty, accounting for 32.1% of the total population in the region (ECLAC, 2022). Furthermore, there are alarming levels of violence and crime, where high homicide rates, gang activities, and drug-related violence are common in the area (Chioda, 2017). According to Chioda (2017), the Latin America and Caribbean region has acquired the title of being the most violent in the world, with 24.7 homicides per 100,000 inhabitants. The magnitude of this issue is staggering and persistent, as evidenced by the fact that 42 of the top 50 most violent cities in the world are in Latin America.

Along with the social and economic factors, the environmental factors should be taken under consideration; Latin America is particularly vulnerable to natural disasters and climate change impacts because its geographic positioning, surrounded by the Atlantic and the Pacific oceans, makes it prone to suffer from climate change-related events. Some of the countries in the region are located within hurricane belts, exposing them to an elevated risk of enduring the devastating consequences of tropical storms and hurricanes. The United Nations Office for the Coordination of Humanitarian Affairs (OCHA) reported an average of 17 hurricanes annually in Latin America between 2000 and 2019 (OCHA, 2023).

Countries like Mexico, Honduras, and Brazil can serve as examples to show the region's vulnerability related to natural disasters. For instance, Mexico is

Table 1. 2022 temperature ranking (1900-2022) and anomalies for LAC (°C, difference from the 1991-2020 and 1961-1990 averages)

Region	Temperature	Anomaly (°C)	
		1991-2020	1961-1990
Mexico	6th-15th warmest	0.23 [0.12-0.34]	0.96 [0.61-1.07]
Central America	10th-16th warmest	0.09 [0.02-0.16]	0.59 [0.46-0.73]
Caribbean	15th-31st warmest	-0.02 [-0.13-0.06]	0.50 [0.20-0.65]
South America	12th-25th warmest	-0.04 [-0.09-0.08]	0.50 [0.39-0.67]
LAC	12th-21st warmest	0.00 [-0.06-0.10]	0.55 [0.46-0.70]

Note: Data are from the following six data sets: Berkeley Earth, ERA5, GISTEMP, HadCRUT5, JRA-55, NOAAGlobalTemp. For details regarding the data sets, see *The WMO State of the Climate in Latin America and the Caribbean 2022 report.*

located amidst five tectonic plates and faces constant risks such as seismic activity, landslides, and floods. Additionally, Mexico's coastal areas occasioned the threat of hurricanes and tropical storms. Similarly, Honduras, situated in a region prone to natural disasters, including hurricanes, floods, and droughts, exhibits vulnerability. Meanwhile, Brazil ranks among the top 15 countries in the world with the most significant population exposed to river flood risk. (OCHA,2023).

Latin America has been experiencing a warming trend in recent years, exacerbating or accelerating phenomena like the one described previously. This is reflected in the table elaborated by Berkeley Earth and presented by the World Meteorological Organization in *The WMO State of the Climate in Latin America and the Caribbean 2022 report*. This report shows that Between 1991 and 2022, the region experienced its warmest trend since 1900, with temperatures rising by about 0.2 °C or more per decade, as shown below (WMO, 2023).

In Latin America, the natural phenomenon "El Niño" is widely recognized as a significant driver of climate variability. As Takahashi & Martinez (2019) explain, El Niño Southern Oscillation (ENSO) is a natural climate event suffered in the Pacific Ocean area of Latin America. It occurs when sea surface temperature increases and the trade winds weaken, generating abnormal conditions that cause climate variations and rainfalls in the region. This unique set of meteorological events profoundly impacts various aspects of society, including social dynamics, economic activities, and public health. For instance, ENSO is known to be one of the factors responsible for severe droughts and floods in the Amazonian region, including Colombia, Peru, and Brazil (Takahashi & Martinez, 2019).

Due to changing climatic conditions, there are other relevant climate change-related events, and the Central American Dry Corridor is one of them. It is a stretch of land of 1,600 kilometers long and 100 to 400 kilometers wide that concentrates 90% of the population of Central America and the main capitals of this geographical region (Solera, 2022). The Dry Corridor extends from the Pacific Coast of Guatemala to the north of Costa Rica. In this area, people suffer the effects of droughts characterized by extended periods of unusually arid weather when there is not enough rain, resulting in low agricultural productivity. This significantly impacts crops and livestock, food insecurity, and other related issues like widespread unemployment, mainly in rural communities. By 2019, this phenomenon had left 1.2 million people at risk due to food and resource scarcity (UNEP, 2023).

In addition to the social and economic challenges, the Latin American region is vulnerable to natural disasters, and communities in the region are also affected by the problems of resource scarcity. In recent decades, critical natural resources have become increasingly scarce (Hall & Hall, 1984). Resource scarcity indicates a shortage in the availability of natural resources needed for human survival and well-being, such as water, land, energy, and food (ECLAC, 2022). Climate change can exacerbate resource scarcity by altering ecosystems and disrupting the availability of these resources, being a driver for climate migration.

Water is critical for human well-being, and the impossibility of access to affordable, adequate, reliable, and safe water is known as water insecurity (Stoler, 2021). In Latin America, around 150 million people live in areas where water is scarce, and 400 million people do not have proper sanitary conditions (Wellenstein, 2022). An example of this situation can be found in Colombia, where, due to the weather changes and variable availability in water reservoirs, communities living in rural areas are forced to endure long journeys by boat or tertiary roads to access drinkable water (Rodríguez, 2013). Water insecurity, as described before, acts as a driver for migration, and it is increased by climate variations, adding pressure to the social and political phenomena of the region (Stoler, 2021).

Human mobility has been a form of adaptation since the beginning of time, and it can be characterized in multiple ways. It can be seasonal or permanent, internal or international, and triggered by multiple situations, like socioeconomic and political reasons; these situations are known as drivers (Pan, 2022). It is challenging to have the exact number of immigrants that come into and leave Latin America and the reasons behind the migration process, let alone the portion that emigrated due to climate change-induced events, because there is a lack of precise data. Migration has proved to be a fluctuant phenomenon, and due to the multiple possible drivers that can motivate an individual at the same time, it is difficult to determine the precise reason for it. Nevertheless, governments and non-governmental organizations have produced data to study the trend of migration; for instance, the World Bank estimates there will be between 16.2 and 9.4 million climate migrants by 2050, as shown in Figure 1 (World Bank Group, 2018).

Figure 1. Projected total numbers and shares of internal climate migrants in Latin America under three scenarios by 2050

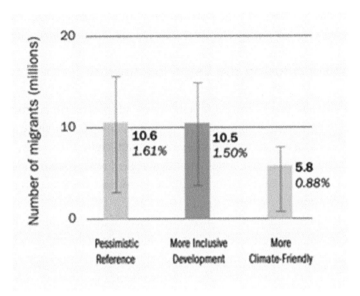

According to the World Bank Group (2018), Latin America will face severe impacts because of climate change. Specifically, the projected number of internal climate migrants is anticipated to reach up to 16.2 million migrants. Nevertheless, under the more climate-friendly scenario, the estimated number of climate migrants is expected to be up to 9.4 million. In this context, it is evident that migration levels could decrease if steps are implemented to mitigate and adapt to climate change in the region. Considering, climate migration is a phenomenon that requires a robust legal framework in Latin America (World Bank Group, 2018).

Although migration has proven to be linked to multiple drivers, and it is difficult to determine the exact reason for an individual to migrate, being Latin America a vulnerable region to the adverse effects of climate change, this phenomenon should be considered as one of the drivers for migration in the region. For instance, a recent study by the International Organization for Migration (IOM, 2019) has shown a direct link between changes in weather patterns in Central America's Dry Corridor and migration trends in recent years, mainly because the region is dependent on agriculture, which is susceptible to weather changes, which can cause resource scarcity. This link between climate-related drivers and migration is aligned with the predictions of the World Bank Group, which show an increasing trend of climate migrants in Latin America.

In summary, this section of the chapter has briefly explored the Latin American region, provided the social, political, and economic context, but also explained the environmental context and the connection with climate change, exposing the different weather-related events that have affected the other countries in the region.

Section Two: Exploring the Legal Framework

At the international level, soft and hard laws address various migration and environmental law issues. There are essential mechanisms that serve as a crucial framework for ensuring the protection of human rights. Treaties, customary international law, general principles, and domestic laws provide guidelines and standards that countries should use as a guide to address the emerging challenges of climate migration.

As discussed in this chapter, the different effects of climate change have proven how drivers can generate human displacement and threaten the enjoyment of human rights. As was described previously in this chapter, Latin America is a vulnerable region due to social and economic factors, so the effects of climate change will likely have a more significant impact than in more developed regions. The reason is that in areas where human rights are already precarious, and protection is weak, these states have less capacity to respond to possible threats (UNHCR, 2011).

Refugee is the most elevated protection category attributed to a migrant. Its definition was laid down in the 1951 Refugee Convention, later complemented by the 1967 Protocol. Under the Convention, the category of refugee only applies to international migrants who have been subject to persecution on account of an individual's race, religion, nationality, political opinion, or membership in a particular social group. The individual is outside their home country and unwilling or unable to seek protection in the countries of transit and the destination country (UN, 2020). This definition rules out almost immediately the application of the refugee category for people affected by climate change, better known as climate migrants.

As explained by McAdam (2011), multiple courts worldwide stated that victims of natural disasters induced by climate change could not be protected as refugees unless, for example, a government targets particular groups by attacking their means of survival by maximizing or accelerating climate change consequences. Given this exclusion, it is relevant to explore the possible protection that climate migrants might have under human rights law, especially considering that fundamental human rights, such as life and health, are endangered by natural disasters and resource scarcity. One way to grant protection is by applying what is known as complementary protection, which means human rights protection outside the Refugee Convention's scope (McAdam, 2011).

The human right to life has been considered the most essential guarantee states should provide for everyone, citizen or not. The human right to life encompasses the basic definition of not being unjustly deprived of life and the right to exist in human dignity and with the minimum necessities of life. According to the United Nations Commission on Human Rights, one of the obligations states acquire is to take positive measures to protect it, for which they must improve their inhabitant's living conditions (UNHCR, 2011). For instance, in cases of extreme pollution, a person's living conditions can seriously deteriorate, with long-term and short-term health effects, and even pose a threat to life, so a state should act to reduce such risks. The same Commission analyzed and indicated that environmental pollution threatens the right to life if there is evidence of long-term health effects and enough contaminants have reached the human environment. This pollution must not transgress the public policy of the country where it is happening, meaning that the country does not have appropriate measures or standards to reduce pollution (UNHCR, 2011). If these conditions are fulfilled, an individual can migrate, escape from them, and be protected under the non-refoulment principle due to the risk it poses for his fundamental right to life (McAdam, 2011).

The European Human Rights Court (2008) has expressed a similar line of thought, asserting that the right to a healthy environment is linked to the right to life. Therefore, it has emphasized the importance of including safeguards against environmental harm within this right. This approach could protect climate migrants from being returned, considering the possible harm they would suffer if they go back to their place of origin, where environmental hazards will threaten their lives. The notion or concept of threat should be broadened to include, for example, victims of natural disasters. However, it will not provide the same special protection that refugees receive under the 1951 Refugee Convention and the 1967 Protocol.

In the context of legal regional frameworks and domestic developments to enhance the protection of climate migrants, a significant regional example from the global south is the African region. Soon after independence, many African countries faced the challenge of rebuilding their nations and the need to protect, assist, and find durable solutions for refugees displaced by South Africa's war of liberation and resistance to apartheid (Moses, 2014).

In 1969, the Convention of the Organization of African Union, in its preamble, recognized that the humanitarian approach is the best way to solve the problems of refugees, first by defining the term refugee and establishing the well-founded fear of being persecuted outside their country of origin and even recognizing that in some cases they are forced to leave their habitual residence (OAU Convention, 1969). Additionally, Article I of this Convention was the first regional instrument to broaden the refugee concept and added foreign occupation or domination or events seriously disturbing public order as a factor for displacement due to external aggression.

The protection mechanism that the member states of the Organization of African Union must adopt for refugees is asylum, which is established as a peaceful and humanitarian act, preventing people from being sent back to their country of origin or denied admission at the borders, therefore applying the principle of non-discrimination, adopting an "open-door" policy. Ethiopia and Uganda are both examples of the African region where they have adopted this open-door policy. This policy refers to the countries' disposition towards hosting and assisting refugees. Between 2009 and 2014, Ethiopia introduced the out-of-camp policy under which refugees are allowed to live in the outside camps provided and support themselves, and the country received nearly 450,000 refugees (Moses, 2014, pp. 71). On the other hand, Uganda also implemented a policy of welcoming refugees, allowing them to cultivate land, among other open-migratory practices. These instances serve as commendable examples that should be promoted and supported (Moses, 2014).

After these regional attempts to grant climate migrants protection, international efforts have also been made as part of international treaties and conventions related to climate change and environmental conservation. In 2010, during the Conferences of the Parties (COP) to the United Nations Framework Convention on Climate Change (UNFCCC), the UNFCCC started addressing the crucial link between climate change, natural resources, food scarcity, and migration. This acknowledgment marked a significant advance in raising awareness of climate migration. In 2015, COP 21 adopted the Paris Agreement, a binding agreement on climate change. Article 2 of the Paris Agreement aimed to limit the increase in global temperature to below 2°C. (UNFCCC, 2016). It emphasized the social impacts of climate change and resulted in the establishment of the Task Force on Displacement. This initiative is responsible for generating recommendations to prevent, reduce, and address displacement caused by the adverse effects of climate change (IOM, 2018).

From international treaties, a series of critical guiding principles in the environmental context emerge. The structural principles can be listed as follows: globalization, sustainability, shared responsibility, and subsidiarity (Valverde, 1996). On the other hand, functional principles derive from the broad idea of sustainable development, which can be considered a broad-reaching principle with social, physical, environmental, and economic implications (Voigt, 2013). Functional principles include the precautionary, polluter pays, and intergenerational equity and integration principles. They are a fundamental piece that defines the legal framework of environmental law. In this sense, these principles should be followed as a guideline to create policies that regulate the migratory movement that occurs due to climate change because they derive from international instruments that are specifically oriented to the protection of the environment, addressing the problem of climate change and at the same time recognizing the protection of the human rights of the people affected. For instance, the Rio Declaration establishes the importance of sustainable development, placing human beings at the center of concerns and maintaining the premise of ensuring fundamental human rights, such as the right to a healthy and productive life in harmony with the environment (Rio Declaration on Environment and Development, 1992). Likewise, the Paris Agreement recognizes climate change as a common concern of humanity. It suggests that the Parties adopt measures to address climate change without leaving aside their responsibilities to respect and promote their human rights obligations and with special protection for the rights of indigenous peoples, migrants, and other vulnerable groups (Paris Agreement, 2015).

Climate change is a global issue affecting countries and regions worldwide. The structural principles of globality and sustainability emphasize the need for international cooperation and long-term planning to address the environmental challenges associated with climate change, including its impact on migration patterns. Climate migration is often driven by the shared responsibility of nations to mitigate greenhouse gas emissions and adapt to the changing climate. The principle of shared responsibility highlights the need for countries to collaborate to address climate change's causes and consequences, including its impact on human displacement (Nollkaemper, 2020).

Additionally, both the subsidiary and the precautionary principles call for proactive measures to address the potential displacement in the context of climate migration. Migration patterns have intergenerational implications, as future generations will continue facing environmental degradation consequences (Venn, 2019). Similarly, the integration principle seeks to integrate environmental, social, and economic considerations into migration policies, ensuring a holistic approach that addresses the various challenges and opportunities associated with climate-induced migration (Nollkaemper, 2001). Under the legal framework perspective, by incorporating these principles into the regional policy, countries can strive to create comprehensive and sustainable solutions that protect the rights and well-being of those affected by climate-induced migration.

Section Three: Exploring the Legal Framework in Latin America

Latin America has developed various regulations related to the protection of refugees. In 1889, the Regional Treaty on Criminal Law established asylum as an inviolable standard for individuals facing persecution for political reasons. This treaty included the concept of asylum as humanitarian and inviolable. Subsequently, the International Protection of Refugees in Latin America, forged in 1981 in Mexico, is a previous step to the Declaration of Cartagena that advocated for safeguarding migrants' rights (Sarmiento, 2014). Late in the 1980s, when civil wars affected El

Salvador, Guatemala, and Nicaragua, countries in the region worked together to create a protection framework.

The Latin American region developed the Cartagena Declaration in 1984, which broadened the refugee definition. The concept of refugee now includes people fleeing threats to their lives, security, or freedom due to widespread violence, conflicts, human rights abuses, or other situations disrupting public order (ACNUR, 2014). Likewise, incorporating non-disruption or disturbance of the public order into the refugee concept was considered for the Convention of the Organization of African Union in 1969. The Cartagena Declaration on Refugees holds significant importance in the region as several countries have incorporated its principles into the national legislation, addressing new challenges and aligning with the Inter-American Court of Human Rights doctrine on non-refoulement. This declaration provided a more robust protection for the refugees in Latin America.

According to Corti, an expanded definition of a refugee has the potential to offer protection to climate migrants. This expanded definition enables countries to apply the principle of non-refoulment to individuals or groups who must migrate due to natural disasters that disrupt public order (Corti, 2021). A notable example of applying the non-refoulment principle occurred during the 2010 earthquake in Haiti, where member states of the Union of South American Nations (USAN) recognized the urgent need for coordinated migration mechanisms to respond to the disaster. The USAN parties emphasized the significance of taking prompt action in emergent scenarios related to natural disasters. In response to this crisis, different countries in the region created responsive emergency measures. One example is Brazil, which took proactive measures by establishing a provisional National Commission for Refugees (CONARE). Similarly, countries such as Peru, Panama, and Ecuador adopted a flexible interpretation of the asylum definition to protect climate migrants affected by the earthquake.

Additionally, in the region, an example is the Declaration and Plan of Action of Mexico to Strengthen the International Protection of Refugees in Latin America in 2004, and this instrument emphasizes the need for concrete collaboration to protect the migrants. It also recognized the importance of improving national and regional networks involving organizations, states, international bodies, civil society, and the Inter-American Court System (Sarmiento, 2014). While the region has made efforts to promote the protection of refugees, it is crucial to note that the Declaration of Cartagena on Refugees is a non-binding regional instrument. It holds importance in the region due to its expanding definition of a refugee. However, as a soft law instrument, countries can choose whether to adhere to its principles. Furthermore, it does not explicitly address the protection of climate migrants. Although these international and regional instruments signify an essential development for protecting climate migrants, gaps have not yet been filled, especially in Latin America. The regional advances are mainly domestic constructions that aim to solve specific needs that the countries had at the time. However, there is not an organized and binding regional instrument. This situation calls for harmonization initiatives that protect climate migrants consistently in Latin America.

It is also essential to consider that Latin American countries are part of the civil law tradition, inherited from continental European countries like Spain and France, so the developments and legal debates are going to be reflected in domestic decrees, laws, or international instruments, rather than in case law, as would be the case with common law countries. It is also relevant to note that judicial precedent is not binding across all Latin American countries, and the precedents of regional tribunals are not either. Given this, looking for answers in judge-made law would not be as effective as going to the binding primary sources of law.

Argentina is an example of countries trying to adapt domestic laws to international legal frameworks regarding climate migration. It was the first country in the region to settle a general rule to guarantee protection because of humanitarian reasons, with Decree 616/2010, which establishes that the Republic of Argentina has reformulated the objectives of its migration policy to adjust it to the framework of the Latin American region, taking into account respect and harmony with human rights while considering the mobility of migrants (Decree 616/2010, 2010) Likewise, this Decree recognizes the need for international cooperation between the Southern Common Market countries (MERCOSUR). This regional integration process is constituted by different countries, including Argentina, Brazil, Paraguay, and Uruguay, an economic integration initiative in South America (MERCOSUR, 2023). This National Decree includes in its plans the recognition of climate migrants and their protection. Its initial part recognizes the importance of the migration issue and how it has been reformed, leaving aside the more restrictive previous framework. According to this new legal framework, in case of contradictions with other legal instruments, what is more favorable to the migrant must be applied.

The purpose of this Decree is to integrate migrants into society and grant them access to the fundamental rights included in the spectrum of human rights, such as health, education, access to justice, work, and employment, all on equal terms with nationals in the Argentine territory, demonstrating an example of the principles of non-discrimination and equal treatment that are characteristic of immigration law, which are factors of protection for migrants that this nation recognizes. In the context of climate migration, Article 24 of the Decree relates to foreigners who enter the country as temporary residents and who could be admitted into the national territory in special cases. Although this condition does not merit or require international protection, it accepts the reality of these migrants who cannot return to their countries of origin because of humanitarian conditions triggered by natural or environmental disasters (Decree 616/2010, 2010)

In this sense, Bolivia has taken significant steps in addressing climate migration by implementing its Migration Law No. 370 in 2013. Its primary objective is to establish institutional coordination spaces that ensure the rights of both Bolivian and foreign migrants following the country's Constitution and international human rights instruments ratified by Bolivia. This law mentions different principles the government must follow in migration, including non-discrimination and equal treatment. As enshrined in the Political Constitution, Bolivia is committed to guaranteeing all individuals, regardless of their sex, color, age, origin, culture, nationality, language, religion, economic, social, or political condition, or any other factor, the full enjoyment and exercise of their rights. Furthermore, Article 2 of the Migration Law outlines that Bolivia promotes a harmonious relationship with nature. The principle of living well is defined as living in harmony with the cycles of Mother Earth, the cosmos, life, and the historical memory that shapes the future (Migration Law No. 370, 2013).

According to Article 6 of the law, climate migrants are individuals compelled to relocate from one State to another due to the adverse impacts of climate-related factors. They form groups that seek new environments and communities due to the challenges posed by climate change. These factors may include natural disasters, environmental crises, nuclear incidents, chemical hazards, or famine. Following the same line of thought, this definition emphasizes the importance of promoting the ratification of international conventions and agreements on climate change and environmental issues with other countries. Additionally, in Article 65, the law encourages the coordination of public policies that facilitate the admission of individuals displaced by climate effects when there is a risk or threat to life, whether due to natural causes or environmental, nuclear, chemical, or famine disasters. Bolivia's Migration Law is committed to addressing climate migration while promoting non-discrimination and living in harmony with nature (Migration Law No. 370, 2013).

Meanwhile, Mexico is working to align its domestic legislation with international legal frameworks to address the pressing issue of climate migration. The General Guidelines for Visa of 2014 in Mexico promote safe and positive migration practices to facilitate mobility within the country (Secretaria de Gobernacion, 2014). With these guidelines, Mexico aims to achieve effective migration management by prioritizing and fostering international cooperation and promoting border and human security. Simultaneously, the guidelines emphasize the importance of ensuring safe and efficient global mobility. These guidelines reinforce international mobilization efforts in Mexico and highlight the country's commitment to effective migration by adhering to facilitation principles and international co-responsibility (Alleyne, 2013).

The National Institution for Migration (INM) in Mexico recognizes the importance of caring for and addressing the necessities of individuals affected by natural disasters (Secretaria de Gobernacion, 2014). To qualify for assistance, migrants must provide evidence that they have experienced a natural disaster or that their lives are at risk due to such an event. The institution may also extend protection to family members of the victims. Mexico introduced a visa in 2014 that allows individuals compelled to leave their home countries due to catastrophes or natural disasters to stay in the country for one year, with the possibility of renewal. The visa application can be solicited through a written document signed by the applicant, stating that a natural catastrophe has impacted their family members or is facing threats to their life or well-being due to a natural disaster (Secretaria de Gobernacion, 2014).

Another example in the region is Peru, which since 2015, with Decree No. 1236, has included the temporal status of humanitarian migration. It shall apply to applicants for refugee and asylum or those who have migrated for reasons of natural and environmental disasters, which justifies the reform of the existing immigration law for citizen security and to strengthen the fight against violence, insecurity, and organized crime. This Decree has the objective of generating and approving new provisions for the regulatory framework for immigration matters and also regulating the entry and exit of nationals and foreigners (Decree N° 1236, 2015).

Likewise, this regulatory law recognizes principles applicable to migration processes. The first one is the principle of recognition of the contribution of migrants in the development of the country, which is relevant because international migrants add value to the culture and, in general, to the development of the country. Second, the principles of free transit and the respect for human rights, which are principles that derive from International Law, through which the State guarantees foreigners the respect of their fundamental rights. Third, the principle of integration of the migrant goes hand in hand with recognizing the contribution that migrants make to the country, but also ensuring the comprehensive protection of the individual and their families. Lastly, the non-criminalization of irregular migration generally refers to the movement of people who cross international borders without complying with legal migration requirements; this protectionist principle goes together with the international principle of non-discrimination. In addition to the above principles, it introduces the principle of migratory formalization. This innovative principle ensures that the State promotes the necessary measures to achieve in a regular manner and following established processes, the formalization of foreigners who wish to enter and remain in the national territory (Decree N° 1236, 2015).

Although the aforementioned domestic acts signify an essential development for protecting climate migrants in Latin America, most countries in the region still lack recognition of climate change as a significant driver for migration; hence, the protection that they provide for migrants only extends to the category of refugee, leaving climate migrants unprotected and in a vulnerable situation. Some countries like Colombia and Honduras have shown interest in creating and adapting their public policies to address migration. These domestic approaches are consistent with the active participation that Latin American countries have had in the drafting of various international instruments and their subsequent incorporation into national legislation. However, these frameworks do not address the specific issue of climate migration and lack proper protection for those forced to move due to the consequences of climate change.

In the case of Colombia, although it has ratified international conventions and treaties such as the Paris Agreement and the Rio Declaration, no specific legal framework protects climate migrants. Historically, Colombia has had one of the most stringent regimes concerning migration issues, limiting the possibility of obtaining refugee status exclusively to those who suffer from persecution as was drafted in earlier international treaties, which excludes climate migrants and victims of natural disasters (Sarmiento-Erazo, 2018). Colombia's closest domestic legal instrument for protection in favor of climate migration is Law 1523 of 2012, adopted by the Colombian Congress, which set the grounds for Colombia's Public Policy for the Prevention and Attention of Natural Disasters. This law also includes a protection regime for the victims of natural disasters, granting them aid for three months after the catastrophic event. Nevertheless, these measures do not directly address the situation of climate migrants, nor do they contribute to giving them protection as refugees; these are just the government's response to natural disasters. In summary, Colombia's legal framework focuses on internal migration due to violence and on protecting international refugees who are suffering from political persecution or whose life is threatened, and recently recognized protection for victims of natural disasters. Still, there are no clear and substantive laws that protect climate migrants (Sarmiento-Erazo, 2018).

In 2022, the National Congress of Honduras approved The Law for the Prevention, Care, and Protection of Internally Displaced Persons. This law is the first legal framework adopted by Honduras that offers a comprehensive response to internal displacement. However, this law addresses forced internal displacement caused by generalized violence since the country faces the issue of organized crime, like neighboring countries that include El Salvador and Nicaragua. (UNODC, 2007) Still, more factors generate displacement in Honduras, and generalized violence is only one of them. Involuntary migration due to climate change is not a determining factor that the Honduran government has taken under consideration, and climate migration still needs to be recognized. Additionally, in the regional context of Latin America, the Comprehensive Regional Protection and Solutions Framework (MIRPS) also promotes response to forced displacement in Belize, Costa Rica, El Salvador, Guatemala, Honduras, Panama, and Mexico. This is an attempt at a regional framework for Central America. However, this only covers migration because of other drivers, like political, economic, and security issues. Nevertheless, even with climate-related events and most of these countries suffering from the effects of climate change, climate migration is still not a topic to be recognized and covered.

This section of the chapter has explained and provided examples of the Latin American region, where countries like Argentina, Bolivia, Mexico, and Peru have addressed climate migration through their domestic legal framework, enhancing special protection for those displaced due to climate change's impacts, like natural and environmental disasters. This section has also explored countries like Colombia and Honduras, where, although there are some developments, there is a legal gap in the region's climate migration framework, and climate migrants are unprotected. As a consequence of this gap, the Office of the High Commissioner of the United Nations has encouraged the governments of the region to provide adequate protection to people displaced across international borders due to climate change since these people are not defined as refugees in the UN Convention Relating to the Status of Refugees and therefore lack complete protection of their rights.

CONCLUSION

This chapter of the book has described how climate change, natural disasters, and resource scarcity are significant factors that actively drive migration. Climate migration refers to the movement of individuals or communities, either voluntarily or involuntarily, from their place of residence within the same country or internationally. The displacement mentioned in this chapter, categorized as climate migration, directly results from changes in the individual's living conditions caused by climate change. Climate migrants are vulnerable to human rights violations, especially if they come from already vulnerable contexts due to social and economic factors, like in most of the global south countries. For instance, regions such as Latin America are keen to experience pronounced impacts from climate migration because they grapple with various economic, social, and political issues.

As discussed in this chapter, Latin America is highly susceptible to natural disasters and climate change impacts due to its location. For instance, natural phenomena significantly contribute to the region's climate variability, leading to temperature alterations, precipitation patterns, rains, and droughts. Furthermore, more frequent extreme climate change-related events directly affect resource management, resulting in most of the countries' resource scarcity, particularly water shortage, a prevailing issue throughout the region. It is essential to acknowledge climate change's role as a migration driver, given that migration has multiple drivers, and it is difficult to differentiate the exact reason for an individual to migrate. This chapter has clearly expressed that in Latin America, adding vulnerability due to location, it is crucial to focus on the emerging issue that climate migration poses for the region. Additionally, it is a global phenomenon, but it mainly affects developing countries.

In light of exploring the issue of climate migration in a global and general context for the international panorama, legal advances are addressing this issue, including incorporating international law, treaties, regional conventions, domestic laws, and generally applicable principles and guidelines. The Refugee Convention of 1951 initially defined refugees, but this definition only covered factors such as race, religion, nationality, political opinion, or membership in a specific social group. Nevertheless, over time, regional instruments such as the 1969 Convention of the Organization of African Union and the 1984 Cartagena Declaration have broadened this definition, including factors such as external aggression, foreign occupation, domination, or events seriously disturbing public order that are the modifications taken under consideration for eventually adapting the legal framework for the integration of climate migration and protection of the individuals included under the category of climate migrants.

The legal framework in Latin America has some advances in protecting climate migrants. For example, in 2010, Argentina was the first country in the region to settle a general rule to guarantee protection because of humanitarian reasons due to the consequences generated by natural or environmental disasters. In addition, in 2013, Bolivia took significant steps in addressing climate migration by encouraging the coordination of public policies that facilitate the admission of individuals displaced by climate effects when there is a risk or threat to life. Moreover, in 2014, Mexico allowed individuals compelled to leave their home countries due to catastrophes or natural disasters. In addition, since 2015, Peru has included the temporal status of humanitarian migration.

The purpose of establishing the vulnerability of the global south through the Latin American region in this chapter is to recognize the emerging situation of climate migration and how it affects individuals and communities, which, in the long run, also affects the country because people are forced to leave. This exposes the vulnerability of both people and nations, and it is clear that mitigation actions in the climate change sphere are not enough at this point. Instead, this is an evident call for the need to have an action plan to protect climate migrants, who are portrayed as vulnerable people affected by climate change impacts.

To effectively address the risks and violations of human rights faced by climate migrants and put an action plan in their favor under work, some countries have made efforts, but it is imperative to establish a harmonized regional legal framework in Latin America. This framework should emphasize the urgent need for comprehensive strategies to have unification in the region; following the examples of Mexico, Bolivia, Argentina, and Peru, creating a regional legal instrument could benefit greatly. In addition, it is crucial to implement adaptive measures and promote specific data focused on climate migration in the region. Moreover, international cooperation plays a vital role in safeguarding the rights and protection of climate migrants and addressing the root causes of climate migration related to climate change. It would be an ideal strategy that could work out in favor of having regional protection in Latin America for climate migration.

However, if a regional commitment like a convention cannot be reached, the idea of having a bilateral treaty among neighboring nations facing the impacts of climate migration would be a significant step forward in protecting climate migrants. Currently, there is no specific legal framework related to climate migrants. Although, there are legal frameworks related to the environment and the impact of climate change, as well as there are domestic laws in the region that show the effort to address this emerging challenge.

To conclude, it is important to remark on the crucial role that international cooperation plays in reaching a harmonious legal framework that recognizes and defines climate migration, which is an understudied issue that is supposed to be a major threat to climate migrants and their human rights, having under consideration international principles into policy frameworks, countries can strive to create comprehensive and sustainable solutions that protect the rights and well-being of those affected by climate-induced migration. Acknolodewing the relevance that a holistic approach is needed to better understand and promote the protection of vulnerable communities and individuals in Latin America and the global south.

REFERENCES

Chioda, L. (2017). *Stop the Violence in Latin America: A Look at Prevention from Cradle to Adulthood.* https://doi.org/ doi:10.1596/978-1-4648-0664-3

Corti, J. (2021) *Regional Protection of Climate Migrants in Latina America* https://www.jstor.org/stable/pdf/27074037.pdf?refreqid=fastly-default%3Af5b8701ed37f67737b376369e3935f68&ab_segments=&origin=&initiator=&acceptTC=1

Darwin, C. (1984). *Concepts and Measures of Natural Resource Scarcity with a Summary of Recent Trends'. Journal of Environmental Economics and Management, 11*(4), 363–379. doi:10.1016/0095-0696(84)90005-6

Economic Commission for Latin America and the Caribbean. (2022). *Social Panorama of Latin America and the Caribbean.* Cepal. https://repositorio.cepal.org/server/api/core/bitstreams/a1208761-efa2-4f3a-8be9-bc9368c370c0/content

El Presidente de la Republica. Peru. (2015). *Decreto Legislativo de Migracion, Decreto Nº 1236.* Acnur. https://www.acnur.org/fileadmin/Documentos/BDL/2015/10203.pdf

European Parliament. (2023). *News European Parliament*. European Parliament. https://www.europarl.europa.eu/news/en/headlines/world/20200624STO81906/exploring-migration-causes-why-people-migrate

Internal Displecement Moitoring Centre. (2021). *Global Report on Internal Displacement 2021*. Internal Displacement. https://www.internal-displacement.org/global-report/grid2021/

International Organization for Migration. (2016). *IOM Handbook On Protection And Assistance For Migrants Vulnerable To Violence, Exploitation And Abuse*. IOM. https://publications.iom.int/books/iom-handbook-migrants-vulnerable-violence-exploitation-and-abuse

International Organization for Migration. (2019). *Climate Change And Migration In Vulnerable Countries*. Switzerland: International Organization for Migration. https://publications.iom.int/system/files/pdf/climate_change_and_migration_in_vulnerable_countries.pdf

International Organization for Migration. (2020). *Task Force on Displacement*. IOM. https://environmentalmigration.iom.int/task-force-displacement

Kirmayer, L. J., Narasiah, L., Munoz, M., Rashid, M., Ryder, A. G., Guzder, J., Hassan, G., Rousseau, C., & Pottie, K. (2011). Common mental health problems in immigrants and refugees: General approach in primary care. CMAJ. *Canadian Medical Association Journal*, *183*(12), E959–E967. doi:10.1503/cmaj.090292 PMID:20603342

La Asamblea Legislativa Plurinacional. (2023) *Law No. 370 de 2013, Ley de migración*. Ref World. https://www.refworld.org/docid/55b636204.html

MacAdam, J. (2011) *Climate Change Displacement and International Law: Complementary Protection Standards*.

Matthew, R. (2008). *Resource Scarcity Responding to the Security Challenge*. iPinst. https://www.ipinst.org/wp-content/uploads/2015/06/rscar0408.pdf

Ministerio de Justicia y Derechos Humanos. (2010). *Decreto 616/2010*. InfoLeg. https://servicios.infoleg.gob.ar/infolegInternet/anexos/165000-169999/167004/norma.htm

Moses, O. (2014). *The 1969 O.A.U. Convention and the continuing challenge for the African Union*. FMR Review. https://www.fmreview.org/faith/okello

Nollkaemper, A. (2001). *Three Conceptions of the Integration Principle in International Environmental Law*. Environmental Policy Integration.

Nollkaemper, A., Ahlborn, C., Boutin, B., Nedeski, N., Plakokefalos, I., & Jacobs, D. (2020). Guiding Principles on Shared Responsibility in International Law. *European Journal of International Law*, *31*(1), 15–72. doi:10.1093/ejil/chaa017

Observer Research Foundation. (2023), *It's time for climate justice- A Global South perspective on the fight against the climate crisis.* Observer Research Foundation. https://www.orfonline.org/research/a-global-south-perspective-on-the-fight-against-the-climate-crisis/

Oficina del Alto Comisionado de las Naciones Unidas para los Refugiados. (2014) *Conmemoración del 30 Aniversario de la Declaración de Cartagena "Cartagena +30".* Acnur. https://www.acnur.org/fileadmin/Documentos/BDL/2014/9780.pdf

Organization of African Unity. (1968). *Convention Governing the Specific Aspects of Refugee Problems in Africa ("OAU Convention").* RefWorld. https://www.refworld.org/docid/3ae6b36018.html

Pan, E. (2020). *Reimagining The Climate Migration Paradigm: Bridging Conceptual Barriers To Climate Migration Responses.* JSTOR.

Reuveny, R. (2007). Climate change-induced migration and violent conflict. *Political Geography*, *26*(6), 656–673. doi:10.1016/j.polgeo.2007.05.001

Rodríguez, N., Restrepo, S., & Zambrano, I. (2013). The lack of water and its implications regarding feeding practice in Turbo, Antioquia. *Revista de Salud Publica (Bogota, Colombia)*, *15*(3), 421–433. PMID:25124000

Sarmiento, K. (2014). *Iniciativa Cartagena +30.* Acnur. https://www.acnur.org/fileadmin/Documentos/Publicaciones/2014/9793.pdf

Sarmiento-Erazo, J. P. (2018). Migración por cambio climático en Colombia: Entre los refugiados medioambientales y los migrantes económicos. *Revista Jurídicas*, *15*(2), 53–69. doi:10.17151/jurid.2018.15.2.4

Solera, E. (2021). *Habitat for Humanity International, Characterization of the Dry Corridor in Central America's Northern Triangle.* Habitat. https://www.habitat.org/sites/default/files/documents/Qualitative%20housing%20deficit%20in%20El%20Salvador%2C%20Guatemala%20and%20Honduras%20exceeds%203.9%20million%20houses.pdf

Soto, M. V. (1996). *General Principles Of International Environmental Law,* I.L.S.A. *Journal of International & Comparative Law*, *3*(1), 10. https://nsuworks.nova.edu/ilsajournal/vol3/iss1/10

Takahashi, K., & Martínez, A. G. (2019). The very strong coastal El Niño in 1925 in the far-eastern Pacific. *Climate Dynamics, 52*(12), 7389–7415. doi:10.1007/s00382-017-3702-1

The European Court Of Human Rights. *Budayena and Others v. Russia,* (March 20, 2008). 15339.

The Southern Common Market. (2023) *¿Qué es el MERCOSUR?* The Southern Common Market. https://www.mercosur.int/quienes-somos/en-pocas-palabras/

The United Nations Environment Programme. (2023) *Helping farmers beat the Climate crisis in Central America's Dry Corridor.* UNEP. https://www.unep.org/news-and-stories/story/helping-farmers-beat-climate-crisis-central-americas-dry-corridor

The White House. (2021). *Report on the Impact of Climate Change on Migration.* The White House. https://www.whitehouse.gov/wp-content/uploads/2021/10/Report-on-the-Impact-of-Climate-Change-on-Migration.pdf

United Nations. (2020). *Retrieved from United Nations Peace, dignity and equality on a healthy planet.* UN. https://www.un.org/en/global-issues/migration#:~:text=Today%2C%20more%20people%20than%20ever,estimated%20to%20be%20281%20million

United Nations Conference on Environment and Development. (1992). *Rio Declaration on Environment and Development.* UN. https://www.un.org/en/development/desa/population/migration/generalassembly/docs/globalcompact/A_CONF.151_26_Vol.I_Declaration.pdf

United Nations Educational, Scientific and Cultural Organization. (2021). *Reporting on Migrants and refugees Handbook For Journalism Education.* United Nations Educational.

United Nations Framework Convention on Climate Change. (2015). *Paris Agreement.* UN. https://unfccc.int/sites/default/files/english_paris_agreement.pdf

United Nations Framework Convention on Climate Change. (2016). *Paris Agreement.* UN. https://unfccc.int/process-and-meetings/the-paris-agreement/the-paris-agreement

United Nations High Commissioner for Refugees. (1977). *Note on Non-Refoulement (Submitted by the High Commissioner) EC/SCP/2.* UN. https://www.unhcr.org/publications/note-non-refoulement-submitted-high-commissioner

United Nations High Commissioner for Refugees. (2011). *The legal framework for protecting refugees*. UN. https://www.unhcr.org/sites/default/files/legacy-pdf/4ec262df9.pdf

United Nations Office for the Coordination of Humanitarian Affairs. (2019). *Natural Disasters in Latin America and the Caribbean*. UN.

United Nations Office for the Coordination of Humanitarian Affairs. (2023). *Regional Office for Latin America and the Caribbean*. UN. https://www.unocha.org/latin-america-and-caribbean

United Nations Office on Drugs and Crime. (2007). *Crime and Development in Central America*. UN. https://www.unodc.org/pdf/research/Central_America_Study_2007.pdf

Venn A. (2019). *Social justice and climate change, Managing Global Warming*. Academic Press. doi:10.1016/B978-0-12-814104-5.00024-7

Voigt, C. (2013). *The principle of sustainable development: Integration and ecological integrity*. Cambridge University Press. doi:10.1017/CBO9781107337961.012

Wellenstein, A. (2022). *The Latin American climate crisis is also a water crisis. How do we move forward?* World Bank. https://blogs.worldbank.org/latinamerica/latin-american-climate-crisis-also-water-crisis-how-do-we-move-forward

World Bank Group. (2018) *Internal Climate Migration in Latin America*. World Bank. https://documents1.worldbank.org/curated/en/983921522304806221/pdf/124724-BRI-PUBLIC-NEWSERIES-Groundswell-note-PN3.pdf

World Meteorological Organization. (2021). *Weather-related ease over past 50 years, causing more damage but fewer deaths*. WMO. https://public.wmo.int/en/media/press-release/weather-related-disasters-increase-over-past-50-years-causing-more-damage-fewer#:~:text=Climate%20change%20has%20increased%20extreme,many%20parts%20of%20the%20world

World Meteorological Organization. (2022). *State of the Climate in Latin America and the Caribbean 2022*. WMO. https://library.wmo.int/viewer/66252/download?file=1322_State_of_the_Climate_in_LAC_2022_en.pdf&type=pdf&navigator=1

World Meteorological Organization. (2022). *State of the Climate in Latin America and the Caribbean 2022*. WMO. https://library.wmo.int/viewer/66252/download?file=1322_State_of_the_Climate_in_LAC_2022_en.pdf&type=pdf&navigator=1

World Metereological Organization. (2014). *The Impact of Climate Change: Migration and Cities in South America*. WMO. https://public.wmo.int/en/resources/bulletin/impact-of-climate-change-migration-and-cities-south-america

Wyman, K. (2013). Responses to climate migration. *The Harvard Environmental Law Review*, *37*(1), 167–216.

KEY TERMS DEFINITIONS

Climate Migration: movement of individuals or communities, either voluntarily or involuntarily, from their place of residence within the same country or internationally due to the impacts of climate change.

Global South: Developing countries that have political, social, and environmental issues and struggle more to overcome than developed countries, mainly because of the economic factor. Countries in Latin America are included under this concept.

Harmonized Legal Framework: A legal framework that provides a uniform and single set of rules that different countries can apply. It seeks to avoid conflicts of law and guarantee the same treatment and result regardless of where it is applied, promoting international cooperation.

Migration Drivers: Factors or forces that motivate individuals or groups of people to move from one location to another.

Natural Disasters: Catastrophic and unpredictable events caused by natural forces that can affect the living conditions of individuals and communities.

Resource Scarcity: The lack of natural resources or services to provide the essential basic needs (water, food, shelter, etc) of a specific community or individual.

Vulnerability: The position to be susceptible to different phenomena, endangering the well-being and survival of a country or individual.

ENDNOTES

[1]   For methodological purposes; this chapter will not dive into the conceptual and linguistic debates surrounding environmental displacement, climate migration, environmental refugees, climate refugees and climate-induced migration.

Chapter 4
Role of Urban Local Bodies in Ensuring Primary Healthcare:
A Case of Bangladesh

Parimal Kumar Roy

(iD) https://orcid.org/0000-0002-0461-2587
Bangladesh Public Administration Training Centre, Bangladesh

ABSTRACT

This study reflected the author's one-decade professional journey in Bangladesh when he worked on the urban local body. Nevertheless, the author's sensuality with high empathy is that alleviating the urban primary health issues requires a governing department—Urban Health Unit. The urban local body is always under capacity to provide health services in terms of sustainability. In this sense, development agencies like ADB, DFID, and UNFPA anticipated the projects and accelerated the primary health care services under urban local bodies' capacities to downsize health pressure in secondary and tertiary health levels. As a result, assertive public participation and time-befitting policy implications were shaky to do so. For this drive, this study dives into ethnographic methods—participant observation and in-depth interviews with project personnel and public representatives in five urban local bodies of Bangladesh to write this chapter for policy recommendations, ab initio, on urban health issues to establish an Urban Health Unit to achieve SDG 3.

INTRODUCTION

In Bangladesh, we have 341 municipalities and 12 city corporations (www.lgd.gov.bd); all are part of urban local bodies popularly known as Municipality and City

DOI: 10.4018/979-8-3693-1178-3.ch004

corporations under the Ministry of Local Government & Cooperatives. However, this study was concentrated on four municipalities—Bogra, Madhobdi, Kushtia, Sirajgnaj and one city corporation—Narayanganj. However, according to the 2022 census, 31.5% of people live in urban areas (BBS, 2022). To ensure urban health, we see public and private interventions trying to turn any unturned stone to minimise the health hazards in Bangladesh, but the Covid -19 failed all attempts. It is interesting that the Global Health Index Report 2019 veiled a report based on six themes: which countries are stronger worldwide in health management systems? But COVID-19 proved that the USA was top and shocked much more, like Bangladesh, Sri Lanka, and Bhutan were in the middle despite that these countries' death toll was fewer than the USA (GHI Report,2019). Why? The author personally investigated the matter and noticed a strong health management system in South Asia (Roy, 2023a, b; Roy, 2022), which needs to improve public health management over the course of time. Against this backdrop, the Government of Bangladesh (GoB) has yet to be able to effectively utilise its local government institutions to control the spread of a pandemic like Covid-19. Three hundred forty-one urban local bodies (logged on 09 June 2023 www.lgd.gov.bd) have a full-fledged health department with a workforce and budget to provide logistics; all these institutions have a little alternative in Bangladesh to prevent the catastrophic disaster of primary health care in urban areas of Bangladesh, even this continent (Siraz et al.,2020).

In the current local government act of the country (LGD Act, 2009), these bodies are supposed to play a significant role in implementing primary health care services, clean water, urban waste management, faecal management, population control, and immunisation programs for 31.5% of urban residents. What is happening at all? To avoid a devastating situation, GoB, with the collaboration of development agencies; for example, in 1996, launched the Urban Primary Health Care Project (UPHCP) under the leadership of the Asian Development Bank with the financial and technical support of UNFPA, Swedish SIDA, DFID, and Orbis International to strengthen the urban health sector of the local government bodies like City corporation and Municipalities. The project takes the opportunity of the Local Government Act 1977; now it is 2009 (amended). After many setbacks, the scheme is still being implemented in selected municipalities and all city corporations, but instead of strengthening the health department, it has gradually weakened itself regarding budget, logistics support, and human resources. That is a different story and context, but the author still explores it as a strategically important part of Bangladesh's health policy interventions aligned with Health Policy 2011. Because " The government health system is weak, with inadequate attention given to the delivery of basic health care to slum-dwellers. For the past 15 years [it's a legacy of British rule], the Local Government Division has been responsible for providing primary health care services to poor urban populations, but it has been unable to meet their needs and demands adequately" (Afsana & Wahid, 2013).

The primary responsibility of the urban local body (hereafter ULB) is to disseminate the information and principles of the Government in promoting health and hygiene practices among urban dwellers. However, the informants claim while interviewing that ULB performances are shallow regarding these issues, almost yet to be done. Against this backdrop, the Covid pandemic has proven that the health system or institutions were looming in managing any epidemic. So, to improve the efficiency and effectiveness of secondary and tertiary institutions, we must pay attention to stopping the primary source of disease. To connect this, if we ensure primary health care services and sustainable environment-friendly sanitation practices, fewer patients will be in the secondary and tertiary health centres to get health care services (Roy et al., 2022, 2023) for attending the SDGs 3. According to the law, the Government of Bangladesh is working on this policy issue to make LGD responsible and accountable for primary health care to the urban people. The Government's main objective is far-reaching public welfare, which applies to all levels. As part of that continuum, the enhanced form of the Urban Primary Healthcare Services Delivery [present name of UPHCP] scheme is effectively implemented in selected urban local bodies to strengthen their health department realistically.

However, this study investigated the two health projects' base activities of the ULB— UPHCP [second phase] and UPHCSDP interventions to find the loopholes in urban healthcare systems at the country level. Here lies the merits of this chapter as a policy recommendation to set up an Urban Health Unit (UHU) like the Local Government Engineering Department (LGED), which removes the rural road maintenance setbacks in Bangladesh. In this regard, there are mushroom-based health services to the urban people, and there are many agencies or authorities to maintain urban health; running a UHU can improve urban health calamities by having a controlling power per se its discretion. There is a need for simple, practical, and user-friendly solutions, as well as strengthened partnerships, strong leadership, and government commitment to face the upcoming pandemic and ensure good health and quality of sound environment-friendly life in urban settings as well as sustainable community development framework—SCDF (Roy, 2024).

Before discussing the SCDF, Bangladesh has a legacy of local government divisions and Health systems; both are interconnected to ensure the people's health. Indeed, the Bangladesh Health Policy 2011 envisages the national health as like to take the initiative the protective and prevention strategy for all. Alternative medical care systems are also available in the health policy to make good health at a low cost (Roy, 2023). Nevertheless, apparently, it is an odd matter because the Ministry of Local Government division instead of the Ministry of Health. But strategically, both ministries are well interconnected to implement the Health Policy 2011 and

LGD Act 2009 due to the legacy of the East India Company regime in the present governance system. So, it is obvious to carry out the health management system to meet the future pandemic in Bangladesh.

ETHNOGRAPHICAL JOURNEY WITH URBAN LOCAL BODY

In August of 2006, I started with the second Urban Primary Health Care Project as an employee to monitor and coordinate the project activities in the Bogura Municipality, Bangladesh. This project delved into giving primary health care services to the urban people according to the LGD Act 2009 (amendment), especially the poor and hard-core poor in the vicinity. Consequently, I had to coordinate also with public representatives to run the activities smoothly. Every ULB has a Health department with well-appointed human resources. This health department's functions are— immunisation, ensuring sanitary and conservancy practices, and managing urban waste hygienically. Nevertheless, the challenge is that this department is always neglected and underestimated in the organization, even the people. In this scenario also, the author gets experience with five urban local bodies till 31 May 2015.

In the Bogra Municipality, I started the journey with the Project at the beginning of the second phase of 2006. This Municipality was big, neat, almost clean, and had a strong health department with the presence of a medical doctor. The authority was sincere in giving an allotment of 1% of the total budget as a sustainable fund— is formed per se the project instruction to reserve a good fund to lead the project if the agencies fund lay off, for further project runs. Finally, they did that. The public representatives of the Municipality were sincere in improving urban health. Then, the Mdhobdi Municipality I was transferred there in July 2009. This Municipality was tiny and situated within the Union Parishad boundary. The authors (Ahmed & Paul, 2012) express with grief that the policymakers should think twice about establishing a municipality like it. This authority finally consented to make a sustainable fund for sustainable urban health, but before that, I was again transferred to Sirajganj Municipality in 2010, ending a one-year journey there. This institution was a budget-deficient municipality; when her employees did not get a salary for 9 to 11 months, it was a dream to give health services to the urban people.

Nevertheless, one chief executive officer deputed from the government worked splendidly to overcome the budget deficiency issue and updated the salary. In this context, the urban health project works to improve the health status of the people by providing logistics and technical support. Under this Project and LGD Act 2009, the project established one Comprehensive Reproductive Health Care Center (CRHCC) for Fifty thousand inhabitants and one Primary Health Care Centre (PHCC) for Ten thousand people. According to this calculation, this Municipality belongs to one

CRHCC and four PHCCs with medical doctors and paramedics in this vicinity. This project runs the health department with a good swing. After five years, I moved to another city corporation —Narayanganj, in February 2015. This is a juicy city corporation with a plentiful budget to lead its health department, but the medical doctors were not to carry the jobs for a limited scope of career development. Narayanganj City Corporation and Sirajgnaj Municipality are examples that if the elected Mayor would have good faith to do good, then the budget is not a matter for people's welfare. Finally, in June 2015, I left the Project with a vote of thanks to all concerned but evaluated the Policy loopholes in the urban health sector in Bangladesh for scaling up my career in another sector and place.

COVID-19: WHAT WE LEARN FROM IT

Covid-19 has shown us that our health system is more vulnerable to face health crises and falsifies the Global Health Index report-2019. Its effects on health and economies are widening the sorrows and sufferings (Khatun et al., 2023). Now, our existing resources and budget are appropriately utilised as the sustainable solution to face the Covid experiences. However, Covid-19, mainly spread among urban people in Bangladesh, lacks personal health and hygiene practices. On the other hand, the ULB is responsible for ensuring its inhabitants' primary health and hygiene practices. In that case, without strengthening the health department of the municipality and city corporation, the Government of Bangladesh took a tour of another luxurious way like setting up a new hospital, appointing medical staff, and purchasing personal protection equipment (PPE) and vaccinations. Ironically, almost all municipalities and city corporations needed a medical doctor to give people health services and ensure sanitation practices, but almost all these positions are vacant for those not interested in joining, like demotivational posting. Asian Development Bank (ADB) approved credit and assistance to strengthen the ULB's health department in 1998. Although the respective health department did not attain the target; as a result, they did not show effective performance during the Covid-19 pandemic in Bangladesh. So, we need to use the existing resources properly to avoid any upcoming pandemic that we learn from the pandemic of 2020.

URBAN PRIMARY HEALTH CARE: WHY WITH LOCAL GOVERNMENT DIVISION

According to the Cabinet Rules of Business1996 (revised 2008), the Urban Local Body is mandated to provide urban public health care services through the ULBs.

On the other hand, according to the allocation of business among different ministries and departments of Schedule-1 of the Rules of Business, the Ministry of Local Government, Rural Development, and Cooperatives will provide the necessary budget allocation and management logistics through the local government division. Not only this, all these institutions (City corporations, Municipalities) will provide primary health care, establish health centres and charitable clinics and promote them in addition to promoting urban primary health care services. The law indicates that the local government division will ensure the immediate health care environment of the city and town dwellers through these urban local bodies within its jurisdiction. The local government division will monitor the activities of all these urban local bodies. In this context, it is believed that this organization needs to monitor the urban healthcare delivery activities through its subordinate organizations for three reasons. The reasons are —i. Recently, rapid urbanization has been associated with health problems. ii. The local government division is extensive in work, with thousands of priority tasks, and iii. The local government division needs more resources to provide urban healthcare services and also needs rural areas to improve primary healthcare services, aligning environmental waste management (Rahman & Roy, 2022).

HISTORICAL LEGACY OF LOCAL BODY

Strengthening local government institutions is the desired goal of the people. Demands for democracy and local Government have always driven each other. A representative of a local body based on democratic ideals can represent the people's interests. It is essential to link local government bodies with the elected administration at every level.

Articles 59 and 60 of the constitution of Bangladesh contain an outline of local Government, which describes the functioning of management with elected representatives so that the administration can effectively involve the people for each unit. It is imperative to ensure the functioning of effective local government institutions in proportion to constitutional requirements and to institutionalize democratic aspirations in all regions.

EVOLUTION OF LOCAL GOVERNMENT IN BANGLADESH

The history of local Government in Bangladesh shows that different organizations have been established at different times, and governments have been established at different times. Legislation / Ordinances have been framed for forming local bodies at village, thana, district and divisional levels within the period. After establishment, local government institutions often change their functions and responsibilities.

The current structure of local Government in Bangladesh emerged during the British colonial period. The first attempts to establish local Government were made in the late 19th century. The structure, function and financial management of local government institutions today have undergone many changes compared to the British colonial era.

Historically, the villages were self-reliant before the colonial rule. Each village had its community-based organization known as Panchayat. All the adult members of the village society constitute it. Apart from making decisions on social issues, he was also responsible for maintaining law and order. Panchayats could collect and use resources for the performance of their traditional functions. Panchayat naturally fulfils the social needs of society based on public opinion. They had no legal basis or authority behind them.

During British rule, the Village Chowkidari Act of Bengal was passed in 1870 with administrative, economic and political objectives. Then, the establishment of local government bodies started according to the law. Under this Act, a Union and Chowkidari Panchayat (Organization) is formed in each Union. The Chowkidari Panchayat consisted of five members the Government appointed for three years. Panchayats appointed Chowkidars (village police) to maintain law and order. Chowkidari village police are paid by collecting taxes from villagers.

Under the Chowkidari system, members should be government employees rather than villagers' representatives. Panchayats were mainly used to help the administration to maintain law and order and collect taxes. They have no role in development activities. For this reason, changes were being felt in the Chowkidar Panchayat system to fulfil more responsibilities of the local government bodies; in this context, the authorities passed the Bengal Local Self Government Act in 1885. Union Committees, Local Government Boards and District Boards were set under this Act.

The Bengal Village Self-Government Act of 1919 abolished Chowkidar Panchayats and Union Committees and replaced them with Union and District Boards. The nomination system of two-thirds elected and one-third nominated union board was abolished in 1946. The main activities of the Union Board were law and order, maintenance of roads and bridges, provision of health care, charitable hospitals and primary schools, water supply to District Boards and assistance to District Boards. Union boards could dispose of minor criminal cases and were empowered to enforce union tax rates.

Under the Basic Democracy Order Act of 1959, local government bodies were set up in four tiers in Pakistan. Union Parishad at the Union level, Thana Council at the Thana level, District Council at the District level and Divisional Council at the Divisional level. An average union had 10,000 residents, and the union council consisted of 10 to 15 members. Voters elect two-thirds of the members, and the Government nominates one-third. No system of nomination was abolished after the constitution. Among them were members to elect a Chairman and a Vice Chairman. Apart from maintaining law and order in their area, Union Councils were given 37 functions, which included agricultural development, water supply, education, communication, and social welfare. According to the Muslim Family and Marriage Ordinance Act 1961, the Union Council is empowered to establish conciliation courts and its members are vested with judicial powers. Under the Basic Democracies Ordinance of 1959, the Union Parishad was allowed to levy taxes on property and other sources to raise funds in addition to the existing Chowkidari Fund. Government grants are given for rural programs and the construction of Union Parishad offices.

FUNCTIONS OF LOCAL GOVERNMENT DIVISION

The Government is committed to establishing strong local government institutions at various levels through active participation of elected representatives in governance and development activities. The Local Government Department is implementing various development and service-oriented activities for poverty alleviation and to make the lives of rural people more comfortable, well-organized and meaningful. LGD activities have been promoted to the grassroots level of the country. Union Parishads, Upazila Parishads, Zilla Parishads, Municipalities and City Corporations are local government institutions under this division. In addition, the Local Government Engineering Department (LGED), Directorate of Public Health Engineering (DPHE), Dhaka WASA, Chittagong WASA, Khulna WASA, Rajshahi WASA and National LOCAL GOVERNMENT INSTITUTE Different departments/departments/institutions of this department. Through these departments/organizations, local government departments through resource consolidation, municipalities and city corporations, rural and urban infrastructure development (construction of roads, box culverts, growth centres for expansion of city corporations, bridges, market facilities), supply of safe drinking water, solid waste disposal And providing sanitation services across the country. The LGD is responsible for planning and implementing development projects at the local level, conducting surveys/research on local government issues and training programs to enhance the knowledge and skills of elected representatives. These activities contribute directly and indirectly to the national socio-economic development goals through poverty alleviation, human resource development and employment generation.

A performance appraisal system of local government institutions has been introduced to improve their capacity, accountability, transparency and healthy competition among local government institutions. Based on performance evaluation results, initiatives have been taken for additional allocations and awards for local government institutions.

TO ESTABLISH AN URBAN HEALTH UNIT ON SAFEGUARDING PRIMARY HEALTH CARE: TIME BEFITTING DEMAND

The percentage of the world's population residing in urban areas will increase from an estimated 55% in 2018 to an estimated 68% in 2050, according to the United Nations. The United Nations projects that Bangladesh's urban population will increase from 48 million in 2011 to 84 million in 2030. This development will be driven primarily by internal migration and natural population growth. Ever-increasing numbers of urban residents will reside in slums. Expanding healthcare services is necessary to satisfy the growing urban population's healthcare needs. Currently, Bangladesh provides both public and private health services. However, this chapter is delimited to the public health providers through ULBs.

During the past two decades, the Bangladeshi Government has allocated some public funds to non-governmental organizations. In both nations, health infrastructure and services have consistently improved but still need to be improved to meet the population's needs. In the past several decades, national governments and external partners have yet to make significant efforts to enhance urban health.

The Municipal Administration Act (1960), and The Pauroshava Ordinance Act (1977), The City Corporation Act (1983), these laws are known as the City Corporation Act (2008) and the Local Government Act (2009). Through the implementation of these laws, the Urban Local Body will exercise effective powers to ensure the health rights of its citizens. In the Act, detailed jurisdiction is guaranteed. However, some critical areas of action have been mentioned, given C-19, and proper implementation of these actions would have been helpful enough to combat the Covid-19 pandemic. However, one of the functions of ULB is –

A. Ensure and control food and environment
B. Control sanitation practices.
C. Veterinary and rabbis' control
D. Conservancy services
E. Medical services
F. Promotion of public health and health education
G. Hospitals and dispensaries operation and management.
H. Provision of vaccination and community health
I. Prevention of infectious and communicable diseases.

Looking at the titles of the three job jurisdictions listed in the order F, H, and I, you will notice a proportional relationship and stay up-to-date on current Covid-19 activity. Due to my ethnographical journey and experience working in several urban local bodies, I want to write the budget and implementation of these works in the future. Urban local bodies think development means hardware and software development matters are like stepsons. However, the actions the state took to deal with C-19 today, such as washing hands frequently, staying clean, following social distancing, and using masks to protect from dust, do not fall into the F mentioned above series. Again, quarantine, isolation, and first aid treatment fall under the duties mentioned in the G and I series. Due to needing more capacity, the Government could only consider some of these institutions to deal with the Covid-19 pandemic. What will the public representatives say about the leadership and responsibility of urban local bodies?

Local Government Departments, the Ministry of Health and Welfare, and Non-Governmental Organizations are engaged in modern urban health care. However, they are not able to cope with contemporary health challenges. C-19 is a significant example at the moment. Therefore, even if we cannot stop the source of the disease, we must continue to make every effort to reduce it as much as possible. However, a Second Urban Primary Health Care Project report found that "heterogeneous standards, approaches, overlapping services create scepticism and ambivalence in the public mind. That is why it is said—a weak legal framework and institutional linkages and coordination constrain the stewardship role of the public sector. Therefore, good prevention can improve health.

City or municipal health departments are functioning in all the city corporations and municipalities of the country as the first step to improving the health system and strengthening the prevention of diseases. A Chief Health Officer (City Corporation) and Medical Officer (Municipality) head the Department. In this Department, some more technical and non-technical human resources are provided to the city residents. Through political, financial, and professional problems, this Department has continued its existing services, which are a product of the southern class of the upper class. However, fighting an epidemic like Covid-19 is like treating rheumatism with borrowed ghee. The reason is that primary health care and public health need to get priority in terms of budget and human resource allocation to urban local bodies. In addition, the inadequacy of revenue collection, over-dependence on central government budget allocation, political interference, corruption, and central government interference are all ways of friends. Crossing the path of the Urban Local Body itself is at the danger point.

Moreover, urban primary health care delivery is crucial; every hundred years, it will be a setback for us. In this case, it is vital to construct an institutional health strategy regarding how this service will be provided. Because the current urban health care delivery strategy/approach as it has emerged has yet to be considered to have been developed in a planned way.

Analysing the first and second reasons, in the mid-term evaluation report of the Second Urban Primary Health Care Project-2008, ADB and DFID recommended that the Government would create an Urban Health Unit under the Ministry of Rural Development & Cooperatives like the Department of Local Government Engineering (LGED) to deal with urban primary health care services. Moreover, analyzing the third reason, all urban local bodies will ensure a Fixed Deposit Return of 1% of their own revenue budget as a 'Sustainable Fund' to provide adequate health care services in the future, aligning to strengthen either the Municipality or City corporation health department. Suppose the assistance of development cooperation agencies stops running the project activities further. In that case, the local bodies will use the sustainable fund to provide the services to her people, which is part of the urban healthcare capacity building program. Nevertheless, the reality is different. Why? Because effective health system governance for urban Primary health care coverage.

Leadership and governance involve ensuring that strategic policy frameworks are in place and paying attention to effective oversight, coalition-building, regulation, system design, and accountability. The chapter discusses three main categories of stakeholders who interact with each other to determine the health system and its governance (WHO, 2023)—

i.   State (government agencies and organizations)
ii.   Health service providers (various public and private health service providers and
iii. Citizens (service recipients) who become service users when interacting with health service providers.

In the Sustainable Development Goals agenda framework, WHO works for urban Health Coverage (WHO, 2023) and manages effective health systems, but in this chapter, I would like to focus on forming the Urban Health Unit to address the barriers and challenges of urban primary health care to achieve Universal Urban Health by 2030.

Biswas et al. (2017) discussed the policy-level gaps in improving Bangladesh's non-communicable diseases (NCD). In this article, they defended the health policy, acts, and strategies for covering universal health coverage, but when the service providers are at finger's point, the Government neglects the doorstep services. The following Table 1 shows there are different levels of policy, acts, and strategies, but ULBs need to be stronger, more effective, and efficient in managing the services to provide to the urban people. As a result, my ethnographic journey with ULBs is

Table 1. Policy documents in Bangladesh

Policy / Acts/ Strategy	Policy Documents	Published Year
Policy and Planning Recommendations	—National Health Policy —National Food Policy	2011 2006
Legislation Acts	—Safe food act —Iodine deficiency disease prevention act —Local government (city corporation) Act —Local government (Municipality) Act	2013 1989 2009 2009
Strategic Plans	—Health, nutrition and population strategic investment plan (HNPSIP) —Health Service Delivery Program (NHSDP) —Health, Population and Nutrition Sector Program	2016—2021 2012 2003

Source: Author's compilation

not happy with the public leaders— budget insufficient, mismanagement, and lack of human resources in the health department.

COVID-19: ARE WE READY TO THE NEXT PANDEMIC?

It is worth discussing because the investigation into our continued failure to combat C-19 may help solve our next pandemic! History says so (1920, 1820, 1720). As much as the current C-19 is discussed and criticized, Urban Local Bodies are under-pronounced. However, all these domestic institutions had the opportunity to play an effective and exemplary role.

Those of us who think that the city corporation or the municipalities, apart from making donations, do birth-death certificates, inheritance certificates, and repair of roads because of these trivial tasks, the public forgets the big responsibilities of these bodies. However, all these institutions are statutory to provide urban healthcare facilities. Nevertheless, unfortunately, not only our people but most of our country's representatives need to have the right idea about this (my field experience says so). Now let us look back a bit ---

The three flows of information in this age of globalization suggest that the Plague of 1720, the Cholera in 1820, and the Spanish flu of 1920 have some early similarities to what is now known as Covid-19. For example, all epidemics are infectious diseases, the invention of vaccines is a product of a long-term process, and basic hygiene is the antidote to these diseases. For writing, why are the state institutions so indifferent to following and running these basic hygiene rules, which I, you, or the state have to pay for?

A look at the website of the Local Government Department reveals the names of many projects implemented by Urban Local Bodies. Projects have been implemented, money has been spent, discussion after submission of the evaluation report, and criticism has been made, all within 90-100 per cent. However, C-19 showed that the work cost only money. A decade-long experience working in multiple health-related projects and urban local bodies says so. The public representatives' role is significant in properly implementing projects and preventing corruption. Municipalities and City Corporations have an Administrative Department along with the Health Department. City Corporations have several Administrative Cadre Officers, and Class "A" Municipalities have one Administrative Cadre Officer - Chief Executive Officer. According to the Local Government Act, these officers will occasionally conduct Mobile Courts to ensure law and order, aligning the health and safety of the urban dwellers. Urban local bodies must pay more attention to primary health care and the obligation to comply with basic hygiene regulations.

Many people talk about the need for more health sector budget allocation about the maximum allocation. Many people talk about the prevention of corruption in the health sector. You will find a few people who will talk about spending the portion of health allocation properly and well. Those who favour such expenses are subjected to various consequences at the workplace. Moreover, a part of the self-interested circle is involved in an evil process.

Still waiting for the state allocation, but look at the breakdown of local government allocations and expenditures. In the last five years' budget analysis of the country's four first-class municipalities and a city corporation, we see the picture of disappointment; there is no opportunity to play an influential role in C-19 control. Because 4-5% of the budget is allocated to the health sector. Again, 80% of the allocation goes to the salary and allowances sector. How is it possible to control Covid by allocating 20% (i.e., 5%) of the total allocation to the health sector? There are several reasons for the allocation of expenditure in the health sector. However, the main reason for me is the conceptual problem in the development concept. Municipal authorities or city authorities think development means hardware development, which will be visible. As a result, infrastructure development becomes the main attraction. There are many benefits, including commission and cash withdrawal, reflected in the budget allocation.

On the other hand, public representatives consider software development unnecessarily wasteful, which cannot be exemplified in elections. So this development needs to be addressed, addressed in the budget. You will notice that in municipal or city elections, all candidates, regardless of party affiliation, simultaneously promise hardware development over software development. The reason is easy to imagine. The state is now paying for it. Development must be balanced so local government institutions can deal with situations like Covid-19.

This research recommends going slow when amending or enacting new laws. Because you cannot unequivocally state that most of the laws enacted during the British period are unenforceable. First of all, I am in favour of the proper application and implementation of any law. If its implementation is not considered adequate, we can seek an amendment of the law. For example, rather than going into the matter of the Waste Act referred to, I would like to relate some of my experience with waste and its regulation. Biasedly, I have always favoured political empowerment and the strengthening of local government systems and believe both are important in development.

However, the Local Government Act 2009, a continuation of British legislation, places responsibility for the disposal and management of waste from existing clinics and hospitals in cities or municipalities. Furthermore, the Urban Governance Improvement Project was undertaken to strengthen and strengthen this issue, i.e., waste management. Under the said project and behavioural governance changes of individuals and institutions, waste classification and storage of waste used in homes and institutions is encouraged. Medical, non-medical, hazardous, and non-harmful wastes were collected and disposed of at designated sites. The problem is that the project is for a certain period, and its implementation is no longer ongoing. Why is it not implemented?

Another thing is that as fast as projects are developed, implemented, and released for waste management improvement and construction, projects are developed, implemented, and released for urban beautification much faster than that. Why is that? Because you do not have to be wise to understand. A municipality in the country works on the PPP model in waste management. The exciting thing is that there was a dispute with a country's government agency over where the collected waste would be dumped. Although far from the urban area and owned land of municipal authority. Another municipal authority has received the push to build a waste management facility on its land for proper waste management. Undoubtedly, the city has become comfortable spending money on beautification projects.

CONCLUSION

Today, we can say that rural Bangladesh is arguably an extended part of the urban areas. For that reason, UHU is now an expected authority to protect urban primary health. Legislation and amendment must be matters of urgent and public welfare consideration. Nevertheless, why is it not happening despite the lack of proper implementation of the existing law and having the waste management department under a fully autonomous department under that law? It means that the Department needs to be fixed. For example, while working in an "A" class municipality (in

2006/2007), the authorities asked the author with a camera to see if the waste department properly removed and separated medical and non-medical waste 2 or 3 times a week. I captured the camera in the early morning. That is, if there is any violation of the implementation of the rules, it should be handed over to the authorities. The result of this process was excellent. The city was then a clean city in implementing such decisions of political wisdom under existing laws, which one would like to know if it still exists today.

Laws they made serve as our foundation in all systems, including justice. So, the municipal or city authorities can compel waste removal by operating mobile courts. However, it does not happen. Political interference is a significant hitch here. For all these reasons, considering the existing laws and their implementation results can give us effective results in sound waste management and a clean city where we all live together.

REFERENCES

Afsana, K., & Wahid, S. S. (2013). Health care for poor people in the urban slums of Bangladesh. *Lancet, 382*(9910), 2049–2051. doi:10.1016/S0140-6736(13)62295-3 PMID:24268606

Ahmed, T., & Paul, B. C. (2012). *Nagarayan O Nagar Sarkar: Bangladesh City Corporation*. Prothoma Prokashon.

Biswas, T., Pervin, S., Tanim, M. I. A., Niessen, L., & Islam, A. (2017). Bangladesh policy on prevention and control of non-communicable diseases: A policy analysis. *BMC Public Health, 17*(1), 1–11. doi:10.1186/s12889-017-4494-2 PMID:28629430

Burris, S., Hancock, T., Lin, V., & Herzog, A. (2007). Emerging strategies for healthy urban governance. *Journal of Urban Health, 84*, 154–163.

Global Security Health Index. (2019). *Building Collective Action and Accountability*. John Hopkins, Bloomberg School of Public Health. www.ghsindex.org

Khatun, F., Nawrin, N., Al Kabir, F., & Neelormi, S. (2023). *Financing for Women's Empowerment in the Context of Post-COVID Recovery and LDC Graduation of Bangladesh (No. 46). Centre for Policy Dialogue*. CPD.

Rahman, M., & Roy, P. K. (2022). Challenges to Ensure Healthy Living through Sanitation and Hygiene Coverage: Study on Narail District, Bangladesh. In Effective Waste Management and Circular Economy (pp. 223-232). CRC Press.

Roy, P. (2022). Sensing the Silence: A Case of the Rakhain Community of Bangladesh. *SSRN, 4559157*. www.ssrn.com

Roy, P. (2023a). Conversation with Silence: An Introduction of the Spirituality and Healing System of the Bangladeshi Rakhain Community. *SSRN, 4539913*. www.ssrn.com. doi:10.2139/ssrn.4539913

RoyP. (2023b). Conversation with Silence: The Methodological Exploration to Study the Spirituality and Healing System of the Bangladeshi Rakhain Community (August 13, 2023). https://ssrn.com/abstract=4539816 doi:10.2139/ssrn.4539816

Roy, P. K. (2024). *Customary Law and Sustainable Community Development: A Study of the Santals of Bangladesh*, [PhD Thesis, Universiti Malaya].

Shawar, Y. R., & Crane, L. G. (2017). Generating global political priority for urban health: The role of the urban health epistemic community. *Health Policy and Planning, 32*(8), 1161–1173. doi:10.1093/heapol/czx065 PMID:28582532

Siraz, M. J., Abd Wahab, H., Saad, R. M., & Roy, P. K. (2020). *Globalization to Slowbalization to Indigenous Holism: Combating the Preemptive: Vaccinationalism with the reflection of Saadia Gaon and Al-Farabi*. Virus Economy. Innovation Solution Lab.

ADDITIONAL READINGS

Baumgart, S., Hackenbroch, K., Hossain, S., & Kreibich, V. (2011). Urban development and public health in Dhaka, Bangladesh. *Health in megacities and urban areas*, 281-300.

Roy, P. (2023, February). Reciprocity and its practice in social research. In *Anthropological Forum. 2-4 Park Square, Milton Park, Abingdon Ox14 4rn, Oxon, England: Routledge Journals*. Taylor & Francis Ltd.

Roy, P., Chowdhury, J. S., Abd Wahab, H., Saad, M. R. B., & Parahakaran, S. (2021). Christianity, COVID-19, and marginal people of Bangladesh: An experience from the Santal Community. In Handbook of Research on the Impact of COVID-19 on Marginalized Populations and Support for the Future (pp. 65-82). IGI Global.

Shafique, S., Bhattacharyya, D. S., Anwar, I., & Adams, A. (2018). Right to health and social justice in Bangladesh: Ethical dilemmas and obligations of state and non-state actors to ensure health for urban poor. *BMC Medical Ethics, 19*(1), 61–69. doi:10.1186/s12910-018-0285-2 PMID:29945594

Siraz, J., Wahab, H. A., Saad, R. M., & Roy, P. K. (2020). Volunteering' as Praxis During COVID-19: Experiences from Bangladeshi Migrant Workers in Malaysia and Indigenous Communities of Bangladesh. *Eubios Journal of Asian and International Bioethics; EJAIB, 30*(8).

KEY TERMS AND DEFINITIONS

Local Government Division: It's a division of the Government of Bangladesh, per se, the rules of business to work smoothly to the outreach part of the country. All urban local bodies are under the LGD of the concerned ministry.

Reflected Ethnography: Typically, this chapter is based on personal experiences with ULB in Bangladesh and shared for mitigating the future pandemic for efficient resource management when we have enough to make a decision. For that reason, the author **emphasized** personal reflections rather than academic text citations whilst working on those issues.

Urban Health Unit: This unit has been proposed in this chapter to look after the Urban Health Systems for effective services.

Chapter 5
A Comparative Study of Environmental Impact Assessment (EIA) Practices in India and Canada

Pranjal Khare
O.P. Jindal Global University, India

Hemendra Singh
O.P. Jindal Global University, India

Paridhi Sharma
O.P. Jindal Global University, India

Shalinee Vishwakarma
O.P. Jindal Global University, India

ABSTRACT

This chapter deals with the concept of Environmental Impact Assessment (EIA) in India and Canada. It scrutinizes the effectiveness of EIA regulatory frameworks in both the countries on the touchstone of extent of public participation, engagement with indigenous communities, and the integration of healthcare aspects. The analysis reveals a nuanced landscape wherein Canada serves as a model for comprehensive and well-structured EIA practices, whereas India grapples with challenges in implementation and enforcement. Canada excels in inclusivity by actively involving the public and indigenous communities in decision-making processes. In contrast, India faces hurdles in achieving meaningful public participation particularly in marginalized communities. The study emphasizes the need for contextualization in EIA frameworks and raises questions about improving public engagement and healthcare integration globally.

DOI: 10.4018/979-8-3693-1178-3.ch005

INTRODUCTION

Environmental Impact Assessment (EIA) has evolved as an important tool in modern environmental management. It aims to balance developmental aspirations of nations with environmental sustainability. EIA acts as a foundation in preventing adverse environmental impacts arising from development projects. It basically serves two roles firstly, it predicts the potential consequences of proposed projects and secondly, it aids the decision-makers in devising mitigation strategies. The development of EIA practices has been influenced by a growing understanding of how ecological systems are interconnected and increased awareness of the rights of local communities and indigenous people. With the passage of time, EIA has evolved from being a mere procedural formality to an integral part of the decision-making process.

The evolution of EIA practices in India and Canada reflects their unique historical, regulatory, and cultural contexts. India's journey began with the establishment of the Ministry of Environment, Forest and Climate Change in 1985, which formalized the EIA process in the form of the Environment Protection Act, 1986. Draft notifications of 2006 and 2020 have considerably changed the original legal framework governing EIA in India. In Canada, the Environmental Impact Assessment was adopted in the year 1973 by introducing a Federal Cabinet Directive. Afterwards, the Canadian Environmental Assessment Act was passed in the year 1992 and later replaced by the Canadian Environmental Assessment Act, 2012. EIA practices were initially embedded in broader environmental assessment processes and have evolved with the recognition of Indigenous rights and consultation. Both countries have navigated challenges in striking a balance between development and environmental conservation.

The legal and regulatory frameworks form the foundation of EIA practices in both countries. India's EIA process is governed by the Environmental Impact Assessment Notification, which outlines procedural steps, criteria for project categorization, and requirements for public consultation. Canada, on the other hand, employs a tiered approach where federal, provincial, and indigenous assessment processes interact. This diversity in frameworks reflects the federal-provincial balance in Canada and India's decentralized approach to governance.

In Canada, mechanisms like indigenous knowledge and traditional land use studies coupled with public participation contribute to a more holistic understanding of project impacts. The Canadian approach is more in line with the United Nations Declaration on the Rights of Indigenous People which ultimately aims to secure free, prior and informed consent for decisions that may affect the rights and interests of indigenous people. On the other hand, importance of public participation in India is overlooked by introducing subsequent amendments in 2006 and 2020. It is pertinent to note that the importance of indigenous engagement within EIA processes is profound. In India, indigenous communities often face displacement due to development projects, undermining the need for equal representation of people from these communities. The difference in approaches arises from distinct historical pathways but which ultimately converges in recognizing the rights of indigenous people in shaping projects that affect their lands and cultures.

Comparative analysis of EIA practices reveals both commonalities and disparities. Canada has a well framed and separate enactment to deal with EIA whereas India has a formal legal framework which has been enacted by making an amendment in the Environment Protection Act, 1986. Canada's experience offers valuable lessons. Canada's recognition of indigenous rights can inspire India to further involve indigenous communities in shaping project outcomes. Its public participation mechanism can encourage India to refine its own methods for engaging marginalized populations. This can be achieved by harmonizing traditional knowledge with scientific assessments, enhancing monitoring protocols, and streamlining public participation channels.

The element of health care in environment impact assessment is better in Canada than India. In both the countries, it is the responsibility of the health care professionals to facilitate and advocate for the effective cooperation of health aspect in environment impact assessment.

Strategic Environmental Assessment (SEA) is another mechanism to deal with potential environmental concerns. While EIA is not undertaken until an environmentally relevant project enters the approval stage, SEA is carried out at the planning stage of a project. SEA systematically analyzes the project by identifying the environmental implications and issuing early warning of the cumulative effects.

Canada does not have any separate legal framework which mandates SEA in the country. The requirement of SEA is derived from the "Cabinet Directive on the Environmental Assessment of Policy, Plan and Program Proposals (1990)." The Directive underwent various amendments in 1999 and 2004 which further enhanced transparency in terms of the assessment process. Although, the Directive does not have specific procedures or regulations for each sector, the idea is to maintain flexibility in the broader framework. The federal government agencies and departments must necessarily abide by the Directive but are given flexibility to formulate the guidelines and framework of their own for SEA requirement within their institution. Although, it seems likely that it is beneficial for the government agencies to implement it, yet research and efforts are required to streamline the process for uniform applicability of the Directives throughout the Canada to avoid any disparity anywhere within the agencies of the country. Moreover, Canada does not have a centralized SEA agency. The Canada's Environmental Assessment Agency is the sole agency which offers training and support for other federal departments and agencies.

The Strategic Environment Assessment is yet to be made compulsory in India. India has been using SEA on an ad-hoc basis and there are only few examples where

SEA was carried out either as a funder requirement or on a discretionary basis. India currently has nine SEA practice instances and six SEA related guidelines.

The principal aim of the research is to draw out the similarities and differences between the regulatory framework and nuanced practices of both the countries with respect to environmental impact assessment and strategic environment assessment. The comparative analysis also brings to light the potential lessons that other countries can draw from India and Canada's well-established EIA and SEA framework.

ENVIRONMENT IMPACT ASSESSMENT IN INDIA AND CANADA

India's EIA Framework

India's Environmental Impact Assessment system is outlined in the 1994 Environmental Impact Assessment Notification. This notice has been updated in 2006 and 2020, showing India's evolving environmental conditions. The Ministry of Environment, Forest and Climate Change supervises the EIA system. Below are some key points from the 1994 Environmental Impact Assessment Notification:

1. **Types of Projects:** The notification breaks down projects into two core types. Type one projects need approval directly from the Central Ministry due to their possible serious environmental and social effects. Type two, less impactful, projects can get the go-ahead at the state level, fostering local control.
2. **Screening**: The EIA journey starts with an activity called screening which is all about examining the possibility of environmental effects caused by projects. This involves a basic review process. In this step, projects are classified as First or Second category. This sets the groundwork for the next steps in the assessment.
3. **Scoping**: Once the screening is done, scoping is undertaken. In this stage, the scope and limits of our project review is undertaken. This guarantees that our focus remains on the project's pivotal environmental aspects. As a result, the final assessment of the project is more precise and effective (Yadav, 2018).
4. **Public Consultation**: Involving the public in decision-making processes is crucial to our EIA process in India. It mandates public meetings. This means all the information about proposed projects must be released to the public. This ensures transparency and allows local communities and stakeholders to provide feedback and enhances the democratic legitimacy of the decision-making process.
5. **Appraisal**: At the appraisal stage, all project information is looked at, including public views and possible environmental effects. The Expert Appraisal

Committee (EAC) checks out each project. They give advice based on what they see, which helps decision-making (Parikh, 2019).

6. **Post-clearance Monitoring**: India's commitment to environmental sustainability extends beyond the approval stage. The notification includes provisions for post-clearance monitoring. It ensures that projects adhere to the conditions set during approval. This ongoing monitoring is crucial for assessing the actual environmental impact of projects and verifying the effectiveness of implemented mitigation measures.

India's Environmental Impact Assessment framework, as outlined in the relevant provisions of the Environmental Impact Assessment Notification, 1994, establishes a systematic and legally binding process. The categorization, screening, scoping, public consultation, appraisal, and post-clearance monitoring stages collectively contribute to a comprehensive approach that ensures projects are evaluated thoroughly which promotes responsible and sustainable development (Thakur & Khosravi, 2021).

Canada's EIA Framework

Canada's commitment to environmental stewardship and sustainable development is enshrined in the Impact Assessment Act, which came into force in 2019. This legislation replaced the Canadian Environmental Assessment Act, 2012, and introduced a modernized approach to Environmental Impact Assessment (EIA). Governed by the Impact Assessment Agency of Canada, the statutory framework emphasizes a more inclusive, comprehensive, and adaptive process. Relevant Provisions of the Impact Assessment Act, 2019 are listed below:

1. **Indigenous Involvement:** A defining feature of Canada's EIA framework is the explicit recognition and inclusion of indigenous perspectives. The Impact Assessment Act mandates the consideration of Indigenous knowledge while making sure that there is active participation of indigenous communities in the whole assessment process. This reflects Canada's commitment to reconciliation and respect for the indigenous rights and interests (Tsuji, 2022).

2. **Early Planning and Engagement:** Canada's groundwork includes thinking ahead and involving everyone early on, following the Impact Assessment Act guidelines. This forward-thinking way ensures that we think about what effect our project will have on the environment right from the beginning. It helps everybody work together and sorts out problems before they get bigger.

3. **Regional and Strategic Assessments:** The legislation brings in the idea of looking at specific region and making strategic assessments. It weighs the total effects of several projects all happening in one place. These assessments shows

that there is seriousness about keeping things balanced and making plans for the full landscape.

4. **Planning Phase:** It lays the foundations for judging the project. It pinpoints the assessment's focus, finds out possible environmental impacts, and figures out how everything will be judged. This way of organizing means our process is consistent and focuses on the right things.

5. **Impact Statement:** Project proponents are required to prepare an impact statement. This comprehensive document outlines the potential environmental, social, and health impacts of the proposed project, serving as a crucial tool for decision-makers in the later stages.

6. **Consultation and Engagement:** The legislation places a significant emphasis on consultation and engagement outlining the requirements for public and stakeholder involvement. This inclusive approach ensures that the assessment benefits from a diverse range of perspectives, fostering transparency and informed decision-making.

Canada's EIA framework, as governed by the Impact Assessment Act, 2019, reflects a modern and adaptive approach to environmental assessment. The statutory provisions emphasize Indigenous involvement, early planning, regional assessments, and comprehensive impact statements. This framework underscores Canada's commitment to responsible development that considers the broader environmental, social, and cultural context, setting the stage for a more sustainable future.

Analysis of Contrasting Frameworks of the Two Countries

India's categorization of projects into Category I and II exemplifies decentralized decision-making. For instance, a large-scale industrial project in Maharashtra (Category A) undergoes central ministry's scrutiny, while a smaller-scale project in Karnataka (Category B) allows for state-level approval. The emphasis on public participation is evident in the process. The proposed expansion of a mining project in Odisha underwent public consultation, where local communities expressed concerns about water contamination, leading to modifications in the project plan. The inclusion of post-clearance monitoring was exemplified in the case of a thermal power plant in Madhya Pradesh. Regular monitoring ensured compliance with emission standards, preventing adverse impacts on air quality. Strengthening enforcement mechanisms for post-clearance conditions could be exemplified by increasing penalties for non-compliance, ensuring adherence to mitigation measures.

Canada's commitment to indigenous involvement is seen in the assessment of a pipeline project where indigenous communities were actively engaged. The resulting modifications to the project plan reflected the incorporation of Indigenous knowledge.

The importance of early planning and engagement was evident in a mining project in British Columbia. Early discussions with local communities addressed concerns about water usage and led to mutually agreed-upon mitigation measures. Canada's approach to regional assessments is exemplified in the examination of multiple mining projects in the Yukon region. The cumulative impacts on biodiversity were assessed collectively, influencing regulatory decisions. Ongoing efforts to enhance reconciliation with Indigenous communities could be illustrated through initiatives that bridge historical gaps and promote collaboration, ensuring meaningful participation.

India's future approach could be exemplified through the incorporation of advanced technologies. For instance, the use of satellite imagery for real-time monitoring of deforestation in a proposed industrial zone in Chattisgarh can enhance accuracy in impact assessment. Initiatives to increase public awareness could be showcased through regional campaigns. An example might include educational programs in Kerala to inform communities about the potential impacts of a proposed tourism development project. Future directions could be highlighted through projects incorporating climate change considerations. An example might involve a wind energy project in Tamil Nadu, designed with climate resilience to mitigate potential impacts of extreme weather events.

Ongoing efforts to innovate Indigenous collaboration could be demonstrated through the establishment of joint monitoring programs. For instance, collaborative efforts between Indigenous communities and industry in Alberta could showcase effective data sharing and monitoring initiatives. Strengthening regional assessments could be exemplified through the examination of a series of offshore wind projects in Atlantic Canada. A comprehensive assessment of cumulative impacts could inform decision-making and promote sustainable development. Canada's commitment to global cooperation could be showcased through participation in international partnerships. For example, collaborative efforts with Arctic nations to address transboundary environmental issues, such as the impact of shipping routes, could demonstrate a commitment to global environmental stewardship.

India and Canada, through their specific statutory provisions and examples, offer a rich tapestry of approaches to Environmental Impact Assessment. By learning from each other's strengths and addressing areas for improvement, these nations pave the way for a more sophisticated, inclusive, and technologically advanced future in environmental assessment. As both countries continue to refine their frameworks, the global community can draw inspiration from their experiences in balancing development and conservation for a sustainable future.

Strategic Environmental Assessment

While India's primary focus has been on project-level assessments, strategic environmental assessments (SEA) have gained prominence in recent years. The EIA Notification from 1994 has elements of SEAs. India knows it must study the wider effects of policies, plans, and programs on the environment. For example, Maharashtra made a regional plan. They ran an environmental check on it, thinking about how it will affect land use, biodiversity, and water in the future. India shows its commitment to SEA through its policy framework. The National Environment Policy (2006) openly talks about the need for environmental assessments during planning.

Canada is following the international gold standards by endorsing strategic plans for the environment. The Impact Assessment Act, put into effect in 2019, gives weightage to assessing the wider impacts of policies, plans, and programs. A great example is a land use plan in Alberta. It had a complete review, keeping in mind the effects of various projects on animal habitats and plant life. Canada's method for regional assessments is synced with these strategic environmental pointers. Take for instance a transportation plan in British Columbia. A thorough assessment was conducted to grasp the ripple effects of different transportation projects on things like air quality, natural habitats, and local communities.

India's formal acceptance and adoption of SEA is a vital move. Including SEAs in policies shows a rising knowledge of the need to think about environmental issues on a larger scale. Even though it's still early, India's strategy fits with the worldwide shift for a more thorough environmental thought (Thakur & Rajvanshi, 2021). Canada's sturdy SEA setup, part of the Impact Assessment Act, shows a deep grasp of the need to look at the wider effects of policies and plans. Fuelling SEA into local evaluations guarantees a full study of environmental effects, pushing for a greener future (Noble et al. 2019).

India's future directions could involve strengthening SEA processes by enhancing institutional capacity and creating guidelines for consistent implementation. For instance, the development of a national water policy could undergo a robust SEA to assess the potential impacts on water resources, ecosystems, and communities. Canada's future approach might involve enhanced integration of SEA into decision-making processes (Noble, 2021). An example could be the assessment of a provincial climate action plan, where a strategic environmental assessment informs the policy's potential impacts on greenhouse gas emissions, adaptation strategies, and overall environmental sustainability.

India and Canada, though at different stages in their strategic environmental assessment journeys, share a common recognition of the importance of evaluating policies, plans, and programs for their broader environmental implications. As both nations continue to refine their approaches to SEA, the global community can benefit from their experiences in incorporating strategic environmental considerations into decision-making processes for a more sustainable future.

ASSESSING PUBLIC PARTICIPATION AND INDIGENOUS ENGAGEMENT

Foundation of the concept of EIA in India was laid down back in 1976-77 when the Department of Science and Technology was directed by the planning commission to examine the major projects through environmental angle (Jha-Thakur & Khosravi, 2021). With EIA Notification of 1994 under the Environment Protection Act, 1986 EIA was made mandatory in India. The concept of environmental justice has undergone major changes over the period. Moving away from the traditional understanding three important aspects of environmental justice includes recognitional justice, procedural justice, and distributive Justice. Recognitional justice includes recognition of diversity of experiences and participations of affected communities (Scholsberg, 2007). It is noteworthy that the public participation was not a mandate under EIA until April 1997. It was done through enactment of Public Hearing Notification in April 1997 as an amendment to EIA Notification of 1994. With introduction of requirement of video recording of the proceedings in 2006, the process was made further transparent and strengthened. Public participation *albeit* introduced as the democratic way of decision making, even after mandating it works as one way flow of information by the members of large vocal groups. Thus, inadequate public participation has been major shortcoming of the EIA process in India. This part of the chapter seeks to assess the fundamental principle of EIA process, that is, *Public Participation* which fosters transparency and accountability (Diduck et al., 2013). For fulfilling this objective, the government in India engages in public hearings and consultations as its *modus operandi* to seek participation of the public.

It is pertinent to note that fundamental shortcoming of EIA process in India is that the public participation occurs after the stages of screening and scoping. As by the stage of public hearing the EIA report is already ready, this results in answering of fundamental questions without incorporating any inputs from the directly affected communities and minimal incentive to include public concerns. However, the importance of providing valuable inputs the members of community cannot be disregarded. Thus, these communities also need to have early access to the project details and understanding of environmental processes. A study done on industrial development affecting a wetland and agricultural livelihoods in the state of Gujarat, the authors while focussing on procedural aspects of environmental justice explained and discussed the extent to which concerns of potentially affected communities were addressed by the EIA (Rathi, 2019). Study found lack of public participation opportunities to be one of important trigger for crucial disconnect between the issues resolved through EIA and the actual concerns of the communities leading to the litigation. Such instances highlight the importance of public participation.

Further, notification of 2006 requires the view of all stakeholders to be ascertained during public hearing process for environment impact. However, in India development and socio-economic concerns side line the public concerns and environmental issues. For example, in small hydro-power projects state level approval processes are yet to include local values and knowledge as a requirement (Sinclar & Diduck, 2016). This inadequate participation and ignorance of ascertaining stakeholder's interest affects and questions the credibility and neutrality of the EIA process.

On the other hand, through catena of judicial pronouncements it can be deduced that the input from public participation has majorly influenced the design of the project and subsequent decision-making process. The landmark judgments like Taj Trapezium zone case (MC Mehta v Union of India, 1997), the Kanpur Tanneries case (MC Mehta v Union of India, 1998) and Delhi Vehicular Pollution Case (MC Mehta v Union of India, 1998) are clear instances for effectiveness of participatory mechanism which leads to cognitive improvement of decision making. The judiciary in India along with NGT has been assiduously invalidating the EIA approvals made in disregard of the statutory requirement. For example, in Adivasi Majdoor kisan Ekta Sangathan and Another v. Ministry of Environment and Forest and Others, the NGT declared the approval invalid due to not recording the opposition voiced and not preparing the summary of public hearing in local language.

EIA 2020 and Public Participation: The Draft EIA Notification 2020 draft was presented by the Union Ministry of Environment, Forest, and Climate Change on March 23, 2020 to replace the Notification from 2006. Though expired this draft notification had some very problematic provisions and was labelled to be favouring the industrial practices over environment. The draft guidelines introduced a 4 stage cycle for EIA including screening, scoping public hearing and appraisal. Here in the projects were divided in category A and B. The category A projects needs mandatory clearance thus need not undergo the stage of screening. On the other hand, category B projects are further divided into two categories of B1 & B2, where in projected falling under B2 are exempted from public hearing as they need not seek environment clearance. This was against the very fundamental principle of public participation to maintain accountability and transparency. The notification further decreased the time frame for public hearing or consultation from 30 days to 20 days which is in conflict with Multilateral Environment Agreements and Judicial pronouncements (Centre for Social Justice v. Union of India, 2001).

Considering decades of judicial intervention to bring Indian jurisprudence in consonance with international practices, it won't be incorrect to call the EIA 2020 draft notification counterproductive. With existing laws, the Judiciary and legislature need to establish a strong public participation mechanism that caters to the voice of stakeholders and indigenous people at the preliminary stage to achieve a holistic and transparent Environment Impact Assessment.

Understanding Public Participation Under Canadian Law

Public participation is essential and meaningful part of the Impact Assessment in Canada. Federal Environment Impact Analysis/assessment regime in Canada is governed by the Impact Assessment Act (IAA) of 2019 which replaces the earlier Canadian Environmental Assessment Act, 2012. The Act recognises the importance and requirement of meaningful public participation in accordance with legislations, policies and statutory regulations (Government of Canada, 2021).

Meaningful participation thus means that the members of public willing to participate gets the adequate opportunity and the capacity enabling them to do so in an informed way. Unlike India the IAA of 2019 not only provides for meaningful public participation in the preamble but also throughout the various stages of assessment process like in the Act's purpose, considering factors for Planning Phase, accounting of factors during assessment by Agency and review panel, substitution, participant funding, and the Registry. This is in stark contrast to Indian laws wherein the public hearing or participation comes after the preparation of Draft EIA report.

It is important to note that the Canadian approach is more in line with the *United Nations Declaration on the Rights of Indigenous People* which ultimately aiming to protect interests and rights of indigenous people by securing free, prior and informed consent for decisions making. The commitment of Canadian government to build a holistic relationship catering to the interest and knowledge of Indigenous people can be seen through various provisions discussed under the IAA. The Act requires the Agency to conduct the assessment in a way that advances inter-jurisdictional cooperation, acclaiming Indigenous people's rights, decision-making process through integrating indigenous knowledge (Government of Canada, 2021).

Along with requirement assessment the Act requires the decision makers to address the impact on *"Aboriginal and treaty rights, any considerations related to Indigenous culture and traditional use of lands and resources"*. The efforts to achieve meaningful participation of the indigenous community has led to tailored and flexible approach of *'Spectrum of Engagement'* which allows the indigenous people to participate, collaborate or partner with the agencies to conduct the impact assessment. Best instance to understand this is 2016 Environment Assessment of Blackwater Gold Project wherein Agency signed a MOU with Lhoosk'uz Dené Nation, Ulkatcho First Nation, and B.C.'s Environmental Assessment Office establishing the collaborative government to government approach between the stakeholders.

As discussed, the Act predominantly stress on the important of meaningful public participation during the Impact Assessment that could be observed through brief understanding of the provisions under the IAA discussed herein after

1. Under the Act, Section 6 (1) (h) among various other purposes provides to ensure providing the opportunities for public participation.
2. Section 22 (1) further requires the IAA Agency or the review panel while conducting the Impact assessment to account *"m) community knowledge provided with respect to the designated project n) comments received from the public"*.
3. During planning phase the Act requires the Agency to invite the comments from public by providing appropriate opportunity, to provide for the summary of the issues related to project realised by the indigenous groups consulted under section 12 or by the public, to set out notice addressing the issues and making decision by considering and accounting for the any comments received by the indigenous groups consulted under Section 12 or by public.
4. During the impact assessment by the Agency the Act along with providing meaningful participating opportunity under Section 27 requires the agency to post a draft report on the internet to invite the public comments within a specific time period.
5. Further, under Section 51 the Act requires the review panel to ensure that the information used for conducting impact assessment is made public. It requires the panel to organise haring in such manner that it cater the meaningful participation as within then time specified along with posting the summary report with the comments received from the public.
6. Furthermore, the Act requires the agency to establish and maintain *"Participant funding program"* along with requirement to maintain internet site for the public to access all related data and information.

HEALTH CARE ASPECT OF ENVIRONMENT IMPACT ASSESSMENT

In Canada, environment impact assessment is federally organized in all territories and provinces. It is used to anticipate mitigation and approval of projects. Various reports in Canada have pointed out that the element of health is inconsistently assimilated into environmental assessment which leads to less opportunities for anticipating positive and negative health impacts. Incorporation of the element of health in environmental assessment can assure the decision makers in approving the project to have all the information on environmental, economic impacts and health.

Additionally, the project related economic cost occurred and the negative health impacts incurred for promoting the pragmatic health impact can be decrease after incorporating health in Environmental assessment.

Incorporating health aspects in Environmental Assessment (EA) is still challenging but it can be traced through various cases in Canada. One of the case was in northern Canada where the diamond mining project was performed by Environmental assessment with the help of Public Review Panel that included their representatives who had specialised knowledge in law, services related to economic and geological issue (Kwiatkowski & Ooi, 2003). The panel was answerable for analysing the report of environmental assessment, accepting result from public hearings, and making recommendations. The recommendations included a wider range of considerations related to health. Another case in Alberta where oil pilot project was examined by the multi-disciplinary consultant team and two community based coordinators, throughout the assessment process the consultants collaborated with the coordinators in developing the basic conceptual health assessment models in Environmental assessment.

Following Factors can be considered to adequately assimilate health in Environmental assessment:

- There should be awareness program that spread knowledge related to the benefits of incorporating the element of health into Environmental Assessment amid health professionals, reviewers, the public, consultants, and the decision makers (Health Canada, 2004);
- Various agencies responsible for Environmental Assessment and public health authorities needs to collaborate to achieve the optimum results.
- There should be more hiring of the qualified staff in the public health agencies that engages in environmental assessment. The staff hired should have the knowledge needed to assess the important effects of a health project (Bhatia & Wernham, 2008);
- After the completion of environmental assessment process, to assess the effect on health one should monitor the health parameters of the population. (Health Canada, 2004a);
- To predict and assess the health impact of future projects, development of analytical methods and tools is necessary (Bhatia & Wernham, 2008).

Various survey was conducted in northern Canada by the environmental assessment government practitioner, environmental assessment consultants, regional and federal health practitioners. The survey identifies various barriers that limits the incorporation of health into environmental assessment. The barrier includes "differences in practitioners' understanding of how well health is integrated into

EA, with some EA practitioners and proponents rating it as sufficient, whereas First Nations participants and some health practitioners suggest it is insufficient; limited coordination and communication between health practitioners and those who work in EA; lack of supporting EA methods and frameworks to deal with the complexity of health impacts from environmental effects; limited access to health data; and a lack of financial and time resources" (Noble & Bronson, 2006).

These barriers can be overcome by public health practitioner who specialized in understanding the mechanism of disease and health. Different environmental, social and economic impacts of a proposed project can be connected by understanding of mechanism and the complicated series of potential health impacts.

"Health Impact Assessment" is a handbook published by Health Canada. This exclusive handbook also incorporated the health aspects in environmental impact assessment in Canada. The primary aim of the handbook is to help or assist the public health practitioner to participate in the process of Environmental assessment (Health Canada, 2004). Along with this, the health impact assessment tool can be used for the more structured incorporation of health into environment assessment. To expedite the connection of the environmental, economic and social impacts HIA tools can be used. These can be used to collect the data of health impacts in one document for the comments and review by the public.

The 1992 Rio Declaration and the well-known principle of environmental jurisprudence known as the "Precautionary Principle" are considered as the key fundamentals which has led to the establishment of EIA in 1978 in India. Certain restrictions on the expansion, modernization or construction of specific projects mandating prior approval from the respective government level Environmental Impact Assessment Authority (EIAA) constituted under the Environment Protection Act, 1986 along with the EIA (Birley, 2011). The EIA Notification, 2006 provides for a 4-stage procedure for obtaining environmental clearance namely – Screening, Scoping, Public Consultation and Appraisal. However, recent draft of EIA 2020 sparked concern amongst the public by containing about an 'ex post facto clearance' channel for certain projects without obtaining for clearance subject to the subsequent payment of fines for the violations.

These relaxed perceptions of environmental clearances have led to increased risk of any hazardous implication on health, environment or society at large. It becomes more relevant to stress on the definition of health as given by the World Health Organisation (WHO) has defined health as a "*state of complete physical, mental and social well-being and not merely the absence of disease or infirmity*" (WHO, 2014)

In India Environment impact assessment served under the umbrella of environment protection act and there is no separate provisions to understand health and social impact assessment of projects undergoes environment assessment process, they come under the purview of Environment impact assessment notification 2006.

The health impact in India can be evaluated on the basis of two Environmental impact assessment reports, one is Northern Coalfield Ltd. report, 2005 (NCL) and the other one is National Thermal Power Corporation Ltd. report, 2008 (NTPCL). While undergoing the process of environmental assessment and after giving the clearance, health and health impact is not mentioned in the NTPC report but NCL report mentioned about health and health impact, there is a separate section of health care in the report. Health element is deficient in Environment impact assessment is because of the inadequate involvement of public health professionals. Therefore, to incorporate health in Environment impact assessment, public health professionals should be appointed.

In the year 2020, a major gas leak from a chemical plant of LG Polymers India Pvt Ltd in Andhra Pradesh's Visakhapatnam had occurred affecting thousands of children and significant number of domestic animals, livestock, and plants. Villagers complained repeatedly to the Andhra Pradesh Pollution Control Board, but they received no response. In 2017, the Villagers expressed their concerns to Rajya Sabha MP Subbarami Reddy. But the PCB showed up, checked everything over, and gave LG (Polymers) a clean chit. This case takes us back to a similar Bhopal gas tragedy in 1984, Shriram Foods Case also known as the "Oleum gas leak Case" in the year 1984 had taken a toll on many lives and disabled others. These two cases have partaken in India's legislative machinery of compensation to those affected by serious environmental deviances. These tragedies are still not able to emphasize the importance of public engagement, and worker security especially at a time when labor and environmental rules are being watered down for economic convenience and business profitability.

India, like any other major developing country, has been pushing major infrastructural changes to thrust ahead its economic derivatives but this often puts the environment at stake, as it is implicit that every EIA notification includes every aspect of public health in consideration. Also, the WHO had emphasized the need for collaboration between the environmental and health sectors to be developed in order to carry out an impact assessment. This could be facilitated by promoting increased health-related training and creating possible access points for medical experts into the EIA process. In this case, political backing could encourage procedures that incorporate health into EIA.

The element of health and health care is inadequately dealt in environment impact assessment in the developing country (India) and developed country (Canada). Both the countries have same issues like health professional are not appointed in the EIA team, existing guidelines are insufficient to consider issues related to health within EIA, no separate health impact procedure is defined in any of the legal framework, including health aspect in EIA will make public participation more complicated in incorporating health aspect in Environmental assessment. Canada is better than

India as they have launched handbooks on health care in Environment assessment and many guidelines were evolving which helps to incorporate health in EIA. But in India, while providing clearance to the projects, health concerns are ignored by the EIA team. In both the countries, it is the responsibility of the health care professional to advocate effective incorporation of health aspect in EIA.

CASE STUDIES

These case studies demonstrate how progress of the environment and society interact in India and Canada. In India, the Sardar Sarovar Dam, a hefty and disputed project, treads a fine line between development, environmental conservation, and indigenous rights. The Polavaram Project, also in India, echoes the struggles, underscoring the need for comprehensive environmental evaluations and community involvement. Turning to Canada, the Trans Mountain Pipeline Expansion Project showcases the worldwide task of clubbing economic targets with environmental duties. Lastly, the Site C Clean Energy Project and Bruce Power Nuclear Generating Station show how essential Environmental Impact Assessments (EIA) are guiding green energy progression while reducing environmental and societal effects. These case studies underscore the imperative to forge a responsible path forward, where progress harmonizes with ethical and sustainable practices.

Indian Cases

Sardar Sarovar Dam Project

The Sardar Sarovar Dam, a huge dam in Gujarat, India, sits on the Narmada River. It balances progress, environmental worries, and local's rights. The idea of using the Narmada River for farming and energy began when India was newly independent. Prime Minister Jawaharlal Nehru started the project in 1961. Yet, it faced problems like lack of money, environmental pushback, and relocation issues. Construction picked up speed in 1987 and finished in 2017. The dam's main goal is to bring irrigation water to dry areas in Gujarat, Rajasthan, and Madhya Pradesh.

The Sardar Sarovar reservoir helps fight off drought and supplies steady water for farming, bettering the life of farmers. Activists like Medha Patkar from Narmada Bachao Andolan (NBA), didn't cheer for the dam. They shared worries about moving tribal folks and how the environment might suffer. This thought led to lots of talk about the fine line between improving society and taking care of human rights, especially for the forgotten and indigenous communities.

The EIA analysis delved into the widespread environmental impact of the dam. It outlined that the project not only shifted residents but also upset river ecosystems and habitats, changing the Narmada River's natural rhythm and calling attention to potential harm to biodiversity and ecology downstream. Critics spotlighted possible gaps in managing these problems, like sluggish actions, insufficient offsetting, and inadequacy in being open about the efforts to rehabilitate (Flood, 1997).

The Narmada Control Authority (NCA), overseeing the Narmada Valley Project, played a crucial role in monitoring rehabilitation and mediating state disputes. Despite these efforts, the fairness of rehabilitation for displaced communities remains contentious. The Sardar Sarovar Dam case study reveals the complex dynamics in large scale infrastructure projects, highlighting the challenges of balancing development with environmental sustainability and human rights protection. While contributing to agriculture and energy, controversies around displacement, rehabilitation, and environmental impact emphasize the need for a nuanced and inclusive approach.

The dam serves as a reminder that progress must align with ethical and sustainable practices. It prompts reflection on the broader implications of development initiatives, urging stakeholders to engage in meaningful dialogue for solutions prioritizing progress and the well-being of people and the environment. As the Sardar Sarovar Dam continues shaping Gujarat's landscape, its legacy unfolds not just in concrete and steel but also in the lives it has touched and transformed.

Polavaram Project

The Polavaram Project in Andhra Pradesh, aimed at providing irrigation and hydropower, faced challenges similar to the Sardar Sarovar Dam in terms of environmental and social impacts. The EIA for the Polavaram Project involved assessments of river diversion, displacement of communities, and the project's overall environmental footprint. However, concerns were raised regarding the adequacy of public consultations and the representation of affected communities in decision making processes (Rao, 2006).

The project faced resistance due to the potential submergence of vast forest areas, leading to habitat loss and impacts on biodiversity. Additionally, displacement concerns for tribal communities and inadequate rehabilitation efforts fueled protests. The controversy surrounding the Polavaram Project prompted scrutiny of the EIA process, revealing gaps in addressing cumulative impacts and ensuring genuine public participation. The Polavaram Project highlights the importance of robust public consultation and the need for comprehensive assessments that consider cumulative impacts. It emphasizes the role of EIAs in anticipating and addressing potential environmental and social complexities, thereby contributing to more informed decision making.

Navi Mumbai Airport Project

The Navi Mumbai Airport Project stands as a significant infrastructure development endeavour in India, strategically located in the Konkan region of Maharashtra. Envisioned to alleviate the increasing air traffic congestion in Mumbai, the project aims to cater to the growing demand for air travel in the Mumbai Metropolitan Region. The need for a new airport became evident due to the saturation of the existing Chhatrapati Shivaji Maharaj International Airport. Proposed several decades ago, the Navi Mumbai Airport faced numerous delays and challenges before gaining momentum.

The EIA method works on pinpointing possible pitfalls and hazards the project might deliver. Critical issues include impacts on nearby environments, such as projected alterations to rivers and likely repositioning of neighbouring villages (Kazi *et al*, 2020). This primary stage is vital for comprehending the magnitude of environmental repercussions and leading future preventative steps. In creating strong preventative plans to tackle recognized ecological concerns, the EIA becomes a crucial player. Meticulous planning and introducing ways to lower environmental damage are key parts. The EIA brings to book exact plans designed to safeguard local environments, minimizing changes to rivers, and preventing harmful effects on nearby villages project's planning. This takes careful planning and methods that lessen environmental harm.

The project has hit snags concerning land buying, resettling uprooted communities, and working with diverse stake holders. Running hefty infrastructure projects, like this, needs solid management of social, green, and logistical parts for lasting growth. When it comes to building, the Navi Mumbai Airport needs the making of many runways, traveller lounges, freight features, and tied structures. Modern design and tech used in the airport's growth shoots for world class standards and smooth journeys for passengers.

The Navi Mumbai Airport Project, moving forward, could change the air travel scenery in the Mumbai Metropolitan Region. It can spark financial progress and jobs. Success in our project depends on handling the environment issues, involving the local community, and doing tasks smoothly. The Navi Mumbai airport shows our nation's promise to upgrade its aviation framework. This is important to keep up with the needs of our fast growing economy and city dwellers.

Canadian Cases

The Trans Mountain Pipeline Expansion Project

The Trans Mountain Pipeline Expansion Project is a hot topic and a significant effort in Canada's energy field. It is planned as a growth of the present Trans Mountain Pipeline. The goal of the project is to move more crude oil from Alberta's oil sands to the British Columbia coast, which makes it easier to sell to around the world. The project's focus is on fixing problems in Canada's oil transportation and reaching various global markets. The plan is to double the existing pipeline, increasing its potential from 300,000 to 890,000 barrels daily. As per the note this project is important for our economy. It's a doorway to fresh markets, it's a job creator, and it helps our country's cash flow (Angevine & Green, 2016).

The Trans Mountain Pipeline Expansion Project's Environmental Impact Assessment (EIA) carries major weight. This project's goal is to double its oil-transporting capacity, moving crude oil from Alberta to British Columbia. To address our needs for energy and economic growth. Those who back the project point to its economic upside. But, there are worries about possible environmental damage. Chief among them, is the threat of oil spills that could harm sea creatures. Local Indigenous tribes are worried about effects to their land and customs. The project has faced legal hurdles, like the 2018 court refusal, showing just how much environmental concerns are under the microscope (Jonasson *et al*, 2019). The EIA has an important role. It must juggle the need for economic progress with caring for the environment. It shapes global talks on ethical resource development.

Native tribes, green entities, and small-scale governments are taking legal action. They're poking holes in environmental check-ups and talk sessions. Back in 2018, the higher law court knocked down the first approval. They said the eco check was a bit lacklustre and they ignored the effects on sea life. Now, the project comes with some money matters. Supporters chat up the cash perks, jobs, more government bucks, and a bigger slice of Canada's energy pie. On the other hand, opponents argue that the economic gains may be outweighed by the environmental and social costs, urging a transition toward cleaner and more sustainable energy alternatives.

The Trans Mountain Pipeline Expansion Project exemplifies the intricate balance between economic development, environmental stewardship, and Indigenous rights. The Canadian government's ownership of the project adds a layer of political complexity, as it seeks to reconcile economic interests with a commitment to climate action and reconciliation with Indigenous peoples. As the project continues, navigating the legal, environmental, and social complexities remains paramount. Striking a balance between economic development and environmental responsibility is crucial for the project's success and acceptance among diverse stakeholders. The Trans

Mountain Pipeline Expansion Project underscores the broader global challenge of meeting energy demands while addressing environmental and Indigenous concerns, shaping the discourse around responsible resource development

The Site C Clean Energy Project

The Site C Clean Energy Project in British Columbia, a hydroelectric dam project on the Peace River, aimed to address growing energy demands but faced criticism for its potential impacts on ecosystems and local communities (Dusyk, 2011). The EIA for the Site C project had to carefully evaluate the impacts on local biodiversity, including fish habitats and wildlife. It's about weighing up green energy needs and keeping fragile habitats safe. They had to do heaps of studies and sprinkle in ways to undo any harm.

People were worried about folks being forced to move because of the dam and about losing places that mean something special to their culture. The EIA process included social impact evaluations to understand potential effects on communities. It showed the need for a full overview. The Site C case emphasized the need to evaluate the long term environmental and societal effects of energy projects. It played up the role of EIAs in pushing forward sustainable energy growth while protecting Canada's rich ecosystems (Dubrule, 2018).

Bruce Power Nuclear Generating Station

The Bruce Power Nuclear Generating Station in Ontario, a key component in Canada's nuclear energy scene, showcases the intricacies involved in managing nuclear power and the necessity of thorough environmental checks.

The EIA for the Bruce Power station focused on nuclear safety and tackled issues connected to managing radioactive waste. The examination of our facility was crucial. This check confirmed our commitment to top-notch safety and careful waste management. Because nuclear power does carry some risks, it was vital for the EIA process to engage the public and prepare for any emergencies (Eyles & Fried, 2012). The process involved public discussions and detailed emergency response creation, which were key parts of the exam.

The Bruce Power situation underscores the essential place the EIA holds in the nuclear power field. It points out the importance of openness, community input, and ceaseless observation to guarantee nuclear facilities operate safely and responsibly.

FINAL REFLECTIONS AND FUTURE CONSIDERATIONS

The comparative study underscores the necessity of contextualizing EIA practices within the unique socio-economic and environmental landscapes of each country. Canada emerges as a benchmark for effective EIA practices, while India's experiences serve as a reflective roadmap for refining regulatory frameworks. The analysis contributes to a nuanced global understanding of EIA best practices, emphasizing the ongoing necessity for adaptive governance, collaborative efforts, and a delicate balance between environmental conservation and societal development.

Public participation and indigenous engagement emerge as pivotal facets in evaluating the success of EIA practices. Canada sets a notable standard in inclusivity by actively involving the public and indigenous communities in decision-making processes, fostering transparency and accountability. Conversely, India grapples with enhancing the effectiveness of public participation, particularly in marginalized communities, revealing the imperative for more robust mechanisms that ensure meaningful engagement with diverse stakeholders.

The integration of healthcare considerations within the EIA process underscores the intrinsic link between environmental impact and public health. Canada's proactive inclusion of health aspects contributes to a holistic understanding of project implications on community well-being. In contrast, India's focus on this nexus remains nascent, signalling a potential area for improvement in aligning developmental projects with broader health considerations.

The exploration of case studies provides tangible examples of EIA outcomes in both nations. Canada's success stories exemplify how stringent EIA practices can lead to sustainable development and minimized environmental harm. Conversely, India's challenges in implementation highlight the complexities involved, emphasizing the need for continuous refinement of regulatory frameworks, improved enforcement mechanisms, and heightened community engagement to achieve desired environmental and social outcomes.

As we reflect on the lessons learned, it prompts us to consider the broader implications for global environmental governance and policy-making. What strategies can be devised to bridge the gaps in public participation and indigenous engagement, fostering a more inclusive and equitable decision-making process? How can healthcare considerations be more seamlessly integrated into EIA practices worldwide, ensuring a comprehensive understanding of the interplay between environmental impact and public health?

DEFINITIONS

1.   Environment Impact Assessment- It is a tool to mitigate and assess the environmental impacts of any proposed project.
2.   Strategic Environment Assessment- It is used to assess the environmental impact of the policy, project at planning stage.
3.   Health Impact Assessment- It is a tool that can be used for the more structured incorporation of health care into environmental impact assessment.
4.   Indigenous Engagement- It is the engagement with the people belonging to indigenous communities who live near or in the project area.
5.   Indigenous Knowledge- It refers to the traditional, local, and unique knowledge of indigenous communities regarding environment.
6.   Public Participation- It is the engagement of public into the decision-making process throughout all the stages of environment impact assessment process.

REFERENCES

Angevine, G., & Green, K. P. (2016). *Obstacles Faced by Major Pipeline Projects. In The Costs of Pipeline Obstructionism* (pp. 22–27). Fraser Institute. https://www.jstor.org/stable/resrep33286.9

Bhatia, R., & Wernham, A. (2008). Integrating human health into environmental impact assessment: An unrealized opportunity for environmental health and justice. *Environmental Health Perspectives*, *116*(8), 9911000. doi:10.1289/ehp.11132 PMID:18709140

Birley, M. (2011). *Health Impact Assessment: Principles and Practice* (1st ed.). Earthscan.

Centre for Social Justice v. Union of India, AIR 2001 Guj 71

Diduck, A., Pratap, D., Sinclair, J., & Deanne, S. (2013). Perceptions of impacts, public participation, and learning in the planning, assessment and mitigation of two hydroelectric projects in Uttarakhand, India. *ScienceDirect, 33.* https://www.sciencedirect.com/science/article/abs/pii/S0264837713000197

Dubrule, T., Patriquin, D. L. D., & Hood, G. A. (2018). A Question of Inclusion: BC Hydro's Site C Dam Indigenous Consultation Process. *Journal of Environmental Assessment Policy and Management*, *20*(2), 1–19. https://www.jstor.org/stable/90022924. doi:10.1142/S1464333218500059

Dusyk, N. (2011). Downstream Effects of a Hybrid Forum: The Case of the Site C Hydroelectric Dam in British Columbia, Canada. *Annals of the Association of American Geographers*, *101*(4), 873–881. https://www.jstor.org/stable/27980234. doi:10.1080/00045608.2011.569655

Eyles, J., & Fried, J. (2012). "Technical breaches" and "eroding margins of safety" — Rhetoric and reality of the nuclear industry in Canada. *Risk Management*, *14*(2), 126–151. https://www.jstor.org/stable/23260054. doi:10.1057/rm.2012.1

Flood, L. U. (1997). Sardar Sarovar Dam: A Case Study of Development-induced Environmental Displacement. Refuge: Canada's Journal on Refugees / Refuge. *Revue Canadienne Sur Les Réfugiés*, *16*(3), 12–17. https://www.jstor.org/stable/45411572

Government of Canada. (2021). *Framework: Public Participation Under the Impact Assessment Act.* Government of Canada. https://www.canada.ca/en/impact-assessment-agency/services/policy-guidance/practitioners-guide-impact-assessment-act/framework-public-participation.html

Government of Canada. (2021). *Policy Context: Indigenous Participation in Impact Assessment.* Government of Canada. https://www.canada.ca/en/impact-assessment-agency/services/policy-guidance/practitioners-guide-impact-assessment-act/policy-indigenous-participation-ia.html

Health Canada. (2004). *Canadian handbook on health impact assessment. Volume 1: The basics.* Ottawa, ON: Health Canada. http://www.hc-sc.gc.ca/fniah-spnia/pubs/promotion/_ environ/handbook-guide2004/index-eng.php

Jha Thakur, U., & Rajvanshi, A. (2021). Strategic environmental assessment in India: trends and prospects. In *Handbook on Strategic Environmental Assessment*. Edward Elgar Publishing. doi:10.4337/9781789909937.00039

Jonasson, M. E., Spiegel, S. J., Thomas, S., Yassi, A., Wittman, H., Takaro, T., Afshari, R., Markwick, M., & Spiegel, J. M. (2019). Oil pipelines and food sovereignty: Threat to health equity for Indigenous communities. *Journal of Public Health Policy*, *40*(4), 504–517. https://www.jstor.org/stable/48703582. doi:10.1057/s41271-019-00186-1 PMID:31548588

Kazi, T. A., Syed, A. A. R., Ansari, M. A., Pandya, J. M., & Kuchekar, V. V. (2020). *Navi Mumbai International Airport EIA Report: Case Study.* AIKTC Library. http://ir.aiktclibrary.org:8080/xmlui/handle/123456789/3566

Kwiatkowski, R. E., & Ooi, M. (2003). Integrated environmental impact assessment: A Canadian example. *Bulletin of the World Health Organization*, *81*(6), 434438. http://www.who.int/bulletin/ volumes/81/6/kwiatkowski.pdf PMID:12894328

MC Mehta v Union of India, AIR 1997 SC 734

MC Mehta v Union of India, AIR 1998 SC 1037

MC Mehta v Union of India, AIR 1998 SC 617

Noble, B., & Bronson, J. (2006). Practitioner survey of the state of health integration in environmental assessment: The case of northern Canada. *Environmental Impact Assessment Review, 26*(4), 410424. doi:10.1016/j.eiar.2005.11.001

Noble, B., Gibson, R., White, L., Blakley, J., Croal, P., Nwanekezie, K., & Doelle, M. (2019). Effectiveness of strategic environmental assessment in Canada under directive-based and informal practice. *Impact Assessment and Project Appraisal, 37*(3–4), 344–355. doi:10.1080/14615517.2019.1565708

Noble, B. F. (2021). Strategic environmental assessment in Canada. In *Handbook on Strategic Environmental Assessment*. Edward Elgar Publishing., doi:10.4337/9781789909937.00033

Parikh, M. (2019). Critique of environmental impact assessment process in India. *Environmental Policy and Law, 49*(4-5), 252–259. doi:10.3233/EPL-190171

Rao, P. T. (2006). Nature of Opposition to the Polavaram Project. *Economic and Political Weekly, 41*(15), 1437–1439. https://www.jstor.org/stable/4418082

Rathi, A. K. A. (2019). *Development of environmental management program in environmental impact assessment reports and evaluation of its robustness: an Indian case study.* Taylor & Francis. https://www.tandfonline.com/doi/full/10.1080/1461 5517.2018.1558745

Scholsberg, D. (2007). *Reconceiving Environmental Justice: Global Movements And Political Theories.* Taylor & Francis. https://www.tandfonline.com/doi/citedb y/10.1080/0964401042000229025?scroll=top&needAccess=true

Sinclair, J., & Diduck, A. (2016). *Reconceptualizing public participation in environmental assessment as EA civics.* Elsevier. https://d3n8a8pro7vhmx. cloudfront.net/envirolawsmatter/pages/290/attachments/original/1461095298/ Sinclair_and_Diduck__Reconceptualizing_public_participation_in_EA_as_EA_ civics.pdf?1461095298

Thakur, U. J., & Khosravi, F. (2021). Beyond 25 years of EIA in India: Retrospection and way forward. *Environmental Impact Assessment Review, 87,* 106533. doi:10.1016/j.eiar.2020.106533

Tsuji, S. R. J. (2022). Canada's Impact Assessment Act, 2019: Indigenous Peoples, Cultural Sustainability, and Environmental Justice. *Sustainability (Basel)*, *14*(6), 3501. doi:10.3390/su14063501

WHO. (2014). *Health Impact Assessment*. World Health Organization. http://www. who. int/hia/en/

Yadav, V. S. (2018). Environmental Impact Assessment: A critique on Indian law and practices. *International Journal of Multidisciplinary Research and Development, 5*(1), 01-05.

Chapter 6
An Analytical Study of Biomedical Waste Management in Indian Healthcare

Nishika Bhatia
O.P. Jindal Global University, India

Siddharth Tandon
State Bank of India, India

ABSTRACT

The world is witnessing rapid advancement in healthcare. As a consequence, the amount of biomedical waste generated globally is growing at an exponential rate. However, management of the biomedical waste (BMW) still remains a difficult challenge. Mismanagement of BMW has alarming and life-threatening ramifications to human health and the environment. Key steps of BMW management are waste segregation, collection, treatment, and safe disposal. Leading international health organisations emphasise segregation at source as an important focus point to improve BMW management. In this chapter, the authors will study a BMW management network in an Indian healthcare facility. The different steps of BMW management will be analytically modelled and simulated. The importance of segregation at source will be investigated and a post-segregation policy with a penalty framework will also be suggested. The authors also conduct numerical experiments to test their model and suggestions. This computational study establishes the importance of accuracy in segregation to improve efficiency of BMW management.

DOI: 10.4018/979-8-3693-1178-3.ch006

INTRODUCTION

The healthcare industry is facing a global challenge of managing biomedical waste produced during medical procedures. Biomedical waste comprises of hazardous, infectious, and/or radio-active substances which require to be disposed of safely. Improper treatment of biomedical waste has dangerous and life-threating consequences to human health and the environment. According to the estimations by the World Health Organisation (WHO), every year 5.2 million people, including 4 million children, lose their lives due to erroneous management of medical waste (Rahman et al. 2020). Reports of dangerous levels of air, water and soil pollution have surfaced recently and are directly linked to the failures of waste management (Pandey & Dwivedi 2016, WHO 2018, Kumar & Prakash 2020).

Overall management of waste of any type broadly involves the process of collection, segregation, treatment and safe disposal. Waste management of any form is in itself a complicated and critical process. In addition, the treatment of biomedical waste involves further challenges. The steps of segregation and treatment of the biomedical waste require higher precision since they are more layered, complex and time consuming. There is less room for error in the overall management of medical waste because of the presence of hazardous substances. Moreover, the increasing volumes of biomedical waste levels further pose an alarming threat. In India, approximately 619 tonnes of biomedical waste is generated every day, of which only 544 tonnes is processed and disposed of. Around 74 tonnes of biomedical waste is dumped in unknown and remote locations. Several Indian states report significant amounts of disparity in biomedical waste generation and treatment (Saxena et al. 2022).

The disparity between waste generation and treatment arises because of improper management of biomedical waste. There is inaccuracy in the implementation of waste management steps of collection, segregation, treatment and disposal. According to the Indian Ministry of Environment and Forest, around 28 percent of biomedical waste is left untreated. In other words, only a two-third of the total biomedical waste is treated and the rest is getting mixed with general waste (Economic Times, 2017). There are dire and dangerous consequences of mixing general waste with biomedical waste comprising used syringes, contaminated swabs, expired drugs and anatomical waste. Untreated biomedical waste is not only contaminating but pathogenic as well. A study conducted by an Environment Support Group (ESG) for a treatment plant in Mavallipura, Bengaluru found evidence of hazardous waste in landfills. The study revealed heavy metals being released from landfills to water bodies. They reported how heavy metals are rarely found in municipal waste but are prominent in hazardous waste from Hospitals or industries. They also reported conversation with local garbage-collecting workers who confirmed picking up garbage bags with used syringes, swabs and other biomedical waste (Deccan Herald, 2018).

Several studies report that one of the major reasons behind mismanagement of biomedical waste is lack of strict legal frameworks (Yong et al. 2016). However, India's Biomedical Waste Management Rules 2016 are considered to be a landmark rulebook for management for biomedical waste. It is not only comprehensive and exhaustive but it has been simplified and easy-to-read as well (Singhal, 2017). However, despite advances in legal framework, there is a significant gap between biomedical waste generation and treatment. This happens because the implementation of the BMW Rules still need a lot of improvement. A key area of enhancing overall management of BMW is improving segregation of biomedical waste. Focus on better segregation of biomedical waste should be top priority for medical policymakers. Efficient segregation not only reduces mixing and contamination of waste, it could also reduce operational cost of waste treatment. Duong, 2023 report cost savings of about $100,000 just by doing appropriate segregation of waste.

The key to improving segregation is by focusing on segregation at source done at the time of waste generation. The most basic and efficient way of segregation is simply placing the right kind of waste in the right bin. This can be achieved by ensuring that segregation is strictly done by doctors, nurses or trained technicians. This is even clearly stated in the BMW 2016 Rules. Operating and surgery rooms present the most tremendous opportunity for waste reduction as the doctoral staff can ensure correct segregation there and then (Duong, 2023). However, this is challenging to achieve in an Indian healthcare facility. Indian healthcare facilities face huge shortage of staff, low awareness amongst healthcare workers and general public, lack of sufficient funds for biomedical waste management infrastructure, training, and awareness campaigns, lack of waste storage facilities, and delayed transportation (Salman Zafar 2020). In addition, doctors and nurses are heavily burdened with multiple responsibilities wherein it becomes challenging for them to maintain high accuracy in segregation. In this research, we study and analyse a biomedical waste management network considering imperfect levels of segregation.

In this chapter, we will present an analytical model for the management of biomedical waste in an Indian healthcare facility. We will first discuss various features of biomedical waste management including the existing Indian legal framework structures in place. The challenges and issues arising in the large-scale management of medical waste will also be highlighted. The various steps involved in biomedical waste management will be formulated in a network form. We will then use the technique of simulation to model the working of biomedical waste management network.. The accuracy of the model will be tested in several simulative environments built on real data obtained from the facility. The simulations will also test the effectiveness of existing policies and analyse the penalty-framework. We will also design experiments and derive insights based on discussions with the healthcare managers at the facility.

LITERATURE REVIEW

Research on biomedical waste management problems has gathered significant attention worldwide in the recent years. In this chapter, we investigate the biomedical management process in an Indian set-up using a mathematical simulative model. We consider a healthcare network and model the different steps of waste management process. The focus in our model is towards segregation of waste. Our model also tests the current policy framework to manage inaccurate segregation. Thus, we review research studying the operational process and policy framework of biomedical waste networks. Our research lies at the intersection of research on biomedical waste management problems as well as operational research on general waste management problems. We divide the literature in two sections by discussing research in i) biomedical waste management networks, ii) analytical models for waste management networks.

Biomedical Waste Management Networks

Several research papers on biomedical waste management were focussed on the Covid 19 pandemic. This happened because the pandemic caused a gigantic and unexpected increase in the BMW numbers across the world. The increase in BMW happened because of several reasons, i) alarming number of people falling sick and overloading the hospitals, ii) general public using medical masks, gloves and other sanitation products, iii) overall increase in standards of sanitation across industries. While these reasons were necessary to avoid the spread of the pandemic, it led to a massive increase in quantities of BMW. Many researchers report how medical and waste management systems across the world were not ready to deal with the increase in the wastage numbers. Cooper Parida 2021 provide a recent review of studies related to biomedical waste and solid waste management during Covid 19. In their research, they discuss how the previous guidelines on waste management needed to be revisited and updated during the pandemic. They curated problems as well as recommendations by international competent authorities for waste management. Similarly, Khan et al. 2019 and Rahman et al. 2020 are comprehensive literature reviews of biomedical waste management studies from an Asian perspective. Recommendations specifically for an Indian healthcare set-up are provided by Ilyas et al. 2020, Chand et al. 2021, Kanyal et al. 2021, Manekar et al. 2022, Saxena et al.. 2022, Bagwan 2023, Bansod Deshmukh 2023, and Jindal Sar 2023. We now discuss studies on biomedical waste management for a non-covid and a more general scenario.

Ferronato Torretta 2019 review the impacts of solid waste mismanagement such as open dumping and burning in developing and low income countries with a focus on environmental contamination and social issues. The results further pointed out that the environmental impacts of marine litter, air, soil and water contamination are global, and the direct interaction of waste pickers with hazardous waste is one of the most important issues. While this was more pertaining to a global landscape, D'Souza et al. 2017 did a cross sectional study to investigate the compliance of biomedical waste management at three different hospitals in Udupi, India with respect to BMWM Rules, 2011. They did a retrospective cost analysis of BMW for a one-year time period. They concluded that operating costs had a bigger impact on smaller hospitals than capital costs. They further advised to provide colour coded bags at uniform pricing to bring down the operating costs.

Alam et al. 2018 assess biomedical waste management in different hospitals in Aligarh City. Datta et al. 2018 review and critically analyse the 2016 BMWM rules while discussing the practical problems for its effective implementation, alongwith drawbacks of conventional techniques. They also advocate the need for more studies in the field of developing environmental friendly medical devices and BMW disposal systems. Duong 2023 has calculated the hidden costs of improper segregation of BMW in Canadian hospitals. They also advocate for recycling initiatives and introduction of sustainability administrative positions to reduce these costs significantly. All studies discussed so far emphasise the importance of segregation to improve efficiency of BMW management. Thus, we next review studies focussing on the significance of segregation in BMW and general waste management.

Ferraz and Afonso, 2005, conducted a study in a Portuguese health facility to test the impact of different segregation strategies on atmospheric pollution levels. They stress on the need of better estimation, evaluation and management of atmospheric pollution generated by incineration of incorrectly segregated waste. Yusof et al. 2019, Atienza 2011, and Fraifeld et al. 2021 carry out waste segregation initiatives in different set-ups to improve overall waste management. Yusof et al. 2019 investigated healthcare guidelines in a city in Malaysia. They showcased and discussed several challenges while performing waste segregation at source. Meanwhile, Atienza 2011 have highlighted the role of good governance in waste management in Philippines. Abah and Ohimain 2011 have highlighted the difficulties observed in healthcare management practices in Nigeria and recommended measures to improve them. Mukherji et al. 2016 examined the correlation between various socio economic groups in Delhi and their willingness to participate in waste management. Moriera and Gunther 2012 evaluated improvements derived from implementation of Medical Waste Management Practices in a primary healthcare facility in Brazil.

Fraifeld et al. 2021 carried out a waste segregation initiative in a tertiary care medical centre in US. The results of the initiative showed a statistically significant decrease in the overall weight of regulated medical waste items which further supported an improvement in waste segregation. A more localised example can be found in Qasim et al. 2020 where they studied and assessed the segregation knowledge of healthcare workers in a hospital in Lahore, Pakistan. Meanwhile, Okechukwu et al. 2013 have similarly conducted similar survey studies in six hospitals of Abuja, Nigeria. Sengodan, 2014 has identified and stressed on the enhanced role of training, supervision and responsibility of healthcare personnel in improving biomedical waste segregation. In our research, we have proposed a mathematical framework for biomedical waste management by considering the network of waste generation, segregation, collection, treatment and disposal. Thus in the next section we review the mathematical and statistical studies pertaining to BMW management.

Analytical Models for Waste Management Networks

Operational set-up of any waste management network comprises of a series of complex and challenginges process. In addition, study of a waste management network involves consideration of various factors related to health, environment, technology, economic and legal framework. Thus, it is challenging to mathematically model a waste management problem due to presence of a large number of factors. However, with advancements in technology and computational abilities, modelling and solving complex mathematical problems have become easier than before. Abdallah et al. 2020 provides a review of literature on diverse waste management problems solved using advanced analytical and Artificial Intelligence (AI) techniques. They list different AI models, techniques as well as its applications in waste management problems like forecasting of waste, waste bin level detection, process parameters prediction, and vehicle routing. We will specifically review studies using analytical or simulative modelling techniques to deal with waste management networks.

Niska & Serkkola 2018 developed data analytics based approach to create waste generation profiles for waste management and collection. They develop a k-means algorithm using container-level waste weighting data from Helsinki, Finland. Their results highlight the potential of advanced data analytics approaches in solving complex waste management problems. While Niska & Serkkola 2018's work promotes use of data analytics in a general waste management problem, Xu et al. 2020 tests use of analytics for waste management problem specifically in the construction business. Their research examines the construction waste management efficiency disparity between the public and private sectors in Hong Kong. Their research debunks the notion of private sector being more efficient. The findings of their research state outperformance of private over public in demolition projects while the latter performs better in foundation and new building projects. While there is competition in public and private players in waste management of several sectors like construction businesses, the responsibility of biomedical waste management of the healthcare facilities largely lies with the public government. Thus, we now review studies specific to analytics in biomedical waste management in the healthcare sector.

Ward et al.. 2014, Raghupathi Raghupathi 2014 and Belle et al.. 2015 have conducted research discussing use of data analytics specifically for healthcare management problems. Ward et al.. 2014 states advantage of the extensive information available through healthcare data. They argue the inevitable need of analytical tools to read and study the enormous healthcare data. They also explore several analytical tools used in healthcare and how it can help in achieving key goals of modern healthcare system: high-quality, responsive, affordable, and efficient care. The promise and potential of analytics in health care system is also discussed by Raghupathi Raghupathi 2014. They outline an architectural framework and methodology with examples from literature to use data analytics in healthcare. They describe the benefits as well as challenges of using analytics in healthcare. Challenges and shortcomings of adopting techniques from analytics are also highlighted by Belle et al.. 2015. They report hindrance in research development in this space because of the fundamental problem inherent to the analytics paradigm and structure. Most of data analytical methodologies were originally developed for business-oriented problems. However, healthcare set-ups have a different environmental and separate objectives. The technology behind the analytical methods must be curated and tailored specifically for healthcare systems. This needs a paradigm shift in the algorithm which required an in-depth study of healthcare problems. In other words, analytical models must be built from scratch for healthcare set-ups to take all the necessary conditions and processes in consideration. Therefore, we next review and discuss specific healthcare problems using analytical methods.

A crucial part of BMW is transporting the waste from the healthcare facilities to the treatment facilities. There are several sub-problems with the transportation problem of BMW like allocating available resources, finding best routes or planning transport schedule. Researchers have been successful in designing analytical tools for solving several aspects of the transportation problem of BMW. Rabbani et al. 2019 uses simulation modelling to waste location problem for hazardous industrial waste. They focus on vehicle routing aspects rather than inherent process of waste management. The waste control system is modelled and simulated by Yong et al. 2016. However, their work is limited to energy sector and lacks the essential features needed for the healthcare sector. Aung et al. 2019 studies biomedical waste management in healthcare sector in Myanmar using a multi criteria decision making approach. Their research highlights the need to advance the legal framework for biomedical waste management in Myanmar along with increase in funding towards biomedical waste management. The focus of Aung et al. 2019's work is towards providing suggestions specific to the Myanmar's systems. However, the suggestions will not be useful for Indian context as the BMW 2016 Rules cover all points raised by them.

In this chapter, we study the BMW management problem through its fundamental process of collection, segregation, treatment and disposal. We also investigate the process of segregation by considering two kinds of segregation, segregation at source at time of waste generation and a post-segregation at the treatment facility. The different steps and processes are charted out in a BMW network comprising of healthcare facility and a centralized waste treatment facility. The network and the BMW process is modelling using an analytical approach. We also conduct an extensive simulation study to mimic different environments and evaluate the benefit of increasing the accuracy of segregation. In this next section, we first present the different steps of BMW process, its network and the analytical model.

BIOMEDICAL WASTE MANAGEMENT PROCESS AND NETWORK

We consider a healthcare facility, referred as HCF, with different functional units like beds, surgery rooms, and medical labs. The functional units of HCF generate biomedical waste on a daily basis. The management of HCF aims to process the biomedical waste generated in the best way possible. First and foremost step of processing biomedical waste is segregation at point of generation. In other words, the waste must be segregated at the source when it is generated during the time of treatment at any functional unit (like surgery room, beds, or medical labs) of HCF. Moreover, the segregation must be done by a doctor, a nurse, or a trained technician, who is generating the waste while treating the patient. The waste generated must be segregated in the designated and colour coded bin/ container kept in the function unit of HCF. The biomedical waste is segregated in four different colour coded bins, namely Yellow, Red, and White.

Towards the end of the day, the waste from the different bins in the multiple functional units are collected and transported to a central unit within the HCF. The central unit, also referred as the "Central Waste Collection Room" is a designated location for waste collection within the HCF. The central unit room stores the biomedical waste till the time it is picked up for treatment and disposal by a waste management organisation. Even though the central unit is situated within the HCF premises, it is to be built at a location which is away from the public/ visitors access. An example of the HCF network and its waste management process is illustrated in Figure 1.

The segregated waste in the four bins at the central unit of HCF is then collected by a third-party waste processing organisation, namely Common biomedical waste treatment and disposal facility, referred as CBWTF. The CBWTF is responsible for collection, treatment, processing and disposal of the biomedical waste. When bins are collected at CBWTF, the facility management first examines the segregated waste. Thus, the CBWTF performs another round of segregation for the mixed waste in all the four bins. The second round of segregation is referred as 'post-segregation'. Even though segregation at source is of paramount importance, it is often maintain high accuracy of segregation at the HCF because of various factors like large volumes of waste generation, lack of funds, infrastructure, staff and resources. Due to this several health organisations (Govt of Karnataka, 2018, EMPHNET, 2021, ICRC 2011) highlight the significance of segregation at the treatment facility as well. They emphasise the need for treatment facilities to repeatedly perform segregation to minimize mixing of waste. In other words, a second round of segregation or post-segregation can help in sorting the waste which wasn't segregated properly at the HCF. The need for repeated rounds of waste segregation is also specifically flagged by a performance audit report by Govt of Karnataka, 2018 where they also suggest that if segregation at source is not being done properly, then post-segregation at the collection and treatment facilities becomes even more important.

The aim of multiple rounds of waste segregation is to minimize its mixing as much as possible. Mixed BMW comprises of harmful chemics and toxins making it highly contaminated. In most cases, mixed and contaminated BMW cannot be processed and has to be disposed of. BMW is either disposed by burying it in deep burials or by burning it in an incinerator. Both these processes lead to pollution in the soil, air or/and water. Moreover, if the BMW is not disposed of properly, its toxins might be released spreading diseases. Thus, handling mixed BMW is a huge challenge.

A key solution to reduce mixing of BMW is enhancing focus on segregation at different levels such as source, collection facility, and treatment facility. Ferraz and Afonso, 2005 Conducted a scientific study comparing the impact of different intensities of segregations on atmospheric pollution levels. Their findings report that a rigorous segregation of waste leads to a reduction of 80% in the waste to be sent for incineration. The decrease in amounts sent for incineration further results in a significant decline in the pollution levels as well. Therefore, we have also enhanced focus on segregation in our study by considering segregation at the source (HCF) as well as post-segregation at the treatment facility (CPWTF).

After the segregation of waste, its treatment is done by multiple processes like incineration, gasification, autoclave, microwaving, chemical disinfection, and deep burial. However, mixed and contaminated waste cannot go through the above-mention treatment processes. We refer the waste obtained after segregation at source of HCF as well as post-segregation at CBWTF as the 'pure waste'. Meanwhile, the waste which cannot be segregated and has been contaminated is referred to as 'mixed waste'.

In this chapter, we examine the management of biomedical waste in the healthcare network comprising of a Healthcare Facility (HCF) and a Common biomedical waste treatment and disposal facility (CBWTF). We analytically model the process of waste collection, transfer and segregation across the network. Our model considers both forms of segregation at source in HCF as well as post-segregation at CBWTF.

Figure 1. Biomedical waste management network

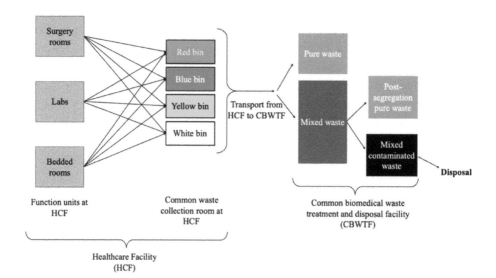

The importance of both forms of segregation is investigated in our modelling framework. The pure and mixed waste are also tracked across the network in our model. Sections 3.1 and 3.2 introduce the biomedical waste management network and its analytical model.

We also conduct a simulation study to test our model in multiple environments and possibilities. Monte Carlo simulations are generated to test the impact of various parameters in our model. The simulation study helps us in deriving insights regarding the management of biomedical waste with a focus on the segregation process. We also suggest a policy framework to enhance the overall efficiency of healthcare network. The simulative study and numerical experiments are provided in sections 4 and 5, respectively.

Modelling Framework for BMW Management

We consider a healthcare network comprising of a healthcare facility (HCF) and a common biomedical waste treatment and disposal facility (CBWTF). Biomedical waste is generated, segregated, collected, treated and disposed of within the healthcare network. Three stages are considered in the healthcare network for waste management,

1. Waste generation at functional units in HCF
2. Waste collection at central waste collection room in HCF
3. Waste treatment at CBWTF

Waste generation at HCF: Biomedical waste is generated at HCF in multiple function units like beds, surgery rooms, operation theatres, and medical labs. In other words, the point of generation is assumed to be the function unit in HCF. After generation, the doctors, nurses or trained technicians will segregate the waste in the four bins, namely red, yellow, black and blue. If the waste is not segregated properly, the different types of waste will get mixed leading to contamination. Contaminated waste is hard to dispose of and is reported to cause dangerous levels of pollution. Thus, the doctors, nurses and technicians are advised to carefully segregated the waste.

Waste collection at central waste collection room in HCF: Once the waste is segregated in various functional units, it is carried to the central waste collection room located within the premise of HCF. The waste from the different bins in functional units is then collected and sealed in bigger bags following the same colour coding. The bigger bags are then sealed and stored till the CBWTF picks it up from the HCF.

Waste treatment at CBWTF: Waste collected from the HCF is treated by CBWTF. Prior to the treatment of waste, CBWTF performs another round of segregation, namely 'post-segregation', to ensure less mixing and contamination of waste. After segregating in the best way possible, the waste is either treated by their respective processes or it is cleaned and disinfected before deep burial.

Mathematical Model for BMW Management

We assume the waste generated at the functional unit in HCF is a random quantity which will be estimated based on historical trends of the HCF. In other words, the waste generation is uncertain and cannot be assumed to be known exactly. The waste generated is denoted as $\tilde{w}$, where $\tilde{}$ represents the uncertainty in waste generation. To account for the randomness and uncertainty in the variable for waste generation, we assume $\tilde{w}$ to follow a known probability distribution. The probability distribution for $\tilde{w}$ will be defined on the basis of real data and reports of biomedical waste generation in Indian health care facilities.

According CPCB (Central Pollution Control Board) health guidelines, biomedical waste is divided in four types of waste as its treatment and disposal methods are different. The different types of biomedical waste is segregated in four bins

1. **Yellow** Bin for anatomical waste, chemical waste, soiled waste, chemotherapy waste, discarded linen and medicines, and laboratory waste.
2. **Red** Bin for contaminated plastic wastes
3. **Blue** Bin for glass waste and metallic implants
4. **Black** Bin for hazardous and other waste

Let n be the total number of bins used for segregation. The four colour coded bins are indexed numerically in our model as $i=1,2,3$, and 4 for yellow, red, blue and black, respectively. The anatomical waste to be put in the yellow bin will be more in quantity on the days higher number of surgeries are conducted. Similarly, on a vaccination campaign day a large number of needles will be used resulting in an increase in the quantity of glass and metallic waste in the blue bin. Thus, the proportion of four kinds of waste can vary across the different days in the HCF. We define $\widetilde{\beta}_i$ as the proportion of ith type of waste in the total waste generated $\tilde{w}$. Similar to $\tilde{w}$, $\widetilde{\beta}_i$ for waste type i is a random variable following a known probability distribution. Since the waste generated will be divided in exactly four types, the proportions for the four bins should sum up to one. The condition of summing up the proportions to 1 can be written mathematically as,

$$\sum_{i=1}^{n} \widetilde{\beta}_i = 1$$

The total amount of waste of type i is represented by b_i. Since the proportions for each type i is defined as $\widetilde{\beta}_i$, its amount is calculated as,

$$b_i = \widetilde{\beta}_i \tilde{w}$$

The segregation of waste $\tilde{w}$ into the four different types is performed by doctors, nurses and trained technicians. They are advised to segregate the waste in the most accurate manner possible. However, several reports highlight the mixing of different types of waste which not only causes mismanagement and contamination of biomedical waste but also leads to extreme levels of pollution. The mixing of waste is reported to happen at the time of generation by the hospital staff. However, given the working conditions at hospitals, it is also unreasonable to expect the hospital staff to be perfectly precise in segregating waste. The hospital staff around the world are usually under tremendous amounts of stress, especially during high-risk surgeries. Several studies suggest the hospital staff can be trained, motivated and incentivized to enhance their accuracy of segregation (Sengodan, 2014, Fraifeld et al.. 2021). In other words, the level with which they segregate the waste may be adjusted and improved. In our modelling framework, we define α as a variable for the accuracy level with which the hospital staff is segregating the waste. The value of α lies between 0 and 1, where $\alpha=0$ and $\alpha=1$ represent the lowest and highest levels of accuracy, respectively. For instance, if the staff is able to segregate 60% of the waste in the correct bins the accuracy level will be $\alpha=0.6$.

If the hospital staff has accuracy level less than 1 ($\alpha<1$), then they will mix the waste of certain type with the others. Thus, a bin i will comprise of pure waste of type i as well as mixed waste. The quantity of the mixed waste will increase with decrease in accuracy levels. On the other hand, higher accuracy levels will minimize the quantity of mixed waste. In other words, the amount of mixed waste is inversely proportional to staff's accuracy level. Thus, we track the mixing of waste in every bin i by defining variables b_i' and b_i^o to represent the pure and mixed waste, respectively. The relationship of accuracy levels with pure and mixed waste can be shown as follows,

$$b_i' = \alpha b_i$$

$$b_i^o = \left(1 - \alpha\right) b_i$$

In the central waste collection room, all the four bins are sealed and stored before the collection by CBWTF. We define c_t as the per unit cost of transporting sealed bins from HCF to CBWTF. The sealed bin comprises of both pure and mixed waste. In other words, the sealed bag has b_i amount of waste of type i comprising of both pure and mixed waste as follows,

$$b_i = b_i' + b_i^o$$

Since there is mixing happening at the source point, the workers at CBWTF will be processing bins with pure and mixed waste. In various treatment processes like microwaving, incineration, autoclaving, only pure waste can be used. Putting mixed waste in some treatment process is prohibited as it may release toxins. For instance, microwaving treatment cannot be used for any radioactive waste, mixed animal carcasses, body parts and large metal items. However, if a worker at CBWTF finds a large metal item in an incorrect bin, they may pick it up and put it in the correct bin. Similarly, if they find a needle or glass waste in the red bin which is for plastics, they may extract it from the red bin and follow procedure to put it in its designated bin. We capture this process in our model by assuming the workers at CBWTF may perform another round of segregation referred to as 'post-segregation' as shown in <fig>. The post segregation will only be done for the mixed waste. We define $\tilde{\gamma}$ as the proportion with which the worker will be able to perform post segregation on the mixed waste. The proportion $\tilde{\gamma}$ is a random variable following a known probability distribution. The amount of ith type of waste post segregated out of the mixed waste b_i^o is $\tilde{\gamma} b_i^o$ and the amount disposed of is $\left(1 - \tilde{\gamma}\right) b_i^o$. The per unit cost of segregation is defined as c_s. Pure waste which was segregated at HCF is treated at a per unit cost of c_s meanwhile the waste segregated by workers at CBWTF go through overtreatment at a per unit cost of c_{ot}. The contaminated waste which is untreatable because of mixing and improper segregation will be disposed of at a per unit cost of c_d.

In this model, we also propose a penalty framework to account for improper segregation. CPCB also defines penalties for not following guidelines related to segregation of BMW. They provide a formula to calculate penalties using various factors like, health risk, size of HCF, type of HCF and environmental compensation. However, their formula doesn't consider the amount of improper segregation. In other words, a HCF which only mixes a small proportion of BMW with other waste will pay the same penalty as a HCF which mixes all its waste. Thus, in this model we propose a penalty framework dependent on the proportion of mixing of waste. This will help us account for the inaccuracy in segregation. We assume CBWTF received waste from HCF through sealed bins. CBWTF then opens the bins, inspect them for purely segregated waste, remove the inaccurately segregated waste, and either treat it (known as overtreatment) or dispose it off. CBWTF performs additional work if they do a round of post segregation. Thus, we propose charging a legal penalty cost of c_l on every unit of mixed waste. The total cost can be calculated as follows,

Total cost = Transportation cost + Cost of treatment of pure waste + Cost of post-segregation of mixed waste + Cost of overtreatment of newly segregated waste + Cost of disposal of untreatable waste + Penalty cost for mixed waste   (1)

Each of the above cost is calculated as follows,

- Transportation cost: wastage in all bins, represented as $\sum_{i=1}^{n} b_i$, will be transported at a per unit cost of c_t. Thus, overall transportation cost is $c_t \sum_{i=1}^{n} b_i$. Similarly, other costs will be calculated as,

- Cost of treatment of pure waste $= c_p \sum_{i=1}^{n} b_i'$

- Cost of post-segregation of mixed waste $= c_s \sum_{i=1}^{n} b_i^0$

- Cost of overtreatment of newly segregated waste $= c_{ot} \sum_{i=1}^{n} \tilde{\gamma} b_i^0$

- Cost of disposal of untreatable waste $= c_d \sum_{i=1}^{n} \left(1 - \tilde{\gamma}\right) b_i^0$

- Penalty cost for mixed waste $= c_l \sum_{i=1}^{n} b_i^0$

Total cost can be written as follows,

$$Total\,cost = \sum_{i=1}^{n} c_t b_i + c_p b_i^i + c_s b_i^0 + c_{ot} \tilde{\gamma} b_i^0 + c_d \left(1 - \tilde{\gamma}\right) b_i^0 + c_l b_i^0 \tag{2}$$

The notations used in the mathematical model are summarized in Table 1. The process of waste management defined above can be briefly written as,

1. Generation and segregation at HCF
2. Collection at waste room to be sent to CBWTF
3. Transportation of waste bins from HCF to CBWTF
4. Post segregation by CBWTF
5. Treatment by CBWTF
6. Disposal by CBWTF

SIMULATION STUDY

In this section, we present the simulation study conducted to test the mathematical model developed for management of BMW. A simulative modelling technique is a way of mimicking an environment existing in the real word. In other words, a reality can be replicated, regenerated and analysed using simulation. The advantage of simulations is creating multiple situations which may happen in future. In a way, creation of different scenarios can help the decision-maker plan for a situation they haven't witnessed it. This will not help the decision-making prepare its system for changes but it will also help in shaping better policies.

In our research, we simulate the waste management process of an Indian set-up. The mathematical model developed in section 3 will be used to represent the waste management process and we will use simulations for the unknown parameter values provided in the model. In particular, we will be using Monte Carlo Simulations to set-

Table 1. Description of notations

Model parameters	
n	Total number of bins for segregation at HCF and CBWTF
$\tilde{w}$	Random waste generation by HCF
$\tilde{\beta}_i$	Random proportion of ith type of waste in the total waste generated $\tilde{w}$
b_i	Total amount of waste of type i
α	Hospital staff's accuracy level of segregating the waste
b_i'	Amount of pure waste of type i
b_i^0	Amount of mixed waste of type i
$\tilde{\gamma}$	Random proportion of performing post segregation on mixed waste
c_t	Per unit cost of transporting wastage from HCF to CBWTF
c_p	Per unit cost of treatment of pure waste at CBWTF
c_s	Per unit cost of segregation of mixed waste at CBWTF
c_{ot}	Per unit cost of overtreatment of new pure waste at CBWTF
c_d	Per unit cost of disposal of untreatable waste at CBWTF
c_l	Per unit cost of a legal penalty for improper segregate at HCF

up the simulative experiment for our model. Monte Carlo method is a computational algorithm which generates number results by repeating the process of random sampling multiple times. It utilizes randomness in parameters to solve problems and test its effectiveness in uncertain environments. In the BMW network model of this chapter, we consider randomness in waste generation by HCF, proportions of different waste types, and post segregation accuracy proportion.

An estimate of the above-parameters is obtained from latest reports and in consultation with an operations head at a hospital in Meerut, Uttar Pradesh, India. Since we are performing a simulative study, we will not use the estimates as is and instead randomize them. We will generate random values around the estimates provided instead of taking any random numbers. It is essential to utilize the information from the estimates to generate the required random numbers. We now define the algorithm for implementing the simulation study. -

Algorithm 1 present a step-by-step process of how we conducted the simulative study for analytical model for management of BMW network. The input data as highlighted comprises of the following,

- Known variable: total number of bins (n) will remain fixed through all experiments
- Control variable: hospital staff's accuracy level of segregating the waste (α) will be changed to investigate its impact over other
- Unknown/random variables: waste generation by HCF $\left(\tilde{w}\right)$, proportion of ith type of waste in the total waste generated $\tilde{w}$

$\left(\widetilde{\beta_i}\right)$, proportion of performing post segregation on mixed waste $\left(\tilde{\gamma}\right)$ are randomly generated using Monte Carlo methods

The input data will be used to obtained output data of waste numbers as well as different cost values. Before starting the algorithm the value of control variable will be set to a certain number as part of initialization. In steps 1 and 2 the values for waste and proportion of post segregation will be selected for each simulation run from a set of random numbers. The values for different types of waste proportions and amounts are obtained for each type in steps 3 and 4. Steps 5 to 11 calculate the different types of waste values at both, HCF and CBWTF. Costs for each type and the simulation run is finally calculated in steps 12 to 15. All values of waste and costs are stored as part of output.

NUMERICAL EXPERIMENTS

In this section, the design and data structure of the numerical experiments will be introduced. We then describe the different numerical experiments undertaken to investigate the impact of segregation over the BMW management process. The computational results obtained from the different set of experiments will be demonstrated and discussed. All the experiments are performed using the simulation algorithm provided in section 4. The algorithm was implemented in MATLAB R2022a.

Design of Experiments and Data

A series of experiments are designed to test the significance of segregation in the BMW management process. We have specifically designed numerical experiments to answer the following questions,

- What is the impact of segregation accuracy levels on different total cost of BMW management process?
- How do the cost related to penalty and overtreatment change with wastage numbers under varying segregation accuracies?

Algorithm 1. Simulative modelling framework for BMW network management

	Input: the input data consists of a known variables, control variable and unknown/random variables
	Output: the output will comprise of different types of waste numbers and cost of BMW process,
	Initialization: set value for total bins n and hospital's accuracy level for segregation α
1:	**for** a simulation run j **do**
2:	Obtain random values for waste $\tilde{w}^j$ and segregation proportion $\tilde{\gamma}^j$
3:	**for** a bin type $i=1,2,\ldots,n$ **do**
4:	Obtain random values for waste proportion $\tilde{\beta}_i^{\,j}$ for type i
5:	Obtain waste values for HCF,
6:	Total amount of waste $b_i^j = \tilde{\beta}_i^{\,j}\,\tilde{w}^j$
7:	Amount of pure waste $b_i^{'j} = \alpha b_i^j$
8:	Amount of mixed waste $b_i^{0j} = \left(1-\alpha\right)b_i^j$
9:	Obtain waste values for CBWTF
10:	Amount of new pure waste after post segregation $= \tilde{\gamma}^j b_i^{0j}$
11:	Amount of disposal waste after post segregation $= (1-\tilde{\gamma}^j)b_i^{0j}$
12:	Calculate costs for each bin
13:	**end for**
14:	Sum up costs for each bin and store waste type information for every bin
15:	**end for**

- Which penalty framework is most suited to enhance overall segregation in the BMW network?

Our experimental design comprises of different values for several parameters. The values for all parameters are selected from multiple CPCB reports, academic papers and news articles (Rao et al. 2004, The Hindu, 2013, Times of India, 2020, Deccan Herald, 2021, BMW Official report 2023). We take three set of values for the segregation parameter α to account for scenarios of low, medium and high precision of segregation. We recall that α lies between 0 and 1, where $\alpha=0$ represents minimum level of segregation accuracy and perfect segregation accuracy is represented by

Table 2. Value of different parameters

Parameter	Value
n	4
$\tilde{w}$	$N(\mu=500,\ \sigma=100)$
$\widetilde{\beta}_i$	(0.45,0.35,0.1,0.1)
α	(0.3,0.6,0.9)
$\tilde{\gamma}$	$N(\mu=0.5,\ \sigma=0.3)$
c_t	Rs 35 per kg
c_p	Rs 10 per kg
c_s	Rs 5 per kg
c_{ot}	Rs 30 per kg
c_d	Rs 50 per kg
c_l	Rs 50 per kg

$\alpha=1$. Therefore, $\alpha=0.3$ is defined as low level of segregation accuracy. Meanwhile, medium and high level of segregation accuracy is characterized by $\alpha=0.6$ and $\alpha=0.9$, respectively. On the other hand, the value of post-segregation parameter is not controlled in similar manner and is assumed to be random. Specifically, we define γ to be a random number following a normal distribution with mean 0.5 and standard deviation 0.3. In one of the experiments we increase the value of post segregation parameter γ by 10% for a penalty framework. Section 5.2 will discuss this in detail. All results are obtained by simulating the parameters over 1000 paths. The parameter values are summarized in Table 2.

Numerical Results and Analysis

In this section, we will present the numerical experiments under two categories: impact of segregation accuracies over different total costs, and investigation of different penalty frameworks.

Impact of Segregation Accuracies Over Different Total Costs

We design experiments to analyse effect of low, medium and high segregation accuracies over total costs. Even though we have considered penalty and overtreatment costs in our model, they are not considered in practice. Thus, we define three different types of total costs to account for inclusion of penalty and overtreatment costs. In other words, we wish to compare our model's suggestions with what happens in practice. The first total cost, denoted as TC1 *is* defined by considering both penalty as well as overtreatment costs. Total cost TC1 *is* evaluated in equation (3) as follows,

$$TC_1 = \sum_{i=1}^{n} c_t b_i + c_p b_i^i + c_s b_i^0 + c_{ot} \tilde{\gamma} b_i^0 + c_d \left(1 - \tilde{\gamma}\right) b_i^0 + c_l b_i^0 \tag{3}$$

The cost of overtreatment will be ignored in second total cost, represented by TC2 as follows,

$$TC_2 = \sum_{i=1}^{n} c_t b_i + c_p b_i^i + c_s b_i^0 + c_d \left(1 - \tilde{\gamma}\right) b_i^0 + c_l b_i^0 \tag{4}$$

The third total cost, denoted as TC_3, excluded both penalty and overtreatment costs. The third total cost TC_3 is close to what happens in practice and is calculated as follows,

$$TC_2 = \sum_{i=1}^{n} c_t b_i + c_p b_i^i + c_s b_i^0 + c_d \left(1 - \tilde{\gamma}\right) b_i^0 \tag{5}$$

According to Algorithm 1, the wastage is simulated in every run and the three total costs defined above are calculated. We plot the total costs with respect to wastage for each run in three scatter plots displayed in left panel of Figure 2. The three different plots refer total cost values with low, medium and high levels of segregation accuracies. We can see as the segregation accuracy increase the values of the different total costs come closer. This happens because increase in segregation accuracy is expected to lessen the penalty as well as overtreatment costs. To further understand why the different total costs are merging, we also plot average values of different waste quantities for each bin. In particular, we consider three types of waste values, i) "pure waste" obtained from segregation at HCF, ii) "post-segregation pure waste" obtained after the second round of segregation at CBWTF, and iii) the left-over "mixed contaminated waste" which is untreatable and will be disposed of by CBWTF. The average waste values of different bins is displayed in the right panel of Figure 2 for different segregation accuracies. At low segregation accuracy, the three types of waste are in similar quantities. In other words, the quantity of pure waste is similar to mixed contaminated waste and the post segregation pure waste. There will be a significant cost incurred to over-treat the waste which will also increase the value of total cost of penalty. Thus, the three costs are scattered in the first case. As the segregation accuracy increases, the quantity of pure waste increases as well. The increasing pure waste results in a lower value of mixed contaminated waste reducing the overtreatment and penalty costs. As a result, the scatter plot showcases the three costs merging. Therefore, an increase in accuracy not only reduces the quantity of mixed contaminated waste but it also reduces overall costs.

Figure 3 display further elements of total cost with overall average waste level across different segregation accuracies. The average penalty and overtreatment is shown on x-axis while the average wastage quantities are shown on y-axis. Similarly, here we see a reduction in costs as well as total mixed waste quantities with increase in segregation accuracies.

Figure 2. Comparison of costs and waste values with varying segregation accuracies

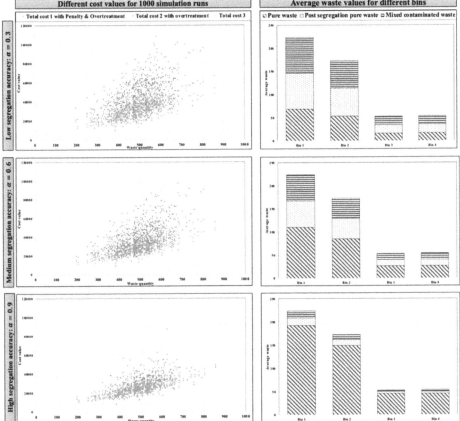

Figure 3. Comparison of penalty, overtreatment and waste values

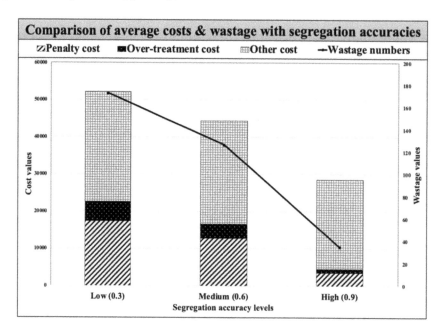

Treatment of Different Penalty Frameworks

In the current model, we have assumed same penalty to be paid for all the mixed waste. In other words, the penalty paid on mixed contaminated waste is same as the one paid on post-segregation pure waste. In a blanket penalty framework like this, there is no incentive for the CBWTF to perform post-segregation activities. Thus, we define different penalty frameworks to encourage post-segregation at CBWTF. In particular we consider three penalty framework, Models 1, 2 and 3, defined as follows,

- Model 1 refers to a blanket penalty framework where same penalty cost c_l is incurred on all the mixed waste b_i^0 for each type of waste.
- Model 2 considers different penalty cost for untreatable waste and post-segregation pure waste. The penalty cost of post-segregated waste is be 20% less than the penalty cost on untreatable waste being disposed of.
- Model 3 has same penalty framework as model 2 along with a 10% increase post segregation proportions

Figure 4 displays penalty and overtreatment costs of the three models across varying segregation accuracies. In all the three cases of different segregation

Figure 4. Comparison of penalty framework models with segregation accuracies

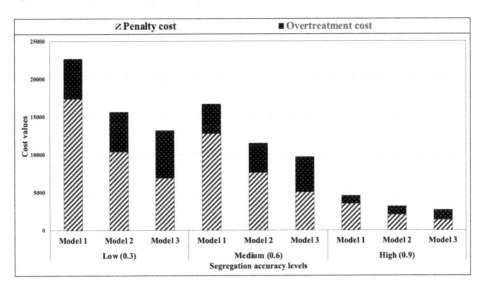

accuracies, there is reduction in costs from Model 1 to Model 2 to Model 3. In other words, as the penalty framework gets more tailored from Models 1 to 3, the costs also reduce. While comparing Model 1 and Model 2, penalty cost decrease in all the three segregation accuracy scenarios. This naturally happens because of a 20% less penalty on the post-segregated treatable waste. However, the overtreatment cost remains same in Models 1 and 2. An increase in overtreatment cost is seen in Model 3. Even though total costs are lowest in Model 3, the overtreatment cost increase. This happens because of increase in post-segregation parameter. In other words, a tailored penalty framework may incentive the process of post-segregation because the overall costs lessen. In addition, increase in overtreatment cost is indicative of more waste being processed and treated well. Therefore, specialized penalty framework will lead to a reduction in overall cost but also encourage stakeholders to reduce segregation as much as possible. Another interest observation from this result is the way cost reduce when there is low accuracy level. The rate of reduction is much higher for a low accuracy level than a higher accuracy level scenario. Thus, a waste-based penalty framework is useful in areas witness low accuracy in segregation abilities.

CONCLUSION

In this chapter, we draw attention to the challenges and nuances present in the large scale management of biomedical waste. As an effort to bridge this gap, we present an analytical model for the management of biomedical waste in an Indian healthcare facility. The steps involved in biomedical waste management are formulated in a network form followed by the use of technique of simulation to analytically model and mimic the workings of a biomedical waste management network. We also design several computational experiments to test the significance of segregation in the BMWM.

As per our findings, accurate segregation not only helps in reducing the impurity of waste but also has the potential to reduce the overall costs incurred drastically. To achieve this, we propose a penalty framework based on the amount of waste improperly segregated, which is different from the existing rules related to penalties in BMWM. Our proposed policy framework builds on the current rules and further incentivises the process of post segregation at the treatment facility. Thus, we suggest that along with segregation at source, there should also be a focus on post segregation at the treatment facility. This will reduce the sole dependency on segregation at source and will also help in reducing contamination of waste.

REFERENCES

Abah, S. O., & Ohimain, E. I. (2011). Healthcare waste management in Nigeria: A case study. *Journal of Public Health and Epidemiology*, *3*(3), 99–110.

Abdallah, M., Talib, M. A., Feroz, S., Nasir, Q., Abdalla, H., & Mahfood, B. (2020). Artificial intelligence applications in solid waste management: A systematic research review. *Waste Management (New York, N.Y.)*, *109*, 231–246. doi:10.1016/j.wasman.2020.04.057 PMID:32428727

Alam, I., Alam, G., Ayub, S., & Siddiqui, A. A. (2019). Assessment of bio-medical waste management in different hospitals in Aligarh city. In Advances in Waste Management: Select Proceedings of Recycle 2016. Springer Singapore. doi:10.1007/978-981-13-0215-2_36

Alvim-Ferraz, M. C. M., & Afonso, S. A. V. (2005). Incineration of healthcare wastes: Management of atmospheric emissions through waste segregation. *Waste Management (New York, N.Y.)*, *25*(6), 638–648. doi:10.1016/j.wasman.2004.07.017 PMID:15993348

Atienza, V. (2011). *Review of the waste management system in the Philippines: initiatives to promote waste segregation and recycling through good governance.* Institute of Developing Economies, Japan External Trade Organization.

Aung, T. S., Luan, S., & Xu, Q. (2019). Application of multi-criteria-decision approach for the analysis of medical waste management systems in Myanmar. *Journal of Cleaner Production, 222*, 733–745. doi:10.1016/j.jclepro.2019.03.049

Bagwan, W. A. (2023). An investigation of the bio-medical waste produced in India during the covid-19 pandemic and maharashtra state (pre-covid-19 and post-covid-19) analysis: A gis-based approach. *Research in Health Services & Regions, 2*(1), 1–18. doi:10.1007/s43999-023-00023-9

Bansod, H. S., & Deshmukh, P. (2023). Biomedical Waste Management and Its Importance: A Systematic Review. *Cureus, 15*(2). doi:10.7759/cureus.34589 PMID:36874306

Belle, A., Thiagarajan, R., Soroushmehr, S., Navidi, F., Beard, D. A., & Najarian, K. (2015). Big data analytics in healthcare. *BioMed Research International, 2015*, 1–16. doi:10.1155/2015/370194 PMID:26229957

Bhawal Mukherji, S., Sekiyama, M., Mino, T., & Chaturvedi, B. (2016). Resident knowledge and willingness to engage in waste management in Delhi, India. *Sustainability (Basel), 8*(10), 1065. doi:10.3390/su8101065

BMW Official report. (2023). TSPCB. https://tspcb.tripura.gov.in/storage/2023/10/BMW-AR-2023.pdf

Capoor, M. R., & Parida, A. (2021). Biomedical waste and solid waste management in the time of covid-19: A comprehensive review of the national and international scenario and guidelines. *Journal of Laboratory Physicians, 13*(02), 175–182. doi:10.1055/s-0041-1729132 PMID:34483566

Capoor, M. R., & Parida, A. (2021). Current perspectives of biomedical waste management in context of COVID-19. *Indian Journal of Medical Microbiology, 39*(2), 171–178. doi:10.1016/j.ijmmb.2021.03.003 PMID:33766404

Chand, S., Shastry, C. S., Hiremath, S., Joel, J. J., Krishnabhat, C. H., & Mateti, U. V. (2021). Updates on biomedical waste management during COVID-19: The Indian scenario. *Clinical Epidemiology and Global Health, 11*, 100715. doi:10.1016/j.cegh.2021.100715 PMID:36032559

D'Souza, B. C., Seetharam, A. M., Chandrasekaran, V., & Kamath, R. (2018). Comparative analysis of cost of biomedical waste management across varying bed strengths in rural India. *International Journal of Healthcare Management, 11*(1), 38–43. doi:10.1080/20479700.2017.1289438

Datta, P., Mohi, G. and Chander, J., (2018). Biomedical waste management in India: Critical appraisal. *Journal of laboratory physicians, 10*(01), 006-014.

Duong, D., (2023). *Improper disposal of medical waste costs health systems and the environment.*

Economic Times. (2017). What makes improper management of biomedical waste so hazardous. *Economic Times.* https://health.economictimes.indiatimes. com/news/industry/what-makes-improper-management-of-biomedical-waste-so-hazardous-/60471726

Ferronato, N., & Torretta, V. (2019). Waste mismanagement in developing countries: A review of global issues. *International Journal of Environmental Research and Public Health, 16*(6), 1060. doi:10.3390/ijerph16061060 PMID:30909625

Fraifeld, A., Rice, A. N., Stamper, M. J., & Muckler, V. C. (2021). Intraoperative waste segregation initiative among anesthesia personnel to contain disposal costs. *Waste Management (New York, N.Y.), 122*, 124–131. doi:10.1016/j.wasman.2021.01.006 PMID:33513532

Herald, D. (2018). *Toxic Waste.* Deccan Herald. https://www.deccanherald.com/india/karnataka/bengaluru/toxic-waste-callous-treatment-1925118

Herald, D. (2021). *Bio Waste.* Deccan Herald. https://www.deccanherald.com/india/karnataka/bengaluru/bio-waste-disposal-costs-up-879340.html

Ilyas, S., Srivastava, R. R., & Kim, H. (2020). Disinfection technology and strategies for COVID-19 hospital and bio-medical waste management. *The Science of the Total Environment, 749*, 141652. doi:10.1016/j.scitotenv.2020.141652 PMID:32822917

Jindal, M. K., & Sar, S. K. (2023). Medical waste management during COVID-19 situation in India: Perspective towards safe environment. *Waste Management Bulletin, 1*(1), 1–3. doi:10.1016/j.wmb.2023.03.002

Kanyal, D., Butola, L. K., & Ambad, R. (2021). Biomedical waste management in India-a review. *Indian Journal of Forensic Medicine Toxicology, 15*(2), 108–113.

Khan, B. A., Cheng, L., Khan, A. A., & Ahmed, H. (2019). Healthcare waste management in Asian developing countries: A mini review. *Waste Management & Research, 37*(9), 863–875. doi:10.1177/0734242X19857470 PMID:31266407

Kumar, M., & Prakash, V. (2020). A review on solid waste: Its impact on air and water quality. *Journal of Pollution Effects & Control, 8*(4), 1–3.

Manekar, S. S., Bakal, R. L., Jawarkar, R. D., & Charde, M. S. (2022). Challenges and measures during management of mounting biomedical waste in COVID-19 pandemic: An Indian approach. *Bulletin of the National Research Center, 46*(1), 1–9. doi:10.1186/s42269-022-00847-4 PMID:35669155

Medical waste assessment. (2011). International Committee of the Red Cross (ICRC). https://www.icrc.org/en/doc/assets/files/publications/icrc-002-4032.pdf

Mojtahedi, M., Fathollahi-Fard, A. M., Tavakkoli-Moghaddam, R., & Newton, S. (2021). Sustainable vehicle routing problem for coordinated solid waste management. *Journal of Industrial Information Integration, 23*, 100220. doi:10.1016/j.jii.2021.100220

Moreira, A. M. M., & Günther, W. M. R. (2013). Assessment of medical waste management at a primary health-care center in São Paulo, Brazil. *Waste Management (New York, N.Y.), 33*(1), 162–167. doi:10.1016/j.wasman.2012.09.018 PMID:23122204

Niska, H., & Serkkola, A. (2018). Data analytics approach to create waste generation profiles for waste management and collection. *Waste Management (New York, N.Y.), 77*, 477–485. doi:10.1016/j.wasman.2018.04.033 PMID:29724480

Okechukwu, E.C., Cyriacus, O.A., Aguora, S.O. & Soni, J.S. (2020). *Segregation Practices by Health Workers in Urban Hospitals-A Step Necessary to Achieve Minimization and Effective Biomedical Waste Management.*

Pandey, S., & Dwivedi, A. K. (2016). *Nosocomial infections through hospital waste.* OMICS. doi:10.4172/2252-5211.1000200

Qasim, S., Momina, A., Zahra, F. T., Qasim, T. B., & Rehman, F. (2020). Knowledge, attitude and practices of healthcare workers regarding biomedical waste segregation at Mayo Hospital Lahore. *The Professional Medical Journal, 27*(12), 2755–2762. doi:10.29309/TPMJ/2020.27.12.3888

Rabbani, M., Heidari, R., & Yazdanparast, R. (2019). A stochastic multi-period industrial hazardous waste location-routing problem: Integrating NSGA-II and Monte Carlo simulation. *European Journal of Operational Research, 272*(3), 945–961. doi:10.1016/j.ejor.2018.07.024

Raghupathi, W., & Raghupathi, V. (2014). Big data analytics in healthcare: Promise and potential. *Health Information Science and Systems, 2*(1), 1–10. doi:10.1186/2047-2501-2-3 PMID:25825667

Rahman, M. M., Bodrud-Doza, M., Griffiths, M. D., & Mamun, M. A. (2020). Biomedical waste amid covid-19: Perspectives from bangladesh. *The Lancet. Global Health*, *8*(10), e1262. doi:10.1016/S2214-109X(20)30349-1 PMID:32798448

Rao, S. K. M., Ranyal, R. K., Bhatia, S. S., & Sharma, V. R. (2004). Biomedical waste management: An infrastructural survey of hospitals. *Medical Journal, Armed Forces India*, *60*(4), 379–382. doi:10.1016/S0377-1237(04)80016-9 PMID:27407678

Saxena, P., Pradhan, I. P., & Kumar, D. (2022). Redefining bio medical waste management during covid-19 in india: A way forward. *Materials Today: Proceedings*, *60*, 849–858. doi:10.1016/j.matpr.2021.09.507 PMID:34660210

Selvakumar, J., Rajasekaran, S., Chitra, S., & Paul, B. (2020). Simulated studies on optimization and characterization of feed and product of melter for safe disposal of high-level radioactive liquid waste. *Progress in Nuclear Energy*, *118*, 103135. doi:10.1016/j.pnucene.2019.103135

Sengodan, V. C. (2014). Segregation of biomedical waste in an South Indian tertiary care hospital. *Journal of Natural Science, Biology, and Medicine*, *5*(2), 378. doi:10.4103/0976-9668.136194 PMID:25097419

Singhal, L., Tuli, A. K., & Gautam, V. (2017). Biomedical waste management guidelines 2016: What's done and what needs to be done. *Indian Journal of Medical Microbiology*, *35*(2), 194–198. doi:10.4103/ijmm.IJMM_17_105 PMID:28681805

Ward, M. J., Marsolo, K. A., & Froehle, C. M. (2014). Applications of business analytics in healthcare. *Business Horizons*, *57*(5), 571–582. doi:10.1016/j.bushor.2014.06.003 PMID:25429161

Wawale, S.G., Shabaz, M., Mehbodniya, A., Soni, M., Deb, N., Elashiri, M.A. and Naved, M., (2022). Biomedical Waste Management Using IoT Tracked and Fuzzy Classified Integrated Technique. *Human-centric Computing and Information Sciences, 12*(32).

WHO. (2018). 'Health-care waste'. WHO. https://www.who.int/news-room/fact-sheets/detail/health-care-waste

Xiao, S., Dong, H., Geng, Y., Tian, X., Liu, C., & Li, H. (2020). Policy impacts on Municipal Solid Waste management in Shanghai: A system dynamics model analysis. *Journal of Cleaner Production*, *262*, 121366. doi:10.1016/j.jclepro.2020.121366

Xu, J., Lu, W., Ye, M., Xue, F., Zhang, X., & Lee, B. F. P. (2020). Is the private sector more efficient? big data analytics of construction waste management sectoral efficiency. *Resources, Conservation and Recycling*, *155*, 104674. doi:10.1016/j. resconrec.2019.104674

Yong, J. Y., Klemeš, J. J., Varbanov, P. S., & Huisingh, D. (2016). Cleaner energy for cleaner production: Modelling, simulation, optimisation and waste management. *Journal of Cleaner Production*, *111*, 1–16. doi:10.1016/j.jclepro.2015.10.062

Yusof, K., Ismail, F., Yunus, J., Kasmuni, N., Ramele, R., Omar, M., & Mustaffa, H. (2019). Community participation and performance of waste segregation program in malacca: Towards sustainable waste management. In *MATEC Web of Conferences* (*Vol. 266*, p. 02003). EDP Sciences.

Zafar, S. (2020). *Medical waste management in developing countries*. BioEnergy Consult.

Chapter 7
"Buried Into Oblivion":
Ecocide as a Crime Against Humanity

Himanshi Bhatia
Symbiosis Law School, Symbiosis International University (Deemed), Nagpur, India & Maharashtra National Law University, Nagpur, India

ABSTRACT

The impact of the environmental deterioration is known to the world with the series of catastrophic damages and events. The discourse on the criminal intent behind man-made disasters is often regarded as a quixotic quest by various scholars and states. This study aims to examine this conundrum concerning the unsuitability of the ecocide as an international crime. It will analyze the profuse hesitation of the states and the international community on preventing environmental destruction. It argues that the presence of inter-linkages of criminal intent and elements while committing the acts deteriorates the environment. The concluding section briefly explores the questions on the urgency of criminalization, the level of regulation, the national and international administrative fallacies on environmental crimes, and above all, the feasibility of "ecocide as an international crime."

ECOCIDE FULFILLING THE FACETS OF CRIME: AN INTRODUCTORY APPRAISAL

"When our legal systems become overly technical and convoluted, they can stray too far from reality. Lawyers and the courts must see to it that their interpretations of the law adhere to reality as closely as possible. Otherwise, legal systems become rudderless and stray, from that single trajectory, which must be towards justice, into technicalities (Oslo Principles on Global Climate Change Obligations, 2015)"

DOI: 10.4018/979-8-3693-1178-3.ch007

The criminalization of any act is based upon the principle of culpability & the intent of the offender. Though, the term *"environmental crime"* is not unknown however it is quite recent as till the 1980s environmental damage was synonymous with civil remedy (Doeker & Gehring, 1990; Woodka, 1992). The paradigm shift towards criminalization of environmental damage occurred with the rise in demand for the incarceration of the polluters by the scholarly work (Faure & Svatikova, 2012; Lopez, 2007) & the public.

International Environmental Law, provides not a single normative framework that lays out what may be defined as rules and principles of criminal liability. Nonetheless, many other areas of international law contain specific provisions & exceptions on the applicability of the criminal principles upon any act or intent. Thus, compulsory framework instruments provide extensive general regulations sufficient to add more precise norms and principles to sectoral or regional texts and promote a sense of community and cooperation. Inevitably, environmental regulation and the gradual deployment of regimes result in certain environmental issues being handled while others are not like environmental crimes.

Herein, the doctrine of *"jus cogens"* i.e., pre-existing norms in international law plays a crucial role to establish the *"obligatio erga omnes"* (It is a term widely used in International Law to establish the legal implications of any act – referring to criminal act here in this chapter, thus it characterizes the state responsibility when a criminal act is committed in its territory towards the International Community) upon the states. According to global environmental regulations, customary international law rules are difficult to determine especially when there is a disconnect between what states claim and what they do. This can be substantiated in the ICJ judgment in Costa Rica/Nicaragua (2015) which summarized the customary international environmental law as follows:

"to fulfill its obligation to exercise due diligence in preventing significant trans-boundary environmental harm, a State must, before embarking on an activity having the potential adversely to affect the environment of another State, ascertain if there is a risk of significant trans-boundary harm, which would trigger the requirement to carry out an environmental impact assessment [...] If the environmental impact assessment confirms that there is a risk of significant transboundary harm, the State planning to undertake the activity is required, in conformity with its due diligence obligation, to notify and consult in good faith with the potentially affected State, where that is necessary to determine the appropriate measures to prevent or mitigate that risk" (Costa Rica v. Nicaragua, 2011)

Consequently, environmental governance has taken the form of statements, guidelines, and recommendations. Being global in application, the non-binding instruments were the safe resort. These instruments have proven to be quite valuable as a guide for both national and international action. Commonly, they serve as a springboard for the eventual establishment and implementation of legally binding rules. Additionally, they are widely used in the context of explaining the interpretation of fundamental parts of multinational environmental treaties. Progressing towards the International Criminal Law, any environmental damage can be attributed as a criminal offense only when it fulfills the existing offenses criteria. Thus, environmental damage per se is not considered a criminal offense in the absence of existing norms or criminal framework.

Although, the emerging study within critical criminology called green criminology is exploring the effects of robust criminal law in subsiding the grave environmental harm like ecocide. The concern of such critical criminologists is on the application of the criminal law on mundane issues while disregarding the larger impact of environmental crimes (Robinson, 2022).

Moreover, while discussing criminal liability of environmental damage during a war, the ICC draft recognized its ramifications under article 8 (2)(b)(iv) as one of the first eco-centric war crimes under the statute. However, the primary argument that emanates from the stated provision, is on sufficiency per se of the prosecution of the long-term environmental damage which is been conducted during peacetime? Additionally, the scholarly critique is majorly based upon the threshold benchmark which is high for environmental damage, the ambiguity of the terms in provision along with the dependence on the proportionality & strict liability regime (Office of Prosecutors, 2016).

Thus, through the above-stated discourse, the chapter intends to explore the applicability of the existing established criminal norms within the ICC framework to the crime of *"ecocide"*. The re-visiting of the conundrum between the International Criminal Law (ICL) with that of traditional criminal law in terms of environmental injury will be the thrust of this particular chapter. To do so, Part II of the chapter will provide an outline of the existing criminal concepts according to which an act is recognized as an offense. The doctrine of harm principle; the nuances of culpability of any offender; mens rea fulfillment and deterrence as an end goal will be discussed particularly. It will also deliberate upon the characteristics of the environmental crimes to appreciate the probable facets of *"ecocide"* as a crime. With the analysis of the degree of complexity, continuity feature, inter-generational loss & aspirational critique of the crime. In Part III, the chapter will attempt to draw an argument on the merits of the criminal enforcement for ecological damages along with a brief discussion on the parallels of both areas of study. It will also include a narrative on civil & criminal deterrence & liability schemes for green crimes. Lastly, through Part V, will deal with the most significant aspect of whether "ecocide" as a crime is an aspirational claim or does it fall within the realistic pattern of criminalization of an act. Therefore, this chapter essentially attempts to explore the dilemma of the international scholars & the states to combat ecocide through the lens of criminal law.

CRIMINAL LAW CORE CONCEPTS AND ECOCIDE: PARALLELS ANALYSIS

The term 'ecocide' came into use in the 1970s primarily after the American-led first planned environmental war on Vietnam (Waugh, 2010). The strategic handling of the *"Agent Orange"* herbicide on the Vietnamese environment under the *"Ranch Hand Operation"* was justified by the American officers under the pretext of managing war victory as an end product (Waugh, 2010). The exposure to the fact that the U.S. Military used the Ph.D. work of Prof. Arthur W. Galston (Plant Biologist) in developing Agent Orange for the war led him to campaign against the practices of the U.S. Authorities (Greene, 2019). He spoke at one of the conferences:

"It seems to me that the wilful and permanent destruction of the environment in which a people can live in a manner of their choosing ought similarly to be considered as a crime against humanity, to be designated by the term ecocide . . . At present, the United States stands alone as possibly having committed ecocide against another country, Vietnam, through its massive use of chemical defoliants and herbicides. The United Nations will indeed seem to be an ideal body for the creation of an anti-ecocide proposal (Fitzgerald, 2012)."

Thus, the Galston voiced for the investigation of Agent Orange's effect on the population led to the coinage of the term "ecocide". However, Galston had no legal background & he was not advocating any legal provision or law for the same (Cho & Byung-Sun, 2000). It was only in 1973 when Prof. Richard A. Falk one of the members of the group called *"Working Group on the Law against Genocide and Ecocide"* (a parallel unofficial community in Stockholm Conference) proposed a draft titled International Convention on the Crime of Ecocide (Cho & Byung-Sun, 2000.

Other than in a legal standard, ecocide is defined as any severe damage or destruction to a certain area's natural environment and ecosystems, to the point where: the habitats are in danger of losing their lives. Some jurists may find it difficult to accept a new phrase like "ecocide". To define the offenses, they recommend a more neutral title, such as serious environmental crimes.

Ecocide, on the other hand, has the advantage of being visually appealing. The concept of ecocide has sparked public and political interest and attention. As opposed to anodyne labeling. The expressive duty of a label is to communicate a message as a legitimate factor and an important function of criminal law. Previously, the terms war crimes and crimes against humanity were used interchangeably. All of these terms, as well as the phrase genocide, were problematic due to their novelty, yet were chosen for their potential to raise public awareness and support (Robinson, 2022)

The Eco-sensitive law was previously codified through international treaties to address the complexity of environmental issues with two aims: to maintain a minimum order of peace & secondly, to establish equity (distributive justice). Additionally, there are several courts or tribunals that have acknowledged that customary international law rules like state responsibility and due diligence exist even for environmental law *(The South China Sea Arbitration (The Republic of Philippines v. The People's Republic of China)*, 2016) *(Pulp Mills on the River Uruguay, Argentina v Uruguay*, 2006) *(International Tribunal for the Law of the Sea, 2011) (Legality of the Threat or Use of Nuclear Weapons, Advisory Opinion,* 1996) *(Dispute concerning Delimitation of the Maritime Boundary Between Ghana and Cote D'ivoire in the Atlantic Ocean) (Ghana/Cote D'ivoire*, 2017). However, due to the significant complexity of environmental issues, the establishment of a legally binding agreement or framework is still an Utopian dream for the world.

There can be an aggressive pursuit of criminal law as an appealing avenue for the attainment of desired results. However, often criminal law principles are taken up as a last resort as being a regressive, exorbitant, bulky tool with lots of nitty-gritty. Thus, the applicability of the criminal law is based upon the worst practices which fulfill the notion of significant harm to society or an individual. The proposal of ecocide being criminalized is based upon a similar analogy of it causing grave harm to the world. Although to be included within the section of international core crimes it must conform with the basic characteristics of the recognized internationally recognized crimes. Thus, following traditional facets of criminal law will be appreciated inasmuch as environmental damage or green crimes.

Harm Principle

According to the criminological element of Harm's Principle, only when the criminal's activity hurts others is the offender obligated to society (Ripstein, 2006). John Stuart Mill was a well-known English philosopher who introduced the utilitarian concept of the Harm Principle. In his well-known work *On Liberty*, he anticipates the idea of a co-relationship between offense and harm in the performance of any act. According to him, the state cannot impose restrictions on liberty-based only on the commission of an offense. As a requirement for restricting the offender's liberty, the offense must be justified by inflicting harm to another person (Macleod, 2016).

Even if certain activities do not endanger others, they are nevertheless criminal under the law. In such cases, the fear of societal harm motivates these sanctions. For instance, ecological harm does not pose an immediate or confirmed threat, yet it may pose an issue in the future. Similarly, under the penal law, certain victimless crimes are designated as aggravated offenses based on the harm, even though there's no harm to another entity.

The premise of the harm principle is hence based upon the central value of balancing the criminal act with the tangible harm to deter future wrongdoing. The utilitarianism in criminal law in the form of retribution, reformation, incapacitation, or deterrence is also a need of an hour for environmental crimes. While acknowledging that the reparative component of the International Criminal Court's system may be conceived and established with a perspective to solve environmental concerns like "ecocide" in a significant way. This is despite the fact that there is some convergence between the aims of criminal justice and environmental preservation specifically.

Three ethical and philosophical justifications for combating crime have historically been put forth: retributivism (just desert), utilitarianism (general welfare & prevention), and expressivist (social rejection and reinforcement) (Duignan & West, 2017). While no doctrine has emerged in international criminal law, as the main reason for imposing individual criminal penalties or sanctions (Office of Prosecutors, 2016). Though, in one of the classic cases by ICTY in Erdemovic (ICTY, 1996), it ruled that deterrence, reprobation, and retribution are components of transnational criminal culpability. Similarly, the ICC Statute's preamble expressly discusses retribution and general prevention of harm while deterrence is established by the retributive assumption of reducing impunity for the most severe offenses will demonstrate potential deterrence for the future perpetrators.

If we study the same implications upon the crime of ecocide, then researcher concur with the discourse on it fulfilling the harm principle doctrine to be criminalized under International Criminal Law. Consequently, the traditional understanding of harm i.e., a concrete commission of an act (offense) that results in noticeable harm has expanded to an extent of "risked harm" as well (Ambos, 2015).

Henceforth, the modern philosophy of "harm principle" embraces the concept & break-through work of *Joel Fienberg* an American philosopher who advocated the usage of three norms for criminalizing a mere risk as follows (Feinberg, 1988): severity and likelihood of the harm, as well as the independent merit of the hazardous activity. The environmental crimes are just another classic example of mere risk & this paradigm shift justifies the recognition of ecocide because it being including the severity & probability of harm parameters.

Similarly, another modern legal philosopher, *Andrew von Hirsch* framed *"Standard Harm Analysis"* (Von Hirsch, 1996) as consisting of three norms: a) first, contemplating the magnitude & the likelihood of the harm; b) balancing the plausibility of criminalization of the actor's concerned actions & the harm of such action upon the society; and c) lastly, evaluating the results of such criminalization on the offender i.e. if it is imposing onerous restrictions irrespective of the gravity or not?

Howbeit, to overcome the issue of wider ambit of the "mere risk" theory as it may attract the criminalization of petty harm on the assumption of prospective damage. The renowned distinguished scholar, *Douglas Husak* recommended the definite norms for the ambiguous "new version of mere risk -harm principle analogy" (Husak, 2007) based on four dimensions as follows:

a)   there shall be *"substantial risk"* from the prohibited act;
b)   the criminalization of action shall be able to achieve the prevention of the crime in the long run;
c)   Also, the prohibition on the alleged harm shall be legitimate;
d)   An offender must act with a certain level of *"culpability"*.

Ecocide and Harm Principle

The rigidity of the archaic criminal core principles is a known fact in International Criminal Law. Though, there is divergence in terms of aims of the international criminal justice & ecological sustainability. Ecological harms are typically irreversible or at least persisting, hence, in the opinion of the *International Court of Justice,* diligence and mitigation be the agenda in dealing with such acts (International Court of Justice, 1997). The tussle between both the approaches can be reiterated from the fact of environmental protection ex post facto remedies & the eventual restoration of the environment when such remedies fail in curbing the menace (Office of Prosecutors, 2016). Thus, the major impediment of the International Criminal Justice mechanism is the insufficient remedies that are restricted to mitigating actions.

Hereafter, on the criterion of the "mere risk"; "substantial risk" or even "tangible harm" acts have been recognized as an offense lately. If we analyze the *Ecocide* attributes it is not alien to the above-stated standards. It is being accepted by a few countries & environmental scholars as to the 'intentional, reckless & substantial harm to the environment' irrespective of war or peacetime commission. The presence of the harm is quite relevant in this context which materializes the claim of it being one of the core crimes under International Criminal Law.

Culpability

Another distinguishing feature of criminal law is "culpability," which is derived from the Latin term *"culpa,"* which essentially means "fault." Despite its status as a philosophical offspring, the concept of responsibility is critical to criminal law theory. The proximity of the concept of culpability to theoretical conceptions such as will and awareness has largely affected its criticism. However, from a legal standpoint, responsibility is proportional to the degree of wrongdoing committed when committing the crime. The use of the term "blame" here reflects societal disapproval of disagreement with communal standards.

Incidentally, several scholarly papers on *mens rea* indicate that criminal accountability should be predicated on the harm done rather than the state of a guilty mind. According to *Baroness Wootton*, the material repercussions of conduct & the justifications for forbidding it are the same whether the purpose is malevolent, criminally inspired, carelessness, or pure curiosity of an offender (Wootton, 1981). He justifies it with an example of a man who is equally dead and his relatives who are grieving now whether he was killed or driven over by a drunken driver or by an ignorant driver makes no difference even if the guilty mind is present or not. Thus, he advocates that it may seem insignificant, yet it would be insane to turn a blind eye to individuals who cause social harm activities that were the result of carelessness, negligence, or just an accident.

Quite the contrary, *Hart* believes in individuals' tendency to participate in decision–making (culpability) plays a crucial role. He claims that it is critical for the law to reflect popular moral judgments, and it is even more vital that, it should accurately represent its judgments on human behavior or decisions that not only underpin morality but also influence our entire society (Hart, 1968). Hart's stance on guilt has been largely accepted in criminal law, with scholars mostly agreeing on the finality of the goal of punishing only those people who have the mental capacity to appreciate the illegality of their conduct, & even then they continue to violate socially acceptable legal boundaries.

Though, the question might arise why culpability concerns for any offense are due to three arguments (O'Hear, 2004). Firstly, it is ethically objectionable to impose punishments without an element of blameworthiness. Secondly, to maintain the proportionality of infliction of punishment with that of the culpability of the offender and lastly, the punishment shall serve the deterrence component considering the *jus desert* principle. It is basically a principle of justice which ensure the application of punishment according to the gravity of the offense.

Ecocide and Culpability

The *"culpability"* is often considered immaterial in ecological crimes due to the strict liability regime which ignores the culpability component when prosecuted under various domestic laws of states. However, the same culpability is expected to be quite high in the sole provision under the ICC statute which creates the individual liability for causing environmental damage. Article 8 (2)(b)(iv) sets the bar for criminal liability with the presence of *"intentional attack & knowledge of causing severe damage to the environment during war-time"*. Henceforth, there is divergence on the nature of culpability in International & domestic laws for environmental damage.

The basic premise of ecocide known for the severe damage with prior knowledge demonstrates the culpability of the probable offenders. The fact, that in Environmental crimes, there is a diffusion of accountability, the continued legitimacy of much organizational activity, the apparent abundance of the violation, and the difficulties in distinguishing individual accountability from societal action are all seem to be particularly relevant factors of such intensity (Office of Prosecutors, 2016). Additionally, there's always a convenient defense of low culpability even when the damage is heinous.

This dilemma can be appreciated with the inclusion of the term *"wanton"* in the definition (Higgins, 2012), as it suggests reckless disdain for the repercussions of someone's conduct or *"callous indifference"* towards the existence, welfare, and protection of human dignity. It entails either understanding of circumstances that render the action illegal or the failure to investigate in a manner that demonstrates an absolute disdain for the law or the harms (*The South China Sea Arbitration (The Republic of Philippines v. The People's Republic of China)*, 2016)(*Pulp Mills on the River Uruguay, Argentina v Uruguay*, 2006) (International Tribunal for the Law of the Sea, 2011) (*Legality of the Threat or Use of Nuclear Weapons, Advisory Opinion*, 1996) (*Dispute concerning Delimitation of the Maritime Boundary Between Ghana and Cote D'ivoire in the Atlantic Ocean Ghana/Cote D'ivoire*, 2017).

However, the culpability can be traced from the eco-cidal act smoothly however the acceptance or recognition of the terms "wrongful" "irresponsible" or "reckless" can cover the most appropriate acts of criminalization which might be controversial for their reasons in the international community. The principle of culpability necessitates a level of wrongdoing and guilt corresponding with a significant offense of international criminality. The ecocide culpability discussion should be comprehensive, taking into account more than just the facilitation of conviction, as well as the idea that everyone should be accountable and the stigmas associated with ICL. It would also be ideal to define and incorporate anything comparable to the common law term of willful blindness, which refers to a situation in which a person lacks knowing primarily due to a conscious endeavour to remain ignorance, even when facts to the contrary are known bring it to their attention need of inquiry. Willful blindness is more than just careless ignorance which subverts a duty of inquiry and necessitates a subjective effort.

Mens Rea

One of the foremost elements to establish any criminal liability except a few is the presence of *mens rea* i.e., guilty mind or intent. As discussed above, the threshold of *mens rea* is quite high in International Criminal Law as the gravity of the offense & its ramifications are sustained globally. *Mens rea* also turned out to be the common justification by the green-crime offenders due to the absence of *mens rea* or chain of causation. It also serves the rationale behind the strict liability regime for environmental damage.

However, in Prosecution within the ICC framework, the mens rea is broadly divided into three kinds: *"dolus directus"* where the repercussions of the act & the intention of the offender are quite clear; *"dolus indirectus"* which involves the offender's knowledge of additional harm as well and lastly, *"dolus eventualis"* where the perpetrator anticipates other harm as a possible or likely result of their behavior and nonetheless acts (Greene, 2021).

The ecocide falls within the ambit of "dolus eventualis" because of the "severe harm" being foreseen by the perpetrator yet commits the crime. Though, the criteria of the *mens rea* in the Rome Statute do not warrant such acts due to the formal recognition of the threshold of intent & knowledge (Rome Statute, Art. 30). On the issue of a higher degree of *mens rea* requirement, the scholars have been proposing a strict liability regime for ecocide or the widening of the ambit to *dolus eventualis*.

The tussle of the requirement of intent was also discussed in the *Lubanga* case (The Prosecutor v. Thomas Lubanga Dyilo, 2007) wherein the chamber unanimously held that Article 30 sets dolus directus of first & second degree as the threshold of *mens rea* & nothing beyond it. Therefore, the threshold of *mens rea* is the same as has been for the other four core crimes which attract criticism due to the complexity of the ecological crimes.

According to the above discussion, it can be inferred that the ecocide at present does not oblige the required threshold of the *mens rea* if the act is the commission in the third degree of *dolus eventualis*. The reason why environmental activists advocate the removal of such limitations of the crimes like ecocide specifically in the form of strict liability or wider interpretation of article 30 of the statute.

MERITS OF CRIMINAL ENFORCEMENT

Even while it is not the only or most effective way to increase environmental protection, international criminal law, when combined with various other areas of international law, may help create a more unified system of protection. There are also other reasons to propel international criminal law toward successful ecological sustainability. There is no convincing basis in international criminal law for a different approach to environmental damage during war versus peacetime. It is also time to shift international criminal law's anthropocentric focus to a more eco-centrism one. As a consequence, the case given in favor of establishing a new international crime against the environment is accepted as reasonable and appropriate. Henceforth, this part will try to put forward the merits & outcomes which may occur if the *ecocide* is criminalized.

Ecocide Not Making Peace With: Peace-Time Environmental Damage

Environmental damage has been recognized under the ICC statute with a subtle pinch of criminalization read with the core crimes. The clause of war-time is pertinent here as apart from the war crimes under art. 8(b)(iv), the remaining crimes can be prosecuted even when committed during peacetime. If we consider other core crimes like *"Crime against Humanity"* under art. 7 & *"Genocide"* under art. 6 of the Statute wherein the ecological damage is recognized only if it causes humanitarian catastrophe or where it establishes the significant *mens rea* threshold respectively. Thus, the peace-time piecemeal approach is among the reason of major obstacles to prosecuting ecocide within the existing criminal justice delivery framework.

International courts have already given an undisputed opinion on the paramountcy of the environment irrespective of its harm being associated with the wartime or peacetime duration (*Gabčíkovo-Nagymaros Project Hungary v. Slovakia,* 1997). If international criminal law regards the environment as worthwhile of preservation above all else during an international armed conflict, it is contextually contradictory to international law to deny such acceptability of protection beyond the warfare instances.

Although the heightened threat to the environment posed by armed conflict is unquestionably one of the driving forces behind specific efforts to preserve the environment during times of armed conflict, it is at least debatable whether this intensified threat can be substantiated in comparison to the environmental degradation that occurs during times of peace. When compared to other environmental dangers that exist during times of peace, the damage done to the environment by armed war is relatively minimal. Environmental crime, whether it is performed during times of war or peace, is a major contributor to the disappearance of wildlife and the destruction of ecosystems.

During times of peace, the economic interests of states and private enterprises give the self-justification that is necessary to address possible environmental risks, even though military considerations may increase these threats. In point of fact, economic reasons constitute a much greater threat to the human and nonhuman habitats of the planet than any military action ever could. This is the case although military action is possible. Therefore, under international criminal law, there is no compelling reason to favor less environmental protection during times of peace over greater environmental protection during times of conflict.

Consequently, the requisite of criminal justification establishes the merits of ecocide to be recognized as a separate core crime. Apparently, ecocide will take into consideration severe ecological damage irrespective of the time frame of its commission i.e., wartime or peace-time here. The undeniable fact that one of the most severe environmental disasters occurred during peacetime can be proved through the following examples (Walters, 2022) which have costed a long-lasting impact on ecological & human health:

"Bhopal Gas Tragedy (1984-India); deadly oil spill in the Niger Delta; the Deepwater Horizon oil leak off the coast of the Gulf of Mexico; and the Pollution in Ecuador's Lago Agrio"

Additionally, the current climate change conundrum is the outcome of events that occurs both in times of peace and in times of conflict. Limiting the Court's duty to environmental harm during warfare highlights the gap between international criminal law and contemporary environmental issues which advances the argument in favor of the application of criminal enforcement for ecocide.

From Anthropocentrism to Eco-Centrism: Non-Human Victims

The concept of preserving nonhuman life, in general, is not novel in international law. Multiple international treaties criminalize damaging specific animal species. For example, the Convention for the Preservation of Fur Seals in the North was established in 1911 (Convention between the United States and Other Powers Providing for the Preservation of Fur Seals, 1957). Other conventions include the conservation of polar bears (Agreement on the Conservation of Polar Bears, 1973), oceans, and marine environments (International Maritime Organization, 1973), among other things.

Despite acknowledging the necessity to safeguard non-human species, such treaties maintain your commitment to the reductionist approach to the environmental law challenge. The encapsulation and disintegration of environmental legislation are both outcomes of the practise of reductionism, which entails the formulation of environmental regulations with the purpose of safeguarding the component parts of ecosystems. Although this approach has a number of positive aspects, its applicability is restricted since it does not take into account the significant degree of interdependence that characterizes ecosystems, in which the role of humans is just a minute one.

To phrase it another way, international law does not have an approach to environmental protection that is based on ecosystems. In contrast to the reductionist approach that is currently taken in international law, the crime of ecocide attempts to incorporate an ecological approach by conceptualizing criminal liability for actions that have an adverse impact on the environment i.e., "severe harm to, destruction of, or loss of ecosystem(s)" (International Maritime Organization, 1973).

The most plausible thrust behind the criminalization of ecological damage is to safeguard human existence. The major force behind the eco-centric approach is also the abundance of the possibility of acts exceeding planetary boundaries, which might have a disruptive effect on the complex global ecosystems that make up the world. This has a direct impact on all living things, including humans and non-humans, although there isn't always a direct link between environmental issues and human lives. The environmental damage to the ecosystem will continue to be neglected as long as environmental crimes are prosecuted solely based on occurrences of harm to individuals. Because of this, there are a few analysts who argue in favour of using an eco-centric approach to environmental ethics and law, which would better address present environmental issues (Waugh, 2010).

Therefore, the key element for the *ecocide per se* criminal enforcement is to guard such vulnerability of the whole ecosystem & not just the minuscule element of humans on this planet. Though, in theory, it might attract criticisms & challenges on its viability of including non-human entities. However, the cessation of the harm to the natural environment is an urgent call to repair the already executed damage. For this purpose, the International Criminal Law can be the last resort as most of the harms are trans-boundary in origin. Subsequently, the criminal sanctions & protection for non-human entities can establish the necessary deterrence & essentially the ecological elements.

Establishment of Direct Accountability of Actors

One of the main justifications for promoting the application of criminal principles is to recognize the role of companies (major actors in ecocide) in some of the most severe cases of environmental harm. However, corporate criminal liability does not come under the purview of the Rome Statute (Art. 30). The recurring issue of widening the ICC jurisdiction to other subjects was raised during the Rome Diplomatic Conference, which concluded with limiting the jurisdiction to individual offenders (Walters, 2022).

Though several factors influenced such outcomes, David Scheffer explains that the traditional practice of prosecuting individuals evidently provides a base for the ICC jurisdiction as well (Scheffer, 2016). Furthermore, it impedes the enforcement of the complementarity principle of the statute when it was being negotiated. However, the number of jurisdictions that recognize a direct criminal liability for companies under their domestic laws has expanded in the years since the Rome Statute came into force. This trend could be interpreted as indicating that the practical obstacles to determining admissibility are unlikely to be as significant as they were when the Rome Statute was written.

Corporate directors have a legal duty to ensure that profit is their main purpose under the current framework, but distinct, revolutionary, radical legislation such as the ones discussed proposed here can readily modify the framework in which corporations operate. By enacting anti-ecocide legislation, corporations would be expected to address environmental factors & implications of their choices. Proponents argue that an ecocide law will hold corporations accountable for environmental devastation, Higgins emphasizes that the current legal structure, in which companies are protected, has a threatening impact concerning "fictional persons" capable of suing, lobbying, and causing harm (Bustami & Hecken, 2021). However, they cannot be prosecuted in a criminal court for the harm they do. As a result, there is an incentive to maximize profit at all costs. Ecocide legislation would impose a duty of care and a contractual obligation on the company's directors, CEOs, and senior officials who might face criminal charges for causing environmental disasters.

This would present an opportunity for businesses to be more environmentally conscious in the future, preventing reckless or profit-seeking behavior that has resulted in a spate of environmental calamities. As a result, criminal enforcement may help to by acting as a check on corporate failure, such calamities can be avoided in the first place. In the long run, it is permissible to include an ecocide crime that applies to businesses in the Rome Statute if there is a way to separate the direct responsibility of corporations for infringements of international law from the requirement of having international legal personality.

CONCLUSION

Ecocide and "climate criminality" are concepts that are still in their infancy in socio-legal and criminological discourse. Legal possibilities for holding political and corporate leaders accountable for environmental harm are expanding as a result of green criminological discourses that try to push the boundaries of what is feasible in green criminology. Thus, this discourse assures that ecocide is not only relevant but also in the dawn of modern security and nature conservation.

Existing ecocide proposals have aroused concerns that they are unduly aspirational, and that "eco-sensitivity" should be explored as a first milestone in the International Criminal Court's efforts to protect the environment & ICC's "greenwashing" (Walters, 2022). Furthermore, there is a widespread perception that proving ecocide under existing international criminal law frameworks based on intent may be difficult. Consequently, the debate over the meaning and framing of ecocide remains contested. An actual incidence of ecocide and climate criminality that can be traced back to a specific political action or omission can serve to increase ecological sensitivity and understanding of climate crime.

To hold individuals accountable for environmental deterioration, it is vital to understand the circumstances under which it occurs, particularly the lived reality. If the International Criminal Court can recognize ecocide as a crime, it must be proved to have definite negative consequences, and evidence of purposeful, malevolent, or careless activities by powerful and political actors which is a debatable ground. A criminological concept has never before tackled the ethical and legal challenges of ecocide. It must be defined, framed, and prosecuted as a new crime under Rome Statute concerning victims' lived trauma, loss, and long-term ecological ramifications (human and non-human). Lastly, His Honour Sir Howard Morrison, a current International Criminal Court judge, has stated the hurdles of ecocide as a fifth crime:

"I'm all in favor of it if it can happen. But to put the fifth offense into the matrix of the ICC means a major change to the Rome Statute, which means, I think, you have to get 75% of the countries to vote for it. That's going to be hard. It may happen because at the moment environment and ecology are in the ascendancy in the minds and philosophy of a lot of people. But I've always said, and I maintain it, that if an environmental offense is egregious enough to affect a large number of people, then why not prosecute it as a crime against humanity, which is already on the statute book of the ICC? (Turok-Squire, 2022)."

ACKNOWLEDGMENT

The author would like to extend heartfelt appreciation to all the anonymous Peer reviewers and Editor for their insightful comments. Particular thanks are due to Mr. Prateek Sikchi (Assistant Professor of Law, Symbiosis Law School, Nagpur) for his enlightening review and time to the research work.

REFERENCES

Agreement on the Conservation of Polar Bears. (1973, November 15). UN. https://treaties.un.org/doc/Publication/UNTS/Volume%202898/Part/volume-2898-I-50540.pdf

Ambos, K. (2015). The Overall Function of International Criminal Law: Striking the Right Balance between the Rechtsgut and the Harm Principles - A Second Contribution Towards a Consistent Theory of ICL. *Criminal Law and Philosophy*, 9(2), 301–329. doi:10.1007/s11572-013-9266-1

Bustami, A., & Hecken, M.-C. (2021). Perspectives for a New International Crime Against the Environment: International Criminal Responsibility for Environmental Degradation under the Rome Statute. *Goettingen Journal of International Law, 1,* 145–189.

Cho, & Byung-Sun. (2000). Emergence of an International Environmental Criminal Law? *UCLA Journal of Environmental Law and Policy, 19*(1), 37.

Dispute concerning Delimitation of the Maritime Boundary Between Ghana and Cote D'ivoire in the Atlantic Ocean (GHANA/CÔTE D'IVOIRE), (INTERNATIONAL TRIBUNAL FOR THE LAW OF THE SEA September 23, 2017). https://www. itlos.org/en/main/cases/list-of-cases/case-no-23/

Doeker, G., & Gehring, T. (1990). PRIVATE OR INTERNATIONAL LIABILITY FOR TRANSNATIONAL ENVIRONMENTAL DAMAGE— THE PRECEDENT OF CONVENTIONAL LIABILITY REGIMES. *Journal of Environmental Law, 2*(1), 1–16. doi:10.1093/jel/2.1.1

Duignan, B., & West, H. R. (2017). Utilitarianism philosophy. In *Encyclopædia Britannica.* https://www.britannica.com/topic/utilitarianism-philosophy

Faure, M. G., & Svatikova, K. (2012). Criminal or Administrative Law to Protect the Environment? Evidence from Western Europe. *Journal of Environmental Law, 24*(2), 253–286. doi:10.1093/jel/eqs005

Feinberg, J. (1988). The Moral Limits of the Criminal Law Volume 4: Harmless Wrongdoing. Oxford University Press. doi:10.1093/0195064704.001.0001.002.003

Fitzgerald, G. J. (2012). The Invention of Ecocide: Agent Orange, Vietnam, and the Scientists Who Changed the Way We Think about the Environment. *The Journal of American History, 99*(2), 677–678. doi:10.1093/jahist/jas292

Greene, A. (2019). The Campaign to Make Ecocide an International Crime. *Fordham Environmental Law Review, 30,* 1–48.

Greene, A. (2021). Mens Rea and the Proposed Legal Definition of Ecocide. *Voelkerreschtsblog.* https://voelkerrechtsblog.org/mens-rea-and-the-proposed-legal-definition-of-ecocide/

Hart, H. L. A., & Gardner, J. (2009). *Punishment and responsibility: essays in the philosophy of law.* Oxford University Press.

Higgins, P. (2012). *Earth is our business: changing the rules of the game.* Shepheard-Walwyn.

Husak, D. N. (2010). *Overcriminalization: the limits of the criminal law*. Oxford University Press.

Lopez, A. (2007). Criminal Liability for Environmental Damage Occurring in Times of Non-International Armed Conflict: Rights and Remedies. *Fordham Environmental Law Review*, *18*(2), 231.

Macleod, C. (2016, August 25). *John Stuart Mill (Stanford Encyclopedia of Philosophy)*. Stanford. https://plato.stanford.edu/entries/mill/

O'Hear, M. M. (2004). Sentencing The Green-Collar Offender: Punishment, Culpability, And Environmental Crime. *The Journal of Criminal Law & Criminology*, *95*(1), 133. doi:10.2307/3491383

Office of Prosecutors. (2016). *Policy Paper on Case Selection and Prioritization, International Criminal Court*. https://www.icccpi.int/sites/default/files/itemsDocuments/20160915_OTP-Policy_Case-Selection_Eng.pdf

Oslo Principles on Global Climate Change Obligations. (2015). Global Justice. https://globaljustice.yale.edu/sites/default/files/files/OsloPrinciples.pdf

Ripstein, A. (2006). Beyond the Harm Principle. *Philosophy & Public Affairs*, 34.

Robinson, D. (2022). Ecocide — Puzzles and Possibilities. *Journal of International Criminal Justice*, *35*(1).

Scheffer, D. (2016). Corporate Liability under the Rome Statute. *Harvard International Law Journal*, *57*(1), 35–38.

The Prosecutor v. Dražen Erdemović, (International Criminal Tribunal for Former Yugoslavia 1996).

The Prosecutor v. Thomas Lubanga Dyilo, Decision on the confirmation of the Charges, ICC-01/04-01/06 (Pre-Trial Chamber I), 119, para. 351 (Jan. 29, 2007).

Turok-Squire, R. (2022, January 16). *Inside the Mind of an International Criminal Court Judge: Sir Howard Morrison QC*. Lacuna. https://lacuna.org.uk/justice/international-criminal-court-icc-judge-sir-howard-morrison-qc/

Von Hirsch, A. (1996). Extending the Harm Principle: "Remote" Harms and Fair Imputation. In A. P. Simester & A. T. H. Smith (Eds.), *Harm and Culpability* (pp. 259–276). Oxford University Press. doi:10.1093/acprof:oso/9780198260578.003.0020

Walters, R. (2022). Ecocide, climate criminals and the politics of bushfires. *British Journal of Criminology*, 1–21.

Waugh, C. (2010). "Only You Can Prevent a Forest": Agent Orange, Ecocide, and Environmental Justice. *Interdisciplinary Studies in Literature and Environment*, *17*(1), 113–132. doi:10.1093/isle/isp156

Woodka, J. L. (1992). Sentencing The CEO: Personal Liability Of Corporate Executives For Environmental Crimes. *Tulane Environmental Law Journal*, *5*(2), 635–666.

Wootton, B. (1981). *Crime and the Criminal Law* (2nd ed.). Steven & Sons.

Chapter 8

Examining the Application and Challenges of the Polluter Pays Principle:
A Focus on India's Environmental Adjudication

Akash Bag
 https://orcid.org/0000-0001-8820-171X
Adamas University, India

Pranjal Khare
O.P. Jindal Global University, India

Paridhi Sharma
O.P. Jindal Global University, India

Souvik Roy
Adamas University, India

ABSTRACT

In India, the idea of the polluter pays principle (PPP) is frequently used in environmental court cases. Though it is widely used, little scholarly research has been done on its conceptual limits and the difficulties it faces when applied to the Indian judicial system. This chapter examines decisions made by the National Green Tribunal (NGT) to close this information gap. This research examines three important aspects of PPP that can be identified from NGT examples. First, it explores how the definitions of "pollution" and "polluter" have changed over time, as demonstrated by several examples. Second, the chapter examines the techniques used by the NGT to determine compensation. Finally, it analyzes the justification for PPP implementation, as explained by the NGT in various instances.
DOI: 10.4018/979-8-3693-1178-3.ch008

INTRODUCTION

The Polluter Pays Principle (PPP), a pivotal environmental policy demanding those responsible for pollution to bear the associated costs and responsibilities, transcends the traditional free market approach by holding polluters accountable for the entire social cost of their actions (Shastri, 2000). Introduced implicitly by the Organisation for Economic Cooperation and Development (OECD) in 1972, the PPP gained prominence due to escalating environmental threats from industrialization (Boyd & Ingberman, 1996). Through the Council on Guiding Principles Recommendation concerning Economic Aspects of Environmental Policies, the OECD emphasized that polluters must cover expenses mandated by public authorities to maintain an environmentally acceptable state. Globally, there is unanimous recognition of atmospheric pollution as an undeniable negative externality resulting from human activities in the global commons, coupled with an acceptance of the limited sink capacity of the atmosphere. However, a contradiction arises within the United Nations Framework Convention on Climate Change (UNFCCC), as the PPP's rational economic and policy sense is not explicitly included in its provisions, highlighting the influence of material power in climate regime formation (Ambec & Ehlers, 2016). As the world grapples with the urgency of addressing climate change, countries, including major emitters, are contemplating the adoption of the PPP in various forms, prompting a global debate on equitable application (Shastri, 2000). This chapter endeavors to analyze the PPP as an economic, ethical, and legal principle, underscoring its potential to comprehensively address climate change issues, encompassing both mitigation and necessary adaptations for the foreseeable future, despite challenges in establishing a timely mitigation regime under the Adhoc Working Group on Durban Platform (ADP).

The Polluter Pays Principle (PPP) is a widely acknowledged concept in environmental law, endorsed internationally and within India. Numerous multilateral environmental treaties on the global stage have integrated PPP, and at the national level, it has been a component of Indian environmental law since the Supreme Court's affirmation in the mid-1990s. The National Green Tribunal Act of 2010 explicitly incorporates PPP into an environmental statute (Centre for Science and Environment, 2018). Despite its apparent clarity, PPP's conceptual boundaries and practical application have evolved complexly, as emphasized by Professor Sadeleer. This chapter delves into the understanding, elaboration, and application of PPP in India, focusing on judgments rendered by the National Green Tribunal (NGT). The analysis spans national judgments from various NGT benches, covering September 2011 to December 2019. The methodology employs a chronological examination of judgments gathered using keywords such as '*polluter pays*,' '*polluter pays principle*,' '*liability*,' '*compensation*,' and '*damages*' from databases like SCC OnLine and

Manupatra. The chapter is structured into five key sections: an introduction and a conclusion; the first section introduces PPP in the Indian domestic context and globally.

The subsequent section addresses definitional challenges related to terms like *'pollution'* and *'polluter,'* drawing insights from NGT judgments. The chapter then explores the methods the NGT employs to calculate compensation for individual victims and restitution costs for damaged property and the environment due to pollution. These approaches range from rough estimations due to data limitations to establishing high-powered committees for precise calculations. The final substantive section examines instances where the NGT extends the scope of PPP beyond its restorative intent, incorporating punitive measures. The concluding section summarizes the key discussions within the chapter. The chapter scrutinizes the nuanced application of PPP in India through the lens of NGT judgments, shedding light on its evolving interpretations and practical implications.

BACKGROUND

The historical foundations of the Polluter Pays Principle (PPP) can be found in both Eastern and Western customs. In The Dialogues, Plato stressed the need for those who purposefully contaminate another person's water to compensate for their losses and purify the water source. Similarly, the Indian philosopher Kautiliya described monetary punishments for environmental damage in his Arthasastra, roughly contemporaneous with Plato (Brooks, 2013). The fines varied according to the extent of the damage, for example, urinating in designated areas or causing damage to agricultural property. PPP was first designed to handle local commons pollution problems, reflecting before global commons issues and private property culture were common (Boyd & Ingberman, 1996). It developed into an economic tool for domestic policy-making, helping distribute pollution control and prevention funds. Government rules were preferred for environmental protection in the 1980s, but a change in focus came in 1992 with the adoption Agenda 21, which emphasized international collaboration through economic tools (Brooks, 2013).

The polluter-pays principle has its roots in the advice of the Organization for Economic Cooperation and Development (OECD) since the early 1970s. The OECD made significant efforts to convert this economic theory into an acknowledged legal basis (Chandani, 2007). The United Nations Conference on Environment and Development, also known as the Rio Declaration, 1992 gave international credence to the polluter-pays principle, formally endorsed by the European Union in the Single European Act of 1987. In some cases, independent governments use direct regulation to impose the polluter-pays concept, generating financial incentives that drive polluters to pay for the damages their operations cause to the environment (Chandani, 2007). This is accomplished by holding the parties that cause pollution liable for their actions. Environmental liability laws, both domestically and internationally, have mostly followed the notion of strict responsibility in the last few decades, emphasizing "*cost internalization*." Making polluters pay for the social cost of their actions helps allocate resources more effectively. The chapter highlights how the strict responsibility approach internalizes non-negligent harm and guarantees that the prices of goods reflect the societal costs associated with pollution, in contrast to the negligence rule. This encourages a more sensible allocation of resources as a result.

On the other hand, the negligence rule, which does not account for non-negligent damages, might encourage too many businesses to enter the market, increasing the likelihood of pollution and environmental harm. One noteworthy observation is that, although many governments follow the stringent polluter-pays concept regarding banned emissions, some nevertheless view permitted pollution as free (Centre for Science and Environment, 2018). This observation highlights how differently the polluter-pays principle is used around the world. Modern environmental policy combines incentives and disincentives to change individual behavior, focusing on prevention as a cost-effective solution. PPP is a brake on the privatization of benefits and socialization of environmental costs. Using it might require the financial assessment of environmental damages using an extended cost-benefit analysis that considers non-marketed environmental products and services (Corvino, 2023). PPP is the most "*economic*" environmental concept, according to Faure and Grimeaud, who also note that this is consistent with its modern origins and representative definitions that support cost internalization (Faure & Grimeaud, 2004). PPP, which started as an economic idea, has developed into a normative theory in environmental law. Following the UN Conference on Environment and Development in Stockholm, the Organization for Economic Cooperation and Development endorsed PPP in 1972. The '*absolute liability*' principle, established in the *M.C. Mehta v. Union of India* case, gave rise to PPP in India (F. Ahmad, 2001). Polluters were ordered by the court to pay fines that were utilized to restore the impacted regions. This was further developed in the *Indian Council for Environment-Legal Action v. Union of India* case, wherein absolute culpability was extended to include compensation for victims of environmental destruction (Shastri, 2000). The Polluter Pays concept was implicitly incorporated since the court determined it had the authority to implement it under the Environment (Protection) Act. Though implicit in constitutional laws, PPP is not specifically referenced in current or prospective legislation, although the courts recognize it.

A significant Indian case implicitly incorporated the Polluter Pays Principle (PPP) into legal doctrine. The court affirmed its jurisdiction to enact measures in line with this concept by citing Sections 3 and 5 of the Environment (Protection) Act of 1986.

This integration was reaffirmed globally at the Rio Summit of 1992, particularly in Principle 16, which states that the polluter should bear most pollution-related expenses (F. Ahmad, 2001). Even though Indian courts have acknowledged PPP, it is noticeably missing from the present and upcoming legislative texts. The court held in the *Vellore Citizens Welfare Forum v. Union of India and Ors*. The case that Articles 48-A and 51-A(g) of the Indian Constitution serve as the foundation for this idea. Significantly, the court emphasized that this idea may be deduced from current laws, highlighting the constitutional foundation of India's Polluter Pays Principle (M. Ahmad, 2022).

FROM THE POLLUTER PAYS PRINCIPLE TO CORPORATE CRIMINAL LIABILITY IN INDIAN ENVIRONMENTAL JURISPRUDENCE

Regulatory authorities have enforced strict criteria for environmental reporting due to the pressing environmental issues to push sectors toward a carbon-neutral economy. A well-known benchmark, the S&P 500 ESG Index, routinely assesses businesses using Environmental, Social, and Governance (ESG) standards and eliminates underperforming ones. As part of its commitment to the global environmental agreements, India has committed to the ambitious Mission 2070 Net Zero objective and is initiating a complete five-decade green revolution (BBC, 2021). Major corporations that perform poorly in terms of the environment may suffer serious consequences, including a decline in support from investors and consumers. According to Forbes India, examples of the importance of governance and the lack of an independent environmental risk assessment for the Mumbai Coastal Road project include Quantum Advisors and Quantum Mutual Fund selling all of their shares in a major engineering and construction company in 2019. These risk evaluations can reduce workplace accidents, improve occupational health and safety procedures, and identify persons who are at risk. Therefore, it is obvious that they are necessary. Sustainability practices are becoming more and more popular with investors and companies. This is demonstrated by the growing popularity of ESG funds worldwide, especially in India (Corvino, 2023).

A notification titled *"Corporate Social Responsibility, Sustainable Development, and Non-Financial Reporting – Role of Banks"* was released by the Reserve Bank of India (RBI) in 2008. This was one of the first initiatives to bring together environmental and social issues to examine records from pollution and environmental authorities, and court rulings reveal that industrial companies are primarily to blame for the environment today (Kumar & Prakash, 2019). Section 3 of the Environment Protection Act 1986 classifies industries that engage in polluting activities (Environment

Protection Act, 1986). Due to their intricate organizational systems, firms are difficult to prosecute. This is especially true when it carries *mens rea* or the intent to conduct an act. As a result, corporate criminal culpability for environmental harm does not now carry much weight (Prabhu, 2022). The *"pay-and-pollute"* mentality of profit-driven enterprises has been affected by civil remedies. Consequently, the gravity of criminal proceedings must be considered to provide justice for environmental crimes (de Sadeleer, 2020). To prosecute those who commit environmental crimes effectively, a liberal interpretation of mens rea and a reevaluation of the valuation of environmental damage are recommended.

The Polluter Pays Principle (PPP), which emphasizes that individuals who cause pollution should pay the external costs rather than burdening the public or the government, is based on the ideas of cost internalization and allocation (Boyd & Ingberman, 1996). According to this principle, polluters must pay for the costs associated with carrying out the measures ordered by the government to preserve a suitable environmental condition, including paying compensation to pollution victims. PPP was first established in India through court rulings, and the National Green Tribunal Act of 2010 codified it. The Supreme Court first applied PPP in the seminal case of the *Indian Council for Enviro-Legal Action v. Union of India* (*"Bichhri"*) (Chandani, 2007). Regarding the contamination of water and land in *Bichhri*, Rajasthan, resulting from untreated wastewater and sludge disposal, the court decided that hazardous activities require the polluter to pay for any damage caused, even if safeguards were taken. Even in cases where a polluter's actions comply with current regulations, courts regularly use the Polluter Pays Principle to hold polluters liable for environmental damage. As an illustration, consider the *Oleum Gas Leak* Case, in which Shriram Industries was found accountable for the environmental effects of the Oleum gas leakage even though it complied with the Air Act 1981 (Chakravarty, 2006). In environmental lawsuits, the courts' main goals are to guarantee that laws are effectively enforced in addition to imposing penalties. The Court in the Indian *Council for Enviro Legal Action v. Union of India* emphasized that it had to intervene because of the enforcement agency's inadequacies, highlighting the judiciary's responsibility to protect fundamental rights when executive duties are compromised (Rengarajan et al., 2018).

The debate over environmental contamination poses an important question: may polluters be held criminally liable, or might civil action against them suffice? Sections 268 and 290 of the Indian Penal Code were used to prosecute people for public nuisances related to environmental issues even before the Stockholm Declaration of 1972 (Smith, 1972). The Stockholm Declaration introduced provisions allowing criminal prosecutions against polluters in the Water (Prevention and Control of Pollution) Act of 1974 and the Air (Prevention and Control of Pollution) Act of 1981. But the real difficulty in India is that the *"polluter pays"* idea seems to have evolved into a dangerous "*pay and pollute*" situation (Sudarshan, 2023). Observers have commented on the principle's insufficient implementation due to the lack of executive action. Notably, there has been little criminal prosecution of polluters; instead, the Pollution Control Board has frequently prioritized monetary fines over punitive measures. Critics have pointed out that this deviates from the original principle. Legal actions are usually referred to the Pollution Control Board, which does not like to take criminal action but does impose fines (Rengarajan et al., 2018). The importance of criminal prosecution in pollution issues has been emphasized by judicial cases, which highlight its deterrent effect. Proponents contend that merely fining offenders does not necessarily affect them, which encourages polluting events to happen again. As a result, it is acknowledged that it is important to start criminal processes to implement punitive measures and a sense of deterrence among potential polluters. The *Vellore Citizens' Forum v. Union of India* case was a major turning point in the legal discussion on environmental protection in India. The Supreme Court's dependence on the constitutional responsibility to protect and improve the environment was highlighted in this case, centering on the discharge of untreated effluent by tanneries in Tamil Nadu (Sudarshan, 2023). According to the Court, the Polluter Pays Principle (PPP) is a cornerstone of Indian domestic environmental law. Furthermore, the court considered PPP an essential component of sustainable development by drawing on customary international law. These instances have been regularly cited in later Indian decisions, establishing PPP's integration into the nation's environmental jurisprudence.

The National Green Tribunal (NGT) was created by the National Green Tribunal Act of 2010 as a specific body for addressing environmental issues in India. With the passage of this legislation, PPP was explicitly acknowledged as the NGT's guiding principle for making orders, judgments, and awards. According to the NGT Act, any relief, payment, or restitution it may provide must be justified in compensating those harmed by pollution, repairing damaged property, and protecting the environment (Bhuvaneshwari et al., 2019). On the other hand, using PPP brings up important issues about its actual application. Important topics include the definitions of "*pollution*" and "*polluter*," the techniques used to calculate compensation, the punitive or restitutive nature of PPP's goal, and the procedures that guarantee recompense to worthy parties or victims of pollution. In the past, companies were exempt from accountability because they were considered interfering with legislative duties. This element complicates the larger conversation about environmental accountability and its real-world ramifications for corporations (Mukherjee, 2023). In legal parlance, corporate criminal liability refers to holding a corporation liable for crimes committed by any person connected to the organization. However, because of its wide application to various actions, determining this liability has grown more difficult. Another difficulty arises from deciding who in the company should take accountability; this decision frequently falls on higher-ranking personnel with significant financial resources.

The court stressed that no business should be immune from major *Standard Chartered Bank and Ors violations. v. Directorate of Enforcement and Ors.* Case. This is especially true where the offenses affect citizens' lives, liberty, and property. Although corporate criminal liability has significant theoretical implications, its practical implementation in the Indian setting is still uncommon (Mukherjee, 2023). Recent conversations have focused on this topic, especially as industrial activity and the law interact. Although courts have fined corporations for environmental offenses, criminal culpability has not been enforced in any significant way. The ultimate punishment for corporations would be to make amends, repair the environment, and act as a warning to other companies not to commit the same crimes (Chandani, 2007). Notably, smaller businesses could find it difficult to absorb environmental expenditures, prompting them to use various pollution-reduction strategies. The difference in resources between large corporations and smaller businesses could be the reason for the unwillingness to apply criminal penalties. This dynamic reflects the continuous conversation about how environmental protection, legal enforcement, and corporate accountability connect (Turaga & Sugathan, 2020).

India has adopted a revolutionary strategy for environmental conservation in recent years, as evidenced by important legislative and administrative actions. Notably, as seen by recent changes highlighted by Jaswal in 2008, the nation has reinterpreted the polluter-pays principle (Gill, 2019). Under this reading, the state must pay victims of environmental harm up front under a system of direct governmental obligation. Subsequently, the government can use a subrogation action to recover these payments from the polluter. The Stockholm Declaration of 1972 served as the basis for the legal system governing the environment in India (Smith, 1972). Due to this international accord, India and 113 other countries committed to environmental protection principles. India saw a proliferation of environmental legislation and regulations to meet these domestic duties. Because of the Stockholm Declaration's significant influence, the constitution was amended to include Articles 48A and 51A (g) (Brooks, 2013). Important environmental laws, including the Water Act of 1974, the Air Act of 1981, and the Environmental Protection Act of 1986, were subsequently passed by the Indian Parliament.

These rules, in line with international norms, gave specialized authorities broad authority, including the capacity to shut down businesses and issue environmental protection directives. However, ineffective administrative practices, common in the larger Indian bureaucracy, made it difficult for these policies to be implemented successfully. As a result, Indian waterways and cities saw unparalleled deterioration. The Indian judiciary has taken a more proactive stance regarding increasing environmental degradation, particularly social justice (Gill, 2019). Acknowledging that individual victims could not bring lawsuits against polluters, the courts forced state governments to compensate for environmental damage. Particular focus was placed on situations in which specialized authorities could not stop injury, requiring local authorities to set up systems for compensation and cleansing (Gill, 2019). The courts even permitted these local authorities to take appropriate legal action in subrogation against the guilty parties. Even when polluters were successfully sued, it was clear that the government was still accountable for any remaining deficiencies. As a result, the involvement of state authorities in handling environmental issues has greatly increased, ranging from designating suitable cleanup agencies to taking direct accountability for victim compensation. The "*government-pays regime*," a paradigm of governmental culpability for environmental harm, is widely hailed as India's ecological savior (Gill, 2019).

NGT'S DYNAMIC APPROACH TO PPP IMPLEMENTATION

The successful implementation of the Polluter Pays Principle (PPP) in India depends on correctly defining pollution and identifying the parties accountable for it (Mukherjee, 2023). Pollution is defined legally with specific constitutive parts in the framework of the three main laws about pollution in the nation: the Environment Protection Act of 1986, the Water (Prevention and Control of Pollution) Act of 1974, and the Air (Prevention and Control of Pollution) Act of 1981 (Chakravarty, 2006). These rules define pollution as the presence of pollutants in solid, liquid, or gaseous form in amounts that can potentially damage the environment. Being harmful to people, other living things, plants, property, or the environment is another definition of this harm. The legal definition also stipulates that the pollution may cause nuisances or endanger public health, safety, domestic, commercial, industrial, agricultural uses, and aquatic species' lives or health. It is important to remember that the legal definition of "*pollution*" is not the same as what is commonly understood (Gill, 2019). According to the law, the pollutants must harm people, property, or the environment at a certain concentration. A threshold limit for this concentration must be established based on data and scientific research. In essence, India's environmental law tries to create an acceptable tolerance threshold rather than preserve an idealized historical condition of the environment (Chandani, 2007). This method emphasizes a practical and scientifically informed approach to environmental management, acknowledging that almost every human action has some environmental consequences. Comprehending the legal notion of "*pollution*" concerning the Polluter Pays Principle (PPP) is crucial for the proper implementation of PPP in legal forums such as the National Green Tribunal (NGT) (Tandon, 2020). But the NGT's methodology shows that there isn't a single, systematic method for identifying *"pollution"* and *"polluter."* Rather, the NGT uses a nuanced and comprehensive interpretation of these concepts.

Sometimes, a unique practice develops where certain activities are regarded as *"deemed to be polluting,"* and the NGT applies PPP following that determination (Tandon, 2020). For example, the NGT ordered the Municipal Corporation of Shimla and Solan to gather financial contributions to dispose of Municipal Solid Waste based on *"Polluter Pays"* in the *Dr. Karan Singh v. State of Himachal Pradesh* case. A similar order was issued in *Kamal Anand v. State of Punjab*, when PPP-compliant homes, businesses, hotels, and industrial buildings were directed to pay specified sums correlated with property taxes. Furthermore, concerning Yamuna River pollution, the NGT allowed the Corporation and the Delhi Jal Board to obtain public monies under PPP. This decision concerned *Manoj Misra v. Union of India* (Mukherjee, 2023). The NGT proposed that a fair criterion for figuring out the amount of environmental compensation that the citizens of Delhi would have to pay may be a specific percentage of their property/house tax. In a different case, the NGT established the *"Green Tax Fund"* to guarantee funding for all-encompassing environmental development and conservation in its *Own motion v. State of Himachal Pradesh*. These cases demonstrate how the NGT's methodology applies PPP dynamically, adjusting to unique situations and adopting creative mechanisms, like the 'Green Tax Fund,' to address environmental issues (Tandon, 2020).

The Rohtang Pass directive from the National Green Tribunal (NGT) is an example of the unique method the Tribunal has used in several cases, which is known as *"deemed to be polluting."* According to the Polluter Pays Principle (PPP), the NGT, in this case, required anyone visiting the Rohtang Pass glacier in a private or public vehicle to pay Rs—50 for light cars and Rs. 100 for large vehicles. In addition, there was an additional charge of Rs. 20 per tourist for electric or CNG buses. The implementation of PPP does not depend on the organizations or individuals involved surpassing a particular pollution threshold (Turaga & Sugathan, 2020). Even though most cars have certifications of pollution clearance, the NGT ordered them to pay for the pollution they produce. All vehicle users in the area, including those who drive electric vehicles, were mandated by the NGT to pay into the Green Tax Fund in the Rohtang Pass case. Although the study advocates for a wider application beyond ecologically vulnerable zones, accepting this strategy is praiseworthy. It adds that such measures should be imposed on every vehicle on the road, admitting that the environmental impact of vehicle emissions is not limited to a specific territory, drawing on the court's case on its *Own motion v. State of Himachal Pradesh*. The case of *Kamal Anand v. State of Punjab* is an example of cost internalization. In this case, waste-generating households, shops, hotels, and industrial buildings were compelled to deposit a certain amount, akin to a property tax. This viewpoint is consistent with the knowledge that the effects of using up natural resources, such as water and air, affect everyone and are not localized.

As demonstrated by several cases, the National Green Tribunal's (NGT) methodology is not dependent on a precise legal definition of pollution. Rather, it is predicated on the idea that some actions are polluting by nature, which leads to implementing the Polluter Pays Principle (PPP). In these situations, proving *"pollution in law"* could be difficult because there isn't a precise legal definition. These situations are unique in that they are ongoing, unlike isolated occurrences like industrial accidents. Moreover, because the pollution process is dispersed, gradual, and ongoing, it is frequently impossible to pinpoint one or more specific polluters. The NGT has adopted the practice of imposing PPP on ongoing, incremental, and decentralized pollution scenarios without necessarily resolving regulatory infractions. In certain cases, the NGT draws attention to pollution before implementing PPP. For instance, the NGT considered the harm an unintentional oil leak caused to mangroves and marine ecosystems in *Samir Mehta v. Union of India*. Similar emphasis was placed on groundwater and air pollution from industrial facilities in *Kasala Malla Reddy v. State of Andhra Pradesh*. Sometimes, the NGT considers breaking the law or not complying with it a legitimate requirement before approving PPP. In the *Gurpreet Singh Bagga v. Ministry of Environment and Forests and Ors.*, the National Green Tribunal ordered businesses to cover the costs of unlawful mining operations without obtaining environmental clearance and State Pollution Control Board approval. The Tamil Nadu Pollution Control Board directed the industry to operate without the necessary consent to pay under PPP, even though no effluents were released in The *Proprietor M/s—Varuna Bio Products v. The Chairman*.

It is clear that after exploring the application of the Polluter Pays Principle (PPP) by the National Green Tribunal (NGT) in various cases, there are three predominant patterns. Firstly, in ongoing activities without identifiable polluters, the NGT deems them as '*deemed to be polluting*' and applies PPP, irrespective of whether they meet the legal definition of pollution (Centre for Science and Environment, 2018). Many of these activities might not violate environmental laws but are considered polluting. Secondly, clear instances of pollution, such as oil spillage, where environmental damage is evident, lead to the explicit application of PPP. Thirdly, there are cases where the NGT acknowledges no discharge by the respondent company, yet PPP is applied due to violations of environmental laws (Mukherjee, 2023). The concern is that relying solely on law violations to apply PPP may inadvertently create a 'right to pollute' for those able or willing to pay. The chapter emphasizes that the ultimate goal is not to accumulate a substantial green fund or increase PPP applications but to promote an eco-friendly way of life. This necessitates a significant shift in current modes of production and consumption towards more sustainable practices. In summary, the chapter scrutinizes the NGT's approach to PPP, highlighting patterns in its application and stressing the need for a broader transition to eco-friendly lifestyles beyond legal remedies (Boyd & Ingberman, 1996).

COMPENSATION CALCULATIONS IN ENVIRONMENTAL ADJUDICATION

In the context of the Polluter Pays Principle (PPP), determining compensation is a crucial step that must come once it has been proven that pollution has happened and the accountable party has been found. This compensation goes beyond simply making reparations to the specific victims; it also includes paying for the expenditures associated with repairing the environment and damaged property. The fundamental presumption is that damages must be measured to calculate the proper reparations and compensation. On the other hand, the approach used by the National Green Tribunal (NGT) in cases such as *Samir Mehta v. Union of India* presents a contrasting image. The National Geographical Survey (NGT) recognized the wide-ranging effects on the marine environment, including seawater, aquatic life, shores, sea bed, mangroves, tourism, and the lives of people living along the shore in Samir Mehta's case, where respondent companies were held accountable for an oil spill and pollution from a sinking ship. Even with these obvious damages, the NGT had trouble putting a number on them for PPP applications. The panel acknowledged that assigning a specific monetary value to damages is challenging, highlighting that some factors, such as harm to marine life, mangroves, seashores, and tourism, are difficult to quantify. The NGT defended its stance by claiming that some conjecture or guessing is necessary in their assessment because of the inherent complexity and intricacy of such damages.

The National Green Tribunal (NGT) recognized that determining the precise monetary value of environmental damages is an inherent issue in this field. In the *Union of India v. Samir Mehta* case, the NGT acknowledged the difficulty in determining damages with *"exactitude and precision"*(Rengarajan et al., 2018). As a result, the Tribunal arrived at a compensation figure of Rs. One hundred crores using a process called *"hypothesizing or guesswork."* Deshpande Jansamsaya Niwaran Samiti v. State of Maharashtra is a different case demonstrating a similar dependence on conjecture. The NGT claimed it must use *"guesswork"* to estimate environmental damages when relevant data is missing due to a lack of accurate information. The responsible agencies' omission of crucial facts and information justified this decision. In this case, the NGT requested information from the Maharashtra Pollution Control Board (MPCB) regarding the air and water quality assessment to comprehend the environmental damage resulting from non-compliance with Municipal Solid Waste operations (Mukherjee, 2023). The MPCB was unable to provide this information, though. The NGT recommended that the MPCB create a specific committee within the company to deal with this issue moving forward. This organization would concentrate on creating innovative, clean technologies as well as scientific and technological research, data analysis, and interpretation related to the environment. The NGT's action in this case was a response to a lack of information, stressing the significance of competent agencies providing sufficient data for correct evaluations rather than an admission of the difficulty of assessing damages (Mukherjee, 2023).

The National Green Tribunal (NGT) encountered difficulties in the *Gurpreet Singh Bagga v. Ministry of Environment and Forests and Ors. The case* when neither the State of Haryana nor the State of Uttar Pradesh could produce a report outlining the harm that illegal sand mining in district Saharanpur—specifically on the Yamuna river's bed and banks—had caused. No document outlining the financial needs for reestablishing, returning, and reviving the environment, ecology, and biodiversity—emphasizing the Yamuna River—was produced in defiance of court orders. In response, the NGT decided to calculate compensation using the guesswork approach. The Tribunal stressed that this should not relieve the defaulting parties of their obligation, even if it recognized the challenge of accurately assessing culpability. The NGT fined each respondent engaged in mineral extraction Rs. Fifty crores and each illegally operating stone crusher/screening unit Rs. 2.5 crores based on the documentation evidence and reports that were available. These fines were imposed due to ongoing defaults, breaking the law and the terms and conditions of the Environmental Clearance (EC), and operating without the required approval from government agencies, such as the State Pollution Control Board (SPCB). This is not the first instance in which guesswork has been used in similar situations; it has also been used in other situations. The NGT validates this technique by citing the Supreme Court's ruling in *AP Pollution Control Board v. Prof. M.V. Nayudu (Retd.)*, emphasizing that the concept of "*limited*" guesswork is a recognized practice. The Supreme Court acknowledged that confusion might result when scientific knowledge is used to inform policy or form the basis of decisions made by agencies or courts.

The difficulty the National Green Tribunal (NGT) faces in rendering verdicts without instruments for calculating damages is covered in the chapter, especially when State government reports are deficient. It's crucial to remember that other approaches are available for determining compensation, even though the NGT has used estimation or guesswork as one of its ways. Compensation decisions have occasionally taken the responding company's size into account. For instance, the NGT considered the business's size while calculating compensation in cases such as *The Proprietor M/s—Varuna Bio Products v. The Chairman Tamil Nadu Pollution Control Board and C. Murugan v. Member Secretary Karnataka*. Furthermore, the NGT has calculated compensation based on the project's cost in certain instances. For example, the NGT ordered M/s. Goel Ganga Developers India Private Limited will pay environmental compensation in *Tanaji Balasaheb Gambhire v. Union of India*, where they were accused of building an unauthorized commercial and residential complex. The compensation amount was fixed at Rs. 100 crores, or five percent of the project's overall cost, whichever was lower. The State Level Express Appraisal Committee (SEAC) will evaluate the claim. This payment was required within a month to restore and restitute environmental damages created by unapproved building operations without prior environmental clearance. The chapter emphasizes how difficult it may be to determine damages when there is insufficient information and how important it is that the NGT look into other ways to calculate compensation.

The chapter discusses a case where the National Green Tribunal (NGT) imposed fines on *M/s. Goel Ganga Developers India Private Limited* for environmental violations during construction. Initially, the NGT ordered a fine of Rs. One hundred crores or 5 percent of the total project cost, whichever is less. The NGT also fined Pune Municipal Corporation (PMC) Rs. 5 lakhs and instructed PMC's Commissioner to act against responsible officers. A review application challenged this order on two grounds. First, it argued that the NGT had initially suggested higher compensation but later softened its stance. Second, it claimed that the lower estimate of damages, Rs. 100 crores, undermined environmental laws. In response, the NGT modified the order to Rs. 190 crores or 5 percent of the project cost, whichever is more, considering damages in terms of Carbon footprint. The Supreme Court (SC) rejected both grounds provided by the review court. It refused to impose special damages, stating that the applicant had a personal interest in the case.

Regarding damages based on carbon footprint, the SC argued that courts can't introduce new assessment concepts without expert evidence or established principles. It emphasized that such methods apply to nations, not individuals violating environmental clearance. The SC ultimately ordered *M/s. Goel Ganga Developers India Private Limited* will pay Rs. One hundred crores or 10 percent of the project cost, whichever is higher, as compensation. The method used by the National Green Tribunal (NGT) to decide compensation in instances involving environmental violations. The NGT has computed fines using various techniques, occasionally tying payments to the size of the project or industry. A ruling on mineral exploitation by the Supreme Court lends legitimacy to this strategy. The NGT has also cited a case involving Sterlite Industries India Ltd., in which the lack of accurate data led to the calculation of damages as five percent of the capital cost. The NGT used fines as initial deposits in multiple cases, imposing fines at a rate of five percent of the project cost. These fines were not altered in the final decisions. Interestingly, the NGT has used strategies other than monetary awards. In several instances, the Tribunal has chosen to forego setting a monetary settlement in favor of ordering polluters to implement corrective measures for environmental restoration, like installing pollution control equipment.

Although this isn't the same as levying financial penalties, it nonetheless supports the larger objective of the Polluter Pays Principle (PPP), which is to repair environmental harm brought on by polluting activities. The National Green Tribunal (NGT) ordered state authorities to order large industries—particularly thermal power plants—to establish reverse osmosis systems to provide uncontaminated drinking water to villages impacted by pollution in the case of *Jagat Narayan Viswakarma v. Union of India*. In this instance, businesses using the Polluter Pays Principle (PPP) had to fix water damage that their effluent discharge had created. Similarly, the NGT mandated that the local enterprises remove slag from the river in *Shiv Prasad v. Union of India*. However, the chapter offers criticism of these methods. The idea of restitution in civil law is considered irreconcilable with the guesswork or approximation method. It is also questioned if heavier fines should be imposed on bigger industries because they might not be commensurate with the degree of harm. According to the author, these approaches can jeopardize the fundamental goal of cost internalization, which holds the polluter accountable for the external pollution costs. The chapter questions whether pragmatism should jeopardize consistency and the rule of law in environmental adjudication in India, notwithstanding the NGT's pragmatic defense of these procedures.

EXPANDING PPP: COMPENSATION AND DETERRENCE

The Polluter Pays Principle (PPP) in Indian environmental law is primarily seen as a mechanism to hold polluters financially accountable for compensating victims, repairing property damages, and addressing environmental harm. In a straightforward interpretation, PPP aligns with civil law principles, emphasizing restoration. Many cases discussed support this vital perspective, focusing on the polluter's responsibility to remedy harm to individuals and the environment. However, there are instances where the National Green Tribunal (NGT) has broadened the scope of PPP to include punitive objectives. In *T.N. Godavarman Thirumulpad v. Union of India and Ors.*, the NGT explicitly highlighted the 'twin objectives' of compensation by polluters: compensating victims for their losses and imposing punitive consequences on the offenders. For example, in *Tanaji Balasaheb Gambhire v. Union of India*, the NGT fined a company Rs. 5 crores for violating environmental laws during construction, exceeding clearance limits, and lacking necessary consent from the regulatory board. This penalty was in addition to the environmental compensation already imposed, showcasing the NGT's willingness to integrate punitive elements into the PPP framework.

The NGT has applied the Polluter Pays Principle (PPP) to impose 'exemplary and deterrent compensation,' as demonstrated in the *Lakhan Singh v. Rajasthan State*

Pollution Control Board and Ors case. Here, the NGT levied a penalty equivalent to one percent of the annual gross turnover on non-compliant units in RIICO Industrial Area Kaladera, Tehsil Chomu, District Jaipur, under the framework of PPP. This interpretation aligns with the Supreme Court's (SC) expansive stance on liability, particularly in hazardous industries. The SC, acknowledging absolute liability in such cases, also endorsed a deterrent objective. According to the SC, compensation should correlate with the enterprise's size and capacity, implying that larger enterprises should bear a higher compensation burden to have a meaningful deterrent impact. The NGT seems to be carrying forward and building upon this understanding articulated by the SC in the late 1980s.

DISCUSSION

This chapter emphasizes how urgent it is for India to pass strict laws requiring companies to report climate-related risks in line with the worldwide trend of required climate disclosure. The Companies Act of 2013 is being completely redrafted to improve business adherence to environmental regulations. According to the first crucial suggestion, the National Green Tribunal Act of 2010 and current environmental regulations should be aligned, emphasizing the NGT's authority to handle complicated environmental matters. Corporate accountability is further reinforced by the NGT's stringent adherence to the environmental compensation framework, as mandated in the *Paryavaran Suraksha Samiti & Anr. v. Union of India & Ors. (2017)* case. To foster cooperation between businesses and the National Chemical Authority and advance openness and efficient chemical management by urging the prompt implementation of the Draft Chemicals (Management and Safety) Rules. These legislative initiatives seek to strengthen India's corporate response to hazards associated with climate change, promote environmental compliance, and bring business practices into line with rapidly changing international norms. A specialized regulatory body must monitor and control corporate environmental operations. The National Green Tribunal and this planned entity are expected to work together smoothly to strengthen the environmental stewardship governance structure.

The Central Pollution Control Board (CPCB) has issued a crucial directive to enterprises under any of the 17 recognized categories of highly polluting substances. These sectors are required to implement an online continuous emission/effluent monitoring system. Most importantly, Section 5 of the Environmental Protection Act (EPA) requires these systems to be closely connected to the servers of State Pollution Control Boards (SPCB) or Pollution Control Committees (PCC). Furthermore, a crucial need is stated, highlighting the requirement that every SPCB publishes its Continuous Emission Monitoring Systems (CEMS) data online. With the abundance of data gathered from these platforms, this transparency initiative aims to make it easier for thorough analyses of regulatory compliance within their different countries. The need for the Supreme Court and High Courts to apply exemplary damages wisely emphasizes the need to intensify penalties for environmental violations. An example of this type of action may be seen in *Sterlite Industries (I) Ltd v. Union of India & Ors. (2013)*, where the company operating without the necessary renewal of its Consent to Operate (CTO) was subject to carefully examining its annual report. Remarkably, in determining compensation, the court used a perceptive methodology to rule that 10% of Profit Before Depreciation, Interest, and Taxes (PBDIT) would be awarded as compensation.

Importantly, the requirement goes beyond sanctions; it also includes that businesses strictly follow the guidelines provided by the Task Force on Climate-related Financial Disclosures (TCFD). These guidelines, which are expansive, discursive, and allow for a high level of discretion, provide a foundation for the thorough disclosure of hazards associated with climate change. One noteworthy proposal advocates for expanding the current system, presenting a fresh approach to climate risk disclosure that is persuasive and flexible. This recalibration is intended to reinforce the effectiveness of the current TCFD Recommendations by promoting a system characterized by rigorous risk assessment and compelling disclosure. Parent firms should be held responsible for any misconduct their subsidiaries commit since they have substantial control over the latter's business operations. This responsibility is suggested by the legal theory of *"piercing or lifting of the corporate veil"*(Mukherjee, 2023). This proposal's reasoning stems from the idea that parent firms invest in subsidiaries and eventually benefit from the profits these subsidiaries make, even though they have limited accountability due to the stock they own in those subsidiaries.

Although the PPP can potentially address a wide range of environmental issues globally, it is not yet widely accepted as an accepted international standard. This lack of recognition results from how governments interpret and apply the PPP according to their internal legal frameworks. This intricacy results from the PPP's wide reach, including the preservation of the environment and public health and financial incentives. The PPP is more of a rule than a principle and has a normative quality (Fitzmaurice, 2013). In contrast to guidelines that direct decision-making when a product's production or consumption incurs costs for a third party, the PPP is intended to impose an immediate obligation on states to guarantee that the responsible party is responsible for paying for the cleanup or prevention of pollution in every instance of environmental harm. According to Sands and Peel (2012), there is still room for interpretation regarding the PPP, especially regarding the kind and scope of expenditures covered and the situations in which the principle might not be applicable (Sands & Peel, 2012).

Notwithstanding these obstacles, the PPP has gained widespread acceptance and is strongly associated with regulations controlling state and civil liability for environmental harm, authorized public subsidies, and recognition of industrialized nations' roles in sustainable development. This link is reflected in the Common But Differentiated Responsibilities (CBDR) idea, which has been incorporated into numerous environmental treaties over the past 30 years. The PPP's significance in global climate change negotiations is also highlighted in the essay, notably in light of loss and damage and the CBDR concept. According to the United Nations Framework Convention on Climate Change (UNFCCC), loss and damage include slow-onset processes and sudden-onset disasters caused by climate change. In discussions concerning who bears the brunt of the negative consequences of climate change, how to pay for projected and actual damages, and how to seek just compensation, the PPP is crucial.

While the PPP is important for combating environmental degradation through international collaboration, the effectiveness of individual countries—where mechanisms like taxation, levies, and liability laws can be implemented—often outweighs the significance of the PPP. The essay emphasizes how the Paris Agreement, where wealthy countries' greenhouse gas emissions have a major impact on global emissions, indirectly incorporates the PPP. But under the PPP model, all signatories to the Paris Agreement—developing nations included—are seen as polluters. As states acknowledge their commitments to addressing climate change and offer strategies to cut emissions, it highlights the relevance of indirect PPP mechanisms in the Paris Agreement, including nationally defined contributions, climate finance obligations, and emission trading schemes. According to the chapter, it is gravely unfair to society for parent firms to absolve themselves of liability for the transgressions done by their subsidiaries. It highlights the need to apply the piercing of the corporate veil theory to prevent parent businesses from being legally insulated from the repercussions of the activities of their subsidiaries. A precedent is set by the Supreme Court's 2010 ruling in the case of *Iridium India Telecom Ltd. v. Motorola Inc.* The court decided that attribution, not vicarious liability, should be used to establish liability without a legislative or common law exception. This emphasizes how crucial it is to examine how conglomerates use the ideas of *"limited liability"* and *"separate legal entities"* to avoid being held legally responsible.

CONCLUSION

Inconsistent behaviors are exposed by the National Green Tribunal's (NGT) adoption of the Polluter Pays Principle (PPP). Notably, the NGT frequently interprets *"pollution in fact"* rather than strictly following environmental statutes' definition of "*pollution in law*." In several instances, compensation decisions under PPP are made without glaring contamination proof. Another controversial issue is figuring out just how much pay is appropriate. Analyzing NGT rulings shows a shift in damage assessment methodology from speculative to expert committees for a more precise estimate of losses and repair expenses. In addition, the NGT has occasionally taken a different approach by directing the polluter to take particular steps instead of receiving monetary compensation. Additionally, there is proof that the NGT supports cost internalization through spot fines, levies, and local authorities creating suitable legislative frameworks. In one instance, the NGT even provided a 10% home/property tax relief to encourage adherence to pollution standards. This diverse approach highlights how the NGT is adapting its PPP application techniques.

By incorporating specialists in the process and moving toward a more uniform methodology for assessing compensation, the National Green Tribunal (NGT) has achieved progress. This action is consistent with the NGT's original goal of integrating expert information into settling environmental disputes. However, there is a need to use the panel of judges' knowledge to increase effectiveness. It's also critical to assess whether the compensation granted to pollution victims benefits them. The National Green Tribunal (Practice and Procedure) Rules, 2011, require, in Rule 35(4), establishing a distinct account to receive and disburse funds associated with NGT orders. Concerns over the effectiveness of the Polluter Pays Principle (PPP) in environmental restoration have been raised by the unfortunate discovery that the Fund Manager hasn't kept a separate account for contributions to the Environment Relief Fund.

India appears to be applying the Polluter Pays Principle (PPP) widely and for various reasons. Nevertheless, there are still questions about its beneficial effects on damage repair and environmental restoration for people and their property. The actual results of PPP seem to differ significantly from its promised benefits. The chapter review emphasizes how the Polluter Pays Principle has only been partially handled by Indian courts, with the criminal responsibility portion being mainly unexplored. Remarkably, there is a shortage of contemporary scholarly works or studies on the Polluter Pays Principle in the second decade of the twenty-first century. In particular, Shibani Ghosh's working chapter addresses problems with the Pollution Control Board and is a noteworthy critique of how the Indian system is now operating (Ghosh, 2015). Recent study publications lack fresh advances or solutions, even after all this time. Although there have been publications written about the subject, they usually restate the findings of previous studies, which indicates that the conversation about the Polluter Pays Principle has not progressed. The Polluter Pays Principle (PPP) has not been widely applied, and its ability to bring about the necessary change is debatable. Criminal culpability is thought to be required to increase its impact, particularly for deterrence. Given the Pollution

Control Board's heavy workload, simplifying the current processes for filing and managing pollution cases is necessary.

The Pollution Control Board has to deal with issues like a backlog of cases and a lack of members. Expanding the membership to enable a more customized reaction to every situation is advised. In addition, the board's duty of providing consent might be streamlined by giving it the authority to issue administrative fines. Victims should be able to contest the board's findings and bring criminal complaints against perpetrators to guarantee justice. This is following 1973's Code of Criminal Procedure, Section 200. The Polluter Pays Principle must be implemented transparently since businesses frequently try to hide the full scope of their pollution, which results in imprecise damage estimates and inadequate societal cost coverage. Although it is acknowledged that the Polluter Pays Principle has to be improved, particularly in the areas listed, actual changes have not yet been noticed. Future research on these topics should analyze them in great detail, acknowledging the Polluter Pays Principle's crucial role in society.

REFERENCES

Ahmad, F. (2001). Origin and Growth of Environmental Law in India. *Journal of the Indian Law Institute, 43*(3), 358–387. https://www.jstor.org/stable/43951782

Ahmad, M. (2022). Ship recycling in India- environmental stock taking. *Indiana Law Review, 6*(3), 465–478. doi:10.1080/24730580.2022.2082100

Ambec, S., & Ehlers, L. (2016). Regulation Via the Polluter-Pays Principle. *Economic Journal (London), 126*(593), 884–906. https://www.jstor.org/stable/24738178. doi:10.1111/ecoj.12184

BBC. (2021, November 1). COP26: India PM Narendra Modi pledges net zero by 2070. *BBC News.* https://www.bbc.com/news/world-asia-india-59125143

Bhuvaneshwari, S., Hettiarachchi, H., & Meegoda, J. N. (2019). Crop Residue Burning in India: Policy Challenges and Potential Solutions. *International Journal of Environmental Research and Public Health, 16*(5), 832. doi:10.3390/ijerph16050832 PMID:30866483

Boyd, J., & Ingberman, D. E. (1996). The "Polluter Pays Principle": Should Liability be Extended When the Polluter Cannot Pay? *The Geneva Papers on Risk and Insurance. Issues and Practice, 21*(79), 182–203. https://www.jstor.org/stable/41954091. doi:10.1057/gpp.1996.13

Brooks, T. (2013). The Real Challenge of Climate Change. *PS, Political Science & Politics*, *46*(1), 34–36. https://www.jstor.org/stable/43284277. doi:10.1017/S1049096512001412

Centre for Science and Environment. (2018). *Review of NGT decisions evoking the Polluter Pays Principle* (GREEN TRIBUNAL, GREEN APPROACH, pp. 8–17) [Policy Report]. Centre for Science and Environment. https://www.jstor.org/stable/resrep38095.4

Chakravarty, B. K. (2006). Environmentalism: Indian Constitution and Judiciary. *Journal of the Indian Law Institute*, *48*(1), 99–105. https://www.jstor.org/stable/43952020

Chandani, A. (2007). Distributive Justice and Sustainability as a Viable Foundation for the Future Climate Regime. *Carbon & Climate Law Review, 1*(2), 152–163. https://www.jstor.org/stable/24323514

Corvino, F. (2023). The forward-looking polluter pays principle for a just climate transition. *Critical Review of International Social and Political Philosophy*, *0*(0), 1–28. doi:10.1080/13698230.2023.2243729

de Sadeleer, N. (2020). The Polluter-Pays Principle. In N. de Sadeleer (Ed.), Environmental Principles: From Political Slogans to Legal Rules (p. 0). Oxford University Press. doi:10.4324/9780367816681-78

Environment Protection Act, ACT NO. 29 OF 1986. (1986).

Faure, M., & Grimeaud, D. (2004). *Financial assurance issues of environmental liability*. Hormone and Metabolic Research - HORMONE METAB RES.

Fitzmaurice, M. (2013). International Environmental Law. By ULRICH BEYERLIN and THILO MARAUHN. *Journal of Environmental Law*, *25*(1), 159–161. doi:10.1093/jel/eqs032

Ghosh, S. (2015). Reforming the Liability Regime for Air Pollution in India. *Environmental Law and Practice Review, 4.*

Gill, G. N. (2019). Precautionary principle, its interpretation and application by the Indian judiciary: 'When I use a word it means just what I choose it to mean-neither more nor less' Humpty Dumpty. *Environmental Law Review*, *21*(4), 292–308. doi:10.1177/1461452919890283

Kumar, K., & Prakash, A. (2019). Examination of sustainability reporting practices in Indian banking sector. *Asian Journal of Sustainability and Social Responsibility*, *4*(1), 2. doi:10.1186/s41180-018-0022-2

Mukherjee, S. (2023). How Much Should the Polluter Pay? Indian Courts and the Valuation of Environmental Damage. *Journal of Environmental Law*, *35*(3), 331–351. doi:10.1093/jel/eqad021

Prabhu, N. (2022, December 12). Criminal Liability of Corporations in India—An Environmental Perspective. *Georgetown Public Policy Review*. https://gppreview.com/2022/12/12/criminal-liability-of-corporations-in-india-an-environmental-perspective/

Rengarajan, S., Palaniyappan, D., Ramachandran, P., & Ramachandran, R. (2018). National Green Tribunal of India—An observation from environmental judgements. *Environmental Science and Pollution Research International*, *25*(12), 11313–11318. doi:10.1007/s11356-018-1763-2 PMID:29572740

Sands, P., & Peel, J. (2012). *Principles of International Environmental Law* (3rd ed.). Cambridge University Press., doi:10.1017/CBO9781139019842

Shastri, S. C. (2000). "The Polluter Pays Principle" and the Supreme Court of India. *Journal of the Indian Law Institute*, *42*(1), 108–116. https://www.jstor.org/stable/43951740

Smith, G. P. (1972). Stockholm. Summer of '72: An Affair To Remember? *American Bar Association Journal. American Bar Association*, *58*(11), 1194–1197. https://www.jstor.org/stable/25726071

Sudarshan, A. (2023). Monitoring Industrial Pollution in India. In T. Madon, A. J. Gadgil, R. Anderson, L. Casaburi, K. Lee, & A. Rezaee (Eds.), Introduction to Development Engineering: A Framework with Applications from the Field (pp. 161–182). Springer International Publishing. doi:10.1007/978-3-030-86065-3_7

Tandon, U. (2020). *Green Justice and the Application of Polluter- Pays Principle: A Study of India's National Green Tribunal* (SSRN Scholarly Paper 3690212). https://papers.ssrn.com/abstract=3690212

Turaga, R. M. R., & Sugathan, A. (2020). Environmental Regulations in India. In Oxford Research Encyclopedia of Environmental Science. doi:10.1093/acrefore/9780199389414.013.417

ADDITIONAL READINGS

Boon, F. K. (1992). The Rio Declaration and Its Influence on International Environmental Law. *Singapore Journal of Legal Studies*, 347–364. https://www.jstor.org/stable/24866183

Brooks, T. (2013). The Real Challenge of Climate Change. *PS, Political Science & Politics*, *46*(1), 34–36. https://www.jstor.org/stable/43284277. doi:10.1017/S1049096512001412

Chandani, A. (2007). Distributive Justice and Sustainability as a Viable Foundation for the Future Climate Regime. *Carbon & Climate Law Review, 1*(2), 152–163. https://www.jstor.org/stable/24323514

Gill, G. N. (2010). A Green Tribunal for India. *Journal of Environmental Law*, *22*(3), 461–474. https://www.jstor.org/stable/44248749. doi:10.1093/jel/eqq014

Sawhney, A. (2003). Managing Pollution: PIL as Indirect Market-Based Tool. *Economic and Political Weekly*, *38*(1), 32–37. https://www.jstor.org/stable/4413042

Singh, C. P. (2010). The Precautionary Principle and Environment Protection. *Journal of the Indian Law Institute*, *52*(3/4), 467–483. https://www.jstor.org/stable/45148535

Stone, C. D. (2004). Common but Differentiated Responsibilities in International Law. *The American Journal of International Law*, *98*(2), 276–301. doi:10.2307/3176729

Subramanian, T. N., & Vakil, R. (2018). The Mechanisms of the National Green Tribunal. *National Law School of India Review, 30*(1), 74–85. https://www.jstor.org/stable/26743934

Walter, I., & Ugelow, J. L. (1979). Environmental Policies in Developing Countries. *Ambio, 8*(2/3), 102–109. https://www.jstor.org/stable/4312437

KEY TERMS AND DEFINITIONS

Corporate Criminal Liability: The concept of holding corporations accountable for crimes committed by individuals connected to the organization has gained importance in environmental law discussions.

Cost Internalization: A principle related to the PPP, where polluters are made to pay for the social costs of their actions, ensuring that the prices of goods reflect the societal costs associated with pollution.

Negative Externality: The harmful side effects or consequences of an activity that affect third parties who did not choose to be involved in that activity, often used to describe environmental harm caused by pollution.

NGT (National Green Tribunal): A specific body in India created by the National Green Tribunal Act of 2010 to address environmental issues, explicitly guided by the PPP in making orders, judgments, and awards.

OECD (Organisation for Economic Cooperation and Development): An international organization that implicitly introduced the PPP in 1972 and emphasized the need for polluters to cover expenses mandated by public authorities to maintain an environmentally acceptable state.

Polluter Pays Principle (PPP): This environmental policy holds those responsible for pollution accountable for all its social costs and responsibilities, ensuring that they bear the financial burden of their actions.

UNFCCC (United Nations Framework Convention on Climate Change): An international treaty addressing climate change, and while it doesn't explicitly mention the PPP, it plays a role in forming global climate regimes.

Chapter 9
Mental Health, SDGs, and Spiritual Care:
A Call for Legal Advocacy

Piyush Pranjal
https://orcid.org/0000-0002-5142-3850
O.P. Jindal Global University, India

Vani Singhal
O.P. Jindal Global University, India

Soumya Sarkar
https://orcid.org/0000-0003-2290-6981
Indian Institute of Management, Ranchi, India

Tanvi Aggarwal
O.P. Jindal Global University, India

ABSTRACT

Mental health illnesses have assumed pandemic proportions, especially post-COVID, adversely impacting society and the global economy. The effect is more pronounced in India, ailing with inadequate mental healthcare infrastructure and management. The mental health illness burden is a drag on the achievement of SDGs as well. Spiritual care, religious-healing, and faith-healing have recently received greater emphasis in research and practice. Several practices within each are either proven support systems or cures. There is, however, a globally recognized downside that it is unregulated, which provides room for misuse and abuse, which are rampant. The current chapter demystifies the nexus between mental health, SDGs, and spiritual care, and necessitates a call for sagacious legal advocacy.

DOI: 10.4018/979-8-3693-1178-3.ch009

MENTAL HEALTH, SDGS, AND SPIRITUAL CARE: A CALL FOR LEGAL ADVOCACY

World Health Organization (WHO) states that nearly one out of every five of the World's children and teenagers has a mental illness and that mental and neurological disorders make up approximately 10% of the global burden of illnesses (Bhatia, 2021). The India numbers are also staggering. One out of every seven Indians has a mental disorder (Bhatia, 2021). Thus, it is crucial to highlight the widespread extent of mental issues pertinent in the World. However, to narrow the scope, the current chapter focuses on issues ailing mental healthcare in India. India is severely inflicted with mental health illnesses, which becomes even more problematic considering the gap in terms of medical professionals available to treat such illnesses. India has a gap of 83%, reflected in having even less than one medical health professional per 100,000 of the Indian population (Sagar & Singh, 2022). The social stigma attached to mental health issues in the country further hinders its diagnosis and treatment. Most people are unaware of the existence of the illness or are hesitant to accept that they or their loved ones may be suffering from mental health issues. According to a Lancet global report, COVID-19 brought these issues to the forefront with a stark increase of 35% in cases of depression and anxiety, thus makingmental health issues a pandemic in their own right (Santomauro et al., 2021). The impact of the mental health pandemic is not limited to the healthcare industry. It has a spillover effect across all sectors and industries. According to the FundaMentalSDG global initiative, poor mental health will result in global financial losses of $6 trillion by 2030 if the current burden continues (The Lancet Global Health, 2020; Votruba et al., 2016). Experts are of the view that given the current global outlook, only 'God'/'Godly' intervention can break the trajectory of the mental health illness burden, more so in India, where the gap between the mental health illness burden and the available infrastructure is immense.

The present chapter attempts to demystify these issues by focusing on the nexus between mental health illness burden, SDGs, and spiritual care–a potential light at the end of a dark tunnel. The chapter then explains the legal framework prevalent in India concerning mental health and calls for intense legal advocacy.

SDGs AND MENTAL HEALTH

Demystifying mental health issues is pivotal to furthering the United Nations Sustainable Development Goals (SDGs), both in direct and indirect forms, and sustainable development in general (WHO, 2019). Under the 3rd goal of the SDG that pertains to 'Good Health and Well Being,' the U.N. advocates for, among other things, reducing one-third of premature deaths from non-communicable illnesses through prevention and treatment and promotion of mental health and well-being (WHO, 2013a). Further, under the SDGs, the United Nations aims to strengthen the prevention and treatment of substance abuse, including narcotic drug abuse and harmful use of alcohol (WHO-GHO, 2023). The explicit focus that the U.N. has shed on the prevention and management of mental health makes it pertinent to demystify mental health issues and make treatment/management more accessible and efficient.

In 1978, the WHO defined health as an amalgamation of mental health and psychological well-being at the core, among other things (Bauer, 2014). Therefore, apart from including mental health as a separate target under the SDGs, the furtherance of health inevitably requires attention to treatment and management of mental health issues. It is considered that over 80% percent of the people suffering from mental health disorders live in lower and middle-income countries (Bhugra et al., 2022). Furthermore, owing to the social stigma attached to mental health issues in these countries and the lack of proper treatment, over 80% of people suffering from severe mental health issues in lower and middle-income countries do not receive any treatment (Bhugra et al., 2022). It also ties into other general parameters related to health, considering that according to the World Report on Disability, over 1 billion people experience disabling conditions worldwide, and 60% percent of the causes are strongly related to mental and neurological conditions and substance abuse (WHO, 2011b).

Furthermore, mental health conditions have not only become a grave cause of significant and long-lasting disability but also have a substantial impact on mortality even in high-income countries, with men suffering from mental health illness dying 20 years earlier and women dying 15 years earlier as compared to mentally healthier people (Lawrence et al., 2013). Mental and Psychological illnesses are the most significant cause of mortality, even more than cancer and cardiovascular illnesses combined, thus making it inevitable and pertinent to demystify mental health issues and ensure their effective management and treatment to further the SDGs above (Whiteford et al., 2013).

The mental health illness burden is also closely related to other SDGs concerning development and the economy. Mental health issues adversely affect the efficiency and productivity of a person who is a vital cog in ensuring the economic growth of a country. It is ratified by how the World Health Organization defines mental health – a state of well-being where individuals realize their potential, cope with everyday life challenges, work productively, and contribute to their community (WHO, 2022). Therefore, to accomplish the SDG goal of 'Decent work and Economic Growth,' it is imperative to ensure efficient treatment of mental health issues. According to estimates, the global cost of mental disorders was measured at $2.5 Trillion in the year 2010. More than half of the cost was borne by low and middle-income countries, thus making it even more critical for these countries to ensure effective management of mental health issues to ensure economic prosperity apart from the social welfare of its citizens (Marquez & Saxena, 2016). Thus, to counter the enormous economic burden that mental health issues pose and can potentially pose to a country's economy, it is essential to further its management and prevention under the U.N. goal of 'Decent Work and Economic Growth.'

The current outlook on the management and treatment of mental health issues is dominated by the rapid westernization that is inundating the country, eventually leading to excessive use of pharmaceuticals, which interacts counter to the SDGs in general and the goals of 'Responsible Consumption and Production' and 'Life on Land.' Under these SDGs, the United Nations pledges to undertake efficient management of natural resources, reducing ecological footprint by changing how we produce and consume goods and resources (Clemente-Suárez et al., 2022). This is so because, with the manufacturing of such medicines, it is inevitable to prevent their emission into the natural environment during production, usage, and disposal, endangering the natural environment and its constituents exposed to such chemicals for extended periods (Boxall, 2004).

Pharmaceuticals are engineered to have a specific mode of action. Even at low levels in water bodies, their existence can negatively impact water organisms, considering that they are exposed to such chemicals for the entirety of their lives (Sehonova et al., 2018).Since the present treatment/management of mental health illnesses involves prescribing medicines/drugs to a majority of patients, it leads to excessive use of resources coupled with toxic waste both in the form of plastic packaging used for medicines and the excessively harmful waste that is generated in the process of manufacturing these medicines. The lack of patience in both the patients and the doctors often leads to the over-prescribing of medicines, further reversing the achievement of the goal of responsible consumption and production. The lack of therapy options further exacerbates these issues (Gupta & Sagar, 2022). Therefore, it is crucial to not only focus on the management and treatment of such mental health issues but also on the practical and sustainable ways of management that minimize the adverse effects of such treatments on the environment and its resources.

MENTAL HEALTHCARE MANAGEMENT IN INDIA: INADEQUACIES

Two significant issues plague mental healthcare management in India – a lack of adequate infrastructure and dependency on spiritual, religious, and faith healers, which are unregulated and often misused.

Lack of Adequate Infrastructure

The Indian medical infrastructure, although increased multifold since the independence of the country, has not been able to match the demands of the country considering the ever-increasing population and the widespread mental health illnesses that plague the country. Access to healthcare facilities in India is urban-biased (Barik & Thorat, 2015). This disparity further widens based on socio-economic differences, especially concerning significant illnesses like hypertension (Barik & Thorat, 2015). So, the people living in rural areas, who are already the more impacted section of the population, are further put in a more vulnerable position by being kept outside proper medical infrastructure. The public health systems responsible for ensuring proper access to medical facilities have been unable to serve the masses adequately, especially those in society who cannot afford the private sector (Barik & Thorat, 2015). This inadequacy has resulted in a sizeable proportion of the Indian population being left untreated due to the unavailability of diagnostic facilities in their vicinity.

According to the World Mental Health Atlas (2020), there are only 0.3 Psychiatrists per 100,000 of the Indian population. The numbers are even lower for Psychologists and Psychiatric Social Workers. The National Health Mission (NHM) is the Government of India's flagship health and family welfare mission. NHM's budget allocation for the financial year 2023-24 has increased by 8% year-on-year to INR 35,947 cr. However, its distribution to various programs within the mission has not been favorable for non-communicable diseases of which mental health illnesses are a part. It was a meager 4% in the financial year 2022-2023.

Owing to the above factors, healthcare infrastructure, and accessibility are still not widely available in India, driving people toward other forms of treatment.

Unregulated Faith-Healing

The second reason deals with the trust and comfort a large population of Indians have in spiritual, faith, and religious leaders and healers for treating various health issues. This segment, however, remains unregulated. Three sub-arguments consolidate this claim: First, the lack of geographical accessibility to medical facilities and trained medical professionals for effective treatment push people toward alternatives (Sagar & Singh, 2022). Second, the ill-informed and rudimentary understanding of mental health issues amplifies the burden of suffering of the patient. Limited information coupled with social stigma has a detrimental impact on the social reputation of the patient, along with doubts over their sanity (Grover et al., 2020). Due to these two reasons, many Indians hesitate to seek professional help. Third, some spiritual, faith, and religious healers provide a comforting escape to the people by transferring the burden of responsibility of having illness to destiny and the wrath of supernatural or divine powers. Often, this 'escapism' creates a sense of false security for the patient, making these healers an easily approachable platform and opening up opportunities for them to exploit patient vulnerabilities.

SPIRITUAL CARE AND HEALING: THE INDIC WAY

Arthur Kleinman, an American Psychiatrist turned Anthropologist, went about questioning or instead restructuring the methodology of treating mental health issues, especially outside the Western World. His research delved into the understanding of 'what matters' regarding moving away from the Western medical view of clinical reality (Kleinman, 1986, 2007).His research was primarily based in China. He hypothesized the amalgamation of what is intellectually or theoretically rigorous and practically relevant, considering that healthcare transactions have various subjective actors affecting the situation, especially ethnographic considerations (Sansom, 1982). He suggested developing medical infrastructure considering three significant parameters – the professional, folk, and popular sectors (Kleinman, 1980).

Although quite relevant for India, the infrastructure, as argued, requires the support of additional sectors (akin to the folk and famous), considering the culture and beliefs prevalent in India along with its pluralistic nature. This additional sector can then act as the necessary support system in managing mental health issues in India, especially considering the country's size, diversity, and lack of adequate infrastructure. Such a support system that subjectivizes the treatment or even the causation comprises, among other things – customs, religion, rituals, symbols, attitudes, knowledge, techniques, and beliefs (Biswal et al., 2017). This additional sector can be called the Classical Sector (Biswal et al., 2017). It is highly subjective and hugely dependent on people's spiritual inclinations, especially in India. This diversity is its biggest strength. It can not only guide the mode of treatment that people prefer and opt for but will also help define the causation of mental health issues subjectively for people. It is for this reason that spiritual care becomes the critical cog in dealing with mental health issues in a diverse country like India.

Spiritual Beginnings

Vedas, four in number and originating in Indian culture and society, are considered pioneers of science and spirituality in the World and the initial 'rulebooks' that guided humankind (Staal, 2008). The Vedas reached the heights of knowledge as Vedanta/Upanishadic teachings. These teachings then gave birth to many complex belief systems, thus forming the cultural backbone of India (Staal, 2008). Thus, looking at the larger picture, barring the nuanced differences, Vedas guided and continue to guide (knowingly or unknowingly) the multiplicity of religions and faiths in present-day India and beyond – making it the way of life. Extending this understanding to mental healthcare and management by including the Classical Sector leads to meaningful learning and can potentially lessen mental health agony. That is – spirituality, and its associated practices can help a person find the true meaning and purpose of life and an associated way of leading it; if a person lives accordingly, then she/he/they have the potential to attain their true self, free of any physical and mental burden/bondage.

To understand the complex human life, Indian scriptures have extensively explored the nexus between mind, body, and consciousness (Rao & Paranjpe, 2016). The body is the physical embodiment; consciousness is the spirit or the subjective self, whereas the brain, which is also a physical embodiment, links the two polar selves of the human ((Rao & Paranjpe, 2016). The transcendental nexus is the connection between the brain and consciousness and helps regulate the meaning of life for a person and the eventual goals and purpose that one aspires to achieve. Whereas the transactional self, which revolves around the nexus of the brain and body, regulates the Karma or the actions of the person during the lifetime to ensure that they are in congruence with the ideologies and beliefs of the person (Rao, 2011). This amalgamation of objectivity and subjectivity is the essence of spirituality, and it has the potential to further the treatment of mental illnesses.

Understanding the two nexus—one which regulates and motivates a person to find a true purpose in life and find one's true self, and the other which regulates the deeds of life- is the key to unlocking solutions for mental health issues. The need to find the meaning of life and its purpose while reaching higher knowledge motivates a person to meditate and focus on the eventual purpose of life rather than getting stuck in the materiality of the World and the sorrows or pain attached to the journey of life. It steers a person to follow good Karma and lead an upright life. Thereby, even after having problems or mental health issues, a person is motivated to believe in eternal knowledge and pursue it. Thus, the nexus of the mind, body, and consciousness is a crucial way to manage mental health better. Spiritual healers can play a crucial role in making people aware of this nexus and guiding them to find the purpose of life.

Folk Rituals and Healing

The non-allopathic forms of medicine can be categorized based on various dimensions. However, one of the most elaborate categorizations leads to two heads – the popular and traditional sectors, subdivided into the religious, folk, and classical sectors. All these sectors have held predominance in India for a very long time. The Indian way of life differs significantly from its Western counterpart. Social ties strongly dominate the way of life in India; hence, the popular sector, dominated by non-professional people to whom a person generally appeals for help owing to emotional connections, becomes essential (Biswal et al., 2017). Family members, colleagues, communities, and the larger society form part of this sector. As a result, not only does the professional sector act as a form of treatment by 'talking it out' to your friends and family, but the people also believe in discussing the matter and seeking solutions from respectable members of the respective communities.

Moreover, people in distress tend to follow beliefs and practices often prevalent in their particular communities, religions, and families before seeking professional help. Also importantly, the popular sector in the country plays a determining role in understanding the causation of mental illnesses, further encouraging the non-traditional methods of treatment, particularly the spiritual, religious, and folk sectors. The popular sector also becomes pertinent as this is the only sector people return to after getting help from other sources. After discussing their treatment with other sources, patients generally tend to consider the opinions of family and friends. The success or failure of every other sector is discussed within the comfort of the Classical Sector, which also leads to the adaptation of other sectors if required (Biswal et al., 2017).

In India, folk and religious-healing is the predominant mode of treatment. According to research, 75% percent of the patients take recourse to folk or religious-healing before resorting to any psychiatric services (Kar, 2008). Places of worship have a long history of trust among people. Most religious and folk-healing practices happen in such places. Religious-healing is based on prayer, meditation, and religious rituals. Prayers in such institutions happen alongside religious rituals like fasting and chanting (Ellison, 1991; Padmavati et al., 2005). According to research, 46% of people believe prayer is one of the only ways to tackle mental health issues (Padmavati et al., 2005). Prayers can act as a source of meaning to life and provide purpose to it. While acting as an effective coping strategy, it has been demonstrated to positively impact people's mental health (Dein, 2020).

Additionally, folk healers are present in communities where certain people are renowned for healing mental illnesses. The nomenclatures are based on their training, functioning, and ceremonies, generally practiced by the same family over generations. They pay attention to physical expressions of illnesses like hands, numerology, and positions of stars and the moon (Biswal et al., 2017). It is a very approachable treatment medium, with research indicating that around 40% of people in India consult them before approaching medical forms of treatment (Campion & Bhugra, 1998; Mukherjee, 2019).

Religious or folk healing also includes practicing rituals, and according to studies, practicing such rituals can reduce anxiety and uncertainty in life, thus providing meaning to life (Hinde & Hinde, 2009). It allows a person to put the uncertainties of life beyond their power, thus allowing and motivating them to lead a life while focusing on the present and not fearing the future or any uncertainty related to such future. Such rituals help to restore social and psychic equilibrium, thus aiding treatment (Turner, 1975). One such ritual practiced in various religions throughout the country is the ritual of confessions (Pennebaker, 2012). It not only helps a person to free oneself of any burden of thought or emotions that they are carrying but also motivates them in the future to lead an upright life and not cause harm to others, thus providing peace to them in the present moment while guiding them about their life ahead.

Often, people also seek help from healers beyond their religion (Campion & Bhugra, 1997). The religion of the healers plays little to no role in people deciding to approach a particular healer. It depends on the faith and acclaim that a particular healer or the place of worship has gained in terms of healing patients with mental health issues rather than the level of education or religion of the healer.

Ayurveda and Yoga: Not Just Buzzwords!

Ayurveda has studied and systematically classified the causation of mental health issues. It attributed the cause to internal (constitutional and psychological) and external (environmental, divine, or demonic) factors (Bagadia et al., 1979). It draws from classical texts such as the Charaka Samhita and Sushruta Samhita. Ayurveda explains that the balance of the three body humor- wind, bile, and phlegm (Vata, Pitta, and Kapha) and the three psychic factors- Sattva, Rajas, and Tamas, keeps a body healthy. It is also essential to balance the 'Panch Bhutas'/five basic elements- Water, Fire, Air, Earth, and the Sky (Suchitra et al., 2010; Wig, 1989). Thereby, Ayurveda explains mental health illnesses as an imbalance of the factors above. The nuanced causative factors of mental health illnesses known as 'Unmada' in Ayurveda are sourced from the Charaka Samhita. These are 1) diet; 2) faulty bodily activity, which encompasses inappropriate thinking or understanding leading to inappropriate action, unfavorable social, personal, or environmental conditions; 3) disrespect to God, elders, and teachers; and 4) mental shock due to emotions such as excessive anguish, pain, joy or anger (Khare & Savanur, 2019; Suchitra et al., 2010). Ayurveda provides a rulebook for leading a healthy life – mentally and physically while trying to control one's emotions regarding oneself and others. All these factors play a crucial role in helping an individual to lead a peaceful and more controlled life wherein, even in moments of despair, the person has a better understanding and control of emotions. The treatment of mental health issues in Ayurveda, among other things, is through a method known as 'Satvavajaya,' which deals with Psychotherapy (Belaguli & Savitha, 2019; Murthy & Singh, 1987). It encompasses spiritual knowledge and moral boosting to cure various illnesses.

Yoga, one of the seven forms of medicine recognized by the Government of India under the AYUSH Ministry, is yet another important method to treat mental health issues. Yoga is a Sanskrit term that means the union of a person's consciousness with the Universal one and is yet another critical methodology for treating mental health issues (Raina & Singh, 2018). It focuses primarily on Pranayama (breathing practices), Dhyana (mediation), and Asanas (body postures), all of which help a person to be calmer, especially helping with neurotic and psychosomatic illnesses (Rout et al., 2013). It is a way of life that focuses on self-development and self-realization; hence, it could be considered a good measure for primary intervention and later for long-term slow and permanent healing procedures (Rout et al., 2013). Regular yoga practice gives rise to specific reactions within the person's body, facilitating quantitative and qualitative improvements in awareness, thus reducing psychological stress and improving health. These forms of treatment gain importance, considering that most people in the country face stress regarding finances, education, employment, and life in general (Padmavati et al., 2005).

MENTAL HEALTH AND LAW

Owing to the reasons outlined in the chapter so far and the vulnerability of the people suffering from such issues and social stigma, some fake healers often misuse people's trust for material benefits (Hardiman, 2013; Macdonald, 2015). There have been several instances of fake healers ruining the lives of people and destroying trust in spiritual care and faith-based healing in India and beyond and across a diversity of religious affiliations (Jain, 2021; Schoonover et al., 2014). It is pertinent to ensure that the vulnerability of people while approaching healers is not misused and that this realm of healthcare is also regulated by law because, in India, religious and spiritual methods of treatment can act as efficient support systems for mental health issues (Avasthi et al., 2013; Kishan, 2020). Hence, it is essential to explore the legal framework available in the country and raise awareness among the Indian populace. It is also crucial to keep advocating for improvements and upgrades in the legal framework to stay abreast with social and cultural realities.

India has had a long journey with laws on mental health (Firdosi & Ahmad, 2016).India initially dealt with people having mental health issues as Lunatics under the India Lunacy Act 1912, wherein Section 3(5) of the said act defined a lunatic as 'an idiot or a person of unsound mind.' The said act worked on the premise that 'lunatics' are dangerous to society, and hence, the main aim of the act was to protect society from such 'lunatic people.'

From the said act, India transitioned into the Mental Health Act of 1987, which, as the Supreme Court of India observed, was a transformative leap in the position of law from treating people with mental issues as lunatics and having no right to life and dignity to being termed as mentally ill persons under Section 2(l), wherein mentally ill persons are defined as "a person who needs treatment because of any mental disorder other than mental retardation." However, even the said act was highly restrictive in that it did not provide a rights-based framework for mental disability but was somewhat restricted to only establishing psychiatric hospitals and psychiatric nursing homes and administrative exigencies of such establishments.

Therefore, although the said act transitioned the law from the idea of protecting society against 'lunatics' to trying to provide them with healthcare, the said act lacked in providing adequate rights and respect to people suffering from mental health issues.

With the progression of time and the ratification of the Convention on the Rights of Persons with Disabilities in 2007, India enacted the Mental Healthcare Act 2017, which repealed the 1987 Act (Duffy & Kelly, 2020). The said act, as observed by the Supreme Court of India, provides a rights-based mental healthcare framework and has a truly transformative potential. In stark difference from the provisions of the 1985 Act, the provisions of the 2017 Act recognize the legal capacity of persons who have mental illness to make decisions and choices on treatment, admission, and personal assistance. Section 2(o) defines mental healthcare diagnosis, treatment, and rehabilitation. Section 4 of the Act states that every person with mental illness shall be 'deemed' to have the capacity to make decisions regarding their mental healthcare and treatment if they can understand the relevant information and the reasonably foreseeable consequence of their decision. Sub-section (3) of Section 4 states that merely because the person's decision is perceived as inappropriate or wrong by 'others,' it shall not mean that the person cannot make decisions. Acknowledging the ability of individuals with mental illness to make well-informed decisions is a crucial first step toward acknowledging their agency.

The act is a significant step towards normalizing the stigma associated with mental health (Duffy & Kelly, 2020); Section 19 (1) mandates not restricting people with mental illness to be segregated from society. It also provides for 11 necessary rights under Chapter 5 of the Act, namely the Right to access mental healthcare under Section 18, the Right to community living under Section 19, Right to protection from cruel, inhuman and degrading treatment, Right to equality and non-discrimination under Section 21, Right to information under section 22, Right to confidentiality under Section 23, Restriction on release of information in respect of mental illness under Section 24, Right to access medical records under Section 25, Right to personal contacts and communication under section 26, Right to legal aid under section 27 and Right to make complaints about deficiencies in provision of services under section 28. These rights form a holistic step towards equal treatment of people under the law, as enshrined under Article 14 of the Indian Constitution (Duffy & Kelly, 2020).

The significant progress that India has witnessed in terms of mental health issues and disabilities in the Mental Healthcare Act, 2017, and the Rights of Persons with Disabilities Act, 2016, renders disability to be a social construct and not merely a medical construct affecting a person. These Acts do not define a mental impairment to constitute a disability solely. Instead, they define disability based on the interaction of the impairment with the barriers that hamper an individual's effective participation in society (Duffy & Kelly, 2020).

This is a highly positive outlook as it now looks upon mental illnesses from the viewpoint of social construct. The hindrance to such affected people is because of the illness in participating in the society, instead of mere theoretical understanding of biology, which eventually helps the state to shift their resources from handling a 'lunatic' as an offender having the potential to cause harm to the society to helping them participate in the community and treating the hindrance in the process of community living (Duffy & Kelly, 2020).

The Supreme Court of India in Ravinder Kumar Dhariwal and Ors v The Union of India discussed the impact of mental disability on termination of service and disciplinary inquiry against a person dealing with disability (Jain & Jain, 2023). The Court recognized disability as a personalized concept devoid of a single jacket formula to identify and solve. It also observed how stigmatization against a person facing any disability by either society or law further deepens the feeling of being disabled, causing agony. The Court thus observed disability to be a social construct dependent on the interplay between mental impairment and barriers such as social, economic, and historical, among other factors; the one-size-fits-all approach can never be used to identify the disability of a person. Disability is not universal but is an individualistic conception based on the impairment a person has and the barriers they face.........what is required is a nuanced and individualized approach to mental disabilities-related discrimination claims, which requires understanding the nature of the disadvantage that such persons suffer.

The Court thus highlighted the individualistic nature of a disability, devoid of any blanket approach toward it (Jain & Jain, 2023). Also, it accentuated the need to consider the individual differences and capabilities of a person who has any mental disability.

THE ROAD AHEAD: INTEGRATING SPIRITUALITY AND TECHNOLOGY

The irony of the situation in India is that despite having a rich spiritual heritage, a considerable chunk of the population is distressed with mental health issues, and only a tiny percentage of people have the means or knowledge to receive even the most basic treatment. Many of them become straight targets of ridicule, stigma, and discrimination, which prevent others from talking about it even if they might be going through similar circumstances (Loganathan & Murthy, 2008; Mathias et al., 2015). There is no simple solution in sight. There is a requirement for technical assistance and considerable financial support through a combined effort of both the private and public sectors. In many countries, mental health advocacy groups have witnessed great success rates and have invited audiences from all classes and groups of the population (Hann et al., 2015). Such groups not only allow a safe space for the people but encourage everyone to come out, own up to who they are, and establish a sense of belongingness. These mental health advocacy groups are still in infancy in India (Kaur et al., 2021). This basic solution has remarkable potential for quick development and spread due to it being related to meager costs and high success rates. Such low-cost solutions become even more critical considering that good healthcare is essentially a luxury in India, more so in the case of mental health. Only recently has India witnessed a rise in social support and solidarity toward mental health issues (Mahajan et al., 2019).

With increasing attention, there have been several upcoming innovative solutions categorized as (a) non-specialist mental health programs, (b) community-based mental health programs, (c) quality improvement mental health programs, (d) mobile-technology mental health programs, (e) tele-mental health programs (Pandya et al., 2020). Mental health advocacy is a combined and concerted effort and cannot be accomplished through individual efforts of a single community or group. It calls for efforts from various stakeholders, including patients' families, non-governmental organizations, health workers, mental health fosterers, bureaucratic decision-makers, policymakers, and planners. In India, the Ministry of Health& Family Welfare plays a significant role as an information disburser and the central authority for the smooth functioning of mental health advocacy groups and to prevent malpractices and ill-doings.

Tele-psychiatry is a possible solution for tackling mental health issues on a large scale basis. In India, it was legalized and entered the bigger picture when the Ministry of Health and Family Welfare released the 'Tele-medicine Practice Guidelines' along with NITI Aayog (Venkatesh et al., 2022). The changes were included as an amendment to the Indian Medical Council (Professional Conduct, Etiquette and Ethics) Regulations, 2002. A medical practitioner has to adhere to severe laws and provisions under various Indian medical acts, along with the Information Technology Acts, to practice Tele-psychiatry in India. Such an innovative practice can be advantageous as it is empowering in the manner that it would allow for early illness detection and consultation. It would help prevent high-grade illnesses and serve as a fitting addition to primitive healthcare services with limited access and scope (Venkatesh et al., 2022). It can be as helpful as face-to-face psychotherapy with significantly lower costs and enhanced access for distressed individuals residing in remote, rural, or low-income suburbs and regions.

However, even with an increase in internet consumption year after year, the National Digital Literacy Mission estimated that digital literacy did not grow at the paramount level (Radovanović et al., 2020). Only about 22% of mobile phone users utilize the internet and its services on their smartphones (Radovanović et al., 2020). Tele-psychiatry, even at its maximum capacity, is the least available where required, leaving it infeasible to a great extent. Moreover, the Indian Medical Council Regulations, 2002 expressly prohibit medical practitioners and their institutions from soliciting patients directly or indirectly through advertisement or publicity, including advertising or selling internet and social media services (Raveesh & Munoli, 2020). Such control prevents a large population from knowing telepsychiatry and how to avail of it. Additionally, privacy and identity theft became noteworthy issues that prevent telepsychiatry from becoming more popular (Raveesh & Munoli, 2020).

Another untapped yet exponential potential is the possibilities and avenues digital tools and technology opened up in today's times, especially those that could cater to the youth (Lehtimaki et al., 2021). To foster early detection and analyze vital symptoms of mental health illness, efficient methods for detection and early diagnosis are incredibly critical. It has to be realized that digital spaces can provide the much-needed first entry point for clinical services, education, and information provision. It can be a step forward toward engaging with and scrutinizing the personal, environmental, social, and physiological predictors of suicidal ideations to open the doors to more specific, personalized, and accurate risk assessment (Parikh et al., 2019).Not only is it limited to this, but it can also help monitor recovery, provide early warning signs of risk or relapse, and offer novel information on functional outcomes (Naslund et al., 2019). Technology and data open opportunities to monitor moods, conditions, reactions, and situations, after which it can determine and prompt corrective measures that need to be taken by an individual, those that can easily be inculcated in their lives through smartphones, laptops, or other devices (Gonsalves et al., 2019; 2021; Naslund et al., 2019).The emerging technology has the innate potential to detect emerging mental ill-health in youth through digital approaches that otherwise may not be detected by conventional services (Gonsalves et al., 2019; 2021; Naslund et al., 2019). However, at the same time, such screening and intervention must be linked with front-line clinical services and characterized by adequate sensitivity and specificity for accurately predicting clinical status and outcomes with minimal magnitude of error.

One of the simplest ways to monitor and treat mental health is the provision of a mobile application that can track one's regular moods and reactions and remind the individual to practice mindfulness, focus more on expressing gratitude, and learn to meditate, all of which have their base in the Indic way (Gonsalves et al., 2019; 2021). Not just general mental health care apps, but there exist disorder-specific apps that can help prevent an illness from developing into a major one at a very early stage (Gonsalves et al., 2019; 2021). The U.S. National Institutes of Health estimated in 2017 that nearly 325,000 health apps, of which approximately 7% were mental-health specific, were available across the most common app stores (Google Play and iOS), an increase of 25% year-on-year (Schueller et al., 2018).All these solutions seem simple and basic; however, one may only indulge in all these practices and habits if there is a constant reminder.

The COVID-19 pandemic took a heavy toll on collective human health, not just physical but also mental. It became difficult to think about anything beyond the pandemic, the magnitude of the illness, and how the infection was spreading from our nearest kin to the farthest possible region of the World. It was then, in 2020, that businesses and companies started turning to technology in a big way for solutions toward improving mental health. In June 2020, the first prescription video game was approved by the USFDA (Asar, 2020). It was designed for young patients to help them focus on multiple quests while playing a simple video game. Virtual Reality, a recent technological development, can be utilized for more than just entertainment purposes. It can be used to simulate popular environments and can be helpful for people, especially children with ADHD, who can practice participating in a simulated classroom (Asar, 2020). It also has the potential to treat anxiety, depression, and other mental illnesses by providing uplifting getaways from reality.

Integrating social work (supported by law), spiritual care, and technological advancements can address mental health issues. Such integration would allow new opportunities for clinical interventions for more efficient and effective mental health treatments, thus allowing for better and improved recovery. The latest enhancements in Neuroscience research, embedded in Indic Psychology, have opened up a new purview of unique opportunities to improve the quality of interventions for those going through mild and severe mental health issues. It can also allow for early detection of people exposed to risk for mental illnesses and can even identify individuals and situations that are irrepressible to mental illnesses and disorders. These public interventions may seem simple, but coupled with Indic spirituality, they can go a long way in exacerbating India's and the World's debilitating mental health illness burden and fostering the achievement of SDGs.

REFERENCES

Asar, A. (2020). Five Tech Innovations That Changed Mental Health in 2020. *Forbes*. https://www.forbes.com/sites/forbestechcouncil/2020/11/25/five-tech-innovations-that-changed-mental-health-in-2020/?sh=289c223b1e9c

Avasthi, A., Kate, N., & Grover, S. (2013). Indianization of psychiatry utilizing Indian mental concepts. *Indian Journal of Psychiatry, 55*(6, Suppl2), S136–S144. doi:10.4103/0019-5545.105508 PMID:23858244

Bagadia, V. N., Shah, L. P., Pradhan, P. V., & Gada, M. T. (1979). Treatment of mental disorders in India. *Progress in Neuro-Psychopharmacology, 3*(1-3), 109–118. doi:10.1016/0364-7722(79)90075-4 PMID:401334

Barik, D., & Thorat, A. (2015). Issues of unequal access to public health in India. *Frontiers in Public Health, 3*, 245. doi:10.3389/fpubh.2015.00245 PMID:26579507

Bauer, G. F., Hämmig, O., & Keyes, C. L. (2014). Mental health as a complete state: How the salutogenic perspective completes the picture. *Bridging occupational, organizational and public health: A transdisciplinary approach*, 179-192.

Belaguli, G., & Savitha, H. P. (2019). An empirical understanding on the concept of Sattvavajaya Chikitsa (Ayurveda Psychotherapy) and a mini-review of its research update. *Indian Journal of Health Sciences and Biomedical Research kleu, 12*(1), 15-20. doi:10.4103/kleuhsj.kleuhsj_175_18

Bhatia, A. (2021 October 8). *World Mental Health Day 2021: Things You Need To Know About The Day*. NDTV. https://swachhindia.ndtv.com/world-mental-health-day-2021-things-you-need-to-know-about-the-day-63554/

Bhugra, D., Moussaoui, D., & Craig, T. J. (Eds.). (2022). *Oxford Textbook of Social Psychiatry*. Oxford University Press. doi:10.1093/med/9780198861478.001.0001

Biswal, R., Subudhi, C., & Acharya, S. K. (2017). Healers and healing practices of mental illness in India: The role of proposed eclectic healing model. *Journal of Health Research and Reviews in Developing Countries, 4*(3), 89–95. doi:10.4103/jhrr.jhrr_64_17

Boxall, A. B. A. (2004). The environmental side effects of medication: How are human and veterinary medicines in soils and water bodies affecting human and environmental health? *EMBO Reports, 5*(12), 1110–1116. doi:10.1038/sj.embor.7400307 PMID:15577922

Campion, J., & Bhugra, D. (1997). Experiences of religious healing in psychiatric patients in South India. *Social Psychiatry and Psychiatric Epidemiology, 32*(4), 215–221. doi:10.1007/BF00788241 PMID:9184467

Campion, J., & Bhugra, D. (1998). Religious and indigenous treatment of mental illness in South India—A descriptive study. *Mental Health, Religion & Culture, 1*(1), 21–29. doi:10.1080/13674679808406494

Clemente-Suárez, V. J., Rodriguez-Besteiro, S., Cabello-Eras, J. J., Bustamante-Sanchez, A., Navarro-Jiménez, E., Donoso-Gonzalez, M., Beltrán-Velasco, A. I., & Tornero-Aguilera, J. F. (2022). Sustainable development goals in the COVID-19 pandemic: A narrative review. *Sustainability (Basel), 14*(13), 7726. doi:10.3390/su14137726

Dein, S. (2020). Religious healing and mental health. *Mental Health, Religion & Culture, 23*(8), 657–665. doi:10.1080/13674676.2020.1834220

Duffy, R. M., & Kelly, B. D. (2020). History of Mental Health Legislation in India. In India's Mental Healthcare Act, 2017: Building Laws, Protecting Rights (pp. 51–59). Springer Singapore. doi:10.1007/978-981-15-5009-6_4

Ellison, C. G. (1991). Religious involvement and subjective well-being. *Journal of Health and Social Behavior, 32*(1), 80–99. doi:10.2307/2136801 PMID:2007763

Firdosi, M. M., & Ahmad, Z. Z. (2016). Mental health law in India: Origins and proposed reforms. *BJPsych International, 13*(3), 65–67. doi:10.1192/S2056474000001264 PMID:29093906

Gonsalves, P. P., Hodgson, E. S., Bhat, B., Sharma, R., Jambhale, A., Michelson, D., & Patel, V. (2021). App-based guided problem-solving intervention for adolescent mental health: A pilot cohort study in Indian schools. *BMJ Mental Health, 24*(1), 11–18. doi:10.1136/ebmental-2020-300194 PMID:33208507

Gonsalves, P. P., Hodgson, E. S., Kumar, A., Aurora, T., Chandak, Y., Sharma, R., Michelson, D., & Patel, V. (2019). Design and development of the "POD adventures" smartphone game: A blended problem-solving intervention for adolescent mental health in India. *Frontiers in Public Health, 7*, 238. doi:10.3389/fpubh.2019.00238 PMID:31508404

Gupta, S., & Sagar, R. (2022). National Mental Health Policy, India (2014): Where Have We Reached? *Indian Journal of Psychological Medicine, 44*(5), 510–515. doi:10.1177/02537176211048335 PMID:36157023

Hann, K., Pearson, H., Campbell, D., Sesay, D., & Eaton, J. (2015). Factors for success in mental health advocacy. *Global Health Action*, *8*(1), 28791. doi:10.3402/gha.v8.28791 PMID:26689456

Hardiman, D. (2013). A subaltern Christianity: faith healing in Southern Gujarat. In *Medical Marginality in South Asia* (pp. 126–151). Routledge. doi:10.4324/9780203112823-13

Hinde, R. A., & Hinde, R. (2009). *Why Gods persist: A scientific approach to religion*. Routledge. doi:10.4324/9780203868751

Jain, A. (2021). Reconciling Illness through Devotion: The Medicalization of Modern Jain Faith Healing Practice through Bhaktāmara Stotra. Florida International University.

Jain, M., & Jain, S. (2023 June 5). A Tale of Empowerment of People with Mental Disability: Part 2. *Supreme Court Observer*. https://www.scobserver.in/journal/a-tale-of-empowerment-of-people-with-mental-disability-part-2/#:~:text=In%20Ravindra%20Kumar%20Dhariwal%20v,employment%2C%20was%20discrim-inatory%20or%20not

Kar, N. (2008). Resort to faith-healing practices in the pathway to care for mental illness: A study on psychiatric inpatients in Orissa. *Mental Health, Religion & Culture*, *11*(7), 720–740. doi:10.1080/13674670802018950

Kaur, A., Kallakuri, S., Kohrt, B. A., Heim, E., Gronholm, P. C., Thornicroft, G., & Maulik, P. K. (2021). Systematic review of interventions to reduce mental health stigma in India. *Asian Journal of Psychiatry*, *55*, 102466. doi:10.1016/j.ajp.2020.102466 PMID:33249319

Keyes, C. L. (2006). Mental health in adolescence: Is America's youth flourishing? *The American Journal of Orthopsychiatry*, *76*(3), 395–402. doi:10.1037/0002-9432.76.3.395 PMID:16981819

Khare, D., & Savanur, P. (2019). Understanding of Unmada in Ayurveda and Rational Application of Herbal Drugs-A Review. *Journal of Ayurveda and Integrated Medical Sciences*, *4*(04), 279–288. 10.21760/jaims.v4i04.676

Kishan, P. (2020). Yoga and Spirituality in Mental Health: Illness to Wellness. *Indian Journal of Psychological Medicine*, *42*(5), 411–420. doi:10.1177/0253717620946995 PMID:33414587

Kleinman, A. (1980). *Patients and healers in the context of culture: An exploration of the borderland between anthropology, medicine, and psychiatry* (Vol. 3). University of California Press. doi:10.1525/9780520340848

Kleinman, A. (1986). *The Social Origins of Distress and Disease: Depression, Neurasthenia, and Pain in Modern China*. Yale University Press.

Kleinman, A. (2007). *What Really Matters: Living A Moral Life Amidst Uncertainty and Danger*. Oxford University Press.

Lawrence, D., Hancock, K. J., & Kisely, S. (2013). *The gap in life expectancy from preventable physical illness in psychiatric patients in Western Australia: Retrospective analysis of population-based registers*. BMJ. doi:10.1136/bmj.f2539

Lehtimaki, S., Martic, J., Wahl, B., Foster, K. T., & Schwalbe, N. (2021). Evidence on digital mental health interventions for adolescents and young people: Systematic overview. *JMIR Mental Health*, *8*(4), e25847. doi:10.2196/25847 PMID:33913817

Loganathan, S., & Murthy, S. R. (2008). Experiences of stigma and discrimination endured by people suffering from schizophrenia. *Indian Journal of Psychiatry*, *50*(1), 39. doi:10.4103/0019-5545.39758 PMID:19771306

Macdonald, H. M. (2015). Skillful Revelation: Local Healers, Rationalists, and Their 'Trickery' in Chhattisgarh, Central India. *Medical Anthropology*, *34*(6), 485–500. doi:10.1080/01459740.2015.1040491 PMID:25897887

Mahajan, P. B., Rajendran, P. K., Sunderamurthy, B., Keshavan, S., & Bazroy, J. (2019). Analyzing Indian mental health systems: Reflecting, learning, and working towards a better future. *Journal of Current Research in Scientific Medicine*, *5*(1), 4–12. doi:10.4103/jcrsm.jcrsm_21_19-

Marquez, P. V., & Saxena, S. (2016, July). Making mental health a global priority. In *Cerebrum: The Dana forum on brain science* (Vol. 2016). Dana Foundation.

Mathias, K., Kermode, M., Sebastian, M. S., Koschorke, M., & Goicolea, I. (2015). Under the banyan tree-exclusion and inclusion of people with mental disorders in rural North India. *BMC Public Health*, *15*(1), 1–11. doi:10.1186/s12889-015-1778-2 PMID:25928375

Mukherjee, P. K. (2019). *Quality control and evaluation of herbal drugs: Evaluating natural products and traditional medicine*. Elsevier.

Murthy, A. R. V., & Singh, R. H. (1987). The concept of psychotherapy in Ayurveda with special reference to satvavajaya. *Ancient Science of Life*, *6*(4), 255. PMID:22557578

Naslund, J. A., Gonsalves, P. P., Gruebner, O., Pendse, S. R., Smith, S. L., Sharma, A., & Raviola, G. (2019). Digital innovations for global mental health: Opportunities for data science, task sharing, and early intervention. *Current Treatment Options in Psychiatry*, *6*(4), 337–351. doi:10.1007/s40501-019-00186-8 PMID:32457823

Padmavati, R., Thara, R., & Corin, E. (2005). A qualitative study of religious practices by chronic mentally ill and their caregivers in South India. *The International Journal of Social Psychiatry*, *51*(12), 139–149. doi:10.1177/0020764005056761 PMID:16048243

Pandya, A., Shah, K., Chauhan, A., & Saha, S. (2020). Innovative mental health initiatives in India: A scope for strengthening primary healthcare services. *Journal of Family Medicine and Primary Care*, *9*(2), 502. doi:10.4103/jfmpc.jfmpc_977_19 PMID:32318372

Parikh, R., Michelson, D., Sapru, M., Sahu, R., Singh, A., Cuijpers, P., & Patel, V. (2019). Priorities and preferences for school-based mental health services in India: A multi-stakeholder study with adolescents, parents, school staff, and mental health providers. *Global Mental Health (Cambridge, England)*, *6*, e18. doi:10.1017/gmh.2019.16 PMID:31531228

Pennebaker, J. W. (2012). *Opening up: The healing power of expressing emotions*. Guilford Press.

Radovanović, D., Holst, C., Belur, S. B., Srivastava, R., Houngbonon, G. V., Le Quentrec, E., Miliza, J., Winkler, A. S., & Noll, J. (2020). Digital literacy key performance indicators for sustainable development. *Social Inclusion (Lisboa)*, *8*(2), 151–167. doi:10.17645/si.v8i2.2587

Raina, M., & Singh, K. (2018). The Ashtanga Yoga Hindi Scale: An assessment tool based on the Eastern philosophy of yoga. *Journal of Religion and Health*, *57*(1), 12–25. doi:10.1007/s10943-015-0096-4 PMID:26215275

Rao, K. R. (2011). Indian Psychology: Implications and applications. In R. M. J. Cornelissen, G. Misra, & S. Verma (Eds.), *Foundations of Indian Psychology: Theories and Concepts* (Vol. 1, pp. 7–26). Pearson.

Rao, K. R., & Paranjpe, A. C. (2016). *Psychology in the Indian Tradition*. Springer India. doi:10.1007/978-81-322-2440-2

Raveesh, B. N., & Munoli, R. N. (2020). Ethical and legal aspects of telepsychiatry. *Indian Journal of Psychological Medicine*, *42*(5, suppl), 63S–69S. doi:10.1177/0253717620962033 PMID:33354067

Rout, O. P., Acharya, R., Gupta, R., Inchulkar, S. R., Karbhal, K. S., & Sahoo, R. (2013). Management of psychosomatic disorders through Ayurvedic drugs-A critical review. *World Journal of Pharmacy and Pharmaceutical Sciences*, *2*(6), 6507–6537.

Sagar, R., & Singh, S. (2022). National Tele-Mental Health Program in India: A step towards mental health care for all? *Indian Journal of Psychiatry*, *64*(2), 117–119. doi:10.4103/indianjpsychiatry.indianjpsychiatry_145_22 PMID:35494321

Sagar, R., & Singh, S. (2022). National Tele-Mental Health Program in India: A step towards mental health care for all? *Indian Journal of Psychiatry*, *64*(2), 117–119. doi:10.4103/indianjpsychiatry.indianjpsychiatry_145_22 PMID:35494321

Sansom, B. (1982). The sick who do not speak. In D. Parkin (Ed.), *Semantic Anthropology* (pp. 183–196). Academic Press.

Santomauro, D. F., Herrera, A. M. M., Shadid, J., Zheng, P., Ashbaugh, C., Pigott, D. M., ... Ferrari, A. J. (2021). Global prevalence and burden of depressive and anxiety disorders in 204 countries and territories in 2020 due to the COVID-19 pandemic. *Lancet*, *398*(10312), 1700–1712. doi:10.1016/S0140-6736(21)02143-7 PMID:34634250

Schoonover, J., Lipkin, S., Javid, M., Rosen, A., Solanki, M., Shah, S., & Katz, C. L. (2014). Perceptions of traditional healing for mental illness in rural Gujarat. *Annals of Global Health*, *80*(2), 96–102. doi:10.1016/j.aogh.2014.04.013

Schueller, S. M., Neary, M., O'Loughlin, K., & Adkins, E. C. (2018). Discovery of and interest in health apps among those with mental health needs: Survey and focus group study. *Journal of Medical Internet Research*, *20*(6), e10141. doi:10.2196/10141 PMID:29891468

Sehonova, P., Svobodova, Z., Dolezelova, P., Vosmerova, P., & Faggio, C. (2018). Effects of waterborne antidepressants on non-target animals living in the aquatic environment: A review. *The Science of the Total Environment*, *631*, 789–794. doi:10.1016/j.scitotenv.2018.03.076 PMID:29727988

Staal, F. (2008). *Discovering the Vedas: origins, mantras, rituals, insights*. Penguin Books India.

Suchitra, S. P., Devika, H. S., Gangadhar, B. N., Nagarathna, R., Nagendra, H. R., & Kulkarni, R. (2010). Measuring the tridosha symptoms of unmāda (psychosis): A preliminary study. *Journal of Alternative and Complementary Medicine (New York, N.Y.)*, *16*(4), 57–62. doi:10.1089/acm.2009.0296 PMID:20423215

The Lancet Global Health. (2020). Mental health matters. *The Lancet Global Health, 8*(11), e1352. doi:10.1016/S2214-109X(20)30432-0

Thirunavukarasu, M., & Thirunavukarasu, P. (2010). Training and national deficit of psychiatrists in India-A critical analysis. *Indian Journal of Psychiatry, 52*(7, Suppl1), 83–88. doi:10.4103/0019-5545.69218 PMID:21836723

Turner, V. (1975). *Drama, Fields, and Metaphors: Symbolic actions in human societies*. Cornell University Press.

Venkatesh, U., Aravind, G. P., & Velmurugan, A. A. (2022). Telemedicine practice guidelines in India: Global implications in the wake of the COVID-19 pandemic. *World Medical & Health Policy, 14*(3), 589–599. doi:10.1002/wmh3.497 PMID:35601469

Votruba, N., & Thornicroft, G. (2016). Sustainable development goals and mental health: Learnings from the contribution of the FundaMentalSDG global initiative. *Global Mental Health (Cambridge, England), 3*, e26. doi:10.1017/gmh.2016.20 PMID:28596894

Whiteford, H. A., Degenhardt, L., Rehm, J., Baxter, A. J., Ferrari, A. J., Erskine, H. E., Charlson, F. J., Norman, R. E., Flaxman, A. D., Johns, N., Burstein, R., Murray, C. J. L., & Vos, T. (2013). Global burden of disease attributable to mental and substance use disorders: Findings from the Global Burden of Disease Study 2010. *Lancet, 382*(9904), 1575–1586. doi:10.1016/S0140-6736(13)61611-6 PMID:23993280

WHO (2011b). *World report on disability*. WHO.

WHO (2013a). *Global action plan for the prevention and control of non-communicable diseases 2013–2020*. WHO.

WHO. (2019, May 2). *The WHO Special Initiative for Mental Health (2019-2023): Universal Health Coverage for Mental Health*. WHO. https://www.who.int/publications/i/item/special-initiative-for-mental-health-(2019-2023)

WHO. (2022, June 17). Mental health: Key facts. WHO. https://www.who.int/news-room/fact-sheets/detail/mental-health-strengthening-our-response

WHO-GHO. (2023). *Target 3.5: Strengthen the prevention and treatment of substance abuse, including narcotic drug abuse and harmful use of alcohol*. WHO. https://www.who.int/data/gho/data/themes/topics/topic-details/GHO/target-3-5-strengthen-the-prevention-and-treatment-of-substance-abuse-including-narcotic-drug-abuse-and-harmful-use-of-alcohol

Wig, N. N. (1989). Indian concepts of mental health and their impact on care of the mentally ill. *International Journal of Mental Health*, *18*(3), 71–80. doi:10.108 0/00207411.1989.11449136

KEY TERMS AND DEFINITIONS

Faith-Healing: The practice of prayer and gestures believed to evoke divine intervention in trying to cure or heal people.

God: A higher power or a divine force, which in Hinduism are many and one, and within all at the same time and every time.

Indic Knowledge: The ancient and traditional knowledge that developed in ancient India.

Karma: The sum of a person's actions in this and previous lives.

Religious-healing: The process of trying to cure people by using the power of prayer and religious belief.

Satvavajaya: A Sanskrit term which refers to conquering the self, strength of mind, or character; later developed into a method for psychotherapy by an ancient Indian Physician, Charaka, wherein a person is trained to restrain themselves from desires for wholesome objects.

Spiritual Care: A set of practices that tend to a person's spiritual needs while coping with illness, grief, or pain. It is known to heal physically and emotionally, rebuild relationships, and regain well-being.

Unmada: Ayurvedic understanding of mental illness comprising three critical entities: buddivikara (deformity of will), manovikara (deformity of mind), and atmavikara (deformity of intellect). Mental illness is a condition where all of the above are found in gradable variations.

Chapter 10
Sustainable Behaviour:
Endorsing Happiness

Kalpana Sharma
Chaudhary Bansi Lal University, Bhiwani, India

ABSTRACT

Sustainable behaviour entails considering the need to protect the environment for current and future generations while also considering economic, environmental, and social development. Also, this is one of the goals of positive psychology to investigate the psychological consequences of such behaviour. As per previous studies, practising pro-environmental and altruistic activities can lead to higher levels of happiness, and thrifty consumption can result in a feeling of fulfilment and intrinsic motivation. For this research, a total number of 200 university students completed general ecological behavioural scale and happiness scale. Statistical analysis includes t, Pearson r, and regression analysis. Results showed that sustainable behaviour had a considerable impact on the "happiness" element. Males are more involved in sustainable behaviours as compared to females, and also had a higher mean score on the happiness scale. Furthermore, the participants' satisfaction was significantly predicted by all elements of sustainable behaviour.

INTRODUCTION

The most pressing worry of the day is the wane of environment, which includes all three levels i.e., atmosphere, soil, and water. Human conduct is crucial in the emergence and perpetuation of environmental issues. Consumerism, waste and resource depletion, pollution, egocentric and inequitable behaviour are all fundamental facets of human behaviour that influence and define environmental quality. In

DOI: 10.4018/979-8-3693-1178-3.ch010

general, sustainable conduct encompasses a set of acts aimed at protecting both the physical and social ecosystems. Behavioural actions like consumption, resource depletion, contamination, egocentric and inequitable behaviour, should be replaced by sustainable behaviour. It entails a series of deliberate and effective measures that result in the environment preservation (both social and physical perspective) for current and future generations.

"Sustainable conduct is defined as a set of acts that aim to protect both the physical and social ecosystems" (Corral-Verdugo et al., 2011). SB (sustainable behaviour) SB is the set of deliberate and effective actions aimed at preserving the ecosystem (both the physical and social) and it results in the conservation of natural and social resources. The inquest of the psychological repercussions of sustainability has recently become a research focus. One of the outcomes stated is subjective well-being or happiness. In reality, governments see achieving happiness for their inhabitants as a goal to pursue as part of their long-term development plans. Happiness is an illusive psychological state that is imprinted by both hereditary and environmental factors. Despite the variation in the theories employed to explain happiness, the findings are very similar. For example, there is unanimity on the fact that heredity has a significant impact on this psychological state. There is consensus on the surprisingly high degree of happiness among individuals, the limitations of money in enhancing happiness, and the importance of social connection to maintain a decent level of good psychological states. There's also consensus that a exact definition of happiness is difficult to come by. The majority of authors in the field of positive psychology propose actions to promote happiness, such as practising altruistic behaviours, learning problem-solving skills, and participating in activities to connect with others. A correlation between sustainable behaviour and happiness is expected since sustainable acts usually result in benefits for oneself and others. This is supported by the available literature.

When confronted with the option to act in an eco-friendly manner, most individual expect unpleasant emotions such as sacrifice, discomfort, or feel embarrassment or guilt as a result of a lack of conservationist effort. Actions that are pro-environmental, thrifty, compassionate, and equitable are examples of virtuous behaviour. Positive psychologists are fascinated with virtues because they are at the heart of personal development, positive social interaction, psychological well-being, and environmental adaptation. (Peterson & Seligman 2004). Furthermore, sustainable activities have a variety of beneficial psychological consequences, and a number of positive emotional states and psychological processes serve as antecedents to long term sustainable behaviours.

Sustainable behaviour is described as "a set of actions aimed at preserving the integrity of this planet's socio-physical resources (Corral-Verdugo et al. 2010)". When people who are committed to sustainability participate in these activities, they

*Figure 1. Model showing correlation between sustainable behaviour and well-being
(Corral-Verdugo, 2012)*

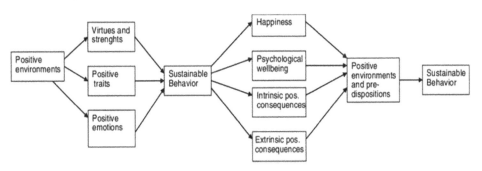

create conditions that allow for fairer utilisation of environmental, economic, and social resources. Their utilisation of those resources is modest, allowing everyone to benefit from them. (De Young 1996). Individuals who are environmentally conscious are also sympathetic and willing to help others people who are in need (Pol 2002), implying that they are altruistically motivated (Schultz 2001); in addition, they are continually engaged in behaviour which are meant for safeguarding the environment (Kaiser 1998). This means that a an individual oriented to sustainable behaviour is at least pro-environmental, thrifty, altruistic, and equitable, and there is research-based evidences that those four categories of sustainable acts have important interrelationships.

According to the study, psychological well-being, human functioning, and performance are all closely linked to people's quality of life. Because India is also dealing with a variety of environmental issues, studies like this one are critical in encouraging future scholars to conduct additional research to better understand the relationship between the environment and psychology. In this study six variables of sustainable behaviour will be examined, including behaviour towards energy conservation, awareness regarding ecological behaviour in mobility and transportation, waste avoidance, consumerism recycling and also social behaviour towards conservation.

OBJECTIVES OF THE STUDY

The major objectives of this study are:

1. To observe correlation between sustainable behaviour and happiness.
2. To assess gender differences in sustainable behaviour of university students.

3. To assess gender differences in happiness of the university students.
4. To find predictive role of sustainable behaviour in promoting happiness.

MATERIALS AND METHODS

Sample selection: Data was collected from different colleges and Universities of Punjab. Two hundred students (both graduates and post graduates) were included in the study ensuring equal participation of males and female. Convenience sampling method was used for data collection.

Tools Used

1. **General Ecological Behavioural Scale:** The General Ecological Behaviour Scale was developed and standardised by Kaiser (1998). It consists of 65 items on a five-point Likert scale, related to six components of sustainable behaviour: energy conservation behaviours (14 items), mobility and transportation (14 items), waste avoidance (six items), consumerism (13 items), recycling (five items), and social behaviours toward conservation (13 items).
2. **Subjective Happiness Scale:** This scale was developed by Lyubomirsky and Lepper (1999). This is a four-item scale to assess subjective happiness of a person.

Procedure: Following the selection and preparation of the objectives, measuring tools, google forms were given to the participants. Informed consent was obtained from subjects before participation. Instructions were given to the participants before the two scales were handed over and the measurement began. For statistical analysis, SPSS was used to tabulate, organize, and compute mean and standard deviations (SDs). Further analysis was done by applying Pearson correlation, and regression analysis.

RESULTS AND INTERPRETATION

Results of Table 1 indicates that males scored significantly higher on the dimension of Mobility and transportation (M =48.84, σ =2.70), waste avoidance (M=18.46, σ =1.43) and social behaviour towards conservation (M=44.17, σ =2.53) as compared to females (M=39.46, σ =3.39); (M=17.18, σ =1.30); (M=37.36, σ =2.07) respectively on the above dimensions. While females scored significantly higher on dimension of recycling (M=17.74, σ =1.24). No significant difference

Table 1. Showing mean, SD, and t-test values of the scores of dimensions of sustainable behaviours of participants

S. no.	Dimensions of GEB Scale	Male		Female		t
		Mean	σ	Mean	σ	
1.	Energy conservation behaviours	42. 82	3.88	42.23	4.25	1.02
2.	Mobility and transportation	48.84	2.70	39.46	3.39	21.64**
3.	Waste avoidance	18.46	1.43	17.18	1.30	6.62**
4.	Consumerism	42.96	2.35	43.54	2.31	1.76
5.	Recycling	12.38	1.21	17.74	1.24	30.93**
6	Social behaviour towards conservation	44.17	2.53	37.36	2.07	20.83**
7.	Sustainable behaviour (Total)	209.63	14.10	197.51	14.56	5.97**

t** = p≤0.01

was found on the dimensions of energy conservation behaviour and consumerism between the two groups.

Table 2 shows that males scored on happiness ($M = 21.96$, $\sigma = 1.43$) in comparison to the female participants ($M = 19.40$, $\sigma = 1.02$). There is a statistically significant ($t = 14.57$) difference between the two groups.

Figure 2. Showing mean values of the dimensions of sustainable behaviours of participants

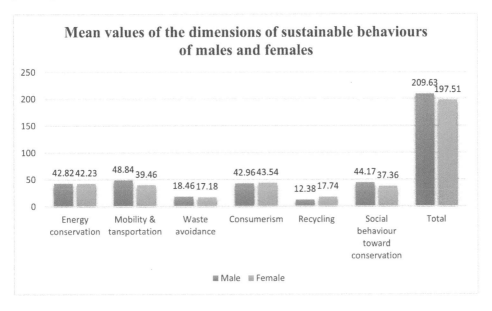

Table 2. The mean, SD and t- values on scale of happiness for males and females

Gender	Happiness score		t
	Mean	σ	
Males	21.96	1.43	14.57**
Females	19.40	1.02	

t**=p≤0.01

Figure 3. Showing mean values of happiness scale for males and females

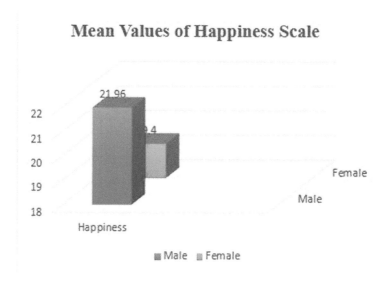

Pearson product correlation method was applied to find the correlation between the variables. Table 3 shows significant correlation between dimension of sustainable behaviour and their corresponding scores on happiness among both the group. Energy conservation behaviour (r=.553, p<0.01; r=.865, p<0.01), mobility and transportation (r=.653, p<0.01; r=.669, p<0.01), waste avoidance (r=.807, p<0.01; r=.776, p<0.01), consumerism (r=.723, p<0.01; r=.860, p<0.01), recycling (r=.932, p<0.01; r=.874, p<0.01), social behaviour towards conservation (r=.564, p<0.01; r=.537, p<0.01). Results clearly indicated that there is a big impact of sustainable behaviour on happiness.

Regression analysis 35.32% of happiness in males and 34.72% in females were predicted by sustainable behaviour. Dimensionally, it was found that in males, 22.41%, 30.79%, 32.52%, 35.01%, 25.18% and 38.02% of happiness was predicted by energy conservation behaviour, mobility and transportation, waste avoidance, consumerism, social behaviour towards conservation respectively. In females 26.71%,

Table 3. The correlations coefficients among the scores of components of sustainable behaviours and happiness

S. No	Dimensions of sustainable behaviour	Happiness	Gender	r
1.	Energy conservation behaviours	Happiness	M-M	.553
			F-F	.865
2.	Mobility and transportation	Happiness	M-M	.653
			F-F	.669
3.	Waste avoidance	Happiness	M-M	.807
			F-F	.776
4.	Consumerism	Happiness	M-M	.723
			F-F	.860
5.	Recycling	Happiness	M-M	.932
			F-F	.874
6.	Social behaviour towards conservation	Happiness	M-M	.564
			F-F	.537

M- Male participants; F-Female participants

35.22%, 34.58%, 30.21%, 37.79%, and 26.21% happiness was predicted by energy conservation behaviour, mobility and transportation, waste avoidance, consumerism, social behaviour towards conservation respectively. Percentage of predictive role of dimensions of sustainable behaviour is clear evidence for its contribution in determining the extent of happiness.

DISCUSSION

The majority of studies on the psychological aspects of sustainability concentrate on the cognitive, affective, and behavioural drivers of sustainable behaviour, with the former serving as precursors to the latter. A thrifty lifestyle (living lightly, minimising waste, and avoiding overconsumption) has also been highlighted as a promoter of happy psychological states. Individual may be involved in sustainable behaviour may be because of external or internal motivation. Materialistic persons (those who are more likely to suffer extrinsic consequences) are less concerned with environmental conservation and are more focused on achieving their goals (money, power) and exploiting natural resources. (Crompton & Kasser, 2009). When we talk about external motivation conservationist acts increase the likelihood of natural resource availability, allowing individuals to use and benefit from them. Many acts that conserve natural resources result in financial savings or tangible gain for individuals who take them. The money saved by conserving water or energy, or the financial benefit that recycling brings to a number of people who sell things to recycling organisations. Individuals may also profit from tax breaks if their acts are environmentally friendly. These are also good extrinsic benefits (Lehman & Geller,2004). But the problem with this type of motivation is that once the consequence is removed, sustainable behaviour become discontinued. Other factors which may promote sustainable behaviour is that of self -determination, a form of internal motivation. Motives related to self-determination are also included in the inherent advantages of sustainable behaviour. One of them is the sense of accomplishment that comes from behaving in a pro-environmental manner (Iwata, 2002).

This study clearly indicates that, sustainable behaviour has a positive impact on happiness. Results of this study are in line with Corral-Verdugo et al. (2011) stating that people who participated in more pro-social and pro-environmental activities reported better levels of psychological well-being. It has also been noted that engaging in pro-environmental activities fosters a sense of competence motivation (akin to self-efficacy), which is fuelled by one's belief in one's own abilities (i.e., knowing than one acted effectively and pro-environmentally). An individual who engages in sustainable activities on a regular basis derives intrinsic joy from his or her pro-environmental expertise, as well as from the experience of doing a pro-environmental activity (de Young, 1996). Thus, Happiness, and the pleasure it entails, may also be an inextricable part of long-term conduct. As a result, promoting the intrinsic motivation and consequences of sustainable behaviour over the use of extrinsic ones is advocated (Ryan & Deci, 2000). This happiness has also been viewed as a source of behavioural self-control, which, combined with emotions of self-efficacy, is an internal positive outcome that motivates people to act in a pro-long-term manner.

Thus, it can be stated that the motivation for sustainable behaviour is rooted in a desire to address environmental, social and economic concerns in a way that preserves resources for future generations. An authentic concern for the environment drives a lot of people. They feel obliged to save the environment, cut back on pollution, and slow down climate change. People who practise sustainable behaviour, such as recycling, using renewable energy, or cutting back on trash, can feel more purposeful and fulfilled since they are helping to conserve the environment. Some people are driven by a desire to improve society as a whole. Since sustainable behaviour can benefit communities, advance social justice, and encourage moral business conduct, it frequently equates with social responsibility. Feelings of satisfaction and social closeness can be strengthened by understanding that one's actions serve the larger good. Economic considerations can also catalyze sustainable practices. For both individuals and organisations, energy efficiency, waste reduction, and responsible usage can result in cost savings. A sense of well-being and contentment may be influenced by having stable finances and the capacity to save money through sustainable practices. People who place a high priority on moral principles like justice, fairness, and integrity could be inspired to adopt sustainable habits as a way to demonstrate their ethical principles. Authenticity and inner pleasure can be increased by acting in a way that is consistent with one's own beliefs.

The pleasure derived from participating in conservation practises was found to be highly and significantly linked to long-term behaviour. Also, self-efficacy is found to be high in people who are involved in conservative behaviour (Hernández et al., 2010).

There is a complicated and individual-specific relationship between sustainable behaviour and subjective satisfaction. However, a positive association is influenced by many factors. People who practise sustainable behaviour frequently feel that their lives have meaning and purpose. One way to improve overall life satisfaction is to contribute to a broader cause, like environmental protection. Feelings of guilt or concern about the environment can be lessened by realising that one is trying to lessen their impact on the environment. Happiness and mental tranquillity may be enhanced by this sense of environmental responsibility. A sense of personal fulfilment can result from acting in ways that are consistent with one's values and beliefs, including sustainability. Happiness and a positive self-perception can be influenced by this alignment. Social ties can be fostered via sustainable behaviours,

Figure 4. Sustainable behavior

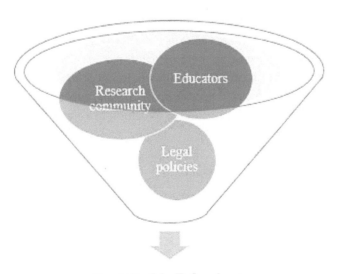

Sustainable Behaviour

particularly those that have a social component (such as participating in community clean-up initiatives). Happiness and well-being are correlated with positive social connections.

This study can be helpful for scientific community, educators and policy makers. The scientific community is expected to design and test interventional programmes of a social and educational nature, as well as provide reliable knowledge about what positive consequences of sustainable behaviour are to be expected by people, the actions these consequences are most associated with, and how they operate. The educational sector has the responsibility of incorporating sustainability into the school curriculum and encouraging pupils to engage in daily pro-environmental behaviours (as a part of their training). Policymakers must take responsibility of facilitating considerable investment in research and education, adopting legal legislation to change the current materialistically focused way of life, and rewarding sustainable practises on an individual and collective level.

CONCLUSION

From his or her pro-environmental and pro-social actions, a person engaged in sustainable behaviour appears to derive happiness. These findings are intriguing since these internal repercussions are possible automatic instigators of more sustainable habits. Simply engaging in frugal and equitable activity can lead to good mental states that encourage and sustain environmentalist and pro-social behaviour. Sustainable behaviour is motivated by a variety of factors, including a feeling of purpose, personal fulfilment, social relationships, and environmental responsibility, all of which can favourably impact subjective satisfaction. It is vital to augment external management of people's conduct by assisting them in becoming self-sufficient and responsible persons. In this regard, the research and intervention of the intrinsic consequences of sustainable behaviour, such as happiness, is particularly intriguing due to its novelty and potential implications in the transition to a more sustainable society.

LIMITATIONS OF THE STUDY

There are several limitations of this study. One of them is that the study was conducted on university students which encompasses a limited age range. Also sample size limits the generalization of results in larger population.

ACKNOWLEDGMENT

Author is grateful to all the participants who gave their valuable time for the purpose of this study.

REFERENCES

Corral-Verdugo, V., Frı'as, M., & Garcı'a, C. (2010). Introduction to the psychological dimensions of sustainability. In V. Corral-Verdugo, C. Garcı'a, & M. Frı'as (Eds.), *Psychological approaches to sustainability*. Nova Science Publishers.

Corral-Verdugo, V., González-Lomelí, D., Rascón-Cruz, M., & Corral-Frías, V. (2016). Intrinsic Motives of Autonomy, Self-Efficacy, and Satisfaction Associated with Two Instances of Sustainable Behavior: Frugality and Equity. *Psychology (Irvine, Calif.)*, *7*(5), 662–671. doi:10.4236/psych.2016.75068

Corral-Verdugo, V., Mireles-Acosta, J. F., Tapia-Fonllem, C., & Fraijo-Sing, B. (2011). Happiness as Correlate of Sustainable Behavior: A Study of Pro-Ecological, Frugal, Equitable and Altruistic Actions That Promote Subjective Wellbeing. *Human Ecology Review*, *18*(2), 95–104. https://www.jstor.org/stable/24707465

Corral-Verdugo, V., Montiel, M., Sotomayor, M., Frías, M., Tapia, C., & Fraijo, B. (2011). Psychological Wellbeing as Correlate of Sustainable Behaviors. *International Journal of Hispanic Psychology*, *4*, 31–44.

Crompton, T., & Kasser, T. (2009). *Meeting Environmental Challenges: The Role of Human Identity*. WWF-UK. http://assets.wwf.org.uk/downloads/meeting_environmental_challenges___the_role_of_human_identity.pdf

De Young, R. (1993). Changing Behavior and Making It Stick: The Conceptualization and Management of Conservation Behavior. *Environment and Behavior*, *25*(3), 485–505. doi:10.1177/0013916593253003

De Young, R. (1996). Some psychological aspects of a reduced consumption lifestyle: The role of intrinsic satisfaction and competence motivation. *Environment and Behavior*, *28*, 358–409. doi:10.1177/0013916596283005

Gyanesh K.T (2016). Sustainable Behaviors and Happiness: An Optimistic Link, *The International Journal of Indian Psychology 4*(1), 75.

Hernández, B., Tabernero, C., & Suárez, E. (2010). Psychosocial Motivations and Self-Regulation Processes That Activate Environmentally Responsible Behavior. In J. Valentín & L. Gámez (Eds.), *Environmental Psychology: New Developments* (pp. 109–126). Nova Science Publishers.

Iwata, O. (2002). Coping Style and Three Psychological Measures Associated with Environmentally Responsible Behavior. *Social Behavior and Personality*, *30*(7), 661–669. doi:10.2224/sbp.2002.30.7.661

Kaiser, F. G. (1998). A general measure of ecological behavior. *Journal of Applied Social Psychology*, *28*(5), 395–442. doi:10.1111/j.1559-1816.1998.tb01712.x

Lyubomirsky, S., & Lepper, H. (1999). A measure of subjective happiness: Preliminary reliability and construct validation. *Social Indicators Research*, *46*(2), 137–155. doi:10.1023/A:1006824100041

Peterson, C., & Seligman, M. E. P. (2004). *Character strengths and virtues: A handbook and classification*. American Psychological Association.

Pol, E. (2002). The theoretical background of the city-identity-sustainability network. *Environment and Behavior*, *34*(1), 8–25. doi:10.1177/0013916502034001002

Ryan, R., & Deci, E. (2000). Self-Determination Theory and the Facilitation of Intrinsic Motivation, Social Development, and Well-Being. *The American Psychologist*, *55*(1), 68–78. doi:10.1037/0003-066X.55.1.68 PMID:11392867

Schultz, P. W. (2001). The structure of environmental concern. Concern for self, other people, and the biosphere. *Journal of Environmental Psychology*, *21*(4), 327–339. doi:10.1006/jevp.2001.0227

Chapter 11
Technology as a Means to Bridge the Gap Between Humans and Nature

Richa Kapoor Mehra

https://orcid.org/0000-0002-5420-8179
O.P. Jindal Global University, India

ABSTRACT

Historically, evidence is available to make us understand the fact that nature has also played a therapeutic role in our lives by benefiting our mental health as well as physical health. The present study will address a concern: How can nature healing occur if a person suffers from chronic disease or is disabled? Through this chapter, an attempt has been made to provide a solution via digital or virtual reality tools, equip disabled patients, and give them a reel feeling of nature. Those who cannot go out and get the real feel of nature can make use of virtual reality tools to heal themselves with technology. Also, the present chapter will address the question, can virtual exposure to nature be equivalent to real exposure? Further, an attempt is made to discover how technological advancement is benefiting our lives, equipping us in the best possible ways. The prime concern here is to unfold how technological advancement and digital revolution have influenced the way we relate to the environment.

INTRODUCTION

Nature is the buzzword these days; saving nature, loving nature, and embracing it are on everyone's lips; it is the need of the hour to protect nature. Numerous

DOI: 10.4018/979-8-3693-1178-3.ch011

advertisement campaigns and write-ups are available to spread awareness about the significance of nature. Various fairy tale books have showcased the importance of nature and tamed tender minds from the beginning. "The best remedy for those who are afraid, lonely, or unhappy is to go outside…I firmly believe that nature brings solace in all troubles." — Anne Frank. These lines clearly express the firm belief that nature is one of the best ways to nurture humans.

The term *greening of the soul*- a term coined by Hilarion Petzold. 'Green is a 'color metaphor' for vitality, health, growth, life force, hope, the 'green side' of young love, and green is more than that: it is the existential feeling of life…" (Petzold, 2023). Nature is our lives; we are nature; this expresses the interconnectedness of nature and human beings. Nature is with us every moment: in our breath, our blood, our cells, the water we partake of and are made up of, and all our life processes are part of nature. We call our earth the mother earth as it gives riles to life and nurtures us with everything we need to survive- air, water, food, and shelter. One has to be mindful of the fact that we are one of the most essential aspects of life and cannot exist without the complex matrices of life, which comprise many things. As we grow and start realizing the richness of nature, we find that we are always, in fact, "in nature," along with many other essential things surrounding us. Thus, our existence in nature is as significant as the existence of many different things co-existing with us. Mindful watching of the things around us allows us to know ourselves more clearly and distinctly. Just as the earth hosts the creative expression of life, women host the creative expression of human life, providing oxygen, fluids, and shelter to growing babies in the womb- much like the earth, offering physical support to optimize the well-being of our offspring growing within us. Understanding our connection and responsibility towards natural environment is our prime task as individuals and communities.

NATURE THE MAGIC HEALER

Just as love is natural, so is grief; pleasure and pain are like two sides of the coin; it is natural and undeniable to feel pain since it is an inevitable part of life. Happy times vanish so fast; however, it becomes difficult to face painful times. Pain may occur due to many reasons; it may be due to loss of any kind, death, divorce, illness, or due to any other unwanted circumstances. It is understandable that no one wants to remain in a state of pain; all beings desire relief from pain. Seeks coping mechanisms to overcome the state of pain; these coping mechanisms are diverse in nature. Some may distract themselves from pain by engaging themselves with technology and entertainment; for some, traveling is the best way to eliminate pain; others may keep themselves busy to get rid of agony; for some, going out in nature works as therapy and healing people from pain. Most of us have witnessed the healing aspect of nature during the hard COVID-19 times when people were in social isolation; closeness to nature was the only remedy for healing and gaining solace, although this opportunity was available only to rural people. On the other hand, being increasingly disconnected from nature gives rise to anxiety, stress, and many health issues. Since its inception, nature has been a great healer, and such healing techniques are evident in the religious texts and scriptures.

Many scientists now believe that human beings are genetically and evolutionarily programmed to connect with nature. In his bestselling 2005 book *Last Child in the Woods,* author Richard Louv coined the term 'nature deficit disorder' to describe the consequences of humanity's modern-day alienation from nature. He believes that a lack of connection with nature has caused widespread anxiety, depression, and attention disorders. This has been witnessed by most of us during the challenging COVID-19 pandemic time; people suffered from anxiety and stress due to the forced lockdown where people were compelled to stay indoors. Humans have experienced closeness to nature, which makes us more relaxed and uplifts our mood. More time spent in nature helps us focus better and enhances the efficiency of individuals.

When plants are grounded, growing up out of the earth, they grow two to three times as tall and bloom more, and eventually blossom. When humans are grounded, we feel much more energetic, healthy, and spirited. Scientists were interested in unfolding the surprising and powerful connection between nature and humans. Nothing else allows us to become the pure buoyant vessel of well-being the way grounding does. Studies have claimed that grounding helps resolve the issue of insomnia. Doctors suggest the most basic yet effective way for good sleep at night is grounding. Medical literature claims that grounding calms brain waves, deepens sleep, normalizes cortisol, and makes sleep more restorative. Doctors also claim grounding immediately stabilizes the autonomic nervous system; calm our heart and stabilizes racing heartbeats. Grounding is an effective tool to provide immediate support during anxiety, anytime, anywhere. Research have suggested during panic attacks touching earth has resulted in calming the patient and helps in relaxing them. Taking the feel of nature has been proved therapeutically healing and have resulted in stabilizing anxious mind. It has been found that getting close to nature is anti-inflammatory and have helped in boosting mood and energy levels of many. One must choose hobbies that are focused on outside routinely, such as gardening, which is a beautiful choice, whether it is flowers, herbs, or vegetables. Performance of activities like bird watching, stretching, photography, walking barefoot on grass have helped in healing individuals. Meditation is one of the most traditional therapeutic approaches which has resulted in calming mind and focusing on the breath, has shown phenomenal results, has improved deeper sleep, lower stress hormones, and can provide relief in the face of trauma.

Medical studies have shown the outstanding results of walking on patients, it improves their sleep quality. Walking has showed positive outcomes on many patients and have helped them in recovering faster. Thus, practising walking can be one of the best ways to improve health along with the medication prescribed by the doctor.

THERAPEUTIC POTENTIAL OF WORKING OUTDOORS

In India, since its inception, nature prescriptions and naturopathy have been referred to as one of the best methods to naturally cure a being. Naturopathy finds its roots in the ancient Indian system of medicine known as Ayurveda. Out of the four major scriptural texts of Hinduism, the Atharvaveda is one of the oldest texts. It is also known as the science of Indian medicine. Atharvaveda comprises of various verses and mantras for curing various physical and mental diseases. The Atharvaveda also highlights the significance of spending time in nature and have shown its health benefits. Walk in nature have resulted in lowering the level of stress and anxiety in human beings, thus helping develop a sound mind and healthy body.

As part of urban settings, our exposure to technology and gadgets is at its peak; due to overexposure to gadgets, our mind stops thinking and becomes over-exhausted. In such situations, nature has been the best healer of the human mind, as our mind gets fresh and feels liberated when it is close to nature. Spending time with nature helps improve sleep quality because the body's exposure to sunlight during the daytime helps to regulate the sleep cycle of a being. While entering the forest, one can stroll and follow the sounds and smells and get completely absorbed by the beauty of nature. 'The key to unlocking the power of nature is in the five senses. Let nature enter through eyes, ears, nose, mouth, hands and feet" (Le Dac-Nhuong, Le Chung Van, Tromp Jolanda G & Nguyen Gia Nhu, 2018). While being in contact with nature, all our five sense organs become activated and work simultaneously; it is believed that walking barefoot in grass improves the health of a person because while walking barefoot, one can listen to the chirping of birds and feet come into contact with the grass, one can smell the earthy smell of wet mud as well as get mesmerized with the smell of flowers in the garden. The sight of beautiful plants and flowers boosts the mood of a being. Gazing at the sky or viewing the waves in the river/ocean has been phenomenally good ways of calming our minds and making us thought-free, hence giving rise to immense peace.

As per the results of one study, children least exposed to greener space developed fifty percent of more diseases than those who were kept close to the nature. Have you ever noticed how easy it becomes to stop a crying child when exposed to nature? A walk outside under the moon and stars can give relief to a crying baby. Walking in nature have resulted in quick change in mood and have resulted in reduction of negative emotions, giving rise to positive emotions of self-love and even boosts self-esteem. Nature walk has been the easiest way to negate negative emotions in individuals. Children who are allowed to play freely in natural spaces are better able to connect socially in natural settings. Moving freely in natural space can also act as the pragmatic way of teaching young minds where they get the chance to explore flowers, plants and many other things like butterflies, bees etc. By looking at the open wide sky one can learn about the beauty of Divine creation; sky gazing can also make them feel how small and interconnected we are with the minutest things of this cosmic reality. It also makes us realize that there is a protection or umbrella above our head which will protect us from all evils in the world.

Due to the therapeutic nature of environment, meditation has been a common practice of all saints and seers. It helps in balancing the mind and makes the body healthy, a balanced mind is the one with balanced flow of emotions. Spiritual guru Ram Dass suggested that we should accept each other and ourselves in the same way that we accept trees:

"When you go out into the woods, and you look at the trees, you see all these different trees. And some of them are bent, and some of them are straight, and some of them are evergreens, and some of them are whatever. And you look at the tree, and you allow it. You see why it is the way it is. You sort of understand that it didn't get enough light, and so it turned that way. You appreciate the tree. "The minute you get near humans, you lose all that. And you are constantly saying, 'You are to this, or I'm to this.' That judgment mind comes in. And so, I practice turning people into trees. Which means appreciating them just as they are." (Wolfelt Alan, 2021).

He suggests us as wonderful and worthy, just as we are. We are a singular part of nature, just like a unique tree. Spending time among trees will help reinforce this crucial message. This clearly shows our dependability and an unbreakable bond between nature and human beings.

HEALTH MEETS TECHNOLOGY

Technology plays a vital role in our lives; it has been widely used for work, study, connection with people, and entertainment, and the use of technology for health is not an exception. The revolutionary acceleration in the use of technology has been witnessed during the Covid-19 pandemic. The immense use of technology has had a profound impact on health care during the pandemic times. From advanced diagnosis analysis tools to smart wearables, to monitor our health, calories consumed, and the amount and quality of sleep have been widely adopted by us. Advancement in technology reduces or even excludes the need for a patient to go to the hospital for health checkups, as monitoring a patient's health remotely by accessing in real-time is possible. Technology plays a vital role in empowering patients by providing access to a wide range of medical information via the internet and by providing social media platforms where medical information is shared with a desire to support each other.

Further patient empowerment has been witnessed with the increasing use of smart wearable home sensor technologies. These wearables give users full insight and control over their health, thus allowing them to adjust and target their activities to reach optimal fitness. Real-time health feedback is extremely significant in bringing in behavior change and motivating users regarding exercise. However, technology has been extremely helpful to medical students; with the help of virtual reality, medical students can now learn and practice operations.

With digital revolution and advancement in technology there have been revolutionized growth in many sectors today, one such sector is the healthcare sector. Healthcare industry has shown a tremendous advancement due to increased use of technology. Now robotic surgery and virtual trainings of surgeons through virtual reality tools is giving rise to smooth learning. Use of technology in care management has been irreplaceable, it is used extensively for giving therapies, guiding Autistic patients, and assisting patients in their day-to-day activities. With the help of virtual reality tools and techniques, delicate and complicated surgeries have become less complex. With the help of technology, doctors can prepare patients as well as their team of other doctors by showing surgery related information pre-surgery by using technology.

Digital Gaming Technology

Digital gaming technology is a new way where health issues are tackled with the help of games. With the changing times, people prefer staying indoors, which is giving rise to various health issues like diabetes, obesity, etc. Exergaming is an innovative way to help users do physical activities by engaging them in a game and ensuring the physical movement of their body. The central notion of exergaming is to involve users in energetic body activities with the expectation of succeeding in the sedentary lifestyle and providing entertainment to the users.

Phobia

We have witnessed people experiencing extreme anxiety about a certain stimulus; the stimulus might be any animal, height, driving, swimming, or any other situation. Such situations give rise to extreme stress, anxiety, or discomfort like sweating, fast heartbeat, or high blood pressure. Virtual reality technology can act as an effective tool to give a virtual feel to its users, which can help in overcoming the various phobias a person may be having. For example, if a person has a phobia of any animal, VR tools can help them combat such phobia by familiarizing them with a certain type of animal in virtual space. Such VR technologies can be effectively used by various therapists, which may assist them in their therapy sessions.

Community Health Care

Health care facilities are on the lower side in rural areas; hence, there is an urgent need to reform the healthcare sector. Technology can act as a blessing in providing healthcare facilities in remote areas; it helps in maintaining community health by providing easy monitoring, especially in rural areas. The structure of community health care can be seen as a 'virtual hospital.' This virtual assistance via technology can bring impactful change in society by virtually guiding patients at the primary level and preparing them for the next level of treatment. It acts as the cheapest and one of the most reliable options for medical assistance.

Medical Training Assistance

With the advancement of technology, there are various apps available to give training and help trainers learn the treatment in an emergency. Through various 3D images, learning becomes much simpler, interesting, and easily accessible.

With the advancement of technology, the field of medicine and healthcare is rapidly expanding, and technology is acting as a means to bridge the gap between humans and nature. One can sense a strong interconnectedness between humans, nature, and technology. Nature represents a shared world where interaction between technology and human beings takes place.

TRIPARTITE RELATION BETWEEN NATURE, HUMANS AND TECHNOLOGY

"Man inhabits two worlds. One is the natural world of plants and animals, of soil and airs and waters which preceded him by billions of years and of which he is a part. The other is the world of social institutions and artifacts he builds for himself, using his tools and engines, his science, and his dreams to fashion an environment obedient to human purpose and direction" (Ward and Dubos, 1972).

Nature gives us a life-supporting fabric, and it is impossible for us to think of our survival without nature. It often refers to the creator of this universe and is indicated by the name 'mother nature.' Our existence without nature is impossible; nature shapes us and nurtures us; it also provides us with things that are needed for our survival, like air, water, shelter, and food. Research has shown that nature has been a great healer, and at times, patients' interaction with nature has reduced their medication. In 1984, environmental psychologist Roger Ulrich studied the medical records of patients recovering from gallbladder surgery at a suburban Pennsylvania hospital. After accounting for all the possible variables, Ulrich and his team discovered that the patients who had bedside windows looking out on leafy trees not only recovered from surgery one day faster, but they also needed a lot less pain medication and had fewer postsurgical complications than the patients whose only view was a brick wall. Since then, numerous additional studies have documented that merely looking at landscapes- whether from a window, an outdoor vantage point, or even on a computer screen helps people think better, feel better, and heal faster. Having a window beside each patient in the hospital is not a practical way out; instead, augmented reality (Augmented reality technology is regarded as a combination of virtual information and real-world information, which opens wide possibilities in various medical activities like surgery, education, consultancy, etc.). Technology can be used as a great source in giving a reel form of nature to patients who cannot go out in nature nor can view nature from their hospital rooms.

We all depend on the earth to be healthy, to be alive, and to feel balanced and fulfilled; we need to have contact with the earth. Empirically, it has been observed that grounding has supported the health of many patients by giving them a sense of deep comfort, the satisfied craving, and the energetic boost that grounding brings. It has been witnessed that patients who feel depressed, lost, hopeless, or disheartened become uplifted, found, energized, and warmed by time spent connecting to the nurturing flow of the earth. The vibrancy of life can be maintained through connecting to nature.

As human beings became more urbanized, the method of self-discovery while going to nature became most popular. Since time immemorial, the relationship between nature and human beings has been understood as spiritual and culturally uplifting. It has been observed that being outdoors is therapeutic in nature and facilitates human potential to flourish.

Carl Rogers proposed that people flourish when good psychological conditions are in place. Carl Rogers, the well-known psychologist and theorist, wrote of finding a sack of potatoes in a dark corner of his family's cellar. Although they had no soil or water and little light, the old, shriveling potatoes were covered in a tangle of white roots. They had sprouted. Rogers was struck by the miracle of life energy represented by those potatoes. This image of resilience inspired him as he started to reflect on the human process and how therapy could best be of help to people. Despite the adverse conditions, the potatoes were striving towards the light. They seemed to have an inbuilt tendency towards growth. Perhaps humans had the same potential (Rogers, 1980).

The conditions were unfavorable, but the potatoes would begin to sprout – pale, white sprouts, unlike the healthy green shoots they sent up when planted in the soil in the spring. But these sad, spindly sprouts would grow 2 or 3 feet in length as they reached toward the distant light of the window. The sprouts were, in their bizarre, futile growth, a sort of desperate expression of the directional tendency I have been describing (Rogers, 1980).

Rogers drew a parallel between those stunted potatoes trying to grow in such impoverished circumstances and the experiences of the many troubled people with whom he worked in his psychotherapy practice. He recognized that, despite sometimes living in the most awful circumstances, these people had remarkable resilience, carrying on with their lives, albeit sometimes in limited or distorted ways, despite their unhappiness.

Whilst he was a realist and recognized how far short of their potential many people fell and how, like the potatoes in the cellar, their lives often became grotesque parodies of what they might otherwise have been, Rogers nevertheless believed that the life force, which he termed the self-actualizing tendency, was ever-present, leading people to make the best of whatever opportunities they had. Whether people flourished did not depend on their innate nature but, rather, on the conditions in which they lived. Like plants, people need good conditions to reach their full potential. Given the right circumstances, they could be trusted to find this.

Rogers' life work centred on identifying, practicing, and teaching the conditions that he saw as being most conducive to the process of actualization. It was in this work that his therapeutic model, known as the person-centred approach, was based.

For Rogers, the story of potatoes depicts the importance of favourable conditions for growth. Just as a plant needs adequate conditions to grow into a tree, it needs adequate water, healthy soil, and proper sunlight. Similarly, humans also need conditions to grow; without an adequate physical, psychological, and spiritual environment, growth may not take place.

Technology is integrated into the lives of human beings; technologies of every conceivable kind are used everywhere by human beings to provide food, shelter, transportation, and all other basic material appurtenances of life (C. Freeman, 1974). Recent technological advancements have made our lives easy and comfortable. We have witnessed the relevance of technology during the challenging times of the pandemic; telecare/ telemedicine turned out to be the lifeline during the difficult times of COVID-19. The most promising application for telemonitoring is by providing virtual consultancy to patients suffering from chronic diseases. With the advances in technology, many wearable devices are readily available for monitoring the working of the human body. Homes are becoming smart with the use of smart gadgets for purposes like opening/closing doors, switching lights on/off, temperature control, and communicating with the outside world. The advanced features of technology have been a saviour in sensing emergencies, preventing, and detecting falls, etc. Digital technologies are part of our life flow. We use them to study and work, to connect with people, and to do our grocery shopping, entertain ourselves, and find love.

Future scenarios ensure friendly internet connectivity with guaranteed social connectedness to the outside world. People wearing 'smart' clothes/ gadgets result in prompt monitoring activities and their health. With the advancement of technology in almost all spheres of life, there is a requirement to move out of the traditional care settings of going out in nature since reaching out to nature becomes tough in the case of patients suffering from chronic diseases. The reel-feel technique helps in curing patients with increased efficiency and equity of quality-oriented healthcare with limited financial resources. However, we also must adapt these technologies to older peoples' self-care processes and coping strategies. Technology should be offered as a choice to patients and should enable them to decide when and which kind of possible technology they want to access. The most striking case of a radical healthcare transformation, from a media point of view, was the launch of the Apple watch on September 9, 2014 (Roberto, 2022).

Technology has been part and parcel of everyone's life, from the time we begin our day, till the time we go off to bed; most of our actions are governed by technology. Virtual space that is created by virtual reality tools gives us mental peace and makes us happy, since it can be controlled and guided by human mind. Reel space which looks like the real space gives us the real feel of the world via virtual space. This development of technology has transformed almost all sectors, one such sector is the healthcare sector where use of artificial intelligence has drastically revolutionized consequences. The most suitable examples of AR in medicine are NuEyes, which are smart, hands-free electronic glasses designed for blind people. ODG R-7 platform facilitates people with low vision to recognize nearby things and easily perform routine tasks. It can be wirelessly operated or via voice commands. Brain Power software technology designed by MIT revolutionized AR-based devices like Google Glass/ Samsung Gear into AI systems to assist people with brain-related issues like Autism. Thus, these technologies help in connecting man, nature, and technology together in one fabric.

Fast urbanization has resulted in diminishing natural surroundings; natural flowers have been replaced by artificial flowers. Water is a natural element that can make an interior space feel like one is outdoors. Studies have shown that viewing nature art yields most of the benefits of spending time in nature. Hanging a natural landscape or painting indoors has a soothing effect on humans. Similarly, watching nature videos and hearing the sounds of ocean waves, mountain forests, etc., can calm the mind and have similar effects. Integration of Technology into the lives of human beings has been witnessed post-COVID-19 pandemic. Technology of every conceivable kind are used everywhere by human beings to provide food, shelter, transportation, and all other basic material appurtenances of life (Baark. Erik & Svedin, Uno, 1988).

IS REEL EXPOSURE EQUIVALENT TO REAL EXPOSURE?

As the popularity of reel videos grows, we find ourselves caught under the vicious cycle of reel vs real life. Our exposure to the reel life is at its peak; it becomes hard to differentiate between the two. Reel exposure immerses us in the created world in such a way that, at times, we fail to differentiate between the reel and real life. It is an undeniable fact that reel-life exposure to nature can never replace the real-life feel of nature, but reel-life exposure to nature can undoubtedly act as a good resource in the field of healthcare to heal and recover patients. Reel exposure to nature can give a 'reel' feel to the patients from the place they belong to, be it a hospital bed or home, which helps them speed up recovery. It also helps them temporarily forget the pain they are undergoing during their treatment. However, the use of natural medicinal herbs has turned the world for health from the beginning. Knowledge of medicinal herbs and other healing plants can make them more valuable and effective, which cannot be replaced by the reel healing effect.

REFERENCES

Ascione, R. (2022). *The Future of Health How Digital Technology will Make Care Accessible, Sustainable, and Human.* Wiley.

Ascione, R. (2022). *How Digital Technology Will Make Care Accessible, Sustainable, and Human.* Wiley.

Baark. Erik & Svedin, Uno. (1988). *Man, Nature, and Technology Essays on the Role of Ideological Perceptions.* Macmillan Press.

Brazier, C. (2018). *Ecotherapy in Practice A Buddhist Model.* Routledge.

Brian, A. (2009). *The Nature of Technology.* Allen Lane.

Cobern, W. (2000). *Everyday Thoughts about Nature.* Springer.

Freeman, C. (1974). *The Economics of Industrial Innovation.* Penguin.

Gillette, A. (2007). *Eugenics and the Nature-Nurture Debate in the Twentieth Century.* Palgrave Macmillan.

Hsiao-Yean, C. (2015). Walking Improves Sleep in Individuals with Cancer: A Meta-Analysis of Randomized, Controlled Trials. *Oncology Nursing Forum, 42*(2).

Inger. Thune & Anne-Sofie. Furberg. (2002). Physical Activity and Cancer Risk: Dose-Response and Cancer, All Sites and Site-Specific. *Medicine and Science in Sports and Exercise, 33.* . doi:10.1097/00005768-200106001-00025

Le Dac-Nhuong, L. C. V. (2018). Emerging Technologies for Health and Medicine Virtual Reality, Augmented Reality, Artificial Intelligence, Internet of Things, Robotics, Industry 4.0. Scrivener Publishing LLC, Wiley.

Moolilahad & Berger. (2013). The Healing Forest in Post-Crisis Work with Children A Nature Therapy and Expressive Arts Program for Groups. Jessica Kingsley Publishers.

Rogers, C. (1995). *A Way of Being.* Open Road Integrated Media.

Sandford, N. (2018). Non- Trauma-Focused Meditation versus Exposure Therapy in Veterans with Post-Traumatic Stress Disorder: A Randomised Controlled Trial. *Lancet Psychiatry, 5.*

Susan, S. S. (2003). *Healing with Nature.* Helios Press.

Ward, B. & Rene, D. (1972). *Only One Earth: The Care and Maintenance of a Small Planet.* London: Andre Deutsch.

Watzening, P. (2023). The healing effect of the forest in integrative therapy with numerous exercise examples for practice. Springer.

Wolfelt, A. (2021). *Nature Heals: Reconciling Your Grief through Engaging with the Natural World (Words of Hope and Healing).* Companion Press.

Chapter 12
Synergizing Horizons:
The Tech-Driven Unification of Health, Environment, and the Law

Anupreet Kaur Mokha

ⓘ https://orcid.org/0000-0003-0822-2807
SGTB Khalsa College, University of Delhi, India

ABSTRACT

The chapter explores the transformative implications of the tech-driven unification of health, environment, and legal domains, emphasizing the profound impact on societal well-being. It delves into the ethical considerations that arise, balancing the collective good with individual privacy rights, addressing biases in artificial intelligence, and ensuring transparent and inclusive technological practices. Global collaboration, exemplified by India's contributions, becomes pivotal in addressing challenges that transcend borders. Looking ahead, the chapter envisions a future of innovation with advancements in predictive technologies, interoperability, and immersive experiences. It underscores the necessity of a human-centric approach, drawing insights from India's diverse landscape. The conclusion is not a static endpoint but a juncture where collaborative efforts paint a vision of a harmonious, resilient, and sustainable future, with India playing a crucial role in this ongoing narrative of global collaboration and responsible technological integration.

INTRODUCTION

For decades, the domains of health, environment, and law have operated within distinct silos, their interactions often characterized by unintended consequences and

DOI: 10.4018/979-8-3693-1178-3.ch012

missed opportunities. This fragmented approach, however, is increasingly untenable in the face of complex, interconnected challenges (Eva et al., 2022). Fortunately, the digital age presents a potent opportunity: to weave these threads together into a unified tapestry of well-being. The rise of sophisticated technologies, from big data analytics to blockchain, offers unprecedented capabilities for synergistic action. Environmental monitoring systems, empowered by sensors and satellite data, can provide real-time insights into air quality, water contamination, and other environmental factors demonstrably impacting human health. This data, seamlessly integrated with personalized healthcare platforms, can inform targeted interventions and preventive measures, ensuring a more proactive approach to public health (Naithani et al., 2023).

Furthermore, legal frameworks can leverage the transparency and immutability of blockchain technology to enhance environmental governance (Jutel, 2021). Smart contracts, self-executing agreements built on blockchain, can incentivize sustainable practices and hold polluters accountable with greater efficiency and precision (Chakrabarti & Ray, 2023). This convergence of technology and law has the potential to reshape environmental regulation, fostering a culture of responsible stewardship. However, technology alone is not a panacea. To fully realize this transformative potential, a paradigm shift is necessary. We must move beyond siloed thinking and embrace a holistic understanding of the interconnectedness of these domains. This requires active collaboration among governments, civil society, industries, and individuals. Governments must craft policies that address the intricate web of relationships between environmental health and legal frameworks. Civil society must advocate for environmental justice and hold stakeholders accountable. Industries must prioritize sustainable practices, employing the power of technology for good and individuals must become active participants in shaping a more sustainable (Jatav, 2023). The digital age presents a unique opportunity to weave a new tapestry, one where health, environment, and law are not disparate threads, but rather, a vibrant symphony of well-being. By embracing collaboration, innovation, and a holistic perspective, we can unlock a future where technology acts as the weaver, crafting a more equitable and sustainable world, thread by thread.

As we stand at the nexus of a transformative era, where technology orchestrates the convergence of health, environment, and law, we must navigate the ethical currents that rise from this confluence. Data privacy, informed consent, environmental stewardship, and responsible technological integration become the guiding principles, the ethical barometers, for charting our course through these uncharted waters (Khang et al., 2023). This chapter embarks on a critical exploration of this imperative, delving into the intricate web of relationships that bind these domains and illuminating the transformative potential of technology to forge a more sustainable future.

LITERATURE REVIEW

The convergence of health, environment, and law in the digital age presents a complex and dynamic landscape, prompting a critical review of existing literature. David (2017) and Bublitz (2019) both highlighted the transformative potential of technological innovation, particularly in the areas of environmental enforcement and health research. Environmental monitoring systems, empowered by sensors, satellites, and big data analytics, have emerged as critical sentinels, providing real-time insights into air and water quality, deforestation patterns, and climate change impacts. Das et al., (2022) highlight the effectiveness of these systems in predicting and mitigating health risks associated with environmental hazards. For instance, air quality monitoring data can be integrated with respiratory health surveillance systems to trigger targeted interventions during pollution peaks. The convergence of environmental data and personalized healthcare platforms offers a unique opportunity for targeted interventions. Pristner and Warth (2022) explored how individual environmental exposures can be factored into healthcare plans to optimize treatment and prevention strategies. For example, individuals with asthma residing in areas with high air pollution levels might benefit from personalized air filtration devices or medication adjustments based on real-time air quality data.

Khang et al., (2023) highlighted the potential of AI-powered environmental monitoring in predicting health risks, while Batko and Ślęzak (2022) showcased personalized healthcare platforms integrating environmental data for targeted interventions. Gao et al., (2021) emphasized the role of remote sensing in tracking deforestation and its impact on public health, while Lan and Chen (2020) demonstrated the effectiveness of telemedicine in bridging healthcare gaps in environmentally vulnerable regions. Manisalidis et al., (2020) analyzed the challenges in aligning environmental regulations with health considerations, while Nomani (2011) proposed a framework for integrating environmental impact assessments into legal frameworks.

Mukherjee (2020) further underscored the role of data analytics, big data, artificial intelligence, and deep learning in driving these advancements. However, the ethical, legal, and social implications of these technologies cannot be overlooked, as emphasized by Cordeiro (2021). Blockchain technology, with its immutable ledger, presents an avenue for enhancing environmental governance and legal frameworks. Allena (2020) explored how blockchain can track polluters, manage permits, and facilitate environmental justice initiatives. For instance, blockchain-based waste management systems can track the movement of hazardous materials, ensuring responsible disposal and holding violators accountable. Tripathi et al. (2023) explored the potential of blockchain in transparent environmental regulation, while Ayan et al. (2022) discussed the use of smart contracts for incentivizing sustainable practices and enhancing accountability.

The tension between the promises of digital health and the challenges it presents, including patient autonomy, equity, and data protection, is a critical consideration in this evolving landscape. As we embrace this tech-driven convergence, ethical considerations emerge as crucial guiding principles. Data privacy, informed consent, environmental ethics, and the responsible use of technology become the cornerstones for shaping a sustainable and equitable future. Natalia et al., (2019) raised concerns about data privacy violations in environmental monitoring systems, while MacIntyre et al., (2023) discussed ethical considerations in AI-driven healthcare platforms. Miya et al. (2023) highlighted the potential for technological advancements to exacerbate existing inequalities in access to healthcare and environmental resources, while Wu and Liu (2023) emphasized the need for inclusive governance models. The need for a unified vision in addressing the health and environmental concerns of disadvantaged communities is also underscored by Lee (2002).

Reviewing these studies collectively underscores the potential of technology in unifying health, environment, and legal considerations, while also emphasizing the need for a holistic and ethical approach.

SYNERGISTIC TECHNOLOGIES

Health and Environment

The rise of powerful technologies like AI, big data, and remote sensing is revolutionizing our understanding of the intricate link between environmental factors and human health (Batko & Ślęzak, 2022). By connecting environmental data with health outcomes, we can unlock a new era of personalized interventions and preventive measures. Here are some key ways technology facilitates this convergence:

Environmental Monitoring and Data Collection

- **Sensor networks:** Dense networks of sensors can monitor air quality, water quality, noise levels, and other environmental factors in real-time, providing granular data on environmental exposures.
- **Satellite and aerial imagery:** Remote sensing technologies can track deforestation, changes in water resources, and agricultural practices, offering broader insights into environmental changes impacting health.
- **Wearable devices:** Personal air pollution monitors, smartwatches, and other wearable devices can track individual exposure to environmental hazards, providing personalized data for health assessments.

Data Integration and Analysis

- **Big data analytics:** Powerful algorithms can analyze vast datasets of environmental and health data, identifying patterns and correlations between specific exposures and health outcomes. This allows for targeted interventions and risk assessments for specific populations or individuals.
- **Machine learning:** Machine learning models can predict future health risks based on real-time environmental data and individual health histories, enabling proactive preventive measures.
- **Geographical Information Systems (GIS):** Mapping tools can visualize the spatial distribution of environmental hazards and health outcomes, revealing hotspots and informing targeted interventions.

Personalized Interventions and Preventive Measures

- **Environmental alerts and advisories:** Real-time air quality alerts can inform individuals with asthma or respiratory issues to take precautions, while alerts on water contamination can prompt public health interventions.
- **Location-based health recommendations:** Smartphone apps can provide personalized recommendations based on individual exposure to environmental hazards, suggesting alternate routes, or suggesting protective measures.
- **Precision medicine:** Environmental data can be integrated into personalized health plans, allowing for tailored interventions and preventative measures based on individual genetic and environmental susceptibilities.

Public Health Surveillance and Policy

- **Early warning systems:** Real-time monitoring of environmental data can provide early warnings of potential health threats like outbreaks of mosquito-borne diseases, enabling timely public health interventions.
- **Targeted environmental policies:** Data-driven insights can inform evidence-based environmental policies, focusing on reducing specific exposures linked to health problems in specific regions or populations.
- **Community engagement:** Public dashboards and visualizations of environmental data can empower communities to understand local environmental risks and advocate for change.

By harnessing the power of technology, we can bridge the gap between environmental data and health outcomes, paving the way for a healthier future for individuals and communities alike.

Environment and Legal

The current state of environmental governance faces significant challenges: opaque monitoring systems, lagging enforcement, and inadequate incentives for sustainable practices (Jutel, 2021). Fortunately, the rise of technology, particularly blockchain, offers promising solutions to these challenges, fostering a new era of transparent oversight and incentivized sustainability.

Blockchain for Transparent Monitoring

- **Immutable Data Records:** Blockchain technology provides an immutable and tamper-proof ledger for environmental data, from pollution levels to resource extraction. This ensures data integrity and transparency, preventing manipulation or greenwashing.
- **Decentralized Monitoring Systems:** Sensor networks and satellite imagery can be integrated with blockchain, allowing real-time data collection and verification by independent nodes, eliminating dependence on centralized authorities.
- **Traceability and Auditing:** Blockchain enables the tracking of resources through supply chains, from raw materials to finished products. This transparency empowers consumers to make informed choices and holds corporations accountable for their environmental footprint.

Smart Contracts for Sustainable Incentives

- **Conditional Payments:** Smart contracts, self-executing agreements on the blockchain, can automate payments based on environmental performance. For example, farmers who implement sustainable practices could receive automatic payments for carbon sequestration or biodiversity conservation.
- **Decentralized Marketplaces:** Blockchain can facilitate peer-to-peer trading of environmental credits, allowing companies and individuals to offset their emissions or invest in sustainable projects directly.
- **Incentivized Data Sharing:** Smart contracts can incentivize individuals and organizations to share environmental data, creating a richer pool of information for better decision-making and policy development.

Health and Legal

The intersection of healthcare and legal systems often presents a chasm for individuals facing environmental harm (Miya et al., 2023). Lack of access to healthcare can exacerbate health impacts, while legal recourse for environmental damage can be complex and inaccessible However, the rise of technology offers innovative solutions to bridge this gap and ensure both healthcare access and environmental justice.

Telemedicine and Remote Sensing

- **Telemedicine platforms:** Online consultations and remote patient monitoring can expand access to healthcare in underserved areas, particularly those affected by environmental hazards. This can be crucial for communities facing pollution-related respiratory illnesses, waterborne diseases, or mental health impacts.
- **Remote sensing and AI-powered health surveillance:** Satellite imagery and AI analysis can track environmental changes and predict outbreaks of diseases linked to environmental factors. This can trigger preventive healthcare interventions and resource allocation to vulnerable populations.

Legal Tech Platforms and AI-powered Case Management

- **Legal chatbot and knowledge bases:** Online platforms equipped with AI-powered chatbots and knowledge bases can provide accessible legal information and self-help tools, empowering individuals to navigate environmental legal issues and seek legal recourse.
- **AI-driven case management and evidence gathering:** AI algorithms can analyze large datasets of environmental data and legal documents, identifying potential cases of environmental harm and streamlining the process of gathering evidence for legal action.

Blockchain for Secure Data Sharing and Transparency

- **Secure data sharing platforms:** Blockchain technology can facilitate secure and transparent sharing of medical records and environmental data between healthcare providers, legal professionals, and individuals. This can improve case-building and ensure fair compensation for victims of environmental harm.

- **Decentralized crowdfunding and resource allocation:** Blockchain-based crowdfunding platforms can enable individuals and communities affected by environmental harm to raise resources for legal action and environmental remediation, fostering collective action and empowerment.

Personalized Legal Assistance and Advocacy

- **AI-powered legal bots and virtual assistants:** Personalized legal bots can provide initial assessments of environmental harm cases, suggest potential legal avenues, and guide individuals through the legal process, reducing barriers to access to justice.
- **Online communities and advocacy platforms:** Technology can create online spaces for individuals and communities affected by environmental harm to connect, share experiences, and amplify their voices, fostering collective advocacy and pressure for policy change.

Nexus between Health, Environment and Legal

In today's interconnected world, the fields of health, environment, and law are increasingly interdependent. Technological advancements have played a significant role in linking these domains, creating new opportunities for collaboration and integration. Businesses, government agencies, healthcare sectors, community organizations, and individuals are recognizing the importance of addressing the social determinants of health systematically and strategically. The social determinants of health refer to the social, economic, and environmental factors that influence individual and population health outcomes (Yang et al., 2013). Collaboration in healthcare settings requires a flexible and boundary-spanning workforce that can accommodate diverse disciplines, education, and demographic characteristics (Brown et al., 2019). Understanding the social determinants of health is crucial in identifying and addressing the underlying causes of health disparities. By adopting a tech-driven approach, we can synergize the horizons of health, environment, and law to create a comprehensive and holistic understanding of the factors that affect individual and population well-being. The social determinants of health framework recognize that the environment in which individuals live, work, and play has a significant impact on their health (Lan and Chen, 2022).

For example, socioeconomic status, education, employment opportunities, access to healthcare services, and the built environment all play a role in determining health outcomes. By leveraging technology, we can gather and analyze vast amounts of data related to these social determinants and identify patterns and trends that may have otherwise gone unnoticed (Mukherjee, 2020). This information can then be used to inform healthcare policies, interventions, and resource allocation, ultimately leading to improved health outcomes for individuals and communities. Furthermore, technology can facilitate collaboration and communication between different stakeholders working in the fields of health, environment, and law (David et al., 2017). For instance, telehealth and digital health platforms can connect healthcare providers with patients in remote or underserved areas, ensuring access to essential healthcare services.

Additionally, technology can support the integration of environmental data into healthcare practices. This can help healthcare providers understand the impact of environmental factors on health outcomes and make informed decisions to prevent and mitigate potential risks (Batko & Ślęzak, 2022). Moreover, technology can also aid in the enforcement of legal regulations related to health and environmental protection. By utilizing digital tools, such as data analytics and artificial intelligence, we can identify areas with high health disparities and prioritize resources accordingly. By integrating technology into the realms of health, environment, and law, we can create a synergistic approach that maximizes the potential for positive impact (Mukherjee, 2020). This tech-driven unification of health, environment, and law not only enhances our understanding of the complex interplay between these domains but also enables us to develop innovative solutions that address the underlying determinants of health and environmental disparities (Nomani, 2011). By leveraging technology, we can gather and analyze vast amounts of data related to the social determinants of health. This includes factors such as socioeconomic status, education, employment opportunities, access to healthcare services, and the built environment. By collecting and analyzing this data, we can identify patterns and trends that may contribute to health disparities and environmental inequities (Batko & Ślęzak, 2022). For example, we may discover that communities with lower income levels have limited access to healthcare facilities and healthy food options, leading to higher rates of chronic diseases. The nexus between health and law is not a static intersection, but rather a dynamic interplay. Legal frameworks safeguard public health through regulations and ethical considerations in medicine, holding healthcare professionals accountable and protecting vulnerable populations. Yet, health challenges like pandemics and disparities in access inform legal responses, prompting innovations in equitable healthcare and mental health awareness. As artificial intelligence and global health concerns surface, this intricate tapestry demands interdisciplinary collaboration and evolving legal frameworks to ensure health thrives under the aegis of justice.

Therefore, synergizing horizons is not merely a technological endeavor; it is a collective journey towards a future where the health of people, the planet, and prosperity are inextricably linked. The health of our planet, our people, and our legal systems are intricately intertwined. Environmental degradation pollutes our air and water, triggering respiratory illnesses and impacting food security. Laws can protect ecosystems and regulate pollution, but their effectiveness hinges on robust enforcement and equitable access to justice (Nomani, 2011). Meanwhile, legal frameworks that prioritize public health can incentivize green technologies and sustainable practices, creating a virtuous cycle of environmental protection and improved well-being. This nexus between health, environment, and law demands holistic approaches, where legal frameworks safeguard both ecological and human health, fostering a future where environmental justice and public health thrive in harmony (Naithani et al., 2023). This chapter serves as an invitation to embark on this critical exploration, to break down the silos, and to join hands in forging a more sustainable and equitable world. It is a call to action, a clarion cry for a new era of collaboration and unified action.

REAL- LIFE EXAMPLES OF TECH-DRIVEN CONVERGENCE IN ACTION

Air pollution forecasting and asthma management: The AirVisual app by IQAir combines real-time air quality data with individual health profiles to provide personalized asthma alerts and preventative recommendations (IQAir, 2021). This empowers users to adjust their activities based on air quality, reducing exposure and improving health outcomes.

- **Mosquito-borne disease prediction and prevention:** AI-powered platforms like the Mosquito Alert system analyze weather data and satellite imagery to predict mosquito breeding grounds and outbreaks of diseases like dengue fever. This enables targeted public health interventions and community education, saving lives and reducing healthcare costs (Yang et al., 2023).
- **Tracking deforestation and illegal logging:** The World Wildlife Fund's blockchain-based platform, Veriforest, uses satellite data and blockchain technology to track timber supply chains, ensuring sustainable forestry practices and preventing illegal logging (Otieno, 2023). This protects endangered ecosystems and empowers consumers to make informed choices about the products they purchase.
- **Decentralized renewable energy marketplaces:** Platforms like Power Ledger allow individuals to trade directly generated solar energy through blockchain-powered microgrids. This fosters community ownership and promotes decentralized renewable energy solutions, contributing to energy independence and sustainability (Wallet, 2023).

- **Telemedicine for remote communities:** Programs like Project ECHO utilize telemedicine platforms to connect healthcare professionals in urban areas with rural communities, providing access to specialized medical consultations and improving health outcomes in underserved regions McBain et al., (2019).
- **AI-powered legal assistance for environmental justice:** Platforms like LawHelp.org use AI to provide legal information and resources to individuals facing environmental harm. This empowers communities to understand their rights, seek legal recourse, and hold polluters accountable.

These real-world examples demonstrate the immense potential of tech-driven convergence for fostering a healthier, more sustainable, and equitable future. By leveraging technology to bridge the gap between health, environment, and law, we can break down silos, address complex challenges holistically, and weave a brighter future for generations to come.

COLLABORATIVE GOVERNANCE AND STAKEHOLDER ENGAGEMENT

Effectively managing the intricate interplay between health, environment, and legal aspects necessitates collaborative governance models. The Indian government's "National Clean Air Program" exemplifies such collaboration, engaging experts, communities, and industries to devise strategies for improved air quality. Furthermore, stakeholder engagement ensures that the perspectives of communities, NGOs, and businesses are considered, amplifying the efficacy of implemented strategies.

Collaborative Governance

Collaborative governance is a model that involves the joint efforts of multiple stakeholders, including government bodies, non-governmental organizations (NGOs), community representatives, businesses, and experts from various fields. In the context of health, environment, and legal convergence, collaborative governance recognizes that complex challenges require the collective expertise and commitment of diverse stakeholders.

National Clean Air Program (NCAP) in India

The "National Clean Air Program" (NCAP) in India is a noteworthy example of collaborative governance aimed at addressing air quality issues. Launched by the Ministry of Environment, Forest, and Climate Change, NCAP seeks to reduce air pollution levels in the country's most polluted cities. The program sets ambitious targets for the reduction of particulate matter (PM) levels and aims to enhance air quality monitoring, public awareness, and regulatory enforcement (Guttikunda et al., 2023).

Engaging Experts, Communities, and Industries

Collaborative governance involves bringing together experts, communities, and industries to collectively tackle environmental challenges. In the case of NCAP, experts from environmental science, health, and technology contribute their knowledge to formulate evidence-based strategies. (Mishra, 2023). Communities, especially those directly affected by poor air quality, are engaged to provide insights into local dynamics and to ensure that interventions are culturally and contextually appropriate. Industries, a significant source of air pollutants, are also stakeholders, and their collaboration is essential to implement sustainable practices and adhere to regulations (Roy et al., 2023).

Public Participation and Community Engagement

Stakeholder engagement goes beyond traditional governance structures to include public participation and community engagement. NCAP recognizes the importance of involving citizens in decision-making processes related to air quality. This participatory approach ensures that policies and interventions align with the needs and concerns of the people (Guttikunda et al., 2023). Platforms for public awareness, feedback mechanisms, and community-driven initiatives contribute to the success of collaborative governance in improving air quality (Roy et al., 2023).

Role of Non-Governmental Organizations (NGOs)

Non-Governmental Organizations (NGOs) play a crucial role in collaborative governance by acting as intermediaries between communities and government agencies. They often bring grassroots perspectives, advocate for marginalized communities, and contribute to the implementation of projects. In the context of air quality improvement, NGOs may conduct awareness campaigns, monitor pollution levels, and hold stakeholders accountable for their commitments (Kaginalkar et al., 2023).

Business and Industry Involvement

Engaging industries is a key aspect of collaborative governance, especially in sectors contributing significantly to environmental issues. The NCAP recognizes the need to work with industries to adopt cleaner technologies, adhere to emission standards, and invest in sustainable practices. Incentives and regulatory frameworks are designed collaboratively to encourage businesses to align their operations with environmental goals (Roy et al., 2023).

Policy Formulation and Implementation

Collaborative governance extends to the formulation and implementation of policies. In the case of NCAP, stakeholders contribute to the development of air quality improvement strategies. The collaborative approach ensures that policies are not only effective but also feasible and acceptable to all involved parties (Mishra, 2023). Furthermore, continuous dialogue and feedback mechanisms allow for adaptive governance, enabling adjustments to strategies based on real-time data and changing circumstances.

Challenges and Success Factors

While collaborative governance offers numerous advantages, it is not without challenges. Balancing diverse interests, ensuring equitable representation, and managing conflicts are inherent complexities. Success factors include transparent communication, trust-building among stakeholders, and a commitment to shared goals (Mishra, 2023). Regular evaluations and assessments contribute to the refinement and optimization of collaborative governance structures (Roy et al., 2023). Therefore, collaborative governance and stakeholder engagement in the context of health, environment, and legal convergence exemplify a dynamic and inclusive approach to addressing complex challenges. The NCAP in India demonstrates how bringing together experts, communities, industries, and NGOs can lead to more comprehensive and sustainable solutions, fostering a shared responsibility for the well-being of society and the environment (Guttikunda et al., 2023).

ETHICAL CONSIDERATIONS AND CHALLENGES

As we navigate the tech-driven unification of health, environment, and legal domains, a critical facet that demands thoughtful consideration is the ethical dimension. This section explores the myriad ethical considerations and challenges that arise in the integration of technology across these interconnected realms.

Balancing the Greater Good and Individual Privacy Rights

At the heart of ethical considerations lies the delicate balance between pursuing the greater good for society and safeguarding individual privacy rights. In the realm of health, for instance, the collection and utilization of vast datasets, including personal health records and behavioral patterns, raise concerns about potential privacy infringements. Striking a balance between leveraging this data for public health advancements and protecting individuals from unwarranted surveillance requires nuanced ethical frameworks (Yalavarthy, 2023). An example from India is the ongoing debate surrounding the Aadhaar project. While Aadhaar, a biometric identification system, aims to streamline public services and welfare programs, concerns about privacy breaches and the potential misuse of personal data have sparked ethical discussions and legal challenges (Roy, 2023).

Data Ownership, Access, and Informed Consent

The question of who owns health and environmental data and who should have access to it poses significant ethical challenges. In a tech-driven environment, ensuring that individuals retain control over their personal data becomes imperative. Establishing robust mechanisms for informed consent, allowing individuals to understand and control how their data is used, is an ethical cornerstone (Bresnihan & Millner, 2023). India's experience with data ownership is exemplified by its evolving data protection laws. The ongoing development of the Digital Personal Data Protection Bill seeks to establish clear guidelines for data usage, protection, and consent, reflecting the nation's commitment to ethical data practices (Banisar, 2023).

Addressing Bias in Artificial Intelligence

The integration of artificial intelligence (AI) introduces ethical challenges related to bias in algorithms. AI systems trained on biased datasets may perpetuate and exacerbate existing societal biases. In healthcare, for instance, biased algorithms can lead to disparities in diagnosis and treatment, impacting vulnerable populations disproportionately. The controversy surrounding "Caste-Aware Algorithms" in India illustrates this concern. Algorithms that inadvertently perpetuate or reinforce social biases based on caste or other demographic factors highlight the need for rigorous ethical scrutiny in the development and deployment of AI technologies (Mathiyazhagan, 2023).

Ensuring Transparency and Accountability

The ethical use of technology requires transparency and accountability from all stakeholders. This involves clear communication about how data is collected, processed, and used, as well as accountability mechanisms for any unintended consequences or misuse. Transparent governance models, especially in the context of collaborative efforts, are essential for building trust among stakeholders. India's push towards digital transparency in governance is demonstrated by initiatives like the Open Government Data (OGD) Platform. By making government data freely available and accessible, such platforms aim to promote transparency and accountability while adhering to ethical principles (Saxena & Janssen, 2017).

Promoting Inclusivity and Avoiding Technological Exclusion

Ethical considerations extend to ensuring that technological advancements benefit all segments of society and do not inadvertently contribute to exclusion. In the context of health and environmental technologies, there is a risk of creating digital divides where certain populations, due to socioeconomic factors or lack of access, are excluded from the benefits of these advancements (Boeva et al., 2023). India's digital literacy initiatives, such as the National Digital Literacy Mission, underscore the ethical imperative of ensuring that technological benefits are inclusive and reach all strata of society.

Continuous Ethical Oversight and Adaptation

Given the dynamic nature of technology, ethical considerations must be an ongoing focus. Ethical oversight should not be static but rather adapt to the evolving technological landscape. Regular reviews, ethical impact assessments, and responsiveness to emerging ethical challenges are critical components of a robust ethical framework (De, 2023). Hence, the tech-driven unification of health, environment, and legal domains demands meticulous attention to ethical considerations. Striking a balance between societal benefits and individual rights, addressing biases in technology, ensuring transparency and inclusivity, and maintaining continuous ethical oversight is imperative for navigating the ethical complexities of this integrated future. The lessons learned from India's experiences, challenges, and evolving ethical frameworks contribute to a global discourse on responsible and ethical technological integration.

ADDRESSING THE CHALLENGES: SOLUTION FOR A SUSTAINABLE AND EQUITABLE FUTURE

The transformative potential of tech-driven convergence across health, environment, and law is undeniable. However, these vital strands often remain tangled in silos, creating a complex landscape of environmental degradation, health disparities, and social inequities (Brown et al., 2019). This chapter delves into the critical challenges arising from this fragmentation and proposes a framework for holistic solutions, paving the way for a sustainable and equitable future. Here are some solutions to address the challenges and ensure this convergence leads to a sustainable and equitable future:

- **Robust data governance frameworks:** Implement clear guidelines on data collection, storage, use, and sharing, prioritizing transparency, privacy, and security.
- **Bias mitigation in algorithms:** Develop and deploy AI algorithms that are fair, inclusive, and do not perpetuate existing inequalities.
- **Public awareness and education:** Empower individuals to understand their data rights, how their data is used, and how to protect their privacy.
- **Invest in infrastructure and technology access:** Expand broadband access, provide affordable devices, and offer digital literacy training in underserved communities.
- **Develop context-appropriate solutions:** Design technologies that are culturally sensitive, linguistically accessible, and address the specific needs of diverse communities.
- **Promote digital inclusion initiatives:** Foster collaboration between governments, NGOs, and technology companies to bridge the digital divide and ensure equitable access to the benefits of technology.
- **Break down siloes and encourage cross-disciplinary dialogue:** Facilitate collaboration between researchers, policymakers, practitioners, and communities across health, environment, and law.
- **Invest in interdisciplinary research and training programs:** Develop educational initiatives that equip professionals with the skills and knowledge needed to navigate the complexities of tech-driven convergence.
- **Create platforms for co-creation and knowledge sharing:** Establish platforms where stakeholders can share best practices, learn from each other, and co-create solutions to address emerging challenges.
- **Engage in open communication and dialogue:** Foster ongoing communication with the public about the potential benefits and risks of tech-driven convergence.

- **Ensure transparency in decision-making processes:** Make data and algorithms accessible and understandable, allowing for public scrutiny and feedback.
- **Develop robust accountability mechanisms:** Implement mechanisms to hold developers, policymakers, and users accountable for the ethical use of technology.
- **Empower communities to participate in decision-making:** Ensure that local communities have a say in how technology is used to address their specific health, environmental, and legal needs.
- **Support community-driven innovation:** Encourage the development of locally-driven solutions that are tailored to the unique challenges and contexts of specific communities.
- **Promote data sovereignty and ownership:** Empower communities to own and control their data, ensuring they benefit from its value and use.

By addressing the challenges through these proactive solutions, we can ensure that tech-driven convergence fulfills its potential to create a more sustainable and equitable future for all. This is an ongoing process that requires continuous collaboration, adaptation, and a shared commitment to building a future where technology is a tool for positive change, not a source of further inequalities.

FUTURE PROSPECTS

The tech-driven unification of health, environment, and legal considerations propels society into a future defined by boundless potential and transformative possibilities. As we look ahead, several key aspects and prospects emerge, shaping the trajectory of this integration and its impact on global well-being.

Advancements in Predictive Technologies

The future holds the promise of even more sophisticated predictive technologies that leverage artificial intelligence and machine learning (Bhattamisra et al., 2023). AI-driven simulations and predictive analytics will become more refined, enabling more accurate forecasting of environmental trends, public health outcomes, and legal implications (Bresnihan & Millner, 2023). These advancements will empower decision-makers with unparalleled insights into potential challenges and opportunities, allowing for proactive measures and strategic planning.

Global Collaboration for Addressing Global Challenges

The interconnected nature of health, environment, and legal domains calls for enhanced international collaboration. Future prospects involve nations working together to share data, insights, and best practices. Collaborative efforts on a global scale will be instrumental in addressing overarching challenges such as climate change, biodiversity loss, and pandemics. Platforms for information exchange and joint initiatives will emerge, fostering a united approach to issues that transcend national boundaries (Parida et al., 2023). India's participation in global climate initiatives, coupled with its commitment to sustainable development, positions it as a key player in these collaborative efforts (Hussain et al., 2023). The nation's experiences and innovations will contribute to a shared pool of knowledge aimed at addressing pressing global challenges.

Integration of Virtual and Augmented Reality

The integration of virtual and augmented reality technologies holds immense potential for transforming how we perceive and interact with health, environment, and legal data. Future scenarios may involve immersive experiences that allow policymakers, scientists, and legal experts to visualize complex datasets in three-dimensional spaces. This immersive approach enhances understanding and facilitates more informed decision-making processes (Khang et al., 2023).

Enhanced Interoperability and Data Sharing

The future envisions a seamless integration of diverse datasets from health, environment, and legal domains. Improved interoperability standards and secure data-sharing mechanisms will break down silos, allowing for a more holistic understanding of interconnected issues (Chakrabarti & Ray, 2023). Open data initiatives will proliferate, fostering a collaborative environment where researchers, policymakers, and communities can access and contribute to a shared pool of information.

Rapid Response Systems for Emerging Challenges

As technology continues to advance, the development of rapid response systems will become more sophisticated. These systems will be capable of quickly mobilizing resources and implementing targeted interventions in response to emerging health threats, environmental crises, or legal challenges. The integration of real-time data and advanced communication technologies will enable authorities to address issues promptly and effectively (Bresnihan & Millner, 2023).

Ethical and Inclusive Technological Development

Future prospects emphasize an increased focus on ethical considerations in technological development. As society becomes more aware of the potential ethical pitfalls of technology, there will be a concerted effort to ensure that advancements are aligned with principles of fairness, transparency, and inclusivity (Parida et al., 2023). Ethical guidelines and frameworks will evolve to address emerging challenges, and societies will prioritize responsible technological innovation.

Catalyzing Sustainable Development Goals

The integration of health, environment, and legal considerations through technology will play a pivotal role in achieving sustainable development goals (SDGs). Future endeavors will align with SDGs, addressing issues such as good health and well-being, climate action, and justice. The tech-driven convergence becomes a catalyst for positive change, contributing to a more equitable (Ikromjonovich, 2023).

Therefore, the future prospects of the tech-driven unification of health, environment, and legal horizons are marked by innovation, collaboration, and a commitment to addressing complex challenges. As we move forward, the fusion of technology with these interconnected domains holds the potential to shape a future where holistic well-being, environmental sustainability, and justice are central tenets of global progress (Lange, 2023). India's role in these future endeavors will be significant, leveraging its technological expertise and commitment to sustainable development to contribute to a harmonious and thriving world.

CONCLUSION

For centuries, the horizons of health, environment, and law have stood as distinct silos, casting long shadows across our planet and its inhabitants. Fragmented approaches have plagued our efforts to address pressing challenges, leading to environmental degradation, health disparities, and systemic inequities. Yet, on the horizon, a new dawn is breaking, illuminated by the promise of technological convergence. This fusion of data, intelligence, and innovation presents a transformative opportunity, not just to solve isolated problems, but to weave a tapestry of a future where health thrives, the environment flourishes, and justice prevails.

The convergence of health, environment, and law through technology is not merely a collection of disparate tools, but a paradigm shift in our approach to global challenges. By connecting environmental data to health outcomes, we can predict and prevent illnesses, empowering individuals and communities to take proactive steps toward wellness. Blockchain-powered transparency and smart contracts can usher in an era of sustainable practices and environmental justice, ensuring responsible resource management and holding polluters accountable (Khang et al., 2023). By bridging the gap between healthcare and legal systems, we can dismantle barriers to access, guaranteeing equitable healthcare and legal recourse for all.

This convergence is not without its challenges. Concerns about data privacy in environmental monitoring and the ethical use of AI in healthcare platforms must be addressed through robust data governance frameworks, informed consent protocols, and transparent data practices (Das & Chadchan, 2023). We must acknowledge the potential for technological advancements to exacerbate existing inequalities in access to healthcare and environmental resources, ensuring equitable distribution and development of these technologies (Hussain et al., 2023). Collaborative research across disciplines, including health, environment, and law, is crucial to developing solutions that are comprehensive and address the intricate interdependencies between these domains (Eva et al., 2022).

Embracing the transformative potential of tech-driven convergence requires collective action. We must break down the silos that divide disciplines, fostering collaboration between scientists, policymakers, technologists, and communities (Brown et al., 2019). Open dialogue and knowledge exchange are essential to ensure that solutions are informed by diverse perspectives and address the needs of all stakeholders (O. Beyan et al., 2020). Building trust and acceptance for this convergence requires ongoing communication, transparent data practices, and active community engagement in decision-making processes.

This collaborative effort extends beyond the realm of technology. We must advocate for ethical considerations to be embedded in every stage of development and implementation, ensuring responsible data use, mitigating bias in algorithms, and upholding the highest standards of data security. Public education and awareness are crucial to empower individuals to understand the implications of this convergence and participate meaningfully in shaping its future (De, 2023).

Ultimately, the tapestry of a sustainable and equitable future cannot be woven by a single hand. It requires the collective efforts of individuals, communities, and nations united in a common purpose (Bresnihan & Millner, 2023). By embracing the power of tech-driven convergence, prioritizing ethical considerations, and fostering collaboration across all levels, we can transform the fragmented horizons of health, environment, and law into a unified landscape of shared prosperity and well-being.

The convergence of health, environment, and law through technology presents not just a solution to existing challenges, but a chance to rewrite the narrative of our future. By embracing this transformative potential, prioritizing ethical considerations, and fostering collaboration across disciplines and communities, we can weave a tapestry of hope, a future where health, environment, and justice resonate in perfect harmony. This is not just a call for action, but an invitation to participate in the grandest project of our time: weaving a future where every thread, every story, every innovation contributes to a tapestry of sustainable and equitable progress.

REFERENCES

Allena, M. (2020). Blockchain Technology For Environmental Compliance: Towards A "Choral" Approach. *Environmental Law (Northwestern School of Law)*, *50*(4), 1055–1103. https://www.jstor.org/stable/27010194

Ayan, B., Güner, E., & Son-Turan, S. (2022). Blockchain Technology and Sustainability in Supply Chains and a Closer Look at Different Industries: A Mixed Method Approach. *Logistics*, *6*(4), 85. doi:10.3390/logistics6040085

Banisar, D. (2023). *National Comprehensive Data Protection/Privacy Laws and Bills 2023*. Privacy Laws and Bills.

Batko, K., & Ślęzak, A. (2022). The use of Big Data Analytics in healthcare. *Journal of Big Data*, *9*(1), 3. doi:10.1186/s40537-021-00553-4 PMID:35013701

Beyan, O., Choudhury, A., van Soest, J., Kohlbacher, O., Zimmermann, L., Stenzhorn, H., Karim, M. R., Dumontier, M., Decker, S., da Silva Santos, L. O. B., & Dekker, A. (2020). Distributed analytics on sensitive medical data: The personal health train. *Data Intelligence*, *2*(1-2), 96–107. doi:10.1162/dint_a_00032

Bhattamisra, S. K., Banerjee, P., Gupta, P., Mayuren, J., Patra, S., & Candasamy, M. (2023). Artificial Intelligence in Pharmaceutical and Healthcare Research. *Big Data and Cognitive Computing*, *7*(1), 10. doi:10.3390/bdcc7010010

Boeva, Y., Braun, K., & Kropp, C. (2023). Platformization in the built environment: The political techno-economy of building information modeling. *Science as Culture*, 1–28. doi:10.1080/09505431.2023.2237042

Bresnihan, P., & Millner, N. (2023). *All We Want is the Earth: Land, Labour and Movements Beyond Environmentalism*. Policy Press.

Brown, R., Werbeloff, L., & Raven, R. (2019). Interdisciplinary research and impact. *Global Challenges (Hoboken, NJ)*, *3*(4), 1900020. doi:10.1002/gch2.201900020 PMID:31565373

Bublitz, F., Oetomo, A., & Sahu, S., K., Kuang, A., X. Fadrique, L., E. Velmovitsky, P., M. Nobrega, R., & P. Morita, P. (2019). Disruptive technologies for environment and health research: An overview of artificial intelligence, blockchain, and internet of things. *International Journal of Environmental Research and Public Health, 16*(20), 3847. doi:10.3390/ijerph16203847 PMID:31614632

Chakrabarti, M. S., & Ray, M. R. K. (2023). Artificial Intelligence and The Law. *Journal of Pharmaceutical Negative Results*, 87–95.

Chen, Z., Wang, Y., Li, H., & Wu, Y. (2020). Telemedicine for chronic disease management in rural areas: A systematic review. *Journal of Rural Health, 36*(3), 417-426. https://journals.sagepub.com/doi/10.1177/14604582221141835?icid=int.sj-full-text.similar-articles.3

Cordeiro, J. V. (2021). Digital Technologies and Data Science as Health Enablers: An Outline of Appealing Promises and Compelling Ethical, Legal, and Social Challenges. *Frontiers of Medicine, 8*, 647897. doi:10.3389/fmed.2021.647897 PMID:34307394

Das, D. K., & Chadchan, J. (2023). A proposed framework for an appropriate governance system to develop smart cities in India. *Territory, Politics, Governance*, 1–22. doi:10.1080/21622671.2023.2229872

Das, P., Martin Sagayam, K., Rahaman Jamader, A., & Acharya, B. (2022). Remote Sensing in Public Health Environment: A Review. In S. Biswas, C. Chowdhury, B. Acharya, & C. M. Liu (Eds.), *Internet of Things Based Smart Healthcare. Smart Computing and Intelligence.* Springer. doi:10.1007/978-981-19-1408-9_17

David, L., Markell, R. L., Glicksman., & Monteleoni, C. (2017). Technological Innovation, Data Analytics, and Environmental Enforcement. *Ecology Law Quarterly, 44*(41), 41–88. doi:10.15779/Z38C53F16C

De, J. (2023). Rethinking Environmental Governance: Exploring the Sustainability Potential in India. In *The Route Towards Global Sustainability: Challenges and Management Practices* (pp. 1–24). Springer International Publishing. doi:10.1007/978-3-031-10437-4_1

Eva, G., Liese, G., Stephanie, B., Petr, H., Leslie, M., Roel, V., Martine, V., Sergi, B., Mette, H., Sarah, J., Laura, R. M., Arnout, S., Morris, S. A., Jan, T., Xenia, T., Nina, V., Koert, V. E., Sylvie, R., & Greet, S. (2022). Position paper on management of personal data in environment and health research in Europe. *Environment International, 165*, 107334. doi:10.1016/j.envint.2022.107334 PMID:35696847

Gao, Y., Skutsch, M., Paneque-Gálvez, J., & Ghilardi, A. (2020). Remote sensing of forest degradation: A review. *Environmental Research Letters*, *15*(10), 103001. doi:10.1088/1748-9326/abaad7

Guttikunda, S., Ka, N., Ganguly, T., & Jawahar, P. (2023). Plugging the ambient air monitoring gaps in India's national clean air programme (NCAP) airsheds. *Atmospheric Environment*, *301*, 119712. doi:10.1016/j.atmosenv.2023.119712

Hussain, M. M., Pal, S., & Villanthenkodath, M. A. (2023). Towards sustainable development: The impact of transport infrastructure expenditure on the ecological footprint in India. *Innovation and Green Development*, *2*(2), 100037. doi:10.1016/j.igd.2023.100037

Ikromjonovich, B. I. (2023). Sustainable Development in the Digital Economy: Balancing Growth and Environmental Concerns. *Al-Farg'oniy avlodlari*, *1*(3), 42-50.

Jatav, S. (2023). Current Trends in Sustainable Tourism in the Indian Context. In *Handbook of Research on Sustainable Tourism and Hotel Operations in Global Hypercompetition* (pp. 391–412). IGI Global.

Jutel, O. (2021). Blockchain imperialism in the Pacific. *Big Data & Society*, *8*(1). doi:10.1177/2053951720985249

Kaginalkar, A., Kumar, S., Gargava, P., & Niyogi, D. (2023). Stakeholder analysis for designing an urban air quality data governance ecosystem in smart cities. *Urban Climate*, *48*, 101403. doi:10.1016/j.uclim.2022.101403

Khang, A., Abdullayev, V., Jadhav, B., Gupta, S. K., & Morris, G. (Eds.). (2023). *AI-Centric Modeling and Analytics: Concepts, Technologies, and Applications*. CRC Press. doi:10.1201/9781003400110

Lan, Y. L., & Chen, H. C. (2022). Telehealth care system for chronic disease management of middle-aged and older adults in remote areas. *Health Informatics Journal*, *28*(4). doi:10.1177/14604582221141835 PMID:36447304

Lange, E. A. (2023). *Transformative sustainability education: Reimagining our future*. Taylor & Francis. doi:10.4324/9781003159643

Lee, C. (2002). Environmental justice: Building a unified vision of health and the environment. *Environmental Health Perspectives*, *110*(suppl 2), 141–144. doi:10.1289/ehp.02110s2141 PMID:11929721

MacIntyre, M. R., Cockerill, R. G., Mirza, O. F., & Appel, J. M. (2023). Ethical considerations for the use of artificial intelligence in medical decision-making capacity assessments. *Psychiatry Research*, *328*, 115466. doi:10.1016/j.psychres.2023.115466 PMID:37717548

Manisalidis, I., Stavropoulou, E., Stavropoulos, A., & Bezirtzoglou, E. (2020). Environmental and Health Impacts of Air Pollution: A Review. *Frontiers in Public Health*, *8*, 14. doi:10.3389/fpubh.2020.00014 PMID:32154200

Mathiyazhagan, S. (2023). A call for algorithmic justice for SC/STs. (2023, May 14). *The Indian Express*. https://indianexpress.com/article/opinion/columns/a-call-for-algorithmic-justice-for-sc-sts-8607880/

McBain, R. K., Sousa, J. L., Rose, A. J., Baxi, S. M., Faherty, L. J., Taplin, C., Chappel, A., & Fischer, S. H. (2019). Impact of Project ECHO Models of Medical Tele-Education: A Systematic Review. *Journal of General Internal Medicine*, *34*(12), 2842–2857. doi:10.1007/s11606-019-05291-1 PMID:31485970

Mishra, A. (2023). *Clearing the Air: India's National Clean Air Programme and the Path Forward*. Policy.

Miya, T. V., Mosoane, B., Lolas, G., & Dlamini, Z. (2023). Healthcare Transformation Using Blockchain Technology in the Era of Society 5.0. In Z. Dlamini (Ed.), *Society 5.0 and Next Generation Healthcare*. Springer. doi:10.1007/978-3-031-36461-7_11

Mukherjee, S. (2020). Emerging Frontiers in Smart Environment and Healthcare – A Vision. *Information Systems Frontiers*, *22*(1), 23–27. doi:10.1007/s10796-019-09965-3

Naithani, C., Sood, S. P., & Agrahari, A. (2023). The Indian healthcare system turns to digital health: eSanjeevaniOPD as a national telemedicine service. *Journal of Information Technology Teaching Cases*, *13*(1), 67–76. doi:10.1177/20438869211061575

Natalia, A., Zhuravleva, K. C., Miloš, P., & Ivana, P. (2019). Data privacy and security vulnerabilities of smart and sustainable urban space monitoring systems. (2019). *Contemporary Readings in Law and Social Justice*, *11*(2), 56–62. doi:10.22381/CRLSJ11220198

Nomani, M. (2011). Legal Framework for Environment Impact Assessment in India: A Contemporary Appraisal in Corporate Perspective. *The Chartered Accountant Journal*, *59*, 1872–1879.

Parida, R., Katiyar, R., & Rajhans, K. (2023). Identification and analysis of critical barriers for achieving sustainable development in India. *Journal of Modelling in Management, 18*(3), 727–755.

Pristner, M., & Warth, B. (2020). Drug-Exposome Interactions: The Next Frontier in Precision Medicine. *Trends in Pharmacological Sciences, 41*(12), 994–1005. doi:10.1016/j.tips.2020.09.012 PMID:33186555

Roy, A., Nenes, A., & Takahama, S. (2023). *Current gaps in air quality management over India: A study on stakeholder consultation* (No. EGU23-12530). Copernicus Meetings.

Roy, R. (2023). The Development and Comparative Analysis of the Right to Privacy in India and the Need for a Law Governing Policy. *Legal Spectrum J., 3*, 1.

Saxena, S., & Janssen, M. (2017). Examining open government data (OGD) usage in India through UTAUT framework. *Foresight, 19*(4), 421–436. doi:10.1108/FS-02-2017-0003

Tripathi, G., Ahad, M. A., & Casalino, G. (2023). A comprehensive review of blockchain technology: Underlying principles and historical background with future challenges. *Decision Analytics Journal, 9*, 100344. doi:10.1016/j.dajour.2023.100344

Wallet, S. (2023, December 11). Power ledger (Powr): A blockchain solution for the future of energy. *Medium*. https://medium.com/coinmonks/power-ledger-powr-a-blockchain-solution-for-the-future-of-energy-00cfe3e2b639

Wu, Y., & Liu, X. M. (2023). Navigating the Ethical Landscape of AI in Healthcare: Insights from a Content Analysis. *TechRxiv, 42*(3), 76-87. doi:10.36227/techrxiv.22294513.v2

Yalavarthy, A. S. (2023). Aadhaar: India's National Identification System and Consent-Based Privacy Rights. *Vand. J. Transnat'l L., 56*, 619.

Yang, H., Nguyen, T.-N., & Chuang, T.-W. (2023). An Integrative Explainable Artificial Intelligence Approach to Analyze Fine-Scale Land-Cover and Land-Use Factors Associated with Spatial Distributions of Place of Residence of Reported Dengue Cases. *Tropical Medicine and Infectious Disease, 8*(4), 238. doi:10.3390/tropicalmed8040238 PMID:37104363

Yang, Z., Kankanhalli, A., Ng, B. Y., & Lim, J. T. Y. (2013). Analyzing the enabling factors for the organizational decision to adopt healthcare information systems. *Decision Support Systems, 55*(3), 764–776. doi:10.1016/j.dss.2013.03.002

Chapter 13

Preserving Public Health:
Strengthening Hazardous Waste Rules for a Safer Future

Deepayan Malaviya
Jindal Global Law School, O.P. Jindal Global University, India

ABSTRACT

There has been an increase in the hazardous waste trade amongst countries of the world; consequently, two approaches have emerged over time. India follows the principles laid down by the Basel convention and incorporates the safeguard of PIC. The hazardous waste (management and transboundary movement) rules, 2016 incorporates the safeguard and regulates the movement of hazardous waste to and from India. Despite the stringent procedural requirement there have been cases wherein hazardous waste has been dumped in India. Research Foundation for Science Technology and Natural Resources Policy v. Union of India (1995) is one such case wherein waste oil was imported in India while being labelled as lubricating oil. The waste oil had to be destroyed in India by way of incineration because other measures were not deemed feasible by the Apex court. A similar thing happened in 2018 in the case of P.P. Electronics v New Delhi (Import & General). The chapter analyses the law, highlights the gaps and challenges and provides remedy for preserving public health in India.

INTRODUCTION

With the increase in the world population, the consumption is increasing. To fulfill the increasing consumption more raw materials are required to undergo industrial

DOI: 10.4018/979-8-3693-1178-3.ch013

processes so that more finished goods can be produced. Waste is the outcome of certain industrial processes. Since waste is not useful it either needs to be treated and disposed or recycled or reutilized into other processes as raw material. But this reutilizing and recycling also has certain ghost costs which we cannot see, the ghost costs include cost to health, biodiversity, climate change, amenities (UNEP, 2012, p. 24). Above ghost costs are lesser for non-hazardous waste as compared to hazardous waste, especially when the hazardous waste is dumped illegally and without adhering to the law of the land. Africa witnessed this during the late 1900s wherein lot of northern based firms had started to dump hazardous waste in African countries (Jennifer Clapp, 1994, p. 19). What were the reasons for dumping hazardous waste in African countries? The answer is two-fold, first, increased public awareness within industrialized countries and the manifestation of not-in-my-backyard-syndrome and second, the increased cost of disposal in the industrialized countries (Jennifer Clapp, 1994, p. 19). Since Africa had weak regulation and law regarding hazardous waste disposal it quickly became a dumping ground for hazardous waste. Thus, we see a weak regulation coupled with lax policy leading Africa to be perceived as a dumping ground by the developed world. This perception damaged not only the environment of Africa but also the public health of Africa as a whole. Increased awareness and not-in-my backyard syndrome also forced developing countries to export the waste to other countries (MARK N. WEXLER, 1996, p. 93).

The ill effects of dumping were seen by many other developing countries as well, the media publicized it and as a result developing countries had to establish national mechanisms to control the waste trade. The world was divided in two camps when it came to establishing regulatory mechanisms and this came to light during the negotiation of the Basel Convention. The developing wanted a complete ban on the trade of hazardous waste, the reasons for pursuing such approach was that they had already seen the ills of dumping and did not want the practice to continue any longer. The developed countries, on the other hand, involved in waste producing and dealing firms wanted the waste trade to be legal and without restrictions (Jennifer Clapp, 1994, p. 23). The mechanism to regulate the hazardous waste was accepted by the United Nations Environment Program and the Basel Convention was established as a consequence that 'regulated' the transborder movement of hazardous wastes and worked on the principle of Prior Informed Consent (Basel Convention on the Control of Transboundary Movements of Hazardous Wastes and Their Disposal, 1989). Based on this principle, the importing party must be notified about the shipment containing hazardous waste in advance. The transaction can take place only if the importing nation agrees to accept the waste, and ensures that the waste shall be disposed off in an environmentally sound manner (Basel Convention on the Control of Transboundary Movements of Hazardous Wastes and Their Disposal, 1989, art. 2(e), 2(g), 10). African countries were not in agreement with the Basel outcome and therefore created their own convention that showed to the world that Africa would not condone the practice of promoting hazardous waste trade. Africa thus postulated for the Bamako Convention which placed a ban on the import and export of hazardous waste to and from Africa (Bamako Convention on The Ban of The Import into Africa and The Control of Transboundary Movement and Management of Hazardous Wastes Within Africa, 1998, bk. 4(2)(a)). This raises a question, pursuant to the adoption of the Bamako convention, was illegal dumping stopped in Africa? Simply put, dumping of hazardous wastes in Africa has not stopped rather, the waste traders have made the dumping difficult to trace by labelling it as "recycling" and "recovery" These loopholes have plagued both the Basel convention and the Bamako convention equally (Jennifer Clapp, 1994, p. 30). The Abijdan controversy is a standing example of the statement wherein despite the strongly worded Bamako convention, waste was dumped illegally on the Ivory coast in the year 2006.

In 2005, Trafigura bought large amounts of unrefined gasoline and intended to use it as raw material (Amnesty International, 2012, p. 3). Trafigura knew that the waste would be hazardous and that it would require treatment before disposal. On 2nd July 2006 *Probo Koala* reached Amsterdam but the stench emanating from the waste forced the authorities to test the waste, The report revealed that the waste was much more hazardous than what was projected by Trafigura. Consequently, the price for treatment was increased to €1,000 m^3 but was declined (Amnesty International, 2012, p. 8). Instead, Trafigura shipped the hazardous waste out of Amsterdam to Abijdan which it knew did not have "environmentally sound facility" for disposing off the hazardous waste (Amnesty International, 2012, p. 4). On 20th August 2006, people of Abijdan woke up to foul smell that ultimately lead to more than 100,000 people getting sick owing to the toxic waste that is dumped in the city (Amnesty International, 2012, pp. 10, 12).

The central theme of the paper shall be that a strong domestic legal framework is of great importance for securing the public health. In fact, it would be argued that public health and domestic law are directly proportional and international law and international documents are mere guiding principles when it comes to ensuring good health. The paper shall start with the International legal framework governing transborder movement of hazardous wastes, the scope shall be restricted to the Prior Informed Consent safeguard as laid down by the Basel convention. Post this the paper shall address the changing dimensions of the notion of public health and the law governing movement of hazardous waste to and from India. The next section will critically examine the said legal framework. The question that shall be answered, whether the existing legal framework regulating the movement of hazardous waste in India secures public health or compromises it? Pursuant to this section, conclusion and suggestions shall be provided, scope for further study shall also be proposed in this section.

INTERNATIONAL APPROACH WITH RESPECT TO TRANSBORDER MOVEMENT OF HAZARDOUS WASTE

The late 1900s witnessed an increase in illegal and deliberate dumping of hazardous waste by the developed countries within the borders of the developing countries (Chhibber, 2015, p. 87). Consequently, regulatory mechanisms had to be framed to curb the ill effects of illegal dumping of hazardous wastes. The United Nations came up with the Basel convention which sought to regulate the waste trade and prescribed the Prior Informed Consent (PIC) safeguard. The convention was adopted in 1989 and India ratified it in 1992. Similarly, the Rotterdam Convention was adopted in 1998 and came into force in 2004. The convention aims to "to promote shared responsibility and cooperative efforts among Parties in the international trade of certain hazardous chemicals in order to protect human health and the environment from potential harm and to contribute to their environmentally sound use, by facilitating information exchange about their characteristics, by providing for a national decision-making process on their import and export and by disseminating these decisions to Parties" (The Rotterdam Convention on the Prior Informed Consent Procedure for Certain Hazardous Chemicals and Pesticides in International Trade, 2019, art. 1). Additionally, the Stockholm Convention on Persistent Organic Pollutants was adopted in 2001 and enforced in 2004 with the aim to "to protect human health and the environment from persistent organic pollutants" (United Nations Environment Programme, 2019, art. 1). The three legal instruments ensure that the environment and human health are safe from pollutants and hazardous wastes, but the regime laid down by the Basel Convention connected to PIC warrants special discussion here.

BASEL CONVENTION AND THE PIC SAFEGUARD

Basel Convention has had more success when it comes to regulating transborder movement of hazardous wastes. Parties to the convention have acknowledged that the improper disposal of hazardous waste has impacts on the environment and human life and therefore seek to minimize hazardous waste generation and transportation of hazardous waste to developing countries especially for its disposal (Basel Convention on the Control of Transboundary Movements of Hazardous Wastes and Their Disposal, 1989, p. 4). Parties to the convention were also aware of the fact that hazardous waste can be used as raw material and not every country can afford to purchase fresh raw materials, therefore the convention allows for transborder movement for this purpose (Basel Convention on the Control of Transboundary Movements of Hazardous Wastes and Their Disposal, 1989, art. 4(9)(b)). Regarding this type of movement, the convention grants the parties freedom to come up with their own procedures provided that they do not differ from those laid down by the convention (Basel Convention on the Control of Transboundary Movements of Hazardous Wastes and Their Disposal, 1989, art. 4(9)(c)). These standard procedures require the establishment of a competent authority that will facilitate the provisions of the convention (Basel Convention on the Control of Transboundary Movements of Hazardous Wastes and Their Disposal, 1989, art. 5). It is through this competent authority that the state of export notifies to the state of import about the proposed transborder movement of hazardous waste (Basel Convention on the Control of Transboundary Movements of Hazardous Wastes and Their Disposal, 1989, art. 6(1)). The competent authority for the importer gives consent to the competent authority of the exporter based on this notification after taking into account the environmentally sound facilities among other things. Similarly, the state of export is not allowed to start the export until it has received written consent from the state of import and that there is contract between the state of import and state of export and in case the movement is for disposal, the export shall not start unless the disposer specifies that disposal shall be done in environmentally sound manner (Basel Convention on the Control of Transboundary Movements of Hazardous Wastes and Their Disposal, 1989, art. 6(2), 6(3)).

In case of departure from the set procedures the convention also lays down certain remedial safeguards. The first is the duty to re-import, wherein, if the movement of hazardous waste cannot be completed as per contract, the state of export has to take back the goods in question (Basel Convention on the Control of Transboundary Movements of Hazardous Wastes and Their Disposal, 1989, art. 8). Second, illegally dumped hazardous waste are required to be taken back by the state of export within 30 days of the illegal traffic being informed to the state of export (Basel Convention on the Control of Transboundary Movements of Hazardous Wastes and Their Disposal, 1989, art. 9). Such that there is appropriate coordination between the various competent authorities as prescribed by the convention, the convention mandates the establishing of a Secretariat to coordinate and communicate (Basel Convention on the Control of Transboundary Movements of Hazardous Wastes and Their Disposal, 1989, art. 16). Thus, we see that the convention operates on the principle of prior informed consent wherein the importer has to consent to the movement before the hazardous waste is actually moved to the importer's jurisdiction. It can also be observed that in case of deviation from the norms, appropriate sanctions are also imposed on the offending party. Such that the proposed legal framework operates smoothly, state parties are required to frame their own domestic laws that regulate the movement of hazardous waste across borders.

LAW RELATING TO HAZARDOUS WASTE IN INDIA

Initially there was no specific law for regulating or managing hazardous waste in India. What we see today in the form of Hazardous and Other Wastes (Management and Transboundary Movement) Rules, 2016 is a result of evolution that took decades, however the seed of the law were sown as early as 1860 (C.M. Jariwala, 2010, p. 423). The Indian Penal Code had provisions against fouling of water and vitiating atmosphere. Subsequently, the regulations associated with factories and industries also contributed to the growth and development of the law with respect to hazardous wastes. Pursuant to the Bhopal gas tragedy, the rule of absolute liability was incorporated into the Indian law which further strengthened the law regulating the domain of hazardous waste. Also, the Environment (Protection) Act, 1986 was formulated subsequent to the disaster. During this period, the driving force behind formulating of the law and judicial pronouncements were the health and well-being of people residing in the vicinity of industries (C.M. Jariwala, 2010, p. 424). Thus, we see that the protection and preserving of human life and public health were the factors responsible for the development of the law.

Maximum impetus was provided to the hazardous waste laws with the passage of the Hazardous Waste Management Rules, 1989. The rules were created pursuant to the international commitment given at Convention on Hazardous Waste in 1989. The 1989 rules shortly gave way to Hazardous wastes (Management Handling and Transboundary Movement) Rules, 2008 which further evolved to the Hazardous and Other Wastes (Management Handling and Transboundary Movement) Rules, 2016 (hereinafter referred to as HW Rules) as the main law that regulate the movement of hazardous waste to and from India. These rules shall be the scope of the study, they shall be studied from the perspective of safeguarding public health and the general health of the environment.

Even if enacting the HW Rules pursuant to international commitments was not required to safeguard, preserve and protect public health of the country, it has been mandated under the Constitution of India under Part IV of the Constitution of India titled Directive Principles of State Policy (Constitution of India, 1950, n.d., art. 48A). While there has been considerable debate regarding the enforceability of the directives but it they are best understood as "providing the framework of values that structure and constrain the interpretation and construction of fundamental rights" (Bhatia, 2014, pp. 2, 29). This being said, there has been constant expansion of Article 21 that has incorporated clean and healthy environment as a fundamental right (*Maneka Gandhi v Union Of India*, 1978; *M.C. Mehta v. Union of India And Ors*, 1986). What has been stated implicitly in the constitution of India has been made explicit in the HW Rules. Moreover, since India is a developing country that requires raw materials for its industries it has adopted the 'regulation' approach as laid down in the Basel convention and has adopted prior informed consent safeguard in the scheme of HW Rules.

The HW Rules were enacted in exercise of powers conferred by sections 6, 8 and 25 of the Environment Protection Act, 1986 to regulate the Hazardous waste import to and export from India. The Ministry of Environment, Forest and Climate Change (hereinafter MOEFCC) is the nodal ministry to give effect to the Rules in general (Hazardous and Other Wastes (Management and Transboundary Movement) Rules, 2016, sec. 11) The general strategy for import and export of hazardous waste is that no waste will be imported for final disposal however, hazardous wastes may be imported for the purpose of recycling, recovery, utilization and reuse (Hazardous and Other Wastes (Management and Transboundary Movement) Rules, 2016, sec. 12(2)). The Rules provide a detailed procedure for such import and export. It must be mentioned here that there are four parts of schedule III of which hazardous wastes listed under part A require the prior informed consent to be fulfilled. Hazardous wastes under part B can be imported without the requirement of prior informed consent and hazardous wates listed under part D require no permission of the MOEFCC. For the purpose of this paper, procedural and substantive aspects for importing hazardous wastes listed under part A and D shall be given special emphasis.

Users intending to import hazardous wastes listed under part A of schedule III have to apply under form 5 to the MOEFCC and the State Pollution Control Board (hereinafter referred to as SPCB), the SPCB gives its observations and comments on the capacity of the actual user to utilize or recycle the goods purported to be imported (Hazardous and Other Wastes (Management and Transboundary Movement) Rules, 2016, sec. 13). The MOEFCC takes into account these comments and observations and grants permission subject to its satisfaction that the actual user has environmentally sound facilities for the use or recycling (Hazardous and Other Wastes (Management and Transboundary Movement) Rules, 2016, sec. 13(5)). The Central Pollution Control Board (hereinafter referred to as CPCB) also takes into cognizance of the fact whether prior informed consent has been given by the actual user along with the authorization provided by the SPCB (Hazardous and Other Wastes (Management and Transboundary Movement) Rules, 2016, sec. 13(5) (iv)). Subsequent to these procedural requirements the permission is forwarded to the Custom authorities, CPCB and the SPCB to ensure compliance as per schedule VII (Hazardous and Other Wastes (Management and Transboundary Movement) Rules, 2016, sec. 13(6)). Schedule VII mentions the duties and responsibilities of MOEFCC, CPCB, SPCB, Director General of Foreign Trade (hereinafter referred to as DGFT) and the Port Authorities (Hazardous and Other Wastes (Management and Transboundary Movement) Rules, 2016, p. 42). On the perusal of the same, it can be understood that MOEFCC, and the CPCB are concerned with monitoring and licensing while the SPCB and the DGFT are concerned with coordination and granting of permissions concerned with licensing requirements and the Port Authorities which are actually assigned the responsibility of document verification, analyse waste and train officials for the purpose of implementing the requirement of the HW Rules. Further, as a measure to enforce strict compliance, the HW Rules also mandate that "the authority specified in column (2) of Schedule VII *shall* perform the duties as specified in column (3) of the said Schedule subject to the provisions of these rules" (Hazardous and Other Wastes (Management and Transboundary Movement) Rules, 2016, sec. 21).

From the above scheme of the Act, it can be seen that the until and unless India consents to the movement of hazardous waste, it cannot be imported to India. Similarly, it is the Port and Customs Authority that is supposed to verify the documents- to ensure that the shipment is accompanied with the movement documents and the test report of the hazardous waste, and analyse the waste and train personnel to check the incoming hazardous waste. The port and custom authorities are empowered to verify the report in case they feel there is discrepancy between the documents and reports furnished (Hazardous and Other Wastes (Management and Transboundary Movement) Rules, 2016, sec. 13(10)). Studying HW Rules alone is not enough to get a clear understanding of the framework. To get a comprehensive understanding, it is essential that the provisions of Customs Act, 1962 (hereinafter referred to as the Customs Act) and the Indian Ports Act, 1908 (hereinafter referred to as the Port Act) pertaining to enquiry and inspection have to be studied as well, the study will elucidate whether the law is fool-proof and whether it safeguards the public health by restricting illegal dumping of hazardous waste. The reason for this detailed study is that there have been instances in the past where hazardous waste has been labelled as "humanitarian aid and plastic raw material for industrial production" (Krueger, 1998, p. 121) and then dumped. Simply put, labels do not matter, it is the law and how it is executed that answers the questions relating to safeguarding of public health of a country. A detailed study of the Port and Customs Act shall answer the aforementioned questions.

THE FIRST LINE OF DEFENCE: PORT AND CUSTOMS AUTHORITIES

The Port Act creates the conservator and health officer as two authorities and governs the laws relating to ports and port charges (The Indian Ports Act. 1908, secs. 7, 17). The conservator is in charge of creating the port regulations, which are mainly related to the management of the port. This includes defining how and where vessels will be stationed, how they will approach the port, and how they will exit a certain port (The Indian Ports Act. 1908, sec. 8) If the conservator suspects that any violation has occurred, the conservator has the authority to board the ships and enter buildings, moreover, the conservator is also responsible for preventing the spread of any infectious disease from the vessel that has the potential to endanger public health(The Indian Ports Act. 1908, secs. 15, 6(p)). For this purpose, the health officer is required to aid and assist the conservator and is empowered to enter a vessel and require the persons in the vessel to undergo medical examination (The Indian Ports Act. 1908, sec. 17(b)). This is one of the few instances where an authority can enter. Further, the health officer can also require the furnishing of any document that he thinks necessary for ascertaining the medical conditions of those on board the vessel.

The Customs Act unifies and reforms the customs-related laws. Certain aspects of the Customs Act gain significance when considered in the context of schedule VII of the HW Rules. The purpose of the Act is to primarily define the boundaries of the customs area (The Customs Act, 1962, sec. 8). It also makes it possible to identify and stop the disposal of unlawfully imported products (The Customs Act, 1962, Chapter IVA). The Act also allows for the search, seizure, and arrest of violators in order to guarantee compliance. This power is supplemented with the power to inspect, search, and seek information (The Customs Act, 1962, sec. 108A). The prohibitions with respect to making of false declarations and providing false documentation are also crucial since, according to the HW Rules, the movement document must state that no items other than those declared are being imported (Hazardous and Other Wastes (Management and Transboundary Movement) Rules, 2016, pp. 58, 61). In addition to the specified provisions, the Customs Act covers the resolution of disputes dealing with imported and exported products as well as duties that are levied, exempt, and refundable. However, the purview of the Act is limited to the imposition of customs and other duties (The Customs Act, 1962, Chapter V). Dispute resolution is also provided for but it is to determine the duties leviable. The investigation and inspection powers likewise apply exclusively to these issues; no inquiry, investigation, or inspection relating to hazardous waste is necessary. Even for provisions that require the collection of samples, it is restricted for ascertaining the valuation of the consignment (The Customs Act, 1962, sec. 114). Thus, we see that there is no substantive provision in the Port Act or the Customs Act under which consignment can be tested and verified against the claims of the importer.

Therefore, we see that the law relating to importing the hazardous waste in India is construed in a narrow sense. Practice shows that port and custom authorities have to rely on intelligence so as to not allow hazardous waste into Indian territory. The oil furnace case is a relevant illustration for this (*Research Foundation for Science Technology and Natural Resources Policy v. Union of India & Anr.*, 1995, p. 2). In this case, Under the guise of lubricating oil, importers were bringing waste oil into India illegally. The Supreme Court of India ordered the importers to provide justification for why the aforementioned consignment should not be re-imported? why the importers should not be required to pay the costs for laboratory testing? why the polluter pays principle shouldn't be followed? and why should not they be held accountable for any losses or environmental harm done to India? The Supreme Court ordered the Commission of Customs to submit a thorough study in order to determine if the cargo comprised of hazardous waste as defined by the Basel treaty and the national legislative framework. A monitoring committee was also constituted to work with the Commissioner of Customs, the monitoring committee was also tasked to suggest possible solutions.

Pursuant to the direction, the samples were sent to the laboratory for testing and the report of the commission stated "…the importers had therefore imported Hazardous Wastes in complete and flagrant violation of the Law. I, therefore, hold and conclude that the goods, viz. Furnace oil imported and contained in the said 133 containers are hazardous" (*Research Foundation for Science Technology and Natural Resources Policy v. Union of India & Anr.*, 1995, p. 6). It was noted by the court that nothing in the cargo was imported with license and the movement to the country was absolutely illegal and in flagrant violation of the law. The court also noted that the cargo could only be discovered owing to the intelligence inputs that were available to the authorities and in the absence of the inputs it would have been very difficult to catch the illegal movement. That being said, once apprehended, an even bigger challenge lay ahead. The challenge was what was to be done with the hazardous waste? The problem was made more serious because four years had elapsed since the cargo came to India. During this time, drums had exploded which had caused the contents to leak and spread in the environment. The possibility to re-export was considered but ruled out and the court was of the informed opinion that it would only expose the environment to a greater risk. Thus, destruction of the hazardous waste by way of incineration was considered as the best possible solution to the problem. Confirming this line of action, the monitoring committee determined a cost of INR 12 per kilogram to be recovered from the importers (*Research Foundation for Science Technology and Natural Resources Policy v. Union of India & Anr.*, 1995, p. 13).

The need for inspection and verification of consignment and the loophole in the law has yet again been brought by the case of P.P. Electronics v New Delhi (Import & General) 2018. In this case, an electronics store owner imported colour picture tubes and declared them to be new and unused. After inspection by expert the tubes were found to be old, used and hazardous in nature and falling under the category of hazardous waste as laid down by the HW Rules under section 15 of the HW Rules, 2016 and the court directed the importer to re-export the goods (*P.P. Electronics v. New Delhi (Import & General)*, 2018).

DOES THE LAW CHANGE?

From the above paragraphs it can be observed that despite the procedural safeguards, hazardous waste is being brought to India. It appears that history is repeating itself, what has happened in Africa is now happening to India and the reason for this is weak regulation and low cost of disposal. Whatever requirements are stipulated by HW Rules, they are required only on paper and at every step it is the document that is being verified. It is on the basis of the verification of the document that the requirement of prior informed consent is considered complete. Form 5 i.e., the application for import of hazardous and other waste for reuse or recycling or recovery or co-processing or utilization etc., mentions in the form of undertaking that the applicant will be liable to pay fine and imprisonment for submitting a false pre-inspection certificate, but this is nothing but a toothless undertaking since no actual verification takes place by the Port and Customs Authorities. The idea that one needs to keep in mind is that a person can verify something *against* something.

The above problem is complicated for India because the hazardous waste that is sent to India is mixed with other waste. Since this is not detected at the ports it wreaks havoc for the environment initially and the public health subsequently. Trade partners of India take advantage of the loophole in the law and export waste mixed with biomedical waste, metal scrapings and other type of wastes to India. The result of this is that the purpose, i.e., reuse and/or reutilization for importing the waste by the end user, stands frustrated (Pratyush Dayal, 2023). This raises the question, Whether the law in this regard has changed in any respect? Has there any growth, evolution, development in the law? The answer is yes, partially. It must be recalled that till now discussion has taken place on hazardous wastes mentioned under part A of schedule III of HW Rules, the procedural aspects of the law have changed for hazardous wastes mentioned under part D of the HW Rules. At this juncture, it must also be recalled that for hazardous wastes mentioned under part D no prior informed consent is required, what is required is the granting of the pre-shipment inspection certificate (hereinafter referred to as PSIC) by the pre-shipment inspection authority (hereinafter referred to as the PSIA). It should be kept in mind that it is the Director General of Foreign Trade that regulates the whole process by giving license to the PISA to grant PSIC (Director General of Foreign Trade, n.d., pp. 32, 33).

However, the said procedure had to be changed owing to the challenges that came before the DGFT. India was receiving a lot of mixed waste, therefore the scope of PSIA was expanded and it was made mandatory for the PSIA to conduct analysis of waste paper so as to ensure that it is only waste paper and free from any hazardous waste including municipal waste, bio-medical waste etc (Ministry of Commerce and Industry, 2009). This mandatory requirement worked for some time but the scenario changed again. It was subsequently discovered, that certain PSIA are granting fake and false PSIC (Ministry of Commerce and Industry, 2005). To ensure compliance with the improved and stringent procedural aspects of the law, it was made mandatory for the PSIA to execute bank guarantee of INR 10 lakh for Indian firm and USD 20 thousand for a foreign firm (Ministry of Commerce and Industry, 2012). In addition to executing a bank guarantee, additional information is also required to be disclosed that includes details of testing equipment used to test for metal scrap, laboratory facilities, experience in metal inspection, details of inspecting persons, the latest requirements also require prescribing minimum qualifications for inspecting officers (Ministry of Commerce and Industry, 2012). These additional requirements further strengthen the legal regime to import waste in India. The impact of such tightening of regulations was that volume of mixed paper waste received by India drastically reduced, whatever India was receiving it was able to recycle and reutilize. By way of amendment in the policy, India is now able not only to safeguard itself against dangers of illegal dumping but also India's policy on the matter is at par with policies of other leading countries in hazardous waste management in the region (Becky Goodall, 2019, p. 27). Further, under the Foreign Trade (Development & Regulation) Act, 1992, the exporter and importer are jointly and severally responsible for any mis-declaration they make (Director General of Foreign Trade, n.d., p. 33).

Thus, we see that the law and policy have been changed and updated, at least partially, to suit the changing requirements but the same has not translated to the PIC procedure despite the cases that have come up before he various courts of the country including the Supreme Court of India. Further, in the oil furnace case, the need for laboratory testing was hinted towards by Justice Kabir. In a subsequent case wherein, it was prayed that import of all hazardous wastes to India be banned, Justice Kabir while not allowing such prayer reasoned that "…[till] such time as a particular product is identified as being hazardous, no ban can be imposed on its import on the ground that it was hazardous. Accordingly, the general prayer made in the writ petition that the Government of India should put a total ban on all hazardous wastes, can be applied in respect of such hazardous wastes as have been identified by the Basel Convention and its Protocols over the years and/or where import into the country have been restricted by the municipal laws of India…the Central Government is directed to issue appropriate notifications for banning the import of such hazardous substances as well" (*Research Foundation for Science Technology and Natural Resources Policy v. Union of India & Anr.*, 1995, para. 32).

This implies that the list provided by the Basel Convention is not an exhaustive list and more wastes can be added to this list. The question how will such new hazardous wastes be incorporated in list? The answer lies in laboratory testing and conducting pre-delivery inspection. Therefore, in light of the contemporary events and judicial observations the law needs regarding PIC needs to be amended and updated to preserve and protect the environment in generally and public health specifically.

THE EXISTING MECHANISM OF PRIOR INFORMED CONSENT

As per the HW Rules, the existing procedure for import of hazardous waste is such that the actual user has to submit an application under form 5 along with required documents to the MOEFCC and SPCB (Hazardous and Other Wastes (Management and Transboundary Movement) Rules, 2016, sec. 13(1)). Pursuant to the submission of the application to the MOEFCC and the comments and observations of the SPCB the MOEFCC gives the permission to import subject to certain conditions such as, that the importer has environmentally sound facilities to reuse and/or recycle, the importer has adequate mechanisms to dispose off the wastes generated and that the exporting country has consented to the movement of the hazardous waste from the source. (Hazardous and Other Wastes (Management and Transboundary Movement) Rules, 2016, sec. 13(5)). It is regarding this the role of SPCB comes into the picture since it has to give its observations regarding the first two requirements. SPCB has been tasked with an array of duties to discharge regarding this under schedule VII. The SPCB is required to authorize the actual users for reusing or recycling the hazardous waste. This is required to be done pursuant to periodic inspection by the CPCB. Further, the SPCB is required to examine the applications submitted by the importer and provide observations to the MOEFCC. As sanction, the SPCB can take action against violators as well (Hazardous and Other Wastes (Management and Transboundary Movement) Rules, 2016, p. 43).

Duties are not restricted to SCPB rather they extend to the State Government and the CPCB as well and it can be observed that the duties are not independent of each other rather they are closely related. For instance, it is the CPCB which lays down guidelines regarding minimizing waste generation as a result of recycling or reusing the hazardous waste and it is the SPCB that has to implement the guidelines. The co-ordination does not stop here rather it is the CPCB that has to ensure that various SPCBs act in tandem and concerted manner. In short, the duties assigned to authorities under schedule VII run in top-to-bottom fashion with SPCBs being responsible for the execution of the plan (Hazardous and Other Wastes (Management and Transboundary Movement) Rules, 2016, p. 42). From the existing scheme it becomes clear that once the hazardous waste comes into India there is a mechanism to regulate it and ensure that it does not cause any further damage or harms the environment. But herein lies the problem, especially when the waste has been mixed with other different types of waste and no pre-delivery inspection takes place. The framework of the law is such that it comes into action when the hazardous waste is inside India. If the waste does not correspond to the description all subsequent coordination and implementation becomes futile. The cases before the supreme court show this, the contemporary event prove this. Therefore, the law must be amended to suit the current requirements. A mandatory requirement of pre-delivery inspection must be introduced. Relevant provision of the Customs Act must be expanded to incorporate collection of samples for this purpose. Coordination must be established between the SPCB and the Custom authorities in this regard.

CONCLUSION

Today, public health, environment and environmental health have become important guiding principles for the country. It is essential for the Parliament to keep these factors in consideration while framing, revising and amending the law. From being embedded in the Constitution of India to being stated explicitly that right to life includes right to a clean, healthy and conducive environment, Article 21 has come a long way. However, despite this there are instances of violation of the law wherein public health and environment are affected negatively. History seems to be repeating itself. What happened with Africa in the 1980s and 1990s is now happening today with India. Practice of hazardous waste dumping was led by two causes, first, the cheap cost of disposal and second, weak regulation. Whatever be the case, it was the environment that suffered, it was the health of the people that suffered and the public health suffered as a whole. The Abidjan tragedy of 2006 is a standing testament to this fact at a global level and 'the oil furnace' case is a testament to the fact at a national level. Despite the presence of 'strong' international law, no punishment with deterrent effect was imposed on the offenders. HW Rules will only be effective once a requirement of pre-delivery inspection is introduced. This requirement shall make the HW Rules effective in the true spirit and sense. This is because the SPCB is mandated to carry out an independent assessment of the actual user's or importer's capacity with respect to ecologically sound facilities and the handling, storage, and disposal of waste produced during the recycling, repurposing, etc. process. Additionally, the SPCB must provide its input on the aforementioned at the time the MOEFCC requests it, and the MOEFCC must consider the information before approving the import of hazardous waste. This means that the SPCB already has the required facilities for testing the hazardous waste. Only requirement is the coordinating and sharing of such facilities with the Port and Customs Authorities subsequent to the amendment in the law.

This is logical since it is the Port and Customs Authorities that are the first line of defense. This premise leads us to a question, shouldn't port and customs authorities, which serve as the first line of defense against unauthorized dumping and trafficking, be the most powerful? Is there no legal framework that permits the collection of hazardous waste samples? Section 114 of Customs Act permits the gathering of samples, albeit there are particular difficulties. First off, the provision's application is restricted to determining the rate of duty or the consignment's worth. The scope of this rule needs to be expanded to include hazardous wastes because customs is the first line of defense. Second, the authority to collect samples is discretionary; it is only exercised when the customs authorities perceive a disparity in the aspects mentioned earlier. Thirdly, it is unclear how or where the sample taken will be analyzed because there is no cooperation between the SPCB and the customs department under the existing HW Rules. Fourthly, the law does not contain any substantive measures concerned with the training of customs and port authorities on the HW Rules. When these are taken together, the discretionary power mentioned above becomes futile. Considering the fact that the National Hazardous Waste Management Strategy emphasizes and prioritizes the prevention of illegal dumping in India, strengthening the Port and Customs authorities will go a long way in the realization of this national goal along with ensuring protection of the environment and public health in general (Jayanthi Natarajan, n.d., pp. 1, 4). Additional research relevant to various jurisdictions can be conducted in order to create a more comprehensive and stringent regulation to address the issues raised by hazardous waste imports into India. However, the research shall also raise concerns regarding the freightage to be paid for the time the ship remains docked at the port. Further, whatever changes in the law and policy are made need to be made after giving due weightage to the fact that India is a developing country that needs to partake in the hazardous waste trade so that it can be used as raw material in other industries. All these remain open for subsequent researches.

REFERENCES

Amnesty International. (2012). *The Toxic Truth*. Greenpeace. https://www.greenpeace.org/static/planet4-international-stateless/2012/09/9161d5e8-the-toxic-truth.pdf

Bhatia, G. (2014). *Directive Principles of State Policy: Theory and Practice* (*SSRN* Scholarly Paper 2411046). https://papers.ssrn.com/abstract=2411046

Chhibber, B. (2015). Challenges And Policy Responses To Hazardous Waste Management. *World Affairs: The Journal of International Issues*, *19*(2), 86–99.

Clapp, J. (1994). Africa, NGOs, and the International Toxic Waste Trade. *Journal of Environment & Development*, *3*(2), 17–46. doi:10.1177/107049659400300204

Constitution of India, 1950.

Dayal, P. (2023, June 25). Paper trail. *CBC News*. https://www.cbc.ca/newsinteractives/features/paper-trail

Director General of Foreign Trade. (n.d.). *Handbook of Procedures*. Ministry of Commerce and Industry. https://content.dgft.gov.in/Website/dgftprod/6978673f-9c59-4aac-a612-084df7b47e39/HBP2023_Chapter02.pdf

Goodall, B. (2019, December 27). Indian Government to Tighten Restrictions on The Import of Mixed Papers. *Resource*. https://resource.co/article/indian-government-tighten-restrictions-import-mixed-papers#disqus_thread

Jariwala, C. M. (2010). HAZARDOUS SUBSTANCE AND WASTE LAW: LESSONS FOR INDIA. *Journal of the Indian Law Institute*, *52*(3/4), 412–434.

Krueger, J. (1998). Prior Informed Consent and the Basel Convention: The Hazards of What Isn't Known. *Journal of Environment & Development*, *7*(2), 115–137. doi:10.1177/107049659800700203

Maneka Gandhi v Union Of India, (Supreme Court of India).

Mark, W. (1996). A SOCIOLOGICAL FRAMING OF THE NIMBY (NOT-IN-MY-BACKYARD) SYNDROME. *International Review of Modern Sociology*, *26*(1), 91–110.

M.C. Mehta v. Union of India And Ors, (Supreme Court February 17, 1986).

Ministry of Commerce and Industry. (2005). *Policy Circular No. 32 (RE-2005)/2004-09*. https://content.dgft.gov.in/Website/32.pdf

Ministry of Commerce and Industry. (2009). *Policy Circular No. 88 (RE-08)/2004-2009*. https://content.dgft.gov.in/Website/88.pdf

Ministry of Commerce and Industry. (2012). *Public Notice No. 104 (RE2010)/20092014*. https://content.dgft.gov.in/Website/pn10410.pdf

Natarajan, J. (n.d.). *National Hazardous Waste Management Strategy*. Ministry of Environment, Forest & Climate Change, Government of India.

P.P. Electronics v. New Delhi (Import & General), (Customs, Excise & Service Tax Appellate Tribunal 2018). 17 June 2023

Research Foundation for Science Technology and Natural Resources Policy v. Union of India & Anr., Writ Petition (civil) 657 of 1995 (Supreme Court of India 1995). https://main.sci.gov.in/jonew/judis/39386.pdf

The Customs Act, 1962, 52 of 1962 (1962). https://lddashboard.legislative.gov.in/sites/default/files/A1962-52.pdf

The Indian Ports Act. 1908, 15 of 1908 (1908). https://lddashboard.legislative.gov.in/sites/default/files/A1908-15.pdf

UNEP. (2012). *Vital Waste Graphics-3*. UN. https://globalpact.informea.org/pdf.js/web/viewer.html?file=/sites/default/files/documents/UNEP-CHW-EWASTE-PUB-VitalWasteGraphics-3.English.pdf#page=16

United Nations Environment Programme. (2019). *Stockholm Convention on Persistent Organic Pollutants*. UN. https://chm.pops.int/TheConvention/Overview/TextoftheConvention/tabid/2232/Default.aspx

Chapter 14

Guardians of Atolls:
Examining the Paris Agreement's Role in Climate Change Mitigation and Resilience in the Maldives

Siddharth Kanojia

(iD) https://orcid.org/0000-0002-1479-5292
O.P. Jindal Global University, India

ABSTRACT

The Maldives, an island nation with a low elevation, is especially susceptible to the consequences of climate change, including rising sea levels, stronger storms, and coral reef degradation. Thereby, it has been committed to reducing greenhouse gas emissions and adapting to climate change under the terms of the Paris Agreement and has actively participated in the international climate negotiations. In reference to this, this chapter aims to assess the implementation and impact of the Paris Agreement on climate action in small island developing states including the Maldives. The primary objectives of this chapter are to analyze the specific commitments and contributions of the Maldives under the Paris Agreement, to assess the effectiveness of the Maldives' adaptation efforts in response to climate change, and to evaluate the progress made by the Maldives in meeting its mitigation targets.

INTRODUCTION

The Maldives, an untamed archipelago in the midst of the Indian Ocean, is a picture-perfect paradise known for its beautiful seas, vivid coral reefs, and picture-perfect beaches. Underneath this idyllic tropical refuge, however, lurks a tale of existential

DOI: 10.4018/979-8-3693-1178-3.ch014

peril and environmental vulnerability. The majority of the Maldives' islands are only marginally above sea level, making it one of the nations with the lowest elevations in the world (Woodworth 2005). The country's highest natural point is only roughly 2.4 metres i.e., 7.9 feet above the sea level. Consequently, similar to other low-lying island countries, the Maldives has been particularly susceptible to the adverse effects of climate change, especially increasing sea levels. As a result, the stability of the islands is under jeopardy due to expanding erosion of coastal areas caused by increasing sea levels (Khan et. al 2002). The significant climatic changes has placed stress on the Maldives' natural defences i.e., coral reefs and mangroves, which hastens the loss of land. The depletion of these crucial ecosystems has an immediate impact on local fisheries in addition to the tourist sector and the delicate balance of marine life. Likewise, overfishing and unsustainable fishing practices are compromising local populations' means of subsistence. While, both land and marine habitats suffer from inadequate waste management infrastructure. Despite having a limited geographical area, the country serves as an authoritative symbol of the environmental problems spurred on by climate change. As a result of environmental problems and increasing sea levels, the country's fundamental existence is under threat.

Accordingly, the nation presents bothersome and quintessential case study for how the world community must mitigate and adapt to climate change. In this context, the Paris Agreement was hailed as a historic turning moment in the fight against climate change on an international stage when it was approved in 2015 at the 21st United Nations Climate Change Conference (COP21). In addition to pursuing efforts to keep the temperature increase to 1.5 degrees Celsius, this agreement established the framework for international cooperation to keep warming well below 2 degrees Celsius over pre-industrial levels (Gao et. al 2017). It also took cognizance of the disproportionate expense that climate change places on tiny island nations like the Maldives and calls for further assistance to help them deal with its effects. This chapter attempts to investigate and evaluate the Maldives' experience with the implementation of Paris Agreement and its effects on global warming. It is crucial to recognise the particular difficulties, triumphs, and failures Maldives has faced in its fight against climate change. The Maldives' predicament serves as symbolic of the larger global battle to realise the lofty goals of the Paris Agreement, making it a valuable case study for environmental plaintiffs, scholars, and governments everywhere.

OVERVIEW OF MALDIVES

The Dhivehin i.e., people that inhabit the Maldives, are a distinct society with a cultural and ethnographic legacy, and as of 2019, the country has a population of 533,900. The tourist industry, which makes up around 1/3rd of the Maldives' GDP and is the one that is expanding the fastest, is the engine of the nation's economy. Despite their decreased GDP contributions to 3.5% and 1.7%, respectively, agriculture and fisheries remain important sources of income and subsistence for rural areas. Meanwhile, present issues affecting development in the Maldivian region encompass potential threats posed by climate change, resilience to natural disasters, and environmental sustainability with increasing volumes of solid waste (Sovacool 2012). In particular, the nation's civilization and economy are especially exposed to rising sea levels, coastal storms and subsequent flooding, as the vast majority of the infrastructure bolstering the tourism sector, the fishery, the population, housing structures, and the critical infrastructure such as connectivity of international airports with more than 100 harbours are all concentrated in areas within 100 metres of the coast. Consequently, according to the report of Asian Development Bank (ADB)'s economic modelling, the Maldives could be the most severely affected of the six South Asian nations including Bangladesh, Bhutan, India, Nepal, and Sri Lanka in terms of the overall economic loss triggered by climate change; the simulation's mean result indicates that the damage could amount to 2.3% of GDP on average in 2050 (Bansal & Datta 2013).

The tropical monsoon season in the Maldives has profound effects on the region's climate, with warm and humid climatic conditions being prevalent all year round. The typical monthly average temperature fluctuates by no more than 1°C throughout the course of an year, with a mean annual temperature of 27.6°C historically, indicating minimal seasonal variation. Furthermore, interannual variations in temperature and precipitation near the Maldives are closely associated with two global climate circulation phenomena: the Indian Ocean Dipole (IOD) and the El Niño Southern Oscillation (ENSO) (Foley & Kelman 2020). Accordingly, conforming to data retrieved from the World Bank Group's CCKP, Male's yearly average minimum and maximum temperatures indicates a rising trend of 0.07° C and 0.17° C per decade, throughout 1969 and 1999 respectively (Rahman 2022). Whereas, the Berkeley Earth Dataset's historical warming data implies an enormous spike in warming after 1977, with the surrounding Maldivian climate warming by approximately 0.8°C over the subsequent 40 years (Sing et. al 2021). Likewise, owing to the distinct monsoon seasons, the rainfall in the Maldives is generally seasonal once a year, with the southwest monsoon bringing in the most rain. Rainfall estimates are higher on the southern islands than on the northern ones. When the average annual precipitation at Malé for the same period is examined, it becomes evident that only the southwest monsoon season exhibits a declining tendency; the northeast monsoon season shows no discernible trend (Suhaila et al. 2010). Furthermore, the possibility of marine heatwaves can also be taken into account. According to research, there was a 54% increase in the number of annual maritime heatwave days worldwide between 1925 and 2016 with the frequency and length of average marine heatwaves increasing by 34% and 17%, respectively (Suhaila et al. 2010). Although the Maldives have not been particularly stressed as being in danger by this research, the effects of these trends could be disastrous for the region's marine ecosystems, which are adapted to exist under extremely stable temperature regimes.

The most common natural occurrences in the Maldives are floods spurred on by rain. According to future climate projections, acute flooding events could become more frequent as a result of existent climate change. By the end of the century, the northern region's 150 mm of rainfall per day is predicted to have a return period of 23 years instead of 300 years. The Maldives lacks data on flood events and droughts, and it is necessary to set up an appropriate system for gathering and logging this kind of information (Sovacool et al. 2012). In contrast to numerous other little tropical islands the Maldives' cyclone (hurricane or typhoon) risk rating is low (Ranguelov & Shadiya 2018). Based on the available data, there is a 1% probability of wind speeds that could cause damage to the islands during the next ten years ((Ranguelov & Shadiya 2018). As a consequence of northern latitudes' proximity to the cyclone belt, the danger of cyclones is greatest in the north and lowest in the south. Despite this generally mild classification, a few cyclones categorized as very severe cyclonic storm, namely *Ockhi* and *Vayu* have recently affected the Maldives in November 2017 and June 2019 respectively. According to UNDP's risk assessment, the concerned region is susceptible to other dangerous hydrological natural hazards, such as storm surges, tsunamis, and *Udha*. Comprehensive risk assessments for the Maldives indicate that tsunamis, which are expected to reach maximal wave heights of 3.2 to 4.5 metres above mean sea level in some areas (Gan–Part 2007). While, swell waves and storm surges are the next most common natural hazards. Considering their close proximity to the Southern Indian Ocean, more swell waves might be experienced by the western and southern islands of the Maldives. However, the eastern rim islands may still be affected because swell waves propagate through reef passes within atoll lagoons. These climatic conditions may seriously harm vital infrastructure, real estate, groundwater aquifer intrusion, coastal erosion, and livelihood.

IMPACT OF CLIMATIC CHANGES

Owing to its geographical nature in terms of no rivers and lakes, the country grapples with some issues related with fresh water resources. It mainly utilizes groundwater as its main source of freshwater after that. Freshwater lens is formed from layer or fresh water over denser salt water covering the islands. This freshwater lens is tapped using wells as a primary means of providing drinking water to local people. Therefore, as a result scarce freshwater sources, rainwater harvesting in an essential customary practice in this area. Most of the homesteads harvest rain from rooftops and retain it in storage tanks for drinking, cooking, and bathing purposes. The Maldives also have a dearth of fresh water sources which have necessitated the increased provision of desalination (Ibrahim et al. 2002). In some instances, the country also depends on importing the water needed. In most cases, it is done for periods of low water levels and highly congested areas that require more water than is locally available. This makes Maldives susceptible to climate change, specifically sea-level rise, which complicates issues regarding fresh water supply. The freshwater lens will also be unstable during these period changes and hence more salt water will sweep in the ground water. This means that proper water management is a must for the sustainability of Maldivians (Ibrahim et al. 2002).

Additionally, global coastal zones are at risk of substantial physical changes due to constant increase in sea level. Correspondingly, the global mean sea level rise by the end of the twenty-first century is expected to be between 0.44 and 0.74 metres, according to the IPCC's Fifth Assessment Report (Dasgupta 2007). In reference to this the National Adaptation Programme of Action (NAPA) i.e., a strategic document developed by nations which are particularly vulnerable to the adverse impacts of climate change. It is a key component of the United Nations Framework Convention on Climate Change (UNFCCC) process and serves as a roadmap for prioritizing and implementing adaptation actions at the national level. The Maldives has submitted its first NAPA in the year 2007 which discovered that the nation's maximum hourly sea level is rising at a slightly faster rate than the global average, at roughly 7 mm/year (Black et. al 2008). Wherein, the areas close to Malé International Airport Weather Station has a long-term trend of relative sea level of about 1.7 mm/year (Jennath et al. 2021). Whereas. in Hulhulé, the sea level rises by 70 cm on an hourly basis above mean sea level (MSL), once every 100 years, and by 2050, it is expected to occur at least once a year (Jennath et al. 2021). Moreover, by the end of the twenty-first century, sea level rise in South Asia is expected to reach roughly 100–115 cm in a 4° Celsius world and 60–80 cm in a 2° Celsius world, with the Maldives expected to witness the highest values (Nicholls et al. 2011). Thus, as far as the impact of these changes are concerned, the Maldives is especially receptive to significant land inundation concerning its low elevation and topography, making even minor variations in sea level potentially disastrous (Gussmann & Hinkel 2021). Consequently, the coastal infrastructure may eventually be threatened by ongoing flooding. Further, the rise in sea-levels, even modest ones, is expected to exacerbate the islands' current environmental problems, such as the constant flooding (Gussmann & Hinkel 2021).

A remarkable biological diversity and cultural significance make the coral reef ecosystems of the Maldives noteworthy on a global and national scale. The renowned *Thiladhunmathi* and *Huvadhoo* are two of the largest natural atolls in the world, with a combined surface area of 3,788 and 3,278 sq. km (Krishnan 2021). They also make up the world's 7th largest reef system, ranked among the prolific in terms of biodiversity, and play a vital role in coastal protection. Given that corals are extremely sensitive to temperature changes, bleaching will occur more frequently and more intensely as sea surface temperatures rise as predicted. The Maldives have endured several instances of coral mortality and bleaching, including those occured in 1977, 1983, 1987, 1991, 1995, and 1997. In addition to the three global bleaching events which have occurred in 1998, 2010, and 2016 (Häder 2018). It was observed that El Niño-related increases in sea temperature were the cause of each of these global bleaching events. The subsequent changes in weather patterns, such as less wind-driven mixing and more sunshine, combine with the seawater's constant rise in temperature brought on by global warming to kill corals.

Similarly, the core component of the Maldivian economy is the fishing industry as more than 20% of the population used to rely solely on fishing for their income and sustenance (Hohne-Sparborth 2015). When it comes to employment and sustaining the local labour force, fishing is considered as the primary industry. This industry is exceptionally affected by climate change, even though overfishing will likely have a greater effect on lowering levels than climate change's influence on the size of fishing stocks overall. Yet, the key variables most likely to affect fisheries as a result of variations in ocean pH and sea surface temperature are those that tuna is highly acclimated to, specifically the specific biophysical conditions of the ocean environment (Hohne-Sparborth 2015).

The impact of climatic changes is also apparent on the economy of Maldives, the primary economic activity is tourism, which contributed 21.4% of the nation's nominal GDP (gross domestic product) in the year 2021. Because of this, country's economy hinges heavily on tourism, and the sector has a multiplier impact. Over 5% of the workforce is employed in the tourism sector, and 14% of all employed people work in resorts, according to the employment Census (Stojanov 2017). The World Travel and Tourism Council estimated that travel and tourism in the Maldives directly and indirectly supported more 81,000 jobs, with potential for growth in the years to come (Mekharat & Traore 2020). Besides, it also predicted that until 2028, both tourist exports and investments in the tourism sector will substantially increase. In this reference, few studies have claimed that there is a direct correlation between tourism and climate change, while there seem to be several signs suggesting small island nations' tourism industries like the Maldives are especially susceptible to the effects of climate change (Scott et al. 2012). On these lines, the "sun, sea, and sand" tourism product is already being impacted by beach erosion, as reported by roughly 45% of resorts (Ahmed Waheed 2015). Likewise, recreational diving is another sector that could be vulnerable due to environmental degradation, reef loss, and coastal erosion, as some Pacific islands have experienced (Klint et al. 2012). Therefore, it can be contended that without significant adaptation measures, the combined effects of rising sea levels and coastal erosion will eventually reduce the variety and quality of beach space that is available, which could somewhat shrink the nation's appeal as a travel destination.

Furthermore, Agriculture continues to be a vital industry for "national development goals, poverty alleviation and sustainable livelihood, nutritional status of the people, retention of foreign currency, and employment" despite its modest GDP contribution. It is also a primary sector of the economy, and the expansion of other industries such as real estate, financial services, construction, and transportation and communication depends on agriculture. Accordingly, the principal hazards to the nation's food security are the low level of agricultural production, the country's high reliance on imports, storage restrictions, and difficulties with food distribution. This vulnerability is made even more acute by extreme weather events, particularly in light of the localised flooding caused by spikes and disruptions in sea-based transportation. Furthermore, the apprehensive impact of climate change on local and regional fishery systems will have an effect on the Maldivian diet, as the majority of Maldivians rely primarily on fish for their protein needs.

A growing corpus of studies has demonstrated that catastrophes linked to climate change have affected human populations in numerous realms, such as public health, agricultural productivity, food security, and water management. Since most Maldivians rely on tourism or fishing for a living, many are particularly sensitive to the consequences of climate change. Whereas, considering that the lowest-income neighbourhoods and groups have no access to desalinated water sources or other local alternatives for storing rainwater, thus, the impoverished communities in society are likely to be disproportionately affected by climate change. Given that, the water security of island nations is seriously threatened by rising sea levels simply because they have the potential to cause salinity to the sources of drinking water. Hence, as a matter of public health, an increased prevalence of hypertension during pregnancy has been linked to the saline intrusion into drinking water sources (Khan et al. 2011). Moreover, according to research, the human body is capable of controlling its temperature up to 35°C, after which even a brief exposure can result in significant illness or even death (Im, E. S. 2017). Global warming due to climate change will bring temperatures closer to this "danger zone" by increasing the frequency and severity of the heat waves consequently leading to intensifying the onset of warming through an increase in the mean annual temperature. Subsequently, these climate change is likely to put more people at risk for heat-related illnesses, possibly with particular reference to the elderly, children, people with chronic illnesses, socially isolated individuals, and at-risk occupational groups (Im, E. S. 2017).

PARIS AGREEMENT

Prior to the development of the Paris Agreement, there were several significant turning points in international climate diplomacy. The groundwork was established in the year 1992 by the United Nations Framework Convention on Climate Change (UNFCCC), which formed the bedrock for global cooperation in the fight against greenhouse gas emissions. In the meantime, the subsequent Kyoto Protocol in 1997 demanded the developed and privileged nations to reduce their emissions. These early accords underscored the difficulties in gaining widespread participation and commitment while setting the standard for collective action (Depledge 2001). Accordingly, the Paris Agreement has been regarded as a turning point in the global campaign to address climate change. It was adopted in December 2015 at the 21st Conference of the Parties (COP21) and added to the existing UNFCCC, the signing of this agreement signified the collective commitment of 197 countries to mitigate and adapt to climate changes. Essentially, the goal of the Paris Agreement is to limit global warming to well below 2 degrees Celsius above pre-industrial levels while pursuing policies to keep temperature increases to 1.5 degrees Celsius. This extravagant objectives is considered to be justified considering the far-reaching effects of greenhouse gas emissions on the environment and the absolute necessity of reducing them. The implementation of this agreement mandated each ratifying country to submit a Nationally Determined Contribution (NDC), a document that outlines its specific plans and commitments to reduce emissions and adapt to the implications of climate change (Mills-Novoa & Liverman 2021). The strength of this agreement lies in the inclusion of both developed and developing nations, highlighting its universal participation. By spotting historic emissions by developed nations and pledging the active participation and assistance of developing countries, this inclusion encourages collective responsibility in combating climate change. The agreement additionally applies a significant focus on financial assistance from affluent nations to less fortunate countries in order to assist them with their climate initiatives, as well as disclosure, responsibility, and transparency (Bertoldi 2018). Ever since its inception, the Paris Agreement has sparked an increase in awareness and action on climate change. Various countries have submitted their NDCs, which demonstrate their dedication and actions towards reducing emissions. Accordingly, this agreement has paved the way for advancements in renewable energy, technology, and climate finance. Moreover, the worldwide discourse and activism about climate change have experienced a notable surge, cultivating a more comprehensive comprehension of the pressing necessity for action.

The effects of the Paris Agreement have been the focus of several research and evaluations in a multitude of fields, notwithstanding their constant evolution. There are few studies which have assessed how the Paris Agreement would affect greenhouse gas emissions worldwide (Kuramochi et al. 2020). They initiated review of the impact that national commitments and nationally determined contributions (NDCs) have had on global mitigation pathways and attempts to reduce emissions. Various researchers frequently looks at the agreement's objectives in relation to scientific advice and the efficiency of the established targets in reducing climate change (Kuramochi et al. 2020). In addition, they focuses on how the agreement has affected the development of green technology, investments in renewable energy, and shifting to being a low-carbon economy. A great deal of research has been done on how the Paris Agreement will affect resilience-building and adaptation strategies (Piqueres et al. 2020). Few scholars have evaluated the agreement's impact on adaptation-related policies and actions, especially in sectors and regions that are vulnerable (Morgan et al 2019). A decent deal of consideration has been accorded to the manner in which the Paris Agreement will impact the global marketplaces and economic systems. Studies underscore the trend of investing in renewable energy, the rise of low-emission technologies, and the financial consequences of shifting to a sustainable, decarbonized economy (Jafari et al. 2022). Another study also look at how the agreement has affected markets and policy, analysing the effects on the economy and global competitiveness (Palei 2015). Further, there has been discourse about how the implementation of Paris Agreement will promote technological innovation and the transfer of green technologies (Oh, C. 2020). Research evaluates its contribution to the advancement of R&D, technology transfer, and capacity building, particularly in the areas of sustainable practises and renewable energy (Oh, C. 2020).

PARIS AGREEMENT & SMALL ISLAND DEVELOPING STATES

Small Island Developing States (SIDS) face an existential threat from climate change. They have been at the forefront of pushing for robust climate action and increasing public awareness of climate change on a worldwide scale, particularly through the Alliance of Small Island States (AOSIS). The small island states played a pivotal role in the negotiations during the COP21, which led to implementation of the Paris Agreement. In addition to successfully securing their unique status as vulnerable nations and advancing the complex debate of loss and damage, SIDS demonstrated leadership in boosting ambition to reduce greenhouse gas emissions in order to support the audacious long-term temperature goal of keeping global warming to 1.5 °C (Rasheed 2019). The particular requirements and concerns of developing countries are mentioned in Article 4.8 of the UNFCCC. Parties brought about by the negative effects of climate change, particularly on: (a) small island nations; (b) nations having low-lying coastal areas. In order to strengthen the position of Small Island Developing States (SIDS) within the United Nations system, especially in relation to environmental and climate change issues of the day, the Alliance of Small Island States (AOSIS) was established during 2nd World Climate Conference in the year 1990, prior to the official negotiations that resulted in the adoption of the UNFCCC (Thomas et al. 2020). An emergence of such a coalition demonstrates the growing awareness among island communities' leaders of the seriousness of the threats posed by climate change. The long-term viability of human societies on islands is seriously threatened by sea level rise, ocean warming and acidification, increased variability in precipitation and extreme events like cyclones and coral bleaching episodes. These threats are especially present in low-lying atoll reef islands. Accordingly, members of AOSIS have taken the lead in voicing the apprehensions, arguing that they face an existential threat from climate change based on scientific evidence relevant to their unique situation. They have been successful in their attempts to formulate a particular negotiation agenda that addresses issues that they find most important, and they have also been successful in getting those issues included in a legally binding convention of historic significance. This demonstrates AOSIS's dedication to increasing group ambition and converting their economies into low-carbon ones. The Small Islands can emphasise their needs for adaptation and, consequently, for financial provisions for adaptive response measures to the adverse impacts of climate change, such as sea level rise, by drawing attention to their limited leeway for mitigation.

Meanwhile, SIDS have been successful in creating a common dialect in diplomacy and influencing tactics. This was caused, in part, by the rise of several prominent politicians who were well-known in the field of climate change. For instance, Mr. Tony de Brum, the Minister of Foreign Affairs of the Republic of Marshall Islands, Mr. Anote Tong, the President of the Republic of Kiribati, or Mr. Enele Sopoaga, the Prime Minister of Tuvalu and the main spokesperson for AOSIS during the fifteenth conference of the parties (COP15 in Copenhagen in 2009) (Ourbak & Magnan 2018). These leaders have created momentum by organising pre-COP21 meetings, like the one that resulted in the 2013, which has raised awareness of climate change and expectations for COP21 (Ourbak & Magnan 2018). Thereafter, the Maldives held the AOSIS Presidency, the lead originated in the Indian Ocean. A few examples of the significant roles that Ministers Thoriq Ibrahim (Maldives), Vivian Balakrishnan (Singapore), and, to a lesser extent, Jean Paul Adam (Seychelles), played were speaking up at various formal and informal negotiation meetings leading up to and during COP21. Subsequently, considering the small size of AOSIS delegations at COP21, the Paris Agreement is concerned as a decent outcome. During COP21, AOSIS fought to have Small Island nations recognised for their unique needs and circumstances as especially vulnerable nations. Consequently, The Paris Agreement's climate change convention, which represents a first diplomatic win for SIDS, is mentioned in the fifth paragraph of the preamble (Ourbak & Magnan 2018). SIDS and LDCs are mentioned five times in the final text of the Paris Agreement in relation to mitigation, financing, capacity building, and transparency issues. Furthermore, SIDS resisted calls from other regions or groups to be specifically listed as "vulnerable countries" until the very last hours of the negotiations, mainly to ensure their preferential access to climate finance (Ourbak & Magnan 2018). Thus, with regard to the new transparency framework and the reporting system's flexibility, AOSIS was able to maintain their unique circumstances while avoiding any further reporting-related burdens. Besides, AOSIS has been pushing for the adoption of an aggressive temperature target—below 1.5 °C warming by the end of the century relative to pre-industrial levels—as the objective for reducing global emissions. A major achievement for AOSIS in the lead-up to COP21 was to start a structured expert dialogue, which resulted in a final report that included the +1.5 °C target.

One of the main obstacles in 2016 following COP21 and the Paris Agreement's adoption was the ratification procedure. The Paris Agreement (UNFCCC 2015b), Decision 1/CP.21, states that the *"Agreement will come into effect thirty days after the date on which at least fifty-five Parties to the Convention, representing a minimum of fifty-five percent of the estimated total global greenhouse gas emissions, have deposited their instruments of ratification, acceptance, approval, or accession"* (Wewerinke-Singh & Doebbler 2016). However, as only a small portion of global emissions can be attributed to AOSIS, not much could be done to meet the 55% emissions target. Still, Small Island States emerged victorious on the international arena once more. The Republic of the Marshall Islands, Palau, the Maldives, and other nations ratified after Fiji, which had done so first, a few days later. Small island states are not new to this position; the Seychelles and the Marshall Islands swiftly ratified the climate convention after Mauritius did (Yamamoto & Esteban 2013). Hence, by integrating pressure on the main emitters, AOSIS members have increased the number of countries that have ratified by using their moral power. Lately, On November 4, 2016, the Paris Agreement came into effect. By September 27, 2017, 166 parties had ratified it, with only two AOSIS members—Surinam and Trinidad and Tobago—not having done so.

IMPACT OF PARIS AGREEMENT IN MALDIVES

The Republic of the Maldives, Chair of the Alliance of Small Island States (AOSIS) and one of the first nations to sound the alarm about the threat of climate change and sea level rise in the 1980s, had its parliament vote in April 2016 to ratify the historic Paris climate change agreement. The then Minister of Environment and Energy and Chair of AOSIS, Mr. Thoriq Ibrahim has stated *"We have long argued that there was no time to waste in tackling climate change. It is telling that some of the country's most vulnerable to the crisis were the first to approve its ratification. We hope the rest of the world follows our example and, even more* importantly, moves expeditiously to implement climate solutions" (Rasheed 2019). While, 2015 marked the Maldives' first Nationally Determined Contribution (NDC) submission to the UNFCCC. According to this NDC, climate change poses a serious threat to the nation's socioeconomic progress and should be given top priority at the federal level. Thereafter, an updated Nationally Determined Contribution (NDC) was filed in 2020 in compliance with the Paris Agreement, reiterating the urgent need for adaptation planning and action. The Maldives' economy and society are extremely sensitive to and vulnerable to natural disasters, climate change, and climate variability. These vulnerabilities are the basis for the NDC's priority measures for climate change adaption (CCA) in: i) agriculture and food security; ii) infrastructure resilience; iii) public health; iv) water security; v) coastal protection; vi) coral reef biodiversity; vii) tourism; viii) fisheries; ix) early warning and systematic observation; x) disaster risk reduction and management; and xi) the cross-cutting issues of finance, climate governance and capacity building (Roper et al. 2021). This NDC was updated after numerous consultations with direct and indirect stakeholder and an examination of initiatives, projects, and programmes across numerous industries. The contributions rendered in the NDC are compliant with all applicable plans, policies, and strategies of the government. With the exception of agriculture and disaster risk reduction and management in the most recent update, the sectors covered by the NDCs have largely stayed the same, but each one has reaffirmed its commitment to stepping up adaptation efforts.

The country is relentless that appropriate measures must be taken to lower greenhouse gas emissions, lessen vulnerability, and increase resilience in order to adapt to a changing climate. The concerned government has developed National Climate Change Policy Framework referred as Maldives Climate Change Policy Framework (MCCPF) to address the impacts of extreme vulnerability to climate change and to offer a blueprint for building resilience in collaboration with our regional and international partners (Mohamed & King 2017). Thus, it is a set of guidelines for implementing policies that have been adopted, national development plans, strategies, action plans, policies, and pertinent documents as a basis and in accordance with them. The main guiding documents of this policy are Maldives Environment Protection and Preservation Act 1993 with its amendment in 2014, Maldives Tourism Act 1999, The Fisheries Law of Maldives 1987, Strategic Action Plan 2009-2013, National Energy Policy 2010, National Security Policy 2012, Maldives Foreign Policy 2014 and National Sustainable Development Strategy 2009 (Techera & Cannell-Lunn 2019). Besides, the policy strongly on following principles which defines country's approach to tackle climatic changes (*See* Figure 1). (i) A strong political commitment and display of "*climate leadership*" by the president, the cabinet, the parliament, island and atoll council members, and non-governmental organisations; (ii) Preserving the nation's natural resources, or its "*exclusive economic zone*," as well as its social, economic, and national security. While ensuring equitable growth amongst population groups by acknowledging the distinctive qualities of every atoll, the variety of needs, and the availability of opportunities, services, products, and advantages. sensitivity, gender equality, the rule of law, and respect for human rights; (iii) Place an emphasis on direct implementation, integrate climate change concerns into the formulation and execution of sector-specific plans and programmes, and prioritise the core economic and social development goals; (iv) Acknowledge and fulfil the Maldives' international obligations, such as those imposed by the Kyoto

Figure 1. Building blocks of MCCPF 2015

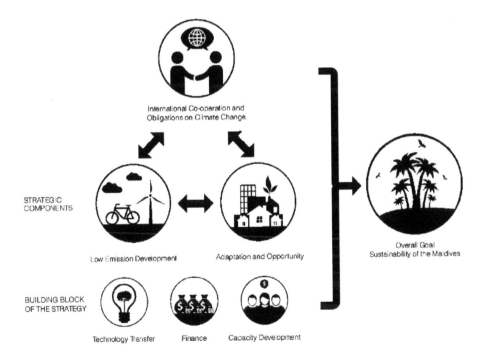

Table 1. Strategies to achieve underlying objectives on MCCPF

Objectives	Strategies			
Low Emission Development	Bolster the legislative and regulatory structure to support conservation, renewable energy, and energy efficiency	Create a system to keep an eye on the energy source composition target in order to sustain low emission development	Use renewable and alternative energy to diversify the technologies used in power generation	Encourage the public and promote EE appliances and measures (through labelling)
Sustainable Finance	Make sure that funds for low-emission development (LED) initiatives, climate change adaptation, and opportunities are allotted within the national budget	Establish supportive conditions to help communities, businesses, NGOs, and the public obtain climate finance	Create a National Implementing Entity (NIE) to guarantee a modality of direct access	Utilise bilateral and multilateral mechanisms to mobilise and realise predictable and sustainable funding for climate change initiatives
Adaptation & Opportunities	Compile evaluations of adaptation vulnerability for the most vulnerable sectors mentioned in NAPAs and the plans and strategies that follow	Discuss climate change projections and scenarios in the field of urban and rural planning	Set up comprehensive island risk assessment plans, instruments, and guidelines for a few Maldivian islands	Deliver a system for managing the availability and supply of fresh water so that communities can adapt to a changing climate and an extended dry spell
Capacity Development	Permit policymakers technical and scientific advice using the proper channels	Serve a means for diverse stakeholders to effectively communicate and network about climate change issues	Inspire students to conduct research on the topic of local climate change and its implications for the societies of the Maldives	Foster Maldives participation in pertinent conferences and international climate negotiations
Fostering Sustainability	Make sure that natural resources are used sustainably and are preserved for future generations	Establish cooperative and coordinated agreements between sectors to ensure respect for human rights, the rule of law, gender equality, and sensitivity. Take into account the National Climate Change Policy in legislative review processes	Make certain that there is national ownership of climate change issues and that a wide range of stakeholders participate in the planning and decision-making process without bias	Design a climate spatial data mechanism for climate-sensitive reporting and climate-informed decision-making

Protocol and the UNFCCC, to the greatest extent feasible; (v) Working together with regional and international partners and organisations, as appropriate and practical, to mobilise resources for the Maldives' climate change agenda and carry out its programmes and projects; (vi) Adoption of environmentally sound practises and technologies (ESTs) to help the economy transition to a low-carbon one. Assist in fulfilling national and international obligations regarding the causes and effects of climate change by fostering the adoption of suitable technologies and practises; (vii) Taking responsibility for the innate complexity of the climate change problem and the necessity of multi-sectoral, multi-focal solutions that are planned and executed with coherence and coordination. Whereas, the strategic component of the policy focuses on attaining atmospheric stabilisation of greenhouse gas concentrations at a level that would shield the climate system from harmful human interference while assuring that food production is not jeopardised and permitting sustainable economic development to continue (Falkner 2016).

It is imperative to strategically address the above-mentioned goals of climate change policy. Accordingly, the policy outframes list of strategies to meet these objectives (See Table 1).

Sectoral Adaption

As stated in the Maldives' Country Programme, the projects, programmes, and initiatives have tackled adaptation planning in the country's priority sectors.

Tourism - A number of initiatives in the tourism industry have been created to support CCA by encouraging integrated water resource management and infrastructure development. For instance, the GEF-financed, UNDP-supported Increasing Climate Change Resilience of Maldives through Adaptation in the Tourism Sector Project (TAP) came to an end in 2016 and addressed important infrastructure issues (Shakeela et al. 2015). The aim of the project was to develop necessary policies, standards, codes, and regulatory guidance to enable the necessary investments to make the infrastructure supporting tourism more resilient to climate change (Shakeela et al. 2015). Another goal of the initiative was to boost the Ministry of Tourism's and tourism businesses' ability to identify climate risks to their business operations and implement suitable adaptation strategies to mitigate those risks. To advocate integrated water management, a community-based adaptation project called Sustainable Water Use Management and Community Awareness was also put into place on Maalhos Island, Baa Atoll (Wolf 2021).

Fisheries - Several plans and policies have been developed within the fisheries sector to support CCA. Recently, the parliament passed the new Fisheries Act, which makes major changes to improve the sectoral governance. In addition, The Ministry of Fisheries and Agriculture also created a Master Plan for Sustainable

Fisheries (MASPLAN) to include the sector's efforts to address the challenges posed by climate change (Edwards et al. 2020). The programme was developed with the assistance of the Marine Research Centre (MRC) and its findings. In order to prevent the unsustainable methods of bait extraction in the Maldives, the MRC has also created a live bait fishery management plan (Edwards et al. 2020).

Water - The National Water and Sewerage Policy (NWSP), which establishes priorities for the provision of water and sewage services as well as the appropriate management of water resources in the Maldives, is one of the policies in the water sector that have been created to support CCA (Solutions 2017). The Maldives Climate Change Policy Framework (MCCPF) is acknowledged in the policy, but the effect of climate change on water supply and access is not given much direct thought. Whereas, in order to increase water security, the Maldives has carried out a number of projects to enhance access to sewage systems and desalinated or rainwater-piped water across a number of islands. Concerns about water security are anticipated to be addressed by a project that uses integrated water resource management (IWRM) to increase climate resilience (Gheuens et al. 2019).

Public Health - A Health National Adaptation Plan (HNAP), created by the Ministry of Health, outlines tactics and initiatives for mainstreaming CCA in the industry. While the HNAP recommends mapping climate-sensitive risks and diseases, it did not carry out any independent, health-oriented vulnerability assessments. Thus, in order to address any new health concerns, the Maldives Health Master Plan (MHMP) for the years 2016–2025 plans to keep an eye on how climate change is affecting people's health (WHO 2015).

CONCLUSION

In conclusion, the chapter implementation and Impact of the Paris Agreement on Climate Change in the Maldives underscores the crucial intersection between global climate action and the peculiar vulnerabilities faced by small island nations. The Maldives which is situated at the forefront of climate change impacts, has demonstrated a committed effort to align its policies with the ambitious goals of the Paris Agreement. The country has adopted a multimodal approach to implementing the Paris Agreement, which includes adaptation strategies, mitigation techniques, a call for global cooperation and advocating for global temperature goals, particularly limiting warming to 1.5 degrees Celsius by shifting to renewable energy sources, and establishing emission reduction targets are all part of mitigation efforts. The aforementioned efforts are not only vital to the country's survival but also show how important it is to include adaptation in climate policies, especially for those that are most directly affected by the effects of climate change. Whereas, by recognising the need for unity in the face of climate change, the Paris Agreement has made it easier to provide the Maldives with financial and technical support. Accordingly, encouraging accountability and fostering a common understanding of the country's progress towards climate goals is the nation's dedication to transparent reporting through Monitoring, Reporting, and Verification mechanisms. Nevertheless, even with its proactive approach, The Maldives still has resource limitations and needs ongoing international assistance to achieve its climate goals. Moreover, issues associated with loss and damage resulting from climate impacts highlight the need for increased international cooperation and innovative proposals. In a broader perspective, the Maldives provide a striking illustration of the world community's shared obligation to confront climate change. In addition to national commitment, the Maldives' ability to successfully implement the Paris Agreement will also depend on ongoing international cooperation and a steadfast commitment to the principles of climate justice. In the pursuit of a sustainable and resilient future, the Maldives' experiences highlight the need for ongoing research, flexible policy, and a steadfast dedication to the common objectives delineated in the Paris Agreement.

REFERENCES

Ahmed Waheed, W., Ali Shareef, S., Mareer Mohamed Husny, H., Mohamed Asif, M., & Zammath Khaleel, K. (2015). *Maldives Climate Change Policy Framework*.

Bansal, A., & Datta, S. (2013). The impact of climate change in South Asia. In *South Asian Security* (pp. 218–234). Routledge.

Bertoldi, P., Kona, A., Rivas, S., & Dallemand, J. F. (2018). Towards a global comprehensive and transparent framework for cities and local governments enabling an effective contribution to the Paris climate agreement. *Current Opinion in Environmental Sustainability*, *30*, 67–74. doi:10.1016/j.cosust.2018.03.009

Black, R., Kniveton, D., Skeldon, R., Coppard, D., Murata, A., & Schmidt-Verkerk, K. (2008). *Demographics and climate change: Future trends and their policy implications for migration. Development Research Centre on Migration, Globalisation and Poverty*. University of Sussex.

Dasgupta, S. (2007). *The impact of sea level rise on developing countries: a comparative analysis* (Vol. 4136). World Bank Publications. doi:10.1596/1813-9450-4136

Depledge, J. J. (2001). *The organization of the Kyoto Protocol negotiations: Lessons for global environmental decision-making.* University of London, University College London.

Edwards, Z., Sinan, H., Adam, M. S., & Miller, A. (2020). State-led fisheries development: enabling access to resources and markets in the Maldives pole-and-line skipjack tuna fishery. *Securing Sustainable Small-Scale Fisheries: Showcasing Applied Practices in Value Chains. Post-Harvest Operations and Trade, 652,* 141.

Falkner, R. (2016). The Paris Agreement and the new logic of international climate politics. *International Affairs, 92*(5), 1107–1125. doi:10.1111/1468-2346.12708

Foley, A., & Kelman, I. (2020). Precipitation responses to ENSO and IOD in the Maldives: Implications of large-scale modes of climate variability in weather-related preparedness. *International Journal of Disaster Risk Reduction, 50,* 101726. doi:10.1016/j.ijdrr.2020.101726

Gan–Part, L. (2007). *Detailed Island Risk Assessment in Maldives.*

Gao, Y., Gao, X., & Zhang, X. (2017). The 2 C global temperature target and the evolution of the long-term goal of addressing climate change—From the United Nations framework convention on climate change to the Paris agreement. *Engineering (Beijing), 3*(2), 272–278. doi:10.1016/J.ENG.2017.01.022

Gheuens, J., Nagabhatla, N., & Perera, E. D. P. (2019). Disaster-risk, water security challenges and strategies in Small Island Developing States (SIDS). *Water (Basel), 11*(4), 637. doi:10.3390/w11040637

Gussmann, G., & Hinkel, J. (2021). A framework for assessing the potential effectiveness of adaptation policies: Coastal risks and sea-level rise in the Maldives. *Environmental Science & Policy, 115,* 35–42. doi:10.1016/j.envsci.2020.09.028

Häder, D. P. (2018). Effects of climate change on corals. In K. Gao (Ed.), *Aquatic Ecosystems in a Changing Climate; Häder, D.-P* (pp. 146–161). doi:10.1201/9780429436130-8

Hohne-Sparborth, T., Shiham Adam, M., & Ziyad, A. (2015). *A socio-economic assessment of the tuna fisheries in the Maldives.* International Pole & Line Foundation.

Ibrahim, S. A., Bari, M. R., & Miles, L. (2002). *Water resources management in Maldives with an emphasis on desalination.* Maldives Water and Sanitation Authority.

Im, E. S., Pal, J. S., & Eltahir, E. A. (2017). Deadly heat waves projected in the densely populated agricultural regions of South Asia. *Science Advances, 3*(8), e1603322. doi:10.1126/sciadv.1603322 PMID:28782036

Jafari, M., Botterud, A., & Sakti, A. (2022). Decarbonizing power systems: A critical review of the role of energy storage. *Renewable & Sustainable Energy Reviews*, *158*, 112077. doi:10.1016/j.rser.2022.112077

Jennath, A., Krishnan, A., Paul, S. K., & Bhaskaran, P. K. (2021). Climate projections of sea level rise and associated coastal inundation in atoll islands: Case of Lakshadweep Islands in the Arabian Sea. *Regional Studies in Marine Science*, *44*, 101793. doi:10.1016/j.rsma.2021.101793

Khan, A. E., Ireson, A., Kovats, S., Mojumder, S. K., Khusru, A., Rahman, A., & Vineis, P. (2011). Drinking water salinity and maternal health in coastal Bangladesh: Implications of climate change. *Environmental Health Perspectives*, *119*(9), 1328–1332. doi:10.1289/ehp.1002804 PMID:21486720

Khan, T. M. A., Quadir, D. A., Murty, T. S., Kabir, A., Aktar, F., & Sarker, M. A. (2002). Relative sea level changes in Maldives and vulnerability of land due to abnormal coastal inundation. *Marine Geodesy*, *25*(1-2), 133–143. doi:10.1080/014904102753516787

Klint, L. M., Jiang, M., Law, A., DeLacy, T., Filep, S., Calgaro, E., Dominey-Howes, D., & Harrison, D. (2012). Dive tourism in Luganville, Vanuatu: Shocks, stressors, and vulnerability to climate change. *Tourism in Marine Environments*, *8*(1-2), 91–109. doi:10.3727/154427312X13262430524225

Krishnan, P., Mukherjee, R., Hari, M. S., & Kantharajan, G. (2021). Streamlining Science-Policy Linkage for Fisheries Management in South Asia: Lessons from Regional Initiatives. *Cross-learning for Addressing Emergent Challenges of Aquaculture and Fisheries in South Asia*, 115.

Kuramochi, T., Roelfsema, M., Hsu, A., Lui, S., Weinfurter, A., Chan, S., Hale, T., Clapper, A., Chang, A., & Höhne, N. (2020). Beyond national climate action: The impact of region, city, and business commitments on global greenhouse gas emissions. *Climate Policy*, *20*(3), 275–291. doi:10.1080/14693062.2020.1740150

Mekharat, N., & Traore, N. (2020). *How the tourism sector in emerging markets is recovering from COVID-19.*

Mills-Novoa, M., & Liverman, D. M. (2019). Nationally determined contributions: Material climate commitments and discursive positioning in the NDCs. *Wiley Interdisciplinary Reviews: Climate Change*, *10*(5), e589. doi:10.1002/wcc.589

Mohamed, I., & King, D. (2017). Legacy of Authoritative Environmentalism and Path-Dependent Historic Institutionalism in the Climate Change Policy Dynamics of the Maldives. *Climate Change Research at Universities: Addressing the Mitigation and Adaptation Challenges*, 211-231.

Morgan, E. A., Nalau, J., & Mackey, B. (2019). Assessing the alignment of national-level adaptation plans to the Paris Agreement. *Environmental Science & Policy, 93,* 208–220. doi:10.1016/j.envsci.2018.10.012

Nicholls, R. J., Marinova, N., Lowe, J. A., Brown, S., Vellinga, P., De Gusmao, D., & Tol, R. S. (2011). Sea-level rise and its possible impacts given a 'beyond 4 C world' in the twenty-first century. *Philosophical transactions of the Royal Society A: mathematical, physical and engineering sciences, 369*(1934), 161-181.

Oh, C. (2020). Discursive Contestation on Technological Innovation and the Institutional Design of the UNFCCC in the New Climate Change Regime. *New Political Economy, 25*(4), 660–674. doi:10.1080/13563467.2019.1639147

Ourbak, T., & Magnan, A. K. (2018). The Paris Agreement and climate change negotiations: Small Islands, big players. *Regional Environmental Change, 18*(8), 2201–2207. doi:10.1007/s10113-017-1247-9

Palei, T. (2015). Assessing the impact of infrastructure on economic growth and global competitiveness. *Procedia Economics and Finance, 23,* 168–175. doi:10.1016/S2212-5671(15)00322-6

Piqueres, S. L., Giuli, M., & Hedberg, A. (2020). *Adapting to change: Time for climate resilience and a new adaptation strategy.* EPC Issue Paper.

Rahman, M. A. (2022). *Nature and causes of climate change: An analysis of global climate and greenhouse emissions data.* Research Gate.

Ranguelov, B., & Shadiya, F. (2018). Fractals, Natural Disasters and Ecological Problems of Maldives. *J. Ecological Eng. and Env. Protection,* 18-25.

Rasheed, A. A. (2019). Role of small islands in UN climate negotiations: A constructivist viewpoint. *International Studies, 56*(4), 215–235. doi:10.1177/0020881719861503

Roper, L. A., Siegele, J. L., & Islands, C. (2021). The Global Goal on Adaptation: a SIDS Perspective.

Scott, D., Gössling, S., & Hall, C. M. (2012). International tourism and climate change. *Wiley Interdisciplinary Reviews: Climate Change, 3*(3), 213–232. doi:10.1002/wcc.165

Shakeela, A., Becken, S., & Johnstone, N. (2015). Gaps and disincentives that exist in the policies, laws and regulations which act as barriers to investing in climate change adaptation in the tourism sector of the Maldives. *Increasing Climate Change Resilience of Maldives through Adaptation in the Tourism Sector.* Research Gate.

Singh, P., Singh, S., Kumar, G., & Baweja, P. (Eds.). (2021). *Energy: crises, challenges and solutions.* John Wiley & Sons. doi:10.1002/9781119741503

Solutions, W. (2017). *Environmental impact assessment for the construction and setup of a sewerage system in Maakurathu Island.* Raa Atoll.

Sovacool, B. K. (2012). Perceptions of climate change risks and resilient island planning in the Maldives. *Mitigation and Adaptation Strategies for Global Change, 17*(7), 731–752. doi:10.1007/s11027-011-9341-7

Sovacool, B. K., D'Agostino, A. L., Meenawat, H., & Rawlani, A. (2012). Expert views of climate change adaptation in least developed Asia. *Journal of Environmental Management, 97*, 78–88. doi:10.1016/j.jenvman.2011.11.005 PMID:22325585

Stojanov, R., Duží, B., Kelman, I., Němec, D., & Procházka, D. (2017). Local perceptions of climate change impacts and migration patterns in Malé, Maldives. *The Geographical Journal, 183*(4), 370–385. doi:10.1111/geoj.12177

Suhaila, J., Deni, S. M., Wan Zin, W. Z., & Jemain, A. A. (2010). Spatial patterns and trends of daily rainfall regime in Peninsular Malaysia during the southwest and northeast monsoons: 1975–2004. *Meteorology and Atmospheric Physics, 110*(1-2), 1–18. doi:10.1007/s00703-010-0108-6

Techera, E. J., & Cannell-Lunn, M. (2019). A review of environmental law in Maldives with respect to conservation, biodiversity, fisheries and tourism. *Asia Pacific Journal of Environmental Law, 22*(2), 228–256. doi:10.4337/apjel.2019.02.03

Thomas, A., Baptiste, A., Martyr-Koller, R., Pringle, P., & Rhiney, K. (2020). Climate change and small island developing states. *Annual Review of Environment and Resources, 45*(1), 1–27. doi:10.1146/annurev-environ-012320-083355

Wewerinke-Singh, M., & Doebbler, C. (2016). The Paris agreement: Some critical reflections on process and substance. *UNSWLJ, 39*, 1486.

Wolf, M. (2021). *Community development initiatives as part of a tourism resort's CSR strategy: examination of a high-end luxury resort in the Maldives.*

Woodworth, P. L. (2005). Have there been large recent sea level changes in the Maldive Islands? *Global and Planetary Change, 49*(1-2), 1–18. doi:10.1016/j.gloplacha.2005.04.001

World Health Organization. (2015). Report of a regional meeting on health of older women: policy, gender and delivery of service issues. World Health Organization.

Yamamoto, L., & Esteban, M. (2013). *Atoll Island States and international law.* Springer-Verlag Berlin An.

Compilation of References

Abah, S. O., & Ohimain, E. I. (2011). Healthcare waste management in Nigeria: A case study. *Journal of Public Health and Epidemiology*, *3*(3), 99–110.

Abdallah, M., Talib, M. A., Feroz, S., Nasir, Q., Abdalla, H., & Mahfood, B. (2020). Artificial intelligence applications in solid waste management: A systematic research review. *Waste Management (New York, N.Y.)*, *109*, 231–246. doi:10.1016/j.wasman.2020.04.057 PMID:32428727

Afsana, K., & Wahid, S. S. (2013). Health care for poor people in the urban slums of Bangladesh. *Lancet*, *382*(9910), 2049–2051. doi:10.1016/S0140-6736(13)62295-3 PMID:24268606

Agreement on the Conservation of Polar Bears. (1973, November 15). UN. https://treaties.un.org/doc/Publication/UNTS/Volume%202898/Part/volume-2898-I-50540.pdf

Ahmad, F. (2001). Origin and Growth of Environmental Law in India. *Journal of the Indian Law Institute*, *43*(3), 358–387. https://www.jstor.org/stable/43951782

Ahmad, M. (2022). Ship recycling in India- environmental stock taking. *Indiana Law Review*, *6*(3), 465–478. doi:10.1080/24730580.2022.2082100

Ahmed Waheed, W., Ali Shareef, S., Mareer Mohamed Husny, H., Mohamed Asif, M., & Zammath Khaleel, K. (2015). *Maldives Climate Change Policy Framework*.

Ahmed, T., & Paul, B. C. (2012). *Nagarayan O Nagar Sarkar: Bangladesh City Corporation*. Prothoma Prokashon.

Ahuja, A. (2007). Health Impact Assessment in Project and Policy Formulation. [JSTOR.]. *Economic and Political Weekly*, *42*(35), 3581–3587.

Alam, I., Alam, G., Ayub, S., & Siddiqui, A. A. (2019). Assessment of bio-medical waste management in different hospitals in Aligarh city. In Advances in Waste Management: Select Proceedings of Recycle 2016. Springer Singapore. doi:10.1007/978-981-13-0215-2_36

Allena, M. (2020). Blockchain Technology For Environmental Compliance: Towards A "Choral" Approach. *Environmental Law (Northwestern School of Law)*, *50*(4), 1055–1103. https://www.jstor.org/stable/27010194

Alvim-Ferraz, M. C. M., & Afonso, S. A. V. (2005). Incineration of healthcare wastes: Management of atmospheric emissions through waste segregation. *Waste Management (New York, N.Y.)*, *25*(6), 638–648. doi:10.1016/j.wasman.2004.07.017 PMID:15993348

Ambec, S., & Ehlers, L. (2016). Regulation Via the Polluter-Pays Principle. *Economic Journal (London)*, *126*(593), 884–906. https://www.jstor.org/stable/24738178. doi:10.1111/ecoj.12184

Ambos, K. (2015). The Overall Function of International Criminal Law: Striking the Right Balance between the Rechtsgut and the Harm Principles - A Second Contribution Towards a Consistent Theory of ICL. *Criminal Law and Philosophy*, *9*(2), 301–329. doi:10.1007/s11572-013-9266-1

Amnesty International. (2012). *The Toxic Truth*. Greenpeace. https://www.greenpeace.org/static/planet4-international-stateless/2012/09/9161d5e8-the-toxic-truth.pdf

Angevine, G., & Green, K. P. (2016). *Obstacles Faced by Major Pipeline Projects. In The Costs of Pipeline Obstructionism* (pp. 22–27). Fraser Institute. https://www.jstor.org/stable/resrep33286.9

Asar, A. (2020). Five Tech Innovations That Changed Mental Health in 2020. *Forbes*. https://www.forbes.com/sites/forbestechcouncil/2020/11/25/five-tech-innovations-that-changed-mental-health-in-2020/?sh=289c223b1e9c

Ascione, R. (2022). *How Digital Technology Will Make Care Accessible, Sustainable, and Human*. Wiley.

Ascione, R. (2022). *The Future of Health How Digital Technology will Make Care Accessible, Sustainable, and Human*. Wiley.

Atienza, V. (2011). *Review of the waste management system in the Philippines: initiatives to promote waste segregation and recycling through good governance*. Institute of Developing Economies, Japan External Trade Organization.

Aung, T. S., Luan, S., & Xu, Q. (2019). Application of multi-criteria-decision approach for the analysis of medical waste management systems in Myanmar. *Journal of Cleaner Production*, *222*, 733–745. doi:10.1016/j.jclepro.2019.03.049

Avasthi, A., Kate, N., & Grover, S. (2013). Indianization of psychiatry utilizing Indian mental concepts. *Indian Journal of Psychiatry*, *55*(6, Suppl2), S136–S144. doi:10.4103/0019-5545.105508 PMID:23858244

Ayan, B., Güner, E., & Son-Turan, S. (2022). Blockchain Technology and Sustainability in Supply Chains and a Closer Look at Different Industries: A Mixed Method Approach. *Logistics*, *6*(4), 85. doi:10.3390/logistics6040085

Baark. Erik & Svedin, Uno. (1988). *Man, Nature, and Technology Essays on the Role of Ideological Perceptions*. Macmillan Press.

Bagadia, V. N., Shah, L. P., Pradhan, P. V., & Gada, M. T. (1979). Treatment of mental disorders in India. *Progress in Neuro-Psychopharmacology*, *3*(1-3), 109–118. doi:10.1016/0364-7722(79)90075-4 PMID:401334

Bagwan, W. A. (2023). An investigation of the bio-medical waste produced in India during the covid-19 pandemic and maharashtra state (pre-covid-19 and post-covid-19) analysis: A gis-based approach. *Research in Health Services & Regions*, 2(1), 1–18. doi:10.1007/s43999-023-00023-9

Banisar, D. (2023). *National Comprehensive Data Protection/Privacy Laws and Bills 2023*. Privacy Laws and Bills.

Bank, A. D. (2018). *Health Impact Assessment: A Good Practice Sourcebook*. Asian Development Bank. https://www.adb.org/documents/health-impact-assessment-sourcebook

Bansal, A., & Datta, S. (2013). The impact of climate change in South Asia. In *South Asian Security* (pp. 218–234). Routledge.

Bansod, H. S., & Deshmukh, P. (2023). Biomedical Waste Management and Its Importance: A Systematic Review. *Cureus*, 15(2). doi:10.7759/cureus.34589 PMID:36874306

Barik, D., & Thorat, A. (2015). Issues of unequal access to public health in India. *Frontiers in Public Health*, 3, 245. doi:10.3389/fpubh.2015.00245 PMID:26579507

Barman, M. (2022). Arne Naess Reflection of Eco-Centrism and Deep Ecology with Utilitarian and Deontological Defense against Anthropocentric Theory. *Journal of Positive School Psychology*, 6(3), 8736–8739.

Batko, K., & Ślęzak, A. (2022). The use of Big Data Analytics in healthcare. *Journal of Big Data*, 9(1), 3. doi:10.1186/s40537-021-00553-4 PMID:35013701

Bauer, G. F., Hämmig, O., & Keyes, C. L. (2014). Mental health as a complete state: How the salutogenic perspective completes the picture. *Bridging occupational, organizational and public health: A transdisciplinary approach*, 179-192.

BBC. (2021, November 1). COP26: India PM Narendra Modi pledges net zero by 2070. *BBC News*. https://www.bbc.com/news/world-asia-india-59125143

Belaguli, G., & Savitha, H. P. (2019). An empirical understanding on the concept of Sattvavajaya Chikitsa (Ayurveda Psychotherapy) and a mini-review of its research update. *Indian Journal of Health Sciences and Biomedical Research kleu*, 12(1), 15-20..doi:10.4103/kleuhsj.kleuhsj_175_18

Belle, A., Thiagarajan, R., Soroushmehr, S., Navidi, F., Beard, D. A., & Najarian, K. (2015). Big data analytics in healthcare. *BioMed Research International*, 2015, 1–16. doi:10.1155/2015/370194 PMID:26229957

Bertoldi, P., Kona, A., Rivas, S., & Dallemand, J. F. (2018). Towards a global comprehensive and transparent framework for cities and local governments enabling an effective contribution to the Paris climate agreement. *Current Opinion in Environmental Sustainability*, 30, 67–74. doi:10.1016/j.cosust.2018.03.009

Bettelheim, B., & Zelan, K. (1981). *On Learning to Read: The Child's Fascination with Meaning*. Alfred A. Knopf.

Beyan, O., Choudhury, A., van Soest, J., Kohlbacher, O., Zimmermann, L., Stenzhorn, H., Karim, M. R., Dumontier, M., Decker, S., da Silva Santos, L. O. B., & Dekker, A. (2020). Distributed analytics on sensitive medical data: The personal health train. *Data Intelligence*, 2(1-2), 96–107. doi:10.1162/dint_a_00032

Bhatia, A. (2021 October 8). *World Mental Health Day 2021: Things You Need To Know About The Day*. NDTV. https://swachhindia.ndtv.com/world-mental-health-day-2021-things-you-need-to-know-about-the-day-63554/

Bhatia, G. (2014). *Directive Principles of State Policy: Theory and Practice* (*SSRN* Scholarly Paper 2411046). https://papers.ssrn.com/abstract=2411046

Bhatia, R., & Wernham, A. (2008). Integrating Human Health into Environmental Impact Assessment: An Unrealized Opportunity for Environmental Health and Justice. *Environmental Health Perspectives*, 116(8), 991–1000. doi:10.1289/ehp.11132 PMID:18709140

Bhattamisra, S. K., Banerjee, P., Gupta, P., Mayuren, J., Patra, S., & Candasamy, M. (2023). Artificial Intelligence in Pharmaceutical and Healthcare Research. *Big Data and Cognitive Computing*, 7(1), 10. doi:10.3390/bdcc7010010

Bhawal Mukherji, S., Sekiyama, M., Mino, T., & Chaturvedi, B. (2016). Resident knowledge and willingness to engage in waste management in Delhi, India. *Sustainability (Basel)*, 8(10), 1065. doi:10.3390/su8101065

Bhugra, D., Moussaoui, D., & Craig, T. J. (Eds.). (2022). *Oxford Textbook of Social Psychiatry*. Oxford University Press. doi:10.1093/med/9780198861478.001.0001

Bhuvaneshwari, S., Hettiarachchi, H., & Meegoda, J. N. (2019). Crop Residue Burning in India: Policy Challenges and Potential Solutions. *International Journal of Environmental Research and Public Health*, 16(5), 832. doi:10.3390/ijerph16050832 PMID:30866483

Birley, M. (2011). *Health Impact Assessment: Principles and Practice* (1st ed.). Earthscan.

Biswal, R., Subudhi, C., & Acharya, S. K. (2017). Healers and healing practices of mental illness in India: The role of proposed eclectic healing model. *Journal of Health Research and Reviews in Developing Countries*, 4(3), 89–95. doi:10.4103/jhrr.jhrr_64_17

Biswas, T., Pervin, S., Tanim, M. I. A., Niessen, L., & Islam, A. (2017). Bangladesh policy on prevention and control of non-communicable diseases: A policy analysis. *BMC Public Health*, 17(1), 1–11. doi:10.1186/s12889-017-4494-2 PMID:28629430

Black, R., Kniveton, D., Skeldon, R., Coppard, D., Murata, A., & Schmidt-Verkerk, K. (2008). *Demographics and climate change: Future trends and their policy implications for migration. Development Research Centre on Migration, Globalisation and Poverty*. University of Sussex.

BMW Official report . (2023). TSPCB. https://tspcb.tripura.gov.in/storage/2023/10/BMW-AR-2023.pdf

Boeva, Y., Braun, K., & Kropp, C. (2023). Platformization in the built environment: The political techno-economy of building information modeling. *Science as Culture*, 1–28. doi:10.1080/095 05431.2023.2237042

Boxall, A. B. A. (2004). The environmental side effects of medication: How are human and veterinary medicines in soils and water bodies affecting human and environmental health? *EMBO Reports*, 5(12), 1110–1116. doi:10.1038/sj.embor.7400307 PMID:15577922

Boyd, J., & Ingberman, D. E. (1996). The "Polluter Pays Principle": Should Liability be Extended When the Polluter Cannot Pay? *The Geneva Papers on Risk and Insurance. Issues and Practice*, 21(79), 182–203. https://www.jstor.org/stable/41954091. doi:10.1057/gpp.1996.13

Brazier, C. (2018). *Ecotherapy in Practice A Buddhist Model*. Routledge.

Bresnihan, P., & Millner, N. (2023). *All We Want is the Earth: Land, Labour and Movements Beyond Environmentalism*. Policy Press.

Bretter, C., & Schulz, F. (2023). Why focusing on "climate change denial" is counterproductive. *PNAS Nexus*, 120(10), e2217716120. doi:10.1073/pnas.2217716120 PMID:36853937

Brian, A. (2009). *The Nature of Technology*. Allen Lane.

Brooks, T. (2013). The Real Challenge of Climate Change. *PS, Political Science & Politics*, 46(1), 34–36. https://www.jstor.org/stable/43284277. doi:10.1017/S1049096512001412

Brown, R., Werbeloff, L., & Raven, R. (2019). Interdisciplinary research and impact. *Global Challenges (Hoboken, NJ)*, 3(4), 1900020. doi:10.1002/gch2.201900020 PMID:31565373

Bublitz, F., Oetomo, A., & Sahu, S., K., Kuang, A., X. Fadrique, L., E. Velmovitsky, P., M. Nobrega, R., & P. Morita, P. (2019). Disruptive technologies for environment and health research: An overview of artificial intelligence, blockchain, and internet of things. *International Journal of Environmental Research and Public Health*, 16(20), 3847. doi:10.3390/ijerph16203847 PMID:31614632

Burris, S., Hancock, T., Lin, V., & Herzog, A. (2007). Emerging strategies for healthy urban governance. *Journal of Urban Health*, 84, 154–163.

Bustami, A., & Hecken, M.-C. (2021). Perspectives for a New International Crime Against the Environment: International Criminal Responsibility for Environmental Degradation under the Rome Statute. *Goettingen Journal of International Law*, 1, 145–189.

Campion, J., & Bhugra, D. (1997). Experiences of religious healing in psychiatric patients in South India. *Social Psychiatry and Psychiatric Epidemiology*, 32(4), 215–221. doi:10.1007/BF00788241 PMID:9184467

Campion, J., & Bhugra, D. (1998). Religious and indigenous treatment of mental illness in South India—A descriptive study. *Mental Health, Religion & Culture*, 1(1), 21–29. doi:10.1080/13674679808406494

Capoor, M. R., & Parida, A. (2021). Biomedical waste and solid waste management in the time of covid-19: A comprehensive review of the national and international scenario and guidelines. *Journal of Laboratory Physicians*, *13*(02), 175–182. doi:10.1055/s-0041-1729132 PMID:34483566

Capoor, M. R., & Parida, A. (2021). Current perspectives of biomedical waste management in context of COVID-19. *Indian Journal of Medical Microbiology*, *39*(2), 171–178. doi:10.1016/j.ijmmb.2021.03.003 PMID:33766404

Centre for Science and Environment. (2018). *Review of NGT decisions evoking the Polluter Pays Principle* (GREEN TRIBUNAL, GREEN APPROACH, pp. 8–17) [Policy Report]. Centre for Science and Environment. https://www.jstor.org/stable/resrep38095.4

Centre for Social Justice v. Union of India, AIR 2001 Guj 71

Chakrabarti, M. S., & Ray, M. R. K. (2023). Artificial Intelligence and The Law. *Journal of Pharmaceutical Negative Results*, 87–95.

Chakravarty, B. K. (2006). Environmentalism: Indian Constitution and Judiciary. *Journal of the Indian Law Institute*, *48*(1), 99–105. https://www.jstor.org/stable/43952020

Chandani, A. (2007). Distributive Justice and Sustainability as a Viable Foundation for the Future Climate Regime. *Carbon & Climate Law Review, 1*(2), 152–163. https://www.jstor.org/stable/24323514

Chand, S., Shastry, C. S., Hiremath, S., Joel, J. J., Krishnabhat, C. H., & Mateti, U. V. (2021). Updates on biomedical waste management during COVID-19: The Indian scenario. *Clinical Epidemiology and Global Health*, *11*, 100715. doi:10.1016/j.cegh.2021.100715 PMID:36032559

Chen, Z., Wang, Y., Li, H., & Wu, Y. (2020). Telemedicine for chronic disease management in rural areas: A systematic review. *Journal of Rural Health, 36*(3), 417-426. https://journals.sagepub.com/doi/10.1177/14604582221141835?icid=int.sj-full-text.similar-articles.3

Chhibber, B. (2015). Challenges And Policy Responses To Hazardous Waste Management. *World Affairs: The Journal of International Issues, 19*(2), 86–99.

Chioda, L. (2017). *Stop the Violence in Latin America: A Look at Prevention from Cradle to Adulthood.* https://doi.org/ doi:10.1596/978-1-4648-0664-3

Cho, & Byung-Sun. (2000). Emergence of an International Environmental Criminal Law? *UCLA Journal of Environmental Law and Policy, 19*(1), 37.

Clapp, J. (1994). Africa, NGOs, and the International Toxic Waste Trade. *Journal of Environment & Development, 3*(2), 17–46. doi:10.1177/107049659400300204

Clemente-Suárez, V. J., Rodriguez-Besteiro, S., Cabello-Eras, J. J., Bustamante-Sanchez, A., Navarro-Jiménez, E., Donoso-Gonzalez, M., Beltrán-Velasco, A. I., & Tornero-Aguilera, J. F. (2022). Sustainable development goals in the COVID-19 pandemic: A narrative review. *Sustainability (Basel), 14*(13), 7726. doi:10.3390/su14137726

Cobern, W. (2000). *Everyday Thoughts about Nature.* Springer.

Constitution of India, 1950.

Cordeiro, J. V. (2021). Digital Technologies and Data Science as Health Enablers: An Outline of Appealing Promises and Compelling Ethical, Legal, and Social Challenges. *Frontiers of Medicine,* *8,* 647897. doi:10.3389/fmed.2021.647897 PMID:34307394

Corral-Verdugo, V., Frı'as, M., & Garcı'a, C. (2010). Introduction to the psychological dimensions of sustainability. In V. Corral-Verdugo, C. Garcı'a, & M. Frı'as (Eds.), *Psychological approaches to sustainability.* Nova Science Publishers.

Corral-Verdugo, V., González-Lomelí, D., Rascón-Cruz, M., & Corral-Frías, V. (2016). Intrinsic Motives of Autonomy, Self-Efficacy, and Satisfaction Associated with Two Instances of Sustainable Behavior: Frugality and Equity. *Psychology (Irvine, Calif.), 7*(5), 662–671. doi:10.4236/psych.2016.75068

Corral-Verdugo, V., Mireles-Acosta, J. F., Tapia-Fonllem, C., & Fraijo-Sing, B. (2011). Happiness as Correlate of Sustainable Behavior: A Study of Pro-Ecological, Frugal, Equitable and Altruistic Actions That Promote Subjective Wellbeing. *Human Ecology Review, 18*(2), 95–104. https://www.jstor.org/stable/24707465

Corral-Verdugo, V., Montiel, M., Sotomayor, M., Frías, M., Tapia, C., & Fraijo, B. (2011). Psychological Wellbeing as Correlate of Sustainable Behaviors. *International Journal of Hispanic Psychology, 4,* 31–44.

Corti, J. (2021) *Regional Protection of Climate Migrants in Latina America* https://www.jstor.org/stable/pdf/27074037.pdf?refreqid=fastly-default%3Af5b8701ed37f67737b376369e3935f68&ab_segments=&origin=&initiator=&acceptTC=1

Corvino, F. (2023). The forward-looking polluter pays principle for a just climate transition. *Critical Review of International Social and Political Philosophy, 0*(0), 1–28. doi:10.1080/13698230.2023.2243729

Crompton, T., & Kasser, T. (2009). *Meeting Environmental Challenges: The Role of Human Identity.* WWF-UK. http://assets.wwf.org.uk/downloads/meeting_environmental_challenges___the_role_of_human_identity.pdf

D'Souza, B. C., Seetharam, A. M., Chandrasekaran, V., & Kamath, R. (2018). Comparative analysis of cost of biomedical waste management across varying bed strengths in rural India. *International Journal of Healthcare Management, 11*(1), 38–43. doi:10.1080/20479700.2017.1289438

DanonM. (2019). "From Ego to Eco": The contribution of Ecopsychology to the current environmental crisis management. *Visions for Sustainability,* 12, 8-17. https://doi.org/doi:10.13135/2384-8677/3261

Darwin, C. (1984). *Concepts and Measures of Natural Resource Scarcity with a Summary of Recent Trends'. Journal of Environmental Economics and Management, 11*(4), 363–379. doi:10.1016/0095-0696(84)90005-6

Das, D. K., & Chadchan, J. (2023). A proposed framework for an appropriate governance system to develop smart cities in India. *Territory, Politics, Governance,* 1–22. doi:10.1080/21622671.2023.2229872

Dasgupta, S. (2007). *The impact of sea level rise on developing countries: a comparative analysis* (Vol. 4136). World Bank Publications. doi:10.1596/1813-9450-4136

Das, P., Martin Sagayam, K., Rahaman Jamader, A., & Acharya, B. (2022). Remote Sensing in Public Health Environment: A Review. In S. Biswas, C. Chowdhury, B. Acharya, & C. M. Liu (Eds.), *Internet of Things Based Smart Healthcare. Smart Computing and Intelligence.* Springer. doi:10.1007/978-981-19-1408-9_17

Datta, P., Mohi, G. and Chander, J., (2018). Biomedical waste management in India: Critical appraisal. *Journal of laboratory physicians, 10*(01), 006-014.

David, L., Markell, R. L., Glicksman., & Monteleoni, C. (2017). Technological Innovation, Data Analytics, and Environmental Enforcement. *Ecology Law Quarterly, 44*(41), 41–88. doi:10.15779/Z38C53F16C

Dayal, P. (2023, June 25). Paper trail. *CBC News.* https://www.cbc.ca/newsinteractives/features/paper-trail

de Sadeleer, N. (2020). The Polluter-Pays Principle. In N. de Sadeleer (Ed.), Environmental Principles: From Political Slogans to Legal Rules (p. 0). Oxford University Press. doi:10.4324/9780367816681-78

De Young, R. (1993). Changing Behavior and Making It Stick: The Conceptualization and Management of Conservation Behavior. *Environment and Behavior, 25*(3), 485–505. doi:10.1177/0013916593253003

De Young, R. (1996). Some psychological aspects of a reduced consumption lifestyle: The role of intrinsic satisfaction and competence motivation. *Environment and Behavior, 28,* 358–409. doi:10.1177/0013916596283005

Dein, S. (2020). Religious healing and mental health. *Mental Health, Religion & Culture, 23*(8), 657–665. doi:10.1080/13674676.2020.1834220

De, J. (2023). Rethinking Environmental Governance: Exploring the Sustainability Potential in India. In *The Route Towards Global Sustainability: Challenges and Management Practices* (pp. 1–24). Springer International Publishing. doi:10.1007/978-3-031-10437-4_1

Depledge, J. J. (2001). *The organization of the Kyoto Protocol negotiations: Lessons for global environmental decision-making.* University of London, University College London.

Diduck, A., Pratap, D., Sinclair, J., & Deanne, S. (2013). Perceptions of impacts, public participation, and learning in the planning, assessment and mitigation of two hydroelectric projects in Uttarakhand, India. *ScienceDirect, 33*. https://www.sciencedirect.com/science/article/abs/pii/S0264837713000197

Director General of Foreign Trade. (n.d.). *Handbook of Procedures*. Ministry of Commerce and Industry. https://content.dgft.gov.in/Website/dgftprod/6978673f-9c59-4aac-a612-084df7b47e39/HBP2023_Chapter02.pdf

Dispute concerning Delimitation of the Maritime Boundary Between Ghana and Cote D'ivoire in the Atlantic Ocean (GHANA/CÔTE D'IVOIRE), (INTERNATIONAL TRIBUNAL FOR THE LAW OF THE SEA September 23, 2017). https://www.itlos.org/en/main/cases/list-of-cases/case-no-23/

Doeker, G., & Gehring, T. (1990). PRIVATE OR INTERNATIONAL LIABILITY FOR TRANSNATIONAL ENVIRONMENTAL DAMAGE— THE PRECEDENT OF CONVENTIONAL LIABILITY REGIMES. *Journal of Environmental Law, 2*(1), 1–16. doi:10.1093/jel/2.1.1

Dua, B., & Acharya, A. S. (2014). Health impact assessment: Need and future scope in India. *Indian Journal of Community Medicine, 39*(2), 76–81. doi:10.4103/0970-0218.132719 PMID:24963222

Dubrule, T., Patriquin, D. L. D., & Hood, G. A. (2018). A Question of Inclusion: BC Hydro's Site C Dam Indigenous Consultation Process. *Journal of Environmental Assessment Policy and Management, 20*(2), 1–19. https://www.jstor.org/stable/90022924. doi:10.1142/S1464333218500059

Duffy, R. M., & Kelly, B. D. (2020). History of Mental Health Legislation in India. In India's Mental Healthcare Act, 2017: Building Laws, Protecting Rights (pp. 51–59). Springer Singapore. doi:10.1007/978-981-15-5009-6_4

Duignan, B., & West, H. R. (2017). Utilitarianism philosophy. In *Encyclopædia Britannica*. https://www.britannica.com/topic/utilitarianism-philosophy

Duong, D., (2023). *Improper disposal of medical waste costs health systems and the environment.*

Dupuche, J. R. (2003). Abhinavagupta: The Kula Ritual, as Elaborated in Chapter 29 of the Tantrāloka, Motilal Banarsidass Publishers, ISBN 81-208-1979-9.

Dusyk, N. (2011). Downstream Effects of a Hybrid Forum: The Case of the Site C Hydroelectric Dam in British Columbia, Canada. *Annals of the Association of American Geographers, 101*(4), 873–881. https://www.jstor.org/stable/27980234. doi:10.1080/00045608.2011.569655

Economic Commission for Latin America and the Caribbean. (2022). *Social Panorama of Latin America and the Caribbean*. Cepal. https://repositorio.cepal.org/server/api/core/bitstreams/a1208761-efa2-4f3a-8be9-bc9368c370c0/content

Economic Times. (2017). What makes improper management of biomedical waste so hazardous. *Economic Times.* https://health.economictimes.indiatimes.com/news/industry/what-makes-improper-management-of-biomedical-waste-so-hazardous-/60471726

Edwards, Z., Sinan, H., Adam, M. S., & Miller, A. (2020). State-led fisheries development: enabling access to resources and markets in the Maldives pole-and-line skipjack tuna fishery. *Securing Sustainable Small-Scale Fisheries: Showcasing Applied Practices in Value Chains. Post-Harvest Operations and Trade, 652,* 141.

El Presidente de la Republica. Peru. (2015). *Decreto Legislativo de Migracion, Decreto N° 1236.* Acnur. https://www.acnur.org/fileadmin/Documentos/BDL/2015/10203.pdf

Ellison, C. G. (1991). Religious involvement and subjective well-being. *Journal of Health and Social Behavior, 32*(1), 80–99. doi:10.2307/2136801 PMID:2007763

Environment Protection Act, ACT NO. 29 OF 1986. (1986).

European Parliament. (2023). *News European Parliament.* European Parliament. https://www.europarl.europa.eu/news/en/headlines/world/20200624STO81906/exploring-migration-causes-why-people-migrate

Eva, G., Liese, G., Stephanie, B., Petr, H., Leslie, M., Roel, V., Martine, V., Sergi, B., Mette, H., Sarah, J., Laura, R. M., Arnout, S., Morris, S. A., Jan, T., Xenia, T., Nina, V., Koert, V. E., Sylvie, R., & Greet, S. (2022). Position paper on management of personal data in environment and health research in Europe. *Environment International, 165,* 107334. doi:10.1016/j.envint.2022.107334 PMID:35696847

Eyles, J., & Fried, J. (2012). "Technical breaches" and "eroding margins of safety" — Rhetoric and reality of the nuclear industry in Canada. *Risk Management, 14*(2), 126–151. https://www.jstor.org/stable/23260054. doi:10.1057/rm.2012.1

Falkner, R. (2016). The Paris Agreement and the new logic of international climate politics. *International Affairs, 92*(5), 1107–1125. doi:10.1111/1468-2346.12708

Faure, M. G., & Svatikova, K. (2012). Criminal or Administrative Law to Protect the Environment? Evidence from Western Europe. *Journal of Environmental Law, 24*(2), 253–286. doi:10.1093/jel/eqs005

Faure, M., & Grimeaud, D. (2004). *Financial assurance issues of environmental liability.* Hormone and Metabolic Research - HORMONE METAB RES.

Fehr, R., Viliani, F., Nowacki, J., & Martuzzi, M. (2014). *Health in impact assessments: Opportunities not to be missed.* World Health Organization. Regional Office for Europe; WHO IRIS. https://iris.who.int/handle/10665/137369

Feinberg, J. (1988). The Moral Limits of the Criminal Law Volume 4: Harmless Wrongdoing. Oxford University Press. doi:10.1093/0195064704.001.0001.002.003

Ferronato, N., & Torretta, V. (2019). Waste mismanagement in developing countries: A review of global issues. *International Journal of Environmental Research and Public Health*, *16*(6), 1060. doi:10.3390/ijerph16061060 PMID:30909625

Firdosi, M. M., & Ahmad, Z. Z. (2016). Mental health law in India: Origins and proposed reforms. *BJPsych International*, *13*(3), 65–67. doi:10.1192/S2056474000001264 PMID:29093906

Fitzgerald, G. J. (2012). The Invention of Ecocide: Agent Orange, Vietnam, and the Scientists Who Changed the Way We Think about the Environment. *The Journal of American History*, *99*(2), 677–678. doi:10.1093/jahist/jas292

Fitzmaurice, M. (2013). International Environmental Law. By ULRICH BEYERLIN and THILO MARAUHN. *Journal of Environmental Law*, *25*(1), 159–161. doi:10.1093/jel/eqs032

Flood, L. U. (1997). Sardar Sarovar Dam: A Case Study of Development-induced Environmental Displacement. Refuge: Canada's Journal on Refugees / Refuge. *Revue Canadienne Sur Les Réfugiés*, *16*(3), 12–17. https://www.jstor.org/stable/45411572

Foley, A., & Kelman, I. (2020). Precipitation responses to ENSO and IOD in the Maldives: Implications of large-scale modes of climate variability in weather-related preparedness. *International Journal of Disaster Risk Reduction*, *50*, 101726. doi:10.1016/j.ijdrr.2020.101726

Fraifeld, A., Rice, A. N., Stamper, M. J., & Muckler, V. C. (2021). Intraoperative waste segregation initiative among anesthesia personnel to contain disposal costs. *Waste Management (New York, N.Y.)*, *122*, 124–131. doi:10.1016/j.wasman.2021.01.006 PMID:33513532

Freeman, C. (1974). *The Economics of Industrial Innovation*. Penguin.

Gan–Part, L. (2007). *Detailed Island Risk Assessment in Maldives*.

Gao, Y., Gao, X., & Zhang, X. (2017). The 2 C global temperature target and the evolution of the long-term goal of addressing climate change—From the United Nations framework convention on climate change to the Paris agreement. *Engineering (Beijing)*, *3*(2), 272–278. doi:10.1016/J.ENG.2017.01.022

Gao, Y., Skutsch, M., Paneque-Gálvez, J., & Ghilardi, A. (2020). Remote sensing of forest degradation: A review. *Environmental Research Letters*, *15*(10), 103001. doi:10.1088/1748-9326/abaad7

Gheuens, J., Nagabhatla, N., & Perera, E. D. P. (2019). Disaster-risk, water security challenges and strategies in Small Island Developing States (SIDS). *Water (Basel)*, *11*(4), 637. doi:10.3390/w11040637

Ghosh, S. (2015). Reforming the Liability Regime for Air Pollution in India. *Environmental Law and Practice Review, 4*.

Gilbert, J., Soliev, I., Robertson, A., Vermeylen, S., Williams, N. W., & Grabowski, R. C. (2023). Understanding the Rights of Nature: Working Together Across and Beyond Disciplines in Human Ecology. *Human Ecology: an Interdisciplinary Journal*, *51*(3), 363–377. doi:10.1007/s10745-023-00420-1

Gillette, A. (2007). *Eugenics and the Nature-Nurture Debate in the Twentieth Century.* Palgrave Macmillan.

Gill, G. N. (2019). Precautionary principle, its interpretation and application by the Indian judiciary: 'When I use a word it means just what I choose it to mean-neither more nor less' Humpty Dumpty. *Environmental Law Review*, *21*(4), 292–308. doi:10.1177/1461452919890283

Giménez, T. V. (2023). The rights of Nature: The legal revolution of the 21st century. *MOJ Ecology & Environmental Sciences*, *8*(3), 97–115. doi:10.15406/mojes.2023.08.00280

Glasson, J., Therivel, R., Chadwick, A. J., & Chadwick, A. (2012). *Introduction to environmental impact assessment* (4th ed.). Routledge.

Global Security Health Index. (2019). *Building Collective Action and Accountability.* John Hopkins, Bloomberg School of Public Health. www.ghsindex.org

Gonsalves, P. P., Hodgson, E. S., Bhat, B., Sharma, R., Jambhale, A., Michelson, D., & Patel, V. (2021). App-based guided problem-solving intervention for adolescent mental health: A pilot cohort study in Indian schools. *BMJ Mental Health*, *24*(1), 11–18. doi:10.1136/ebmental-2020-300194 PMID:33208507

Gonsalves, P. P., Hodgson, E. S., Kumar, A., Aurora, T., Chandak, Y., Sharma, R., Michelson, D., & Patel, V. (2019). Design and development of the "POD adventures" smartphone game: A blended problem-solving intervention for adolescent mental health in India. *Frontiers in Public Health*, *7*, 238. doi:10.3389/fpubh.2019.00238 PMID:31508404

Goodall, B. (2019, December 27). Indian Government to Tighten Restrictions on The Import of Mixed Papers. *Resource.* https://resource.co/article/indian-government-tighten-restrictions-import-mixed-papers#disqus_thread

Government of Canada. (2021). *Framework: Public Participation Under the Impact Assessment Act.* Government of Canada. https://www.canada.ca/en/impact-assessment-agency/services/policy-guidance/practitioners-guide-impact-assessment-act/framework-public-participation.html

Government of Canada. (2021). *Policy Context: Indigenous Participation in Impact Assessment.* Government of Canada. https://www.canada.ca/en/impact-assessment-agency/services/policy-guidance/practitioners-guide-impact-assessment-act/policy-indigenous-participation-ia.html

Govindarajan, V. (2018, April 6). *'Every house has a sick person': Why people in Tuticorin are opposing Vedanta's copper smelter.* Scroll.In. https://scroll.in/article/874441/every-house-has-a-sick-person-why-people-in-tuticorin-are-opposing-vedantas-copper-smelter

Greene, A. (2021). Mens Rea and the Proposed Legal Definition of Ecocide. *Voelkerreschtsblog.* https://voelkerrechtsblog.org/mens-rea-and-the-proposed-legal-definition-of-ecocide/

Greene, A. (2019). The Campaign to Make Ecocide an International Crime. *Fordham Environmental Law Review, 30*, 1–48.

Gupta, S., & Sagar, R. (2022). National Mental Health Policy, India (2014): Where Have We Reached? *Indian Journal of Psychological Medicine, 44*(5), 510–515. doi:10.1177/02537176211048335 PMID:36157023

Gussmann, G., & Hinkel, J. (2021). A framework for assessing the potential effectiveness of adaptation policies: Coastal risks and sea-level rise in the Maldives. *Environmental Science & Policy, 115*, 35–42. doi:10.1016/j.envsci.2020.09.028

Guttikunda, S., Ka, N., Ganguly, T., & Jawahar, P. (2023). Plugging the ambient air monitoring gaps in India's national clean air programme (NCAP) airsheds. *Atmospheric Environment, 301*, 119712. doi:10.1016/j.atmosenv.2023.119712

Gyanesh K.T (2016). Sustainable Behaviors and Happiness: An Optimistic Link, *The International Journal of Indian Psychology 4*(1), 75.

Häder, D. P. (2018). Effects of climate change on corals. In K. Gao (Ed.), *Aquatic Ecosystems in a Changing Climate; Häder, D.-P* (pp. 146–161). doi:10.1201/9780429436130-8

Hann, K., Pearson, H., Campbell, D., Sesay, D., & Eaton, J. (2015). Factors for success in mental health advocacy. *Global Health Action, 8*(1), 28791. doi:10.3402/gha.v8.28791 PMID:26689456

Hardiman, D. (2013). A subaltern Christianity: faith healing in Southern Gujarat. In *Medical Marginality in South Asia* (pp. 126–151). Routledge. doi:10.4324/9780203112823-13

Harris-Roxas, B., Viliani, F., Bond, A., Cave, B., Divall, M., Furu, P., Harris, P., Soeberg, M., Wernham, A., & Winkler, M. (2012). Health impact assessment: The state of the art. *Impact Assessment and Project Appraisal, 30*(1), 43–52. doi:10.1080/14615517.2012.666035

Hart, H. L. A., & Gardner, J. (2009). *Punishment and responsibility: essays in the philosophy of law*. Oxford University Press.

Health Canada. (2004). *Canadian handbook on health impact assessment. Volume 1: The basics.* Ottawa, ON: Health Canada. http://www.hc-sc.gc.ca/fniah-spnia/pubs/promotion/_ environ/handbook-guide2004/index-eng.php

Health impact assessment. (n.d.). WHO. https://www.who.int/health-topics/health-impact-assessment

Health impact assessment. A guide for the oil and gas industry. (n.d.). Ipieca. https://www.ipieca.org/resources/health-impact-assessment-a-guide-for-the-oil-and-gas-industry

Herald, D. (2018). *Toxic Waste.* Deccan Herald. https://www.deccanherald.com/india/karnataka/bengaluru/toxic-waste-callous-treatment-1925118

Herald, D. (2021). *Bio Waste.* Deccan Herald. https://www.deccanherald.com/india/karnataka/bengaluru/bio-waste-disposal-costs-up-879340.html

Hernández, B., Tabernero, C., & Suárez, E. (2010). Psychosocial Motivations and Self-Regulation Processes That Activate Environmentally Responsible Behavior. In J. Valentín & L. Gámez (Eds.), *Environmental Psychology: New Developments* (pp. 109–126). Nova Science Publishers.

Hesse, H. (1968). Magister Ludi, Glass beads game, Engl. Transl. by Holt, Rinehart & Winston.

HIA_in_Planning_Exec_Summary.pdf. (n.d.). UK Government. https://assets.publishing.service. gov.uk/media/5f85b628e90e07329a8dbf81/HIA_in_Planning_Exec_Summary.pdf

Higgins, P. (2012). *Earth is our business: changing the rules of the game.* Shepheard-Walwyn.

Hinde, R. A., & Hinde, R. (2009). *Why Gods persist: A scientific approach to religion.* Routledge. doi:10.4324/9780203868751

Hohne-Sparborth, T., Shiham Adam, M., & Ziyad, A. (2015). *A socio-economic assessment of the tuna fisheries in the Maldives.* International Pole & Line Foundation.

Hsiao-Yean, C. (2015). Walking Improves Sleep in Individuals with Cancer: A Meta-Analysis of Randomized, Controlled Trials. *Oncology Nursing Forum, 42*(2).

Husak, D. N. (2010). *Overcriminalization: the limits of the criminal law.* Oxford University Press.

Hussain, M. M., Pal, S., & Villanthenkodath, M. A. (2023). Towards sustainable development: The impact of transport infrastructure expenditure on the ecological footprint in India. *Innovation and Green Development, 2*(2), 100037. doi:10.1016/j.igd.2023.100037

Husserl, E. 2001, [1900/1901]. Logical Investigations. Ed. Dermot Moran. 2nd ed. 2 vols. London: Routledge.p. 168

Ibrahim, S. A., Bari, M. R., & Miles, L. (2002). *Water resources management in Maldives with an emphasis on desalination.* Maldives Water and Sanitation Authority.

Ikromjonovich, B. I. (2023). Sustainable Development in the Digital Economy: Balancing Growth and Environmental Concerns. *Al-Farg'oniy avlodlari, 1*(3), 42-50.

Ilyas, S., Srivastava, R. R., & Kim, H. (2020). Disinfection technology and strategies for COVID-19 hospital and bio-medical waste management. *The Science of the Total Environment, 749*, 141652. doi:10.1016/j.scitotenv.2020.141652 PMID:32822917

Im, E. S., Pal, J. S., & Eltahir, E. A. (2017). Deadly heat waves projected in the densely populated agricultural regions of South Asia. *Science Advances, 3*(8), e1603322. doi:10.1126/sciadv.1603322 PMID:28782036

India-National-Multidimentional-Poverty-Index-2023.pdf. (n.d.). NITI. https://niti.gov.in/sites/ default/files/2023-08/India-National-Multidimentional-Poverty-Index-2023.pdf

Inger. Thune & Anne-Sofie. Furberg. (2002). Physical Activity and Cancer Risk: Dose-Response and Cancer, All Sites and Site-Specific. *Medicine and Science in Sports and Exercise, 33.* . doi:10.1097/00005768-200106001-00025

Internal Displecement Moitoring Centre. (2021). *Global Report on Internal Displacement 2021*. Internal Displacement. https://www.internal-displacement.org/global-report/grid2021/

International Organization for Migration. (2016). *IOM Handbook On Protection And Assistance For Migrants Vulnerable To Violence, Exploitation And Abuse*. IOM. https://publications.iom.int/books/iom-handbook-migrants-vulnerable-violence-exploitation-and-abuse

International Organization for Migration. (2019). *Climate Change And Migration In Vulnerable Countries*. Switzerland: International Organization for Migration. https://publications.iom.int/system/files/pdf/climate_change_and_migration_in_vulnerable_countries.pdf

International Organization for Migration. (2020). *Task Force on Displacement*. IOM. https://environmentalmigration.iom.int/task-force-displacement

Iwata, O. (2002). Coping Style and Three Psychological Measures Associated with Environmentally Responsible Behavior. *Social Behavior and Personality*, *30*(7), 661–669. doi:10.2224/sbp.2002.30.7.661

Jafari, M., Botterud, A., & Sakti, A. (2022). Decarbonizing power systems: A critical review of the role of energy storage. *Renewable & Sustainable Energy Reviews*, *158*, 112077. doi:10.1016/j.rser.2022.112077

Jain, A. (2021). Reconciling Illness through Devotion: The Medicalization of Modern Jain Faith Healing Practice through Bhaktāmara Stotra. Florida International University.

Jain, M., & Jain, S. (2023 June 5). A Tale of Empowerment of People with Mental Disability: Part 2. *Supreme Court Observer*. https://www.scobserver.in/journal/a-tale-of-empowerment-of-people-with-mental-disability-part-2/#:~:text=In%20Ravindra%20Kumar%20Dhariwal%20v,employment%2C%20was%20discriminatory%20or%20not

Jariwala, C. M. (2010). HAZARDOUS SUBSTANCE AND WASTE LAW: LESSONS FOR INDIA. *Journal of the Indian Law Institute*, *52*(3/4), 412–434.

Jatav, S. (2023). Current Trends in Sustainable Tourism in the Indian Context. In *Handbook of Research on Sustainable Tourism and Hotel Operations in Global Hypercompetition* (pp. 391–412). IGI Global.

Jennath, A., Krishnan, A., Paul, S. K., & Bhaskaran, P. K. (2021). Climate projections of sea level rise and associated coastal inundation in atoll islands: Case of Lakshadweep Islands in the Arabian Sea. *Regional Studies in Marine Science*, *44*, 101793. doi:10.1016/j.rsma.2021.101793

Jha Thakur, U., & Rajvanshi, A. (2021). Strategic environmental assessment in India: trends and prospects. In *Handbook on Strategic Environmental Assessment*. Edward Elgar Publishing. doi:10.4337/9781789909937.00039

Jimenez, M. P., DeVille, N. V., Elliott, E. G., Schiff, J. E., Wilt, G. E., Hart, J. E., & James, P. (2021). Associations between Nature Exposure and Health: A Review of the Evidence. *International Journal of Environmental Research and Public Health*, *18*(9), 4790. doi:10.3390/ijerph18094790 PMID:33946197

Jindal, M. K., & Sar, S. K. (2023). Medical waste management during COVID-19 situation in India: Perspective towards safe environment. *Waste Management Bulletin, 1*(1), 1–3. doi:10.1016/j.wmb.2023.03.002

Jonasson, M. E., Spiegel, S. J., Thomas, S., Yassi, A., Wittman, H., Takaro, T., Afshari, R., Markwick, M., & Spiegel, J. M. (2019). Oil pipelines and food sovereignty: Threat to health equity for Indigenous communities. *Journal of Public Health Policy, 40*(4), 504–517. https://www.jstor.org/stable/48703582. doi:10.1057/s41271-019-00186-1 PMID:31548588

Jutel, O. (2021). Blockchain imperialism in the Pacific. *Big Data & Society, 8*(1). doi:10.1177/2053951720985249

Kaginalkar, A., Kumar, S., Gargava, P., & Niyogi, D. (2023). Stakeholder analysis for designing an urban air quality data governance ecosystem in smart cities. *Urban Climate, 48*, 101403. doi:10.1016/j.uclim.2022.101403

Kaiser, F. G. (1998). A general measure of ecological behavior. *Journal of Applied Social Psychology, 28*(5), 395–442. doi:10.1111/j.1559-1816.1998.tb01712.x

Kanyal, D., Butola, L. K., & Ambad, R. (2021). Biomedical waste management in India-a review. *Indian Journal of Forensic Medicine Toxicology, 15*(2), 108–113.

Kar, N. (2008). Resort to faith-healing practices in the pathway to care for mental illness: A study on psychiatric inpatients in Orissa. *Mental Health, Religion & Culture, 11*(7), 720–740. doi:10.1080/13674670802018950

Kaur, A., Kallakuri, S., Kohrt, B. A., Heim, E., Gronholm, P. C., Thornicroft, G., & Maulik, P. K. (2021). Systematic review of interventions to reduce mental health stigma in India. *Asian Journal of Psychiatry, 55*, 102466. doi:10.1016/j.ajp.2020.102466 PMID:33249319

Kazi, T. A., Syed, A. A. R., Ansari, M. A., Pandya, J. M., & Kuchekar, V. V. (2020). *Navi Mumbai International Airport EIA Report: Case Study.* AIKTC Library. http://ir.aiktclibrary.org:8080/xmlui/handle/123456789/3566

Kemm, J. (Ed.). (2013). *Health impact assessment: Past achievement, current understanding, and future progress* (1st ed.). Oxford University Press.

Kemm, J., Parry, J., & Palmer, S. (2004). *Health Impact Assessment.* Oxford University Press. doi:10.1093/acprof:oso/9780198526292.001.0001

Keyes, C. L. (2006). Mental health in adolescence: Is America's youth flourishing? *The American Journal of Orthopsychiatry, 76*(3), 395–402. doi:10.1037/0002-9432.76.3.395 PMID:16981819

Khan, A. E., Ireson, A., Kovats, S., Mojumder, S. K., Khusru, A., Rahman, A., & Vineis, P. (2011). Drinking water salinity and maternal health in coastal Bangladesh: Implications of climate change. *Environmental Health Perspectives, 119*(9), 1328–1332. doi:10.1289/ehp.1002804 PMID:21486720

Khan, B. A., Cheng, L., Khan, A. A., & Ahmed, H. (2019). Healthcare waste management in Asian developing countries: A mini review. *Waste Management & Research*, *37*(9), 863–875. doi:10.1177/0734242X19857470 PMID:31266407

Khanduja, G. (2017). Prakriti and Shakti: An Ecofeminist Perspective. *Jindal Journal of Public Policy*, *3*(1), 105-14. ISSN 2277-8743

Khang, A., Abdullayev, V., Jadhav, B., Gupta, S. K., & Morris, G. (Eds.). (2023). *AI-Centric Modeling and Analytics: Concepts, Technologies, and Applications.* CRC Press. doi:10.1201/9781003400110

Khan, T. M. A., Quadir, D. A., Murty, T. S., Kabir, A., Aktar, F., & Sarker, M. A. (2002). Relative sea level changes in Maldives and vulnerability of land due to abnormal coastal inundation. *Marine Geodesy*, *25*(1-2), 133–143. doi:10.1080/014904102753516787

Khare, D., & Savanur, P. (2019). Understanding of Unmada in Ayurveda and Rational Application of Herbal Drugs-A Review. *Journal of Ayurveda and Integrated Medical Sciences*, *4*(04), 279–288. 10.21760/jaims.v4i04.676

Khatun, F., Nawrin, N., Al Kabir, F., & Neelormi, S. (2023). *Financing for Women's Empowerment in the Context of Post-COVID Recovery and LDC Graduation of Bangladesh (No. 46). Centre for Policy Dialogue.* CPD.

Kirmayer, L. J., Narasiah, L., Munoz, M., Rashid, M., Ryder, A. G., Guzder, J., Hassan, G., Rousseau, C., & Pottie, K. (2011). Common mental health problems in immigrants and refugees: General approach in primary care. CMAJ. *Canadian Medical Association Journal*, *183*(12), E959–E967. doi:10.1503/cmaj.090292 PMID:20603342

Kishan, P. (2020). Yoga and Spirituality in Mental Health: Illness to Wellness. *Indian Journal of Psychological Medicine*, *42*(5), 411–420. doi:10.1177/0253717620946995 PMID:33414587

Kleinman, A. (1980). *Patients and healers in the context of culture: An exploration of the borderland between anthropology, medicine, and psychiatry* (Vol. 3). University of California Press. doi:10.1525/9780520340848

Kleinman, A. (1986). *The Social Origins of Distress and Disease: Depression, Neurasthenia, and Pain in Modern China.* Yale University Press.

Kleinman, A. (2007). *What Really Matters: Living A Moral Life Amidst Uncertainty and Danger.* Oxford University Press.

Klint, L. M., Jiang, M., Law, A., DeLacy, T., Filep, S., Calgaro, E., Dominey-Howes, D., & Harrison, D. (2012). Dive tourism in Luganville, Vanuatu: Shocks, stressors, and vulnerability to climate change. *Tourism in Marine Environments*, *8*(1-2), 91–109. doi:10.3727/154427312X13262430524225

Kochetkova, T. (2022a). Environmental management in transition: Lessons from tantra. In: (Eds.) P. Gupta, S. P. Sahni & T. Bhatnagar, Spirituality and Management: From Models to Applications. Springer Singapore.

Kochetkova, T. (2022b). The impact of ideas on bodily processes. Lessons from mantra techniques. In (Eds). G. Enthoven, S. Rudnicki & R. Sneller, Towards a Science of Ideas, An inquiry into the emergence, evolution and expansion of ideas and their translation into action. Vernon Press.

Krishnan, P., Mukherjee, R., Hari, M. S., & Kantharajan, G. (2021). Streamlining Science-Policy Linkage for Fisheries Management in South Asia: Lessons from Regional Initiatives. *Cross-learning for Addressing Emergent Challenges of Aquaculture and Fisheries in South Asia*, 115.

Krueger, J. (1998). Prior Informed Consent and the Basel Convention: The Hazards of What Isn't Known. *Journal of Environment & Development, 7*(2), 115–137. doi:10.1177/107049659800700203

Kumar, K., & Prakash, A. (2019). Examination of sustainability reporting practices in Indian banking sector. *Asian Journal of Sustainability and Social Responsibility, 4*(1), 2. doi:10.1186/s41180-018-0022-2

Kumar, K., & Shetty, D. R. (2017). Health Impact Assessment: Recent Developments and Challenges. *International Journal of Health Sciences and Research, 7*(11), 296–306.

Kumar, M., & Prakash, V. (2020). A review on solid waste: Its impact on air and water quality. *Journal of Pollution Effects & Control, 8*(4), 1–3.

Kuramochi, T., Roelfsema, M., Hsu, A., Lui, S., Weinfurter, A., Chan, S., Hale, T., Clapper, A., Chang, A., & Höhne, N. (2020). Beyond national climate action: The impact of region, city, and business commitments on global greenhouse gas emissions. *Climate Policy, 20*(3), 275–291. doi:10.1080/14693062.2020.1740150

Kwiatkowski, R. E., & Ooi, M. (2003). Integrated environmental impact assessment: A Canadian example. *Bulletin of the World Health Organization, 81*(6), 434438. http://www.who.int/bulletin/volumes/81/6/kwiatkowski.pdf PMID:12894328

La Asamblea Legislativa Plurinacional. (2023) *Law No. 370 de 2013, Ley de migración.* Ref World. https://www.refworld.org/docid/55b636204.html

Lange, E. A. (2023). *Transformative sustainability education: Reimagining our future.* Taylor & Francis. doi:10.4324/9781003159643

Lan, Y. L., & Chen, H. C. (2022). Telehealth care system for chronic disease management of middle-aged and older adults in remote areas. *Health Informatics Journal, 28*(4). doi:10.1177/14604582221141835 PMID:36447304

Łaszewska-Hellriegel, M. (2023). Environmental Personhood as a Tool to Protect Nature. *Philosophia, 51*(3), 1369–1384. doi:10.1007/s11406-022-00583-z

Lawrence, D., Hancock, K. J., & Kisely, S. (2013). *The gap in life expectancy from preventable physical illness in psychiatric patients in Western Australia: Retrospective analysis of population-based registers.* BMJ. doi:10.1136/bmj.f2539

Le Dac-Nhuong, L. C. V. (2018). Emerging Technologies for Health and Medicine Virtual Reality, Augmented Reality, Artificial Intelligence, Internet of Things, Robotics, Industry 4.0. Scrivener Publishing LLC, Wiley.

Lee, C. (2002). Environmental justice: Building a unified vision of health and the environment. *Environmental Health Perspectives*, *110*(suppl 2), 141–144. doi:10.1289/ehp.02110s2141 PMID:11929721

Lehtimaki, S., Martic, J., Wahl, B., Foster, K. T., & Schwalbe, N. (2021). Evidence on digital mental health interventions for adolescents and young people: Systematic overview. *JMIR Mental Health*, *8*(4), e25847. doi:10.2196/25847 PMID:33913817

Leopold, A. (1949). *A Sand County almanac. And sketches here and there*. Oxford University Press.

Lidke, J. (2017). *The Goddess Within and Beyond the Three Cities: Śākta Tantra and the Paradox of Power in Nepāla-Maṇḍala*. Printworld.

Lidke, J. S. (2009). Towards a Theory of Tantra-Ecology. In C. K. Chapple (Ed.), DANAM Conference. *Yoga and Ecology: Dharma for the Earth: Proceedings of Two of the Sessions at the Fourth DANAM Conference, held on site at the American Academy of Religion*. Deepak Heritage Books, Deepak Heritage Books.

Loganathan, S., & Murthy, S. R. (2008). Experiences of stigma and discrimination endured by people suffering from schizophrenia. *Indian Journal of Psychiatry*, *50*(1), 39. doi:10.4103/0019-5545.39758 PMID:19771306

Lopez, A. (2007). Criminal Liability for Environmental Damage Occurring in Times of Non-International Armed Conflict: Rights and Remedies. *Fordham Environmental Law Review*, *18*(2), 231.

Lü, D., Richard, W., & Jung, C. G. (2014). The secret of the golden flower: a Chinese book of life. Mansfield Centre., OCLC 105755408.

Lyubomirsky, S., & Lepper, H. (1999). A measure of subjective happiness: Preliminary reliability and construct validation. *Social Indicators Research*, *46*(2), 137–155. doi:10.1023/A:1006824100041

M.C. Mehta v. Union of India And Ors, (Supreme Court February 17, 1986).

MacAdam, J. (2011) *Climate Change Displacement and International Law: Complementary Protection Standards*.

Macdonald, H. M. (2015). Skillful Revelation: Local Healers, Rationalists, and Their 'Trickery' in Chhattisgarh, Central India. *Medical Anthropology*, *34*(6), 485–500. doi:10.1080/01459740.2015.1040491 PMID:25897887

MacIntyre, M. R., Cockerill, R. G., Mirza, O. F., & Appel, J. M. (2023). Ethical considerations for the use of artificial intelligence in medical decision-making capacity assessments. *Psychiatry Research*, *328*, 115466. doi:10.1016/j.psychres.2023.115466 PMID:37717548

Macleod, C. (2016, August 25). *John Stuart Mill (Stanford Encyclopedia of Philosophy)*. Stanford. https://plato.stanford.edu/entries/mill/

Mahajan, P. B., Rajendran, P. K., Sunderamurthy, B., Keshavan, S., & Bazroy, J. (2019). Analyzing Indian mental health systems: Reflecting, learning, and working towards a better future. *Journal of Current Research in Scientific Medicine*, 5(1), 4–12. doi:10.4103/jcrsm.jcrsm_21_19-

Maneka Gandhi v Union Of India, (Supreme Court of India).

Manekar, S. S., Bakal, R. L., Jawarkar, R. D., & Charde, M. S. (2022). Challenges and measures during management of mounting biomedical waste in COVID-19 pandemic: An Indian approach. *Bulletin of the National Research Center*, 46(1), 1–9. doi:10.1186/s42269-022-00847-4 PMID:35669155

Manisalidis, I., Stavropoulou, E., Stavropoulos, A., & Bezirtzoglou, E. (2020). Environmental and Health Impacts of Air Pollution: A Review. *Frontiers in Public Health*, 8, 14. doi:10.3389/fpubh.2020.00014 PMID:32154200

Mark, W. (1996). A SOCIOLOGICAL FRAMING OF THE NIMBY (NOT-IN-MY-BACKYARD) SYNDROME. *International Review of Modern Sociology*, 26(1), 91–110.

Marquez, P. V., & Saxena, S. (2016, July). Making mental health a global priority. In *Cerebrum: The Dana forum on brain science* (Vol. 2016). Dana Foundation.

Mathias, K., Kermode, M., Sebastian, M. S., Koschorke, M., & Goicolea, I. (2015). Under the banyan tree-exclusion and inclusion of people with mental disorders in rural North India. *BMC Public Health*, 15(1), 1–11. doi:10.1186/s12889-015-1778-2 PMID:25928375

Mathiyazhagan, S. (2023). A call for algorithmic justice for SC/STs. (2023, May 14). *The Indian Express*. https://indianexpress.com/article/opinion/columns/a-call-for-algorithmic-justice-for-sc-sts-8607880/

Matthew, R. (2008). *Resource Scarcity Responding to the Security Challenge*. iPinst. https://www.ipinst.org/wp-content/uploads/2015/06/rscar0408.pdf

MC Mehta v Union of India, AIR 1997 SC 734

MC Mehta v Union of India, AIR 1998 SC 1037

MC Mehta v Union of India, AIR 1998 SC 617

McBain, R. K., Sousa, J. L., Rose, A. J., Baxi, S. M., Faherty, L. J., Taplin, C., Chappel, A., & Fischer, S. H. (2019). Impact of Project ECHO Models of Medical Tele-Education: A Systematic Review. *Journal of General Internal Medicine*, 34(12), 2842–2857. doi:10.1007/s11606-019-05291-1 PMID:31485970

Medical waste assessment. (2011). International Committee of the Red Cross (ICRC). https://www.icrc.org/en/doc/assets/files/publications/icrc-002-4032.pdf

Mekharat, N., & Traore, N. (2020). *How the tourism sector in emerging markets is recovering from COVID-19.*

Mills-Novoa, M., & Liverman, D. M. (2019). Nationally determined contributions: Material climate commitments and discursive positioning in the NDCs. *Wiley Interdisciplinary Reviews: Climate Change, 10*(5), e589. doi:10.1002/wcc.589

Ministerio de Justicia y Derechos Humanos. (2010). *Decreto 616/2010.* InfoLeg. https://servicios.infoleg.gob.ar/infolegInternet/anexos/165000-169999/167004/norma.htm

Ministry of Commerce and Industry. (2005). *Policy Circular No. 32 (RE-2005)/2004-09.* https://content.dgft.gov.in/Website/32.pdf

Ministry of Commerce and Industry. (2009). *Policy Circular No. 88 (RE-08)/2004-2009.* https://content.dgft.gov.in/Website/88.pdf

Ministry of Commerce and Industry. (2012). *Public Notice No.104 (RE2010)/20092014.* https://content.dgft.gov.in/Website/pn10410.pdf

Mishra, A. (2023). *Clearing the Air: India's National Clean Air Programme and the Path Forward.* Policy.

Miya, T. V., Mosoane, B., Lolas, G., & Dlamini, Z. (2023). Healthcare Transformation Using Blockchain Technology in the Era of Society 5.0. In Z. Dlamini (Ed.), *Society 5.0 and Next Generation Healthcare.* Springer. doi:10.1007/978-3-031-36461-7_11

Mohamed, I., & King, D. (2017). Legacy of Authoritative Environmentalism and Path-Dependent Historic Institutionalism in the Climate Change Policy Dynamics of the Maldives. *Climate Change Research at Universities: Addressing the Mitigation and Adaptation Challenges,* 211-231.

Mojtahedi, M., Fathollahi-Fard, A. M., Tavakkoli-Moghaddam, R., & Newton, S. (2021). Sustainable vehicle routing problem for coordinated solid waste management. *Journal of Industrial Information Integration, 23,* 100220. doi:10.1016/j.jii.2021.100220

Moolilahad & Berger. (2013). The Healing Forest in Post-Crisis Work with Children A Nature Therapy and Expressive Arts Program for Groups. Jessica Kingsley Publishers.

Moreira, A. M. M., & Günther, W. M. R. (2013). Assessment of medical waste management at a primary health-care center in São Paulo, Brazil. *Waste Management (New York, N.Y.), 33*(1), 162–167. doi:10.1016/j.wasman.2012.09.018 PMID:23122204

Morgan, E. A., Nalau, J., & Mackey, B. (2019). Assessing the alignment of national-level adaptation plans to the Paris Agreement. *Environmental Science & Policy, 93,* 208–220. doi:10.1016/j.envsci.2018.10.012

Morgan, R. K. (2012). Environmental impact assessment: The state of the art. *Impact Assessment and Project Appraisal, 30*(1), 5–14. doi:10.1080/14615517.2012.661557

Morley, J. (2008). Embodied Consciousness in Tantric Yoga and the Phenomenology of Merleau-Ponty. *Religion and the Arts*, *12*(1-3), 144–163. doi:10.1163/156852908X270980

Moses, O. (2014). *The 1969 O.A.U. Convention and the continuing challenge for the African Union*. FMR Review. https://www.fmreview.org/faith/okello

Mukherjee, P. K. (2019). *Quality control and evaluation of herbal drugs: Evaluating natural products and traditional medicine*. Elsevier.

Mukherjee, S. (2020). Emerging Frontiers in Smart Environment and Healthcare – A Vision. *Information Systems Frontiers*, *22*(1), 23–27. doi:10.1007/s10796-019-09965-3

Mukherjee, S. (2023). How Much Should the Polluter Pay? Indian Courts and the Valuation of Environmental Damage. *Journal of Environmental Law*, *35*(3), 331–351. doi:10.1093/jel/eqad021

Murthy, A. R. V., & Singh, R. H. (1987). The concept of psychotherapy in Ayurveda with special reference to satvavajaya. *Ancient Science of Life*, *6*(4), 255. PMID:22557578

Naithani, C., Sood, S. P., & Agrahari, A. (2023). The Indian healthcare system turns to digital health: eSanjeevaniOPD as a national telemedicine service. *Journal of Information Technology Teaching Cases*, *13*(1), 67–76. doi:10.1177/20438869211061575

Naslund, J. A., Gonsalves, P. P., Gruebner, O., Pendse, S. R., Smith, S. L., Sharma, A., & Raviola, G. (2019). Digital innovations for global mental health: Opportunities for data science, task sharing, and early intervention. *Current Treatment Options in Psychiatry*, *6*(4), 337–351. doi:10.1007/s40501-019-00186-8 PMID:32457823

Natalia, A., Zhuravleva, K. C., Miloš, P., & Ivana, P. (2019). Data privacy and security vulnerabilities of smart and sustainable urban space monitoring systems. (2019). *Contemporary Readings in Law and Social Justice*, *11*(2), 56–62. doi:10.22381/CRLSJ11220198

Natarajan, J. (n.d.). *National Hazardous Waste Management Strategy*. Ministry of Environment, Forest & Climate Change, Government of India.

Nicholls, R. J., Marinova, N., Lowe, J. A., Brown, S., Vellinga, P., De Gusmao, D., & Tol, R. S. (2011). Sea-level rise and its possible impacts given a 'beyond 4 C world' in the twenty-first century. *Philosophical transactions of the Royal Society A: mathematical, physical and engineering sciences, 369*(1934), 161-181.

Niska, H., & Serkkola, A. (2018). Data analytics approach to create waste generation profiles for waste management and collection. *Waste Management (New York, N.Y.)*, *77*, 477–485. doi:10.1016/j.wasman.2018.04.033 PMID:29724480

Noble, B. F. (2021). Strategic environmental assessment in Canada. In *Handbook on Strategic Environmental Assessment*. Edward Elgar Publishing., doi:10.4337/9781789909937.00033

Noble, B., & Bronson, J. (2006). Practitioner survey of the state of health integration in environmental assessment: The case of northern Canada. *Environmental Impact Assessment Review*, *26*(4), 410424. doi:10.1016/j.eiar.2005.11.001

Noble, B., Gibson, R., White, L., Blakley, J., Croal, P., Nwanekezie, K., & Doelle, M. (2019). Effectiveness of strategic environmental assessment in Canada under directive-based and informal practice. *Impact Assessment and Project Appraisal*, *37*(3–4), 344–355. doi:10.1080/14615517 .2019.1565708

Nollkaemper, A. (2001). *Three Conceptions of the Integration Principle in International Environmental Law*. Environmental Policy Integration.

Nollkaemper, A., Ahlborn, C., Boutin, B., Nedeski, N., Plakokefalos, I., & Jacobs, D. (2020). Guiding Principles on Shared Responsibility in International Law. *European Journal of International Law*, *31*(1), 15–72. doi:10.1093/ejil/chaa017

Nomani, M. (2011). Legal Framework for Environment Impact Assessment in India: A Contemporary Appraisal in Corporate Perspective. *The Chartered Accountant Journal*, *59*, 1872–1879.

O'Donnell, E. L., & Talbot-Jones, J. (2018). Creating Legal Rights for Rivers: Lessons from Australia, New Zealand, and India. *Ecology and Society*, *23*(1), 7. doi:10.5751/ES-09854-230107

O'Hear, M. M. (2004). Sentencing The Green-Collar Offender: Punishment, Culpability, And Environmental Crime. *The Journal of Criminal Law & Criminology*, *95*(1), 133. doi:10.2307/3491383

Observer Research Foundation. (2023), *It's time for climate justice- A Global South perspective on the fight against the climate crisis*. Observer Research Foundation. https://www.orfonline. org/research/a-global-south-perspective-on-the-fight-against-the-climate-crisis/

Office of Prosecutors. (2016). *Policy Paper on Case Selection and Prioritization,* International Criminal Court. https://www.icccpi.int/sites/default/files/itemsDocuments/20160915_OTP-Policy_Case-Selection_Eng.pdf

Oficina del Alto Comisionado de las Naciones Unidas para los Refugiados. (2014) *Conmemoración del 30 Aniversario de la Declaración de Cartagena "Cartagena +30"*. Acnur. https://www.acnur. org/fileadmin/Documentos/BDL/2014/9780.pdf

Oh, C. (2020). Discursive Contestation on Technological Innovation and the Institutional Design of the UNFCCC in the New Climate Change Regime. *New Political Economy*, *25*(4), 660–674. doi:10.1080/13563467.2019.1639147

Okechukwu, E.C., Cyriacus, O.A., Aguora, S.O. & Soni, J.S. (2020). *Segregation Practices by Health Workers in Urban Hospitals-A Step Necessary to Achieve Minimization and Effective Biomedical Waste Management*.

Organization of African Unity. (1968). *Convention Governing the Specific Aspects of Refugee Problems in Africa ("OAU Convention")*. RefWorld. https://www.refworld.org/docid/3ae6b36018. html

Oslo Principles on Global Climate Change Obligations. (2015). Global Justice. https://globaljustice. yale.edu/sites/default/files/files/OsloPrinciples.pdf

Ourbak, T., & Magnan, A. K. (2018). The Paris Agreement and climate change negotiations: Small Islands, big players. *Regional Environmental Change, 18*(8), 2201–2207. doi:10.1007/s10113-017-1247-9

P.P. Electronics v. New Delhi (Import & General), (Customs, Excise & Service Tax Appellate Tribunal 2018). 17 June 2023

Padmavati, R., Thara, R., & Corin, E. (2005). A qualitative study of religious practices by chronic mentally ill and their caregivers in South India. *The International Journal of Social Psychiatry, 51*(12), 139–149. doi:10.1177/0020764005056761 PMID:16048243

Padoux, A. (2017) *The Hindu Tantric World: An Overview*, Chicago University Press, https://doi.org/ doi:10.7208/chicago/9780226424125.001.0001

Palei, T. (2015). Assessing the impact of infrastructure on economic growth and global competitiveness. *Procedia Economics and Finance, 23*, 168–175. doi:10.1016/S2212-5671(15)00322-6

Pan, E. (2020). *Reimagining The Climate Migration Paradigm: Bridging Conceptual Barriers To Climate Migration Responses.* JSTOR.

Pandey, S., & Dwivedi, A. K. (2016). *Nosocomial infections through hospital waste.* OMICS. doi:10.4172/2252-5211.1000200

Pandi-Perumal, S. R. (2022). Sterlite Copper: Much Ado About Nothing, all the while Ignoring the Elephant in the Room? SSRN *Electronic Journal.* doi:10.2139/ssrn.4106810

Pandya, A., Shah, K., Chauhan, A., & Saha, S. (2020). Innovative mental health initiatives in India: A scope for strengthening primary healthcare services. *Journal of Family Medicine and Primary Care, 9*(2), 502. doi:10.4103/jfmpc.jfmpc_977_19 PMID:32318372

Parida, R., Katiyar, R., & Rajhans, K. (2023). Identification and analysis of critical barriers for achieving sustainable development in India. *Journal of Modelling in Management, 18*(3), 727–755.

Parikh, M. (2019). Critique of environmental impact assessment process in India. *Environmental Policy and Law, 49*(4-5), 252–259. doi:10.3233/EPL-190171

Parikh, R., Michelson, D., Sapru, M., Sahu, R., Singh, A., Cuijpers, P., & Patel, V. (2019). Priorities and preferences for school-based mental health services in India: A multi-stakeholder study with adolescents, parents, school staff, and mental health providers. *Global Mental Health (Cambridge, England), 6*, e18. doi:10.1017/gmh.2019.16 PMID:31531228

Pennebaker, J. W. (2012). *Opening up: The healing power of expressing emotions.* Guilford Press.

Peterson, C., & Seligman, M. E. P. (2004). *Character strengths and virtues: A handbook and classification.* American Psychological Association.

Piqueres, S. L., Giuli, M., & Hedberg, A. (2020). *Adapting to change: Time for climate resilience and a new adaptation strategy.* EPC Issue Paper.

Pol, E. (2002). The theoretical background of the city-identity-sustainability network. *Environment and Behavior*, *34*(1), 8–25. doi:10.1177/0013916502034001002

Prabhu, N. (2022, December 12). Criminal Liability of Corporations in India—An Environmental Perspective. *Georgetown Public Policy Review*. https://gppreview.com/2022/12/12/criminal-liability-of-corporations-in-india-an-environmental-perspective/

Pradyumna, A. (2015). Health Aspects of Environmental Impact Assessment Process in India. *Economic and Political Weekly*, *50*(8), 57–64.

Pristner, M., & Warth, B. (2020). Drug-Exposome Interactions: The Next Frontier in Precision Medicine. *Trends in Pharmacological Sciences*, *41*(12), 994–1005. doi:10.1016/j.tips.2020.09.012 PMID:33186555

Qasim, S., Momina, A., Zahra, F. T., Qasim, T. B., & Rehman, F. (2020). Knowledge, attitude and practices of healthcare workers regarding biomedical waste segregation at Mayo Hospital Lahore. *The Professional Medical Journal*, *27*(12), 2755–2762. doi:10.29309/TPMJ/2020.27.12.3888

Rabbani, M., Heidari, R., & Yazdanparast, R. (2019). A stochastic multi-period industrial hazardous waste location-routing problem: Integrating NSGA-II and Monte Carlo simulation. *European Journal of Operational Research*, *272*(3), 945–961. doi:10.1016/j.ejor.2018.07.024

Radovanović, D., Holst, C., Belur, S. B., Srivastava, R., Houngbonon, G. V., Le Quentrec, E., Miliza, J., Winkler, A. S., & Noll, J. (2020). Digital literacy key performance indicators for sustainable development. *Social Inclusion (Lisboa)*, *8*(2), 151–167. doi:10.17645/si.v8i2.2587

Raghupathi, W., & Raghupathi, V. (2014). Big data analytics in healthcare: Promise and potential. *Health Information Science and Systems*, *2*(1), 1–10. doi:10.1186/2047-2501-2-3 PMID:25825667

Rahman, M. A. (2022). *Nature and causes of climate change: An analysis of global climate and greenhouse emissions data*. Research Gate.

Rahman, M., & Roy, P. K. (2022). Challenges to Ensure Healthy Living through Sanitation and Hygiene Coverage: Study on Narail District, Bangladesh. In Effective Waste Management and Circular Economy (pp. 223-232). CRC Press.

Rahman, M. M., Bodrud-Doza, M., Griffiths, M. D., & Mamun, M. A. (2020). Biomedical waste amid covid-19: Perspectives from bangladesh. *The Lancet. Global Health*, *8*(10), e1262. doi:10.1016/S2214-109X(20)30349-1 PMID:32798448

Raina, M., & Singh, K. (2018). The Ashtanga Yoga Hindi Scale: An assessment tool based on the Eastern philosophy of yoga. *Journal of Religion and Health*, *57*(1), 12–25. doi:10.1007/s10943-015-0096-4 PMID:26215275

Ranguelov, B., & Shadiya, F. (2018). Fractals, Natural Disasters and Ecological Problems of Maldives. *J. Ecological Eng. and Env. Protection*, 18-25.

Rao, K. R. (2011). Indian Psychology: Implications and applications. In R. M. J. Cornelissen, G. Misra, & S. Verma (Eds.), *Foundations of Indian Psychology: Theories and Concepts* (Vol. 1, pp. 7–26). Pearson.

Rao, K. R., & Paranjpe, A. C. (2016). *Psychology in the Indian Tradition.* Springer India. doi:10.1007/978-81-322-2440-2

Rao, P. T. (2006). Nature of Opposition to the Polavaram Project. *Economic and Political Weekly*, *41*(15), 1437–1439. https://www.jstor.org/stable/4418082

Rao, S. K. M., Ranyal, R. K., Bhatia, S. S., & Sharma, V. R. (2004). Biomedical waste management: An infrastructural survey of hospitals. *Medical Journal, Armed Forces India*, *60*(4), 379–382. doi:10.1016/S0377-1237(04)80016-9 PMID:27407678

Rasheed, A. A. (2019). Role of small islands in UN climate negotiations: A constructivist viewpoint. *International Studies*, *56*(4), 215–235. doi:10.1177/0020881719861503

Rathi, A. K. A. (2019). *Development of environmental management program in environmental impact assessment reports and evaluation of its robustness: an Indian case study.* Taylor & Francis. https://www.tandfonline.com/doi/full/10.1080/14615517.2018.1558745

Raveesh, B. N., & Munoli, R. N. (2020). Ethical and legal aspects of telepsychiatry. *Indian Journal of Psychological Medicine*, *42*(5, suppl), 63S–69S. doi:10.1177/0253717620962033 PMID:33354067

Rengarajan, S., Palaniyappan, D., Ramachandran, P., & Ramachandran, R. (2018). National Green Tribunal of India—An observation from environmental judgements. *Environmental Science and Pollution Research International*, *25*(12), 11313–11318. doi:10.1007/s11356-018-1763-2 PMID:29572740

Research Foundation for Science Technology and Natural Resources Policy v. Union of India & Anr., Writ Petition (civil) 657 of 1995 (Supreme Court of India 1995). https://main.sci.gov.in/jonew/judis/39386.pdf

Reuveny, R. (2007). Climate change-induced migration and violent conflict. *Political Geography*, *26*(6), 656–673. doi:10.1016/j.polgeo.2007.05.001

Ripstein, A. (2006). Beyond the Harm Principle. *Philosophy & Public Affairs*, 34.

Robinson, D. (2022). Ecocide — Puzzles and Possibilities. *Journal of International Criminal Justice*, *35*(1).

Rodríguez, N., Restrepo, S., & Zambrano, I. (2013). The lack of water and its implications regarding feeding practice in Turbo, Antioquia. *Revista de Salud Publica (Bogota, Colombia)*, *15*(3), 421–433. PMID:25124000

Rogers, C. (1995). *A Way of Being.* Open Road Integrated Media.

Rohr. Fr. R. (2014). *Eager to Love: The Alternative Way of Francis of Assisi.* Hodder & Stoughton.

Roper, L. A., Siegele, J. L., & Islands, C. (2021). The Global Goal on Adaptation: a SIDS Perspective.

Rout, O. P., Acharya, R., Gupta, R., Inchulkar, S. R., Karbhal, K. S., & Sahoo, R. (2013). Management of psychosomatic disorders through Ayurvedic drugs-A critical review. *World Journal of Pharmacy and Pharmaceutical Sciences*, *2*(6), 6507–6537.

Roy, A., Nenes, A., & Takahama, S. (2023). *Current gaps in air quality management over India: A study on stakeholder consultation* (No. EGU23-12530). Copernicus Meetings.

Roy, P. K. (2024). *Customary Law and Sustainable Community Development: A Study of the Santals of Bangladesh*, [PhD Thesis, Universiti Malaya].

Roy, P. (2022). Sensing the Silence: A Case of the Rakhain Community of Bangladesh. *SSRN*, *4559157*. www.ssrn.com

Roy, P. (2023a). Conversation with Silence: An Introduction of the Spirituality and Healing System of the Bangladeshi Rakhain Community. *SSRN*, *4539913*. www.ssrn.com. doi:10.2139/ssrn.4539913

RoyP. (2023b). Conversation with Silence: The Methodological Exploration to Study the Spirituality and Healing System of the Bangladeshi Rakhain Community (August 13, 2023). https://ssrn.com/abstract=4539816 doi:10.2139/ssrn.4539816

Roy, R. (2023). The Development and Comparative Analysis of the Right to Privacy in India and the Need for a Law Governing Policy. *Legal Spectrum J.*, *3*, 1.

Ryan, R., & Deci, E. (2000). Self-Determination Theory and the Facilitation of Intrinsic Motivation, Social Development, and Well-Being. *The American Psychologist*, *55*(1), 68–78. doi:10.1037/0003-066X.55.1.68 PMID:11392867

Sagar, R., & Singh, S. (2022). National Tele-Mental Health Program in India: A step towards mental health care for all? *Indian Journal of Psychiatry*, *64*(2), 117–119. doi:10.4103/indianjpsychiatry.indianjpsychiatry_145_22 PMID:35494321

Sanderson, A. (2017). Ritual Transgression in Kaula Trika, https://amritananda-natha-saraswati.blogspot.com/p/ritual-in-kaula-trika.html

Sandford, N. (2018). Non- Trauma-Focused Meditation versus Exposure Therapy in Veterans with Post-Traumatic Stress Disorder: A Randomised Controlled Trial. *Lancet Psychiatry, 5.*

Sands, P., & Peel, J. (2012). *Principles of International Environmental Law* (3rd ed.). Cambridge University Press., doi:10.1017/CBO9781139019842

Sansom, B. (1982). The sick who do not speak. In D. Parkin (Ed.), *Semantic Anthropology* (pp. 183–196). Academic Press.

Santomauro, D. F., Herrera, A. M. M., Shadid, J., Zheng, P., Ashbaugh, C., Pigott, D. M., ... Ferrari, A. J. (2021). Global prevalence and burden of depressive and anxiety disorders in 204 countries and territories in 2020 due to the COVID-19 pandemic. *Lancet*, *398*(10312), 1700–1712. doi:10.1016/S0140-6736(21)02143-7 PMID:34634250

Sarmiento, K. (2014). *Iniciativa Cartagena +30*. Acnur. https://www.acnur.org/fileadmin/Documentos/Publicaciones/2014/9793.pdf

Sarmiento-Erazo, J. P. (2018). Migración por cambio climático en Colombia: Entre los refugiados medioambientales y los migrantes económicos. *Revista Jurídicas*, *15*(2), 53–69. doi:10.17151/jurid.2018.15.2.4

Saxena, P., Pradhan, I. P., & Kumar, D. (2022). Redefining bio medical waste management during covid-19 in india: A way forward. *Materials Today: Proceedings*, *60*, 849–858. doi:10.1016/j.matpr.2021.09.507 PMID:34660210

Saxena, S., & Janssen, M. (2017). Examining open government data (OGD) usage in India through UTAUT framework. *Foresight*, *19*(4), 421–436. doi:10.1108/FS-02-2017-0003

Scheffer, D. (2016). Corporate Liability under the Rome Statute. *Harvard International Law Journal*, *57*(1), 35–38.

Scholsberg, D. (2007). *Reconceiving Environmental Justice: Global Movements And Political Theories*. Taylor & Francis. https://www.tandfonline.com/doi/citedby/10.1080/0964401042000229025?scroll=top&needAccess=true

Schoonover, J., Lipkin, S., Javid, M., Rosen, A., Solanki, M., Shah, S., & Katz, C. L. (2014). Perceptions of traditional healing for mental illness in rural Gujarat. *Annals of Global Health*, *80*(2), 96–102. doi:10.1016/j.aogh.2014.04.013

Schueller, S. M., Neary, M., O'Loughlin, K., & Adkins, E. C. (2018). Discovery of and interest in health apps among those with mental health needs: Survey and focus group study. *Journal of Medical Internet Research*, *20*(6), e10141. doi:10.2196/10141 PMID:29891468

Schultz, P. W. (2001). The structure of environmental concern. Concern for self, other people, and the biosphere. *Journal of Environmental Psychology*, *21*(4), 327–339. doi:10.1006/jevp.2001.0227

Scott, D., Gössling, S., & Hall, C. M. (2012). International tourism and climate change. *Wiley Interdisciplinary Reviews: Climate Change*, *3*(3), 213–232. doi:10.1002/wcc.165

Sehonova, P., Svobodova, Z., Dolezelova, P., Vosmerova, P., & Faggio, C. (2018). Effects of waterborne antidepressants on non-target animals living in the aquatic environment: A review. *The Science of the Total Environment*, *631*, 789–794. doi:10.1016/j.scitotenv.2018.03.076 PMID:29727988

Selvakumar, J., Rajasekaran, S., Chitra, S., & Paul, B. (2020). Simulated studies on optimization and characterization of feed and product of melter for safe disposal of high-level radioactive liquid waste. *Progress in Nuclear Energy*, *118*, 103135. doi:10.1016/j.pnucene.2019.103135

Sengodan, V. C. (2014). Segregation of biomedical waste in an South Indian tertiary care hospital. *Journal of Natural Science, Biology, and Medicine, 5*(2), 378. doi:10.4103/0976-9668.136194 PMID:25097419

Shakeela, A., Becken, S., & Johnstone, N. (2015). Gaps and disincentives that exist in the policies, laws and regulations which act as barriers to investing in climate change adaptation in the tourism sector of the Maldives. *Increasing Climate Change Resilience of Maldives through Adaptation in the Tourism Sector*. Research Gate.

Shastri, S. C. (2000). "The Polluter Pays Principle" and the Supreme Court of India. *Journal of the Indian Law Institute, 42*(1), 108–116. https://www.jstor.org/stable/43951740

Shawar, Y. R., & Crane, L. G. (2017). Generating global political priority for urban health: The role of the urban health epistemic community. *Health Policy and Planning, 32*(8), 1161–1173. doi:10.1093/heapol/czx065 PMID:28582532

Sherma, R. D. (1998). Sacred Immanence: Reflections of Ecofeminism in Hindu Tantra. In L. E. Nelson (Ed.), *Purifying the Earthly Body of God. Religion and Ecology in Hindu India* (pp. 89–132). SUNY Press.

Shiva, V. (1993). *Ecofeminism*. Zed Books Ltd.

Shiva, V. (2016). *Staying Alive: Women, Ecology and Development*. North Atlantic Books.

Simmel, G. (1950). The Metropolis and Mental Life. In K. H. Wolff (Ed.), *The Sociology of Georg Simmel* (pp. 409–424). The Free Press.

Sinclair, J., & Diduck, A. (2016). *Reconceptualizing public participation in environmental assessment as EA civics*. Elsevier. https://d3n8a8pro7vhmx.cloudfront.net/envirolawsmatter/pages/290/attachments/original/1461095298/Sinclair_and_Diduck__Reconceptualizing_public_participation_in_EA_as_EA_civics.pdf?1461095298

Singh, S., Kaur, A., & Kaur, N. (2010). Environmental Degradation — A Case Study of Ambient Air Quality in Some Industrial Pockets of Punjab, *National Seminar on Management of Natural Resources and Environment in India,* Organized by GAD Institute of Development Studies, Amritsar, (pp. 564-75).

Singhal, L., Tuli, A. K., & Gautam, V. (2017). Biomedical waste management guidelines 2016: What's done and what needs to be done. *Indian Journal of Medical Microbiology, 35*(2), 194–198. doi:10.4103/ijmm.IJMM_17_105 PMID:28681805

Singh, P., Singh, S., Kumar, G., & Baweja, P. (Eds.). (2021). *Energy: crises, challenges and solutions*. John Wiley & Sons. doi:10.1002/9781119741503

Siraz, M. J., Abd Wahab, H., Saad, R. M., & Roy, P. K. (2020). *Globalization to Slowbalization to Indigenous Holism: Combating the Preemptive: Vaccinationalism with the reflection of Saadia Gaon and Al-Farabi*. Virus Economy. Innovation Solution Lab.

Smith, G. P. (1972). Stockholm. Summer of '72: An Affair To Remember? *American Bar Association Journal. American Bar Association*, *58*(11), 1194–1197. https://www.jstor.org/stable/25726071

Solera, E. (2021). *Habitat for Humanity International, Characterization of the Dry Corridor in Central America's Northern Triangle*. Habitat. https://www.habitat.org/sites/default/files/documents/Qualitative%20housing%20deficit%20in%20El%20Salvador%2C%20Guatemala%20and%20Honduras%20exceeds%203.9%20million%20houses.pdf

Solutions, W. (2017). *Environmental impact assessment for the construction and setup of a sewerage system in Maakurathu Island*. Raa Atoll.

Soto, M. V. (1996). *General Principles Of International Environmental Law,* I.L.S.A. *Journal of International & Comparative Law*, *3*(1), 10. https://nsuworks.nova.edu/ilsajournal/vol3/iss1/10

Sovacool, B. K. (2012). Perceptions of climate change risks and resilient island planning in the Maldives. *Mitigation and Adaptation Strategies for Global Change*, *17*(7), 731–752. doi:10.1007/s11027-011-9341-7

Sovacool, B. K., D'Agostino, A. L., Meenawat, H., & Rawlani, A. (2012). Expert views of climate change adaptation in least developed Asia. *Journal of Environmental Management*, *97*, 78–88. doi:10.1016/j.jenvman.2011.11.005 PMID:22325585

Staal, F. (2008). *Discovering the Vedas: origins, mantras, rituals, insights*. Penguin Books India.

Starhawk (1999). *The Spiral Dance*. 20th edition, Harper.

Starhawk (2013) *The Earth Path: Grounding Your Spirit in the Rhythms of Nature,* HarperOne.

Stojanov, R., Duží, B., Kelman, I., Němec, D., & Procházka, D. (2017). Local perceptions of climate change impacts and migration patterns in Malé, Maldives. *The Geographical Journal*, *183*(4), 370–385. doi:10.1111/geoj.12177

Stone, C. D. (1972). Should Trees Have Standing—Toward Legal Rights for Natural Objects. *Southern California Law Review*, *45*, 450.

Suchitra, S. P., Devika, H. S., Gangadhar, B. N., Nagarathna, R., Nagendra, H. R., & Kulkarni, R. (2010). Measuring the tridosha symptoms of unmāda (psychosis): A preliminary study. *Journal of Alternative and Complementary Medicine (New York, N.Y.)*, *16*(4), 57–62. doi:10.1089/acm.2009.0296 PMID:20423215

Sudarshan, A. (2023). Monitoring Industrial Pollution in India. In T. Madon, A. J. Gadgil, R. Anderson, L. Casaburi, K. Lee, & A. Rezaee (Eds.), Introduction to Development Engineering: A Framework with Applications from the Field (pp. 161–182). Springer International Publishing. doi:10.1007/978-3-030-86065-3_7

Suhaila, J., Deni, S. M., Wan Zin, W. Z., & Jemain, A. A. (2010). Spatial patterns and trends of daily rainfall regime in Peninsular Malaysia during the southwest and northeast monsoons: 1975–2004. *Meteorology and Atmospheric Physics*, *110*(1-2), 1–18. doi:10.1007/s00703-010-0108-6

Supran, G. (2023). Assessing ExxonMobil's Climate Change Communication, https://www.europarl.europa.eu/cmsdata/162144/Presentation%20Geoffrey%20Supran.pdf

Susan, S. S. (2003). *Healing with Nature*. Helios Press.

Tabuchi, H. (2023). Maui Sued Big Oil in 2020, Citing Fire Risks and More, The New York Times.

Takahashi, K., & Martínez, A. G. (2019). The very strong coastal El Niño in 1925 in the far-eastern Pacific. *Climate Dynamics*, *52*(12), 7389–7415. doi:10.1007/s00382-017-3702-1

Tandon, U. (2020). *Green Justice and the Application of Polluter- Pays Principle: A Study of India's National Green Tribunal* (SSRN Scholarly Paper 3690212). https://papers.ssrn.com/abstract=3690212

Techera, E. J., & Cannell-Lunn, M. (2019). A review of environmental law in Maldives with respect to conservation, biodiversity, fisheries and tourism. *Asia Pacific Journal of Environmental Law*, *22*(2), 228–256. doi:10.4337/apjel.2019.02.03

Thakur, U. J., & Khosravi, F. (2021). Beyond 25 years of EIA in India: Retrospection and way forward. *Environmental Impact Assessment Review*, *87*, 106533. doi:10.1016/j.eiar.2020.106533

The Customs Act, 1962, 52 of 1962 (1962). https://lddashboard.legislative.gov.in/sites/default/files/A1962-52.pdf

The European Court Of Human Rights. *Budayena and Others v. Russia*, (March 20, 2008). 15339.

The Indian Ports Act. 1908, 15 of 1908 (1908). https://lddashboard.legislative.gov.in/sites/default/files/A1908-15.pdf

The Lancet Global Health. (2020). Mental health matters. *The Lancet Global Health, 8*(11), e1352. doi:10.1016/S2214-109X(20)30432-0

The Prosecutor v. Dražen Erdemović, (International Criminal Tribunal for Former Yugoslavia 1996).

The Prosecutor v. Thomas Lubanga Dyilo, Decision on the confirmation of the Charges, ICC-01/04-01/06 (Pre-Trial Chamber I), 119, para. 351 (Jan. 29, 2007).

The Southern Common Market. (2023) *¿Qué es el MERCOSUR?* The Southern Common Market. https://www.mercosur.int/quienes-somos/en-pocas-palabras/

The United Nations Environment Programme. (2023) *Helping farmers beat the Climate crisis in Central America's Dry Corridor.* UNEP. https://www.unep.org/news-and-stories/story/helping-farmers-beat-climate-crisis-central-americas-dry-corridor

The White House. (2021). *Report on the Impact of Climate Change on Migration.* The White House. https://www.whitehouse.gov/wp-content/uploads/2021/10/Report-on-the-Impact-of-Climate-Change-on-Migration.pdf

Thirunavukarasu, M., & Thirunavukarasu, P. (2010). Training and national deficit of psychiatrists in India-A critical analysis. *Indian Journal of Psychiatry*, *52*(7, Suppl1), 83–88. doi:10.4103/0019-5545.69218 PMID:21836723

Thomas, A., Baptiste, A., Martyr-Koller, R., Pringle, P., & Rhiney, K. (2020). Climate change and small island developing states. *Annual Review of Environment and Resources*, *45*(1), 1–27. doi:10.1146/annurev-environ-012320-083355

Thondoo, M., & Gupta, J. (2021). Health impact assessment legislation in developing countries: A path to sustainable development? *Review of European, Comparative & International Environmental Law*, *30*(1), 107–117. doi:10.1111/reel.12347

Tripathi, G., Ahad, M. A., & Casalino, G. (2023). A comprehensive review of blockchain technology: Underlying principles and historical background with future challenges. *Decision Analytics Journal*, *9*, 100344. doi:10.1016/j.dajour.2023.100344

Tsuji, S. R. J. (2022). Canada's Impact Assessment Act, 2019: Indigenous Peoples, Cultural Sustainability, and Environmental Justice. *Sustainability (Basel)*, *14*(6), 3501. doi:10.3390/su14063501

Turaga, R. M. R., & Sugathan, A. (2020). Environmental Regulations in India. In Oxford Research Encyclopedia of Environmental Science. doi:10.1093/acrefore/9780199389414.013.417

Turner, V. (1975). *Drama, Fields, and Metaphors: Symbolic actions in human societies*. Cornell University Press.

Turok-Squire, R. (2022, January 16). *Inside the Mind of an International Criminal Court Judge: Sir Howard Morrison QC*. Lacuna. https://lacuna.org.uk/justice/international-criminal-court-icc-judge-sir-howard-morrison-qc/

Ulansey, D. (2000). Cultural Transition and Spiritual Transformation: from Alexander the Great to Cyberspace. In T. Singer (Ed.), *The Vision Thing: Myth* (pp. 213–231). Politics, and Psyche in the World.

Ulrich, R. S. (1984). View Through a Window May Influence Recovery from Surgery. *Science*, *224*(4647), 420–421. doi:10.1126/science.6143402 PMID:6143402

UNEP. (2012). *Vital Waste Graphics-3*. UN. https://globalpact.informea.org/pdf.js/web/viewer.html?file=/sites/default/files/documents/UNEP-CHW-EWASTE-PUB-VitalWasteGraphics-3.English.pdf#page=16

United Nations Conference on Environment and Development. (1992). *Rio Declaration on Environment and Development*. UN. https://www.un.org/en/development/desa/population/migration/generalassembly/docs/globalcompact/A_CONF.151_26_Vol.I_Declaration.pdf

United Nations Educational, Scientific and Cultural Organization. (2021). *Reporting on Migrants and refugees Handbook For Journalism Education*. United Nations Educational.

United Nations Environment Programme. (2019). *Stockholm Convention on Persistent Organic Pollutants.* UN. https://chm.pops.int/TheConvention/Overview/TextoftheConvention/tabid/2232/Default.aspx

United Nations Framework Convention on Climate Change. (2015). *Paris Agreement.* UN. https://unfccc.int/sites/default/files/english_paris_agreement.pdf

United Nations Framework Convention on Climate Change. (2016). *Paris Agreement.* UN. https://unfccc.int/process-and-meetings/the-paris-agreement/the-paris-agreement

United Nations High Commissioner for Refugees. (1977). *Note on Non-Refoulement (Submitted by the High Commissioner) EC/SCP/2.* UN. https://www.unhcr.org/publications/note-non-refoulement-submitted-high-commissioner

United Nations High Commissioner for Refugees. (2011). *The legal framework for protecting refugees.* UN. https://www.unhcr.org/sites/default/files/legacy-pdf/4ec262df9.pdf

United Nations Office for the Coordination of Humanitarian Affairs. (2019). *Natural Disasters in Latin America and the Caribbean.* UN.

United Nations Office for the Coordination of Humanitarian Affairs. (2023). *Regional Office for Latin America and the Caribbean.* UN. https://www.unocha.org/latin-america-and-caribbean

United Nations Office on Drugs and Crime. (2007). *Crime and Development in Central America.* UN. https://www.unodc.org/pdf/research/Central_America_Study_2007.pdf

United Nations. (2020). *Retrieved from United Nations Peace, dignity and equality on a healthy planet.* UN. https://www.un.org/en/global-issues/migration#:~:text=Today%2C%20more%20people%20than%20ever,estimated%20to%20be%20281%20million

US EPA. O. (2015, July 15). *Proctor Creek Boone Boulevard Health Impact Assessment (HIA) Final Report* [Reports and Assessments]. EPA. https://www.epa.gov/healthresearch/proctor-creek-boone-boulevard-health-impact-assessment-hia-final-report

Venkatesh, U., Aravind, G. P., & Velmurugan, A. A. (2022). Telemedicine practice guidelines in India: Global implications in the wake of the COVID-19 pandemic. *World Medical & Health Policy, 14*(3), 589–599. doi:10.1002/wmh3.497 PMID:35601469

Venkatraman, A., Nandy, R., Rao, S. S., Mehta, D. H., Viswanathan, A., & Jayasundar, R. (2019). Tantra and Modern Neurosciences: Is there any Correlation? *Neurology India, 67*(5), 1188–1193. doi:10.4103/0028-3886.271263 PMID:31744942

Venn A. (2019). *Social justice and climate change, Managing Global Warming.* Academic Press. doi:10.1016/B978-0-12-814104-5.00024-7

Voigt, C. (2013). *The principle of sustainable development: Integration and ecological integrity.* Cambridge University Press. doi:10.1017/CBO9781107337961.012

Von Hirsch, A. (1996). Extending the Harm Principle: "Remote" Harms and Fair Imputation. In A. P. Simester & A. T. H. Smith (Eds.), *Harm and Culpability* (pp. 259–276). Oxford University Press. doi:10.1093/acprof:oso/9780198260578.003.0020

Votruba, N., & Thornicroft, G. (2016). Sustainable development goals and mental health: Learnings from the contribution of the FundaMentalSDG global initiative. *Global Mental Health (Cambridge, England)*, *3*, e26. doi:10.1017/gmh.2016.20 PMID:28596894

Wallet, S. (2023, December 11). Power ledger (Powr): A blockchain solution for the future of energy. *Medium.* https://medium.com/coinmonks/power-ledger-powr-a-blockchain-solution-for-the-future-of-energy-00cfe3e2b639

Walters, R. (2022). Ecocide, climate criminals and the politics of bushfires. *British Journal of Criminology*, 1–21.

Wang, S., Blasco, D., Hamzah, A., & Verschuuren, B. (2023). Tourists and 'philosophers': Nature as a medium for consciousness and transcendence in spiritual tourism. *Annals of Tourism Research*, *99*, 103543. doi:10.1016/j.annals.2023.103543

Ward, B. & Rene, D. (1972). *Only One Earth: The Care and Maintenance of a Small Planet.* London: Andre Deutsch.

Ward, M. J., Marsolo, K. A., & Froehle, C. M. (2014). Applications of business analytics in healthcare. *Business Horizons*, *57*(5), 571–582. doi:10.1016/j.bushor.2014.06.003 PMID:25429161

Wathern, P. (Ed.). (2004). *Environmental impact assessment theory and practice.* Routledge.

Watts, A. (1969). *Psychotherapy East and West.* Ballantine Books.

Watzening, P. (2023). The healing effect of the forest in integrative therapy with numerous exercise examples for practice. Springer.

Waugh, C. (2010). "Only You Can Prevent a Forest": Agent Orange, Ecocide, and Environmental Justice. *Interdisciplinary Studies in Literature and Environment*, *17*(1), 113–132. doi:10.1093/isle/isp156

Wawale, S.G., Shabaz, M., Mehbodniya, A., Soni, M., Deb, N., Elashiri, M.A. and Naved, M., (2022). Biomedical Waste Management Using IoT Tracked and Fuzzy Classified Integrated Technique. *Human-centric Computing and Information Sciences, 12*(32).

Weber, M. (2004). *The vocation lectures* (D. S. Owen & T. B. Strong, Eds., LivingstoneR., Trans.). Hackett Pub.

Wellenstein, A. (2022). *The Latin American climate crisis is also a water crisis. How do we move forward?* World Bank. https://blogs.worldbank.org/latinamerica/latin-american-climate-crisis-also-water-crisis-how-do-we-move-forward

Wernham, A. (2011). Health Impact Assessments Are Needed In Decision Making About Environmental And Land-Use Policy. *Health Affairs*, *30*(5), 947–956. doi:10.1377/hlthaff.2011.0050 PMID:21555479

Wewerinke-Singh, M., & Doebbler, C. (2016). The Paris agreement: Some critical reflections on process and substance. *UNSWLJ*, *39*, 1486.

Whiteford, H. A., Degenhardt, L., Rehm, J., Baxter, A. J., Ferrari, A. J., Erskine, H. E., Charlson, F. J., Norman, R. E., Flaxman, A. D., Johns, N., Burstein, R., Murray, C. J. L., & Vos, T. (2013). Global burden of disease attributable to mental and substance use disorders: Findings from the Global Burden of Disease Study 2010. *Lancet*, *382*(9904), 1575–1586. doi:10.1016/S0140-6736(13)61611-6 PMID:23993280

White, L. Jr. (1967). The historical roots of our ecological crisis. *Science*, *155*(3767), 1203–1207. doi:10.1126/science.155.3767.1203 PMID:17847526

WHO (2011b). *World report on disability*. WHO.

WHO (2013a). *Global action plan for the prevention and control of non-communicable diseases 2013–2020*. WHO.

WHO. (2014). *Health Impact Assessment*. World Health Organization. http://www.who.int/hia/en/

WHO. (2018). 'Health-care waste'. WHO. https://www.who.int/news-room/fact-sheets/detail/health-care-waste

WHO. (2019, May 2). *The WHO Special Initiative for Mental Health (2019-2023): Universal Health Coverage for Mental Health*. WHO. https://www.who.int/publications/i/item/special-initiative-for-mental-health-(2019-2023)

WHO. (2022, June 17). Mental health: Key facts. WHO. https://www.who.int/news-room/fact-sheets/detail/mental-health-strengthening-our-response

WHO-GHO. (2023). *Target 3.5: Strengthen the prevention and treatment of substance abuse, including narcotic drug abuse and harmful use of alcohol*. WHO. https://www.who.int/data/gho/data/themes/topics/topic-details/GHO/target-3-5-strengthen-the-prevention-and-treatment-of-substance-abuse-including-narcotic-drug-abuse-and-harmful-use-of-alcohol

Wig, N. N. (1989). Indian concepts of mental health and their impact on care of the mentally ill. *International Journal of Mental Health*, *18*(3), 71–80. doi:10.1080/00207411.1989.11449136

Wilber, K. (2001). *Sex, Ecology, Spirituality*. Shambhala.

Wilson, E. O. (1986). *Biophilia. The human bond with other species*. Harvard University Press.

Wolf, M. (2021). *Community development initiatives as part of a tourism resort's CSR strategy: examination of a high-end luxury resort in the Maldives*.

Wolfelt, A. (2021). *Nature Heals: Reconciling Your Grief through Engaging with the Natural World (Words of Hope and Healing)*. Companion Press.

Woodka, J. L. (1992). Sentencing The CEO: Personal Liability Of Corporate Executives For Environmental Crimes. *Tulane Environmental Law Journal, 5*(2), 635–666.

Woodworth, P. L. (2005). Have there been large recent sea level changes in the Maldive Islands? *Global and Planetary Change, 49*(1-2), 1–18. doi:10.1016/j.gloplacha.2005.04.001

Wootton, B. (1981). *Crime and the Criminal Law* (2nd ed.). Steven & Sons.

World Bank Group. (2018) *Internal Climate Migration in Latin America.* World Bank. https://documents1.worldbank.org/curated/en/983921522304806221/pdf/124724-BRI-PUBLIC-NEWSERIES-Groundswell-note-PN3.pdf

World Health Organization. (2015). Report of a regional meeting on health of older women: policy, gender and delivery of service issues. World Health Organization.

World Meteorological Organization. (2021). *Weather-related ease over past 50 years, causing more damage but fewer deaths.* WMO. https://public.wmo.int/en/media/press-release/weather-related-disasters-increase-over-past-50-years-causing-more-damage-fewer#:~:text=Climate%20change%20has%20increased%20extreme,many%20parts%20of%20the%20world

World Meteorological Organization. (2022). *State of the Climate in Latin America and the Caribbean 2022.* WMO. https://library.wmo.int/viewer/66252/download?file=1322_State_of_the_Climate_in_LAC_2022_en.pdf&type=pdf&navigator=1

World Metereological Organization. (2014). *The Impact of Climate Change: Migration and Cities in South America.* WMO. https://public.wmo.int/en/resources/bulletin/impact-of-climate-change-migration-and-cities-south-america

Wu, Y., & Liu, X. M. (2023). Navigating the Ethical Landscape of AI in Healthcare: Insights from a Content Analysis. TechRxiv, *42*(3), 76-87. doi:10.36227/techrxiv.22294513.v2

Wyman, K. (2013). Responses to climate migration. *The Harvard Environmental Law Review, 37*(1), 167–216.

Xiao, S., Dong, H., Geng, Y., Tian, X., Liu, C., & Li, H. (2020). Policy impacts on Municipal Solid Waste management in Shanghai: A system dynamics model analysis. *Journal of Cleaner Production, 262*, 121366. doi:10.1016/j.jclepro.2020.121366

Xu, J., Lu, W., Ye, M., Xue, F., Zhang, X., & Lee, B. F. P. (2020). Is the private sector more efficient? big data analytics of construction waste management sectoral efficiency. *Resources, Conservation and Recycling, 155*, 104674. doi:10.1016/j.resconrec.2019.104674

Yadav, V. S. (2018). Environmental Impact Assessment: A critique on Indian law and practices. *International Journal of Multidisciplinary Research and Development, 5*(1), 01-05.

Yalavarthy, A. S. (2023). Aadhaar: India's National Identification System and Consent-Based Privacy Rights. *Vand. J. Transnat'l L., 56*, 619.

Yamamoto, L., & Esteban, M. (2013). *Atoll Island States and international law*. Springer-Verlag Berlin An.

Yang, H., Nguyen, T.-N., & Chuang, T.-W. (2023). An Integrative Explainable Artificial Intelligence Approach to Analyze Fine-Scale Land-Cover and Land-Use Factors Associated with Spatial Distributions of Place of Residence of Reported Dengue Cases. *Tropical Medicine and Infectious Disease*, 8(4), 238. doi:10.3390/tropicalmed8040238 PMID:37104363

Yang, Z., Kankanhalli, A., Ng, B. Y., & Lim, J. T. Y. (2013). Analyzing the enabling factors for the organizational decision to adopt healthcare information systems. *Decision Support Systems*, 55(3), 764–776. doi:10.1016/j.dss.2013.03.002

Yong, J. Y., Klemeš, J. J., Varbanov, P. S., & Huisingh, D. (2016). Cleaner energy for cleaner production: Modelling, simulation, optimisation and waste management. *Journal of Cleaner Production*, 111, 1–16. doi:10.1016/j.jclepro.2015.10.062

Yusof, K., Ismail, F., Yunus, J., Kasmuni, N., Ramele, R., Omar, M., & Mustaffa, H. (2019). Community participation and performance of waste segregation program in malacca: Towards sustainable waste management. In *MATEC Web of Conferences* (Vol. 266, p. 02003). EDP Sciences.

Zafar, S. (2020). *Medical waste management in developing countries*. BioEnergy Consult.

About the Contributors

Siddharth Kanojia is an Asst. Professor at Jindal School of Banking & Finance. Presently, he is also a visiting professor at IIM, Amritsar and IIM, Sirmaur. He holds a Ph.D in Corporate Law & Governance, LL.M in International Business and Commercial Law, LL.B and BBS in Finance. Before coming to academics, he has worked at Jersey Island based Intellectual Property Management Company as Legal Consultant and Manchester based Start-up Company as Legal Advisor. Till date, he has 15+ publications including the SCOPUS and WoS indexed journals. He is also an active member in Human Development and Capability Association, USA and Development Studies Association, U.K.

***

Tanvi Aggarwal was a Research Intern with the Centre for Advancing Reasearch in Management and Law at the O. P. Jindal Global University. She is currently pursuing her degree in Law at the O. P. Jindal Global University.

Himanshi Bhatia is an Assistant Professor at Symbiosis Law School, Nagpur. She is currently pursuing her Ph.D. from Maharashtra National Law University, Nagpur. She holds an LL.M in Criminal & Security Law from the National University of Juridical Sciences, Kolkata, and an LL.B (Hons) from the University of Delhi. Before joining academics, she worked at the High Court of Uttarakhand as Legal Researcher cum Judicial Clerk to the Hon'ble Chief Justice of the High Court. Her current research interest includes International Criminal Law for Environment, Criminology and Green Victimology.

Maria Camila Duque is a dynamic professional who excels in the fields of law and sociology. She completed her Master of Law at Pennsylvania State University, specializing in Energy and Enviromental law, beyond her academic achievements, she has gained valuable experience researching regulatory trends in Latin America. Furthermore, she has also applied her skills in the corporate realm, working in the field of corporate law. In addition, she hails from Colombia and possesses a strong passion for contributing to academia through her research on gender and inequality.

Pranjal Khare teaches at Jindal Global Law School, O.P. Jindal Global University, Sonipat.

Tatjana Kochtekova, PhD, associate professor at O.P. Jindal Global University. Tatjana obtained her PhD from the Radboud University in the Netherlands in philosophical anthropology. She had research and teaching appointments at several Dutch universities, including Utrecht University for Humanistic and the University of Twente in Enschede for two decades before joining O. P. Jindal Global University. She is the author of several books and a series of articles on applied ethics and philosophy of man and technology, including the book entitled "The Plurality of the Arts of Living" (in Dutch, Garant, Belgium, 2018). Her research focus is in philosophical anthropology, contemporary art of living and environmental philosophy, including the current technogenic transformation of the human condition.

Richa Kapoor Mehra, is working as an Assistant Professor at O.P Jindal Global University, India, she is a PhD in Philosophy from Jawaharlal Nehru University, Delhi. While pursuing PhD, she was recipient of Junior Research Fellowship from prestigious Indian Council of Philosophical Research (ICPR). She has completed Masters and Bachelor's in Philosophy from Miranda House, University of Delhi. She was awarded with Miranda House award and Delhi University rankers prize for scoring highest marks in Bachelor's program. She has also worked at Miranda House, University of Delhi, Amity University, Noida, B.M.L Munjal University and IIIT Kalyani. She has presented several research papers in National and International conferences and have considerable publications to her credit. Her area of specialization is Philosophy of Mind and Philosophy of Language. Her current research interest includes Business Ethics, self-knowledge, Emotional Intelligence, Virtual Reality, Artificial Intelligence and its ethical concerns.

Anupreet Kaur Mokha is working as an Assistant Professor in Department of Commerce, SGTB Khalsa College, University of Delhi for more than 7 years. She has done her Ph.D. in Marketing from Department of Commerce, Delhi School of Economics, University of Delhi. She did her B.Com (Hons.) and M.Com from SGTB Khalsa College, University of Delhi. She is a continuous rank holder throughout the academics. Her area of interest consumer behaviour, electronic customer relationship management, electronic commerce, customer experience and customer loyalty. She has published many research papers in Scopus, ABDC, Web of Science and UGC Care indexed journals and also has been reviewer in many reputed publication houses such as Emerald, IGI Global, Sage publications, etc. She is also invited as a special guest and also delivered many lectures as a keynote speaker in many renowned universities and colleges.

Piyush Pranjal is an Associate Professor and Assistant Director with the Centre for Advancing Research in Management and Law at the O. P. Jindal Global University. He has five articles/papers and two book chapters published to his credit. He has presented his research in several international conferences. His research interests include Popular Culture, Branding, B2B Marketing, Marketing Measurement and Indic Knowledge Systems.

Darsana R S is currently pursuing her Ph.D. under the DPIIT, IPR Chair, Maharashtra National Law University, Mumbai, India. She completed her B.A. LLB (Hons.) from the National University of Advanced Legal Studies, Kochi, India and her LL.M. from Maharashtra National Law University, Mumbai, India.

Parimal Roy started a career in 2006 in the Development sector, collaborating with international development partners like ADB, DFID, UNFPA, SIDA, PKSF, and Orbis International. Nevertheless, he has researched and examined Capabilities, ILO-169, UNDRIP-2007, Sustainable Community Development and decision-making within cultural policy, focusing on the implication of participatory governance for the cultural sector. He has concluded vehemently undergraduate and post-graduated in Anthropology (SUST, Bangladesh) and in Business Administration (BOU, Bangladesh). Furthermore, he is now pursuing a PhD. (expected in 2023) in Community [Indigenous-Santals] Development at Universiti Malaya Malaysia.

Soumya Sarkar is an Associate Professor with the Indian Institute of Management Ranchi. He has twenty-five publications in refereed Journals and conference proceedings. He has also published several case studies with reputed case repositories. He is also the author/editor of two prominent books. His research interests include Pop Culture, Strategic Marketing, B2B Marketing and Branding.

Gianluigi Segalerba was born in Genoa, Italy, on 24 June 1967. He graduated in Philosophy at the University of Pisa in 1991 and obtained his PhD in Philosophy at the University of Pisa in 1998. He was visiting scholar at the Universities of Tübingen, Berne, and Vienna. He taught at the Institute of Philosophy of the University of Vienna. His first publication was Note su Ousia (Pisa 2001). He was then co-editor of the volume Substantia – Sic et Non (Frankfurt on the Main 2008), and he is the author of the book Semantik und Ontologie: Drei Studien zu Aristoteles (Berne 2013). He currently lives and works in Vienna.

Vani Singhal is a Research Associate with the Centre for Advancing Reasearch in Management and Law at the O. P. Jindal Global University. She is currently pursuing her degree in Law at the O. P. Jindal Global University.

Gigimon V. S. is currently the Associate Dean (Academics) and the Chair Professor IPR at Maharashtra National Law University, Mumbai, India. He has completed his Ph.D. in Law from Chanakya National Law University, Patna, India. He has a total of teaching & research experience of close to two decades in various institutions across India. His areas of interest are ADR, IPR, Research Methodology, Consumer Protection, Torts, and Human Rights Law. He has published books and several articles in journals and books of national and international repute.

Index

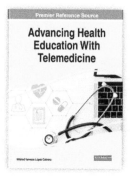

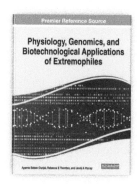

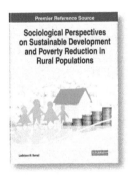